Living Folklore

Living Folklore

*An Introduction to the Study of People
and Their Traditions*

Second Edition

Martha C. Sims
The Ohio State University

Martine Stephens
Ohio Wesleyan University

UTAH STATE UNIVERSITY PRESS
LOGAN, UTAH
2011

Utah State University Press
Logan, Utah 84322-3078
www.usu.edu/usupress

Manufactured in the United States of America
Printed on recycled, acid-free paper

ISBN: 978-0-87421-844-2 (cloth)
ISBN: 978-0-87421-845-9 (e-book)

Second Edition, Revised

The Library of Congress has cataloged the first edition as follows:

Sims, Martha C., 1963-
  Living folklore : an introduction to the study of people and their traditions / Martha C. Sims,
Martine Stephens.
      p. cm.
  Includes bibliographical references and index.
  ISBN 978-0-87421-611-0 (hardcover : alk. paper)
  1. Folklore—Methodology. 2. Folklore—Field work. 3. Folklore—Performance. 4. Manners and
customs. 5.
  Rites and ceremonies. I. Stephens, Martine, 1959- II. Title.
  GR45.S56 2005
  398'.072—dc22
                          2005011837

Contents

Acknowledgments

They say it takes a village to raise a child—well, it takes practically a whole dang planet to write a book about folklore. This book is the result of a collaborative effort that included many more people than just the two of us, and we want to thank our friends, colleagues, families, collaborators, and consultants.

Pat Mullen, Amy Shuman, and Dan Barnes introduced us to the field of folklore and have provided much encouragement and support over the years (and have also shared good ideas, conversation, companionship, parties, stories, and jokes). We are particularly grateful to Pat Mullen, who read drafts of the first edition, asked tough questions, led us to important sources, and always put up with our pestering. Without his ongoing support and input, this book wouldn't have been possible. The second edition of the book also benefitted from the feedback and support of Dorothy Noyes.

Many thanks go to Cynthia Cox, who, through numerous conversations and initial planning sessions, helped get the idea for this book off the ground and onto the page.

Sincere thanks go out to all our readers, whose questions and comments strengthened the final text. Sue V. Lape read just about everything, at just about every stage, and provided invaluable feedback; Kevin Eyster read key chapter drafts; and Jacki Spangler read the very first draft of the introduction and provided practical and emotional support throughout this project. Others who gave serious time and thought to the selections we asked them to read include Erik Bakstrom, Christopher Hyde, Rachel Neeb, Laura Roberts, Gary E. A. Saum, Katherine "Kd" Schuster, Tina Stall, Danny Tuss, and Ohio Wesleyan University students from English 105 classes in Spring and Fall 2004.

Many colleagues nudged this project forward. Our friends and co-workers at the Center for Folklore Studies at Ohio State, the (former) Writing Workshop at Ohio State, and the Writing Center and English Department at Ohio Wesleyan University gave invaluable support. Barbara Pinkele from Ohio Wesleyan brainstormed titles and listened to ideas, and Katey Borland from Ohio State provided insight about the quinceañera (and was a congenial American Folklore Society roommate). Nan Johnson encouraged our commitment to the project and listened when we needed to be listened to. We raise a glass (or two) to our friends and colleagues Rosemary Hathaway, Sheila Bock Alarid, Larry Doyle, Nancy Yan, Kirsi Hänninen, Ann Ferrell, Cassie Patterson, and Kate Parker, who provided support, ideas, and good conversation.

There are many others without whose input and support this work would have been more difficult. We thank Carol Singer, for "tradition." Staut's and Cup o' Joe provided good coffee and a great atmosphere in which to get work done—and the WiFi with which to do it. We also thank the yogis at Yoga on High and Lucinda Kirk (and the "Turning Point" workshop group) for pushing this work through.

We extend thanks to those who shared their time, ideas, words, and collections with us: Patrick Blake, for allowing us to use his essay on food traditions; Adriana Mancillas, for sharing her personal photos and feelings about her own quinceañera and the ritual itself; Charell Albert and Nina Gunnell for their consultation on insider language; Samantha Levanduski, Stephen Smith, and Tema Krempley for ideas (presented in conversation and in academic research) that directed us toward several groups that practice folklore and flourish through online interaction; Barb Vogel, for sharing her collection and photos of Mary Borkowski's quilts; Joyce and Alan Hersh, for sharing their dreidel collection; Charles and Andy Alberts for allowing us to take photos on their property; Bruce and Donna Siple for opening their home to us and Bruce in particular for sharing his art and aesthetic vision; and Randall Schieber for the use of his photographs of Bruce Siple's work. We especially thank the authors of our examples of projects—and their consultants—for so generously permitting us to include their work. We thank Steffani Pealer, Senior Coordinator of Greek Life at the Ohio State University, The Ohio State Office of Student Affairs, and Iota Phi Theta Fraternity, Inc. for providing us with photos of the Ohio State step shows.

Our families tolerated our schedules and supported us in this project in countless ways—both ordinary and extraordinary—that we promise did not always go unnoticed. Beyond their good-natured spousal behavior, Curtis Schieber gave us feedback on drafts and Brian Lovely provided much-needed technical support (and both supplied us with food and wine). And we give extra special thanks to Evan Schieber for his cookies and Flannery Stephens for tasting the Cottage Tuna Loaf. They also provided research and photography assistance—and generally kept us amused and on our toes.

Michael Spooner at Utah State University Press had faith in us and stood by us throughout the genesis of this project and the first edition. We thank him for his sharp editorial eye and friendly encouragement, which kept us going and made this a better book. John Alley worked patiently and diligently to challenge and support us to bring the second edition to press.

Preface

We study folklore because we are interested in the ways that people decorate their yards or use recycled items to create art, in how they use charms to foretell the sex of unborn children, in the cures they create for colds and hangovers, in rumors about government conspiracies circulated through e-mail, in family recipes, in stories about el chupacabra or cry baby bridges—and much more. For us, folklore is a way of understanding people and the wide range of creative ways we express who we are and what we value and believe.

We wrote this book to share our enthusiasm for folklore. We want to give you a sense of the liveliness and immediacy of folklore in our everyday lives as well as at times of celebration and ceremony.

Folklore covers so much territory that we couldn't possibly be specific about every kind of folklore or every type of analysis. We do, however, try to present an overview of most issues and approaches in the field, supported with many different types of examples to give a taste of the wide variety of topics folklorists study. As American folklorists who teach in American universities, we rely primarily on examples drawn from the United States—in all its diversity and complexity. We consider diverse groups from multiple cultures—from groups connected by ethnicity, region, age, gender, and occupation to smaller groups such as families, friends, classmates, and coworkers. The breadth of American culture and cultural experience allows us to talk about such activities as midwestern Thanksgiving traditions, Latina quinceañeras, African American fraternity and sorority step shows, and Apache coming-of-age rituals. Our focus on groups includes discussion of Star Trek fans, Boy Scouts, suburban adolescents, slumber party guests, record store employees, and many others. Each example gives us a window into particular groups and their expressive communication.

Many of the examples in this book will probably be familiar to you, but we hope you will find unfamiliar examples here, too. When you do come across something new, we encourage you to talk with your instructor and classmates and do a little research to learn more. Natural curiosity about what goes on around us and who is doing what is part of what makes folklorists folklorists. And as individuals with unique backgrounds, we each have experiences and cultural knowledge we can share with others, so we encourage you to share examples from your own background with others in your class. We think you'll have fun learning about the varieties of creative ways people express their beliefs, values, and traditions and looking at works of art, listening to jokes and stories, and tasting great new foods. And beyond that, you may find unexpected connections that help you understand yourself—and other people—better.

Because this is, after all, a textbook that is meant to introduce a complex academic subject, we look at definitions of important terms and present a brief overview of the history of folklore study to provide a basic foundation for the more complex discussions later. We frequently introduce a concept early in a chapter and then continue to weave in references to that idea, allowing the definitions and your understanding of those concepts to develop throughout the major chapters. This way, we hope you get a feel for the basics of an idea and can then build on those basics as you read and study further.

It's also important to gain understanding of the people and theories that have influenced the study of folklore. We introduce you in this book to some of the important architects of folklore study and refer frequently to their major works and theories. For each of the primary concepts we discuss, we present overviews of key debates, conflicts, turning points, and critiques and consider scholarly points of view that build on and extend from the foundations—or, in some cases, move away from these foundations in completely different directions. We also delve into some important theoretical issues, not necessarily to solve any of those questions or to merely provide our own assessment of them, but to introduce the issues relevant to the current study of folklore and help you think critically about those issues on your own.

Folklore isn't all theory, though. Once you learn about the field, you will have the opportunity to investigate some folklore yourself. The practice of folklore requires fieldwork and writing about your own research and observations. We devote a chapter to the philosophical and practical aspects of doing fieldwork and ethnographic study and then provide a few examples of projects to illustrate how you might prepare and share your analyses with others. These samples cover a range of topics and have been written by a variety of authors—mostly students, but also professional folklorists. They should help you get ideas for conducting and presenting your own projects. Several suggested assignments appear at the end of the book to support your reading and class discussions and to offer more ideas for writing and fieldwork projects. Some are in-class exercises your instructor may ask you to complete individually or with your classmates; others are potential topics for in-depth research. These assignments are intended to provide fieldwork and research opportunities that allow you to participate fully in folklore study, beyond the words on these pages.

We believe learning about and studying folklore are worthwhile activities in themselves, but folklore also offers many professional possibilities, covering a vast range of material and activities. The careers of those who "do folklore" reflect this same variety.

Many folklorists work in colleges and universities, teaching courses in folklore, cultural studies, comparative studies, religion, languages, history, literature, writing, and a variety of related courses. These academic folklorists usually conduct research projects on topics ranging from folklore and literature to full-scale ethnographic studies in local and distant groups around the world. Most academic folklorists write books and articles to express what they discover about culture, and many are also filmmakers and artists themselves. They are frequently consulted about topics related to folklore by other academics, arts organization workers, journalists, historians, and members of the public.

Other folklorists work outside academia, in arts organizations, museums, government institutions, and businesses.[1] These public sector folklorists often conduct fieldwork or research, as academic folklorists do, but often their work is directed toward different ends and different audiences than the academic world. They might, for instance, teach visitors about the traditions and customs of North Carolina coastal fishermen at a maritime museum or conduct outreach programs about regional folklore with groups of local public schoolchildren. Others might work at places like the Smithsonian Institution or Library of Congress, maintaining catalogs or libraries of materials or designing educational programs or events. The annual Festival of American Folklife sponsored by the Smithsonian Institution, for instance, relies on the research, interpretive, and organizational skills of scores of folklorists. They might help to select performers; organize events; create and produce written, audio, and visual material; or serve as resources to answer questions from festival visitors. Many public sector folklorists work for state arts and humanities organizations assisting folk artists, performers, and groups with gaining funding and resource support for local projects and performances.

There is a lot of overlap within these categories. Many folklorists who work in the public sector also teach courses in universities, and academic folklorists frequently work in public or organizational settings as researchers, project creators and administrators, or consultants. Academic and public sector folklorists often collaborate on projects such as museum exhibits, community festivals that showcase regional food and music, and media projects such as ethnographic documentary films. Public sector folklorists and academic folklorists usually receive their education and training in the same ways: they study folklore in college and/or graduate school and take part in internships or work experiences that allow them to practice fieldwork and analysis. Solid academic background and practical experience are usually necessary for both academic and public sector careers in folklore.

Still others—librarians, music archivists, sociologists, architects, computer programmers, and professionals in a host of other realms—may not be employed strictly as folklorists but consider themselves to be folklorists in terms of the topics they are interested in and how they study those topics. They may have taken a few folklore classes or learned about folklore study in their degree programs and chosen this particular emphasis within their larger professional setting.

For more detail and to get a sense of the range of work conducted by folklorists in academia and the public sector, you might visit the American Folklore Society website and check out the "What Do Folklorists Do?" section as well as the job descriptions in the "Opportunities in Folklore" section (www.afsnet.org).

You may eventually become a practicing folklorist who conducts research, teaches, writes, does fieldwork, and develops public programs, or you may at least go on to take more college courses in folklore. Or perhaps the class you are taking now may be your only academic course in folklore. In any case, we encourage you to see that folklore is not just about time-honored traditions or quaint customs; it is a philosophical approach to understanding people and expressive culture. Above all, we hope you enjoy your introduction to the study of folklore.

CHAPTER 1

Folklore

*W*e know you have heard it before: "It's just folklore." We hear it when news-casters are announcing the report of a popular home remedy that does not really cure people (and may actually harm them). We hear it—or might even say it—when a friend is telling a story about the haunted house on the winding street in our neighborhood. People often call something "folklore" to dismiss the validity of the subject they have been discussing.

To some people, the term *folklore* commonly suggests something untrue, not real—just a story or an old-fashioned belief. But that is a misconception. Some people come to folklore study expecting to learn only about quaint cultures from the past or contemporary cultures of those who are less educated, less fortunate, and less sophisticated than they are—primitive or simpler groups. That, too, is a misconception.

In the following sections we will clear up misconceptions about folklore by considering what folklore is and isn't. We will also look at genres and important concepts of text and context and offer a short history of the study of folklore as a foundation for our own exploration.

What is Folklore?

A Working Definition

Folklore is many things, and it's almost impossible to define succinctly. It's both what folklorists study and the name of the discipline they work within. Yes, folklore is folk songs and legends. It's also quilts, Boy Scout badges, high school marching band initiations, jokes, online avatars, chain letters, nicknames, holiday food, and many other things you might or might not expect. Folklore exists in cities, suburbs, and rural villages; in families, work groups, and residents of college dormitories. Folklore is present in many kinds of informal communication, whether verbal (oral and written texts), customary (behaviors and rituals), or material (physical objects). It exists in the physical world and in virtual settings online. It involves values, traditions, and ways of thinking and behaving. It's about art. It's about people and the way people learn. It helps us learn who we are and how to derive meaning from the world around us.

As we explore some attempts to define the field of *folklore*, we want to ask you to expand your concept of folklore or at least to let go of any preconceived ideas of what folklore means. One of the most useful ways we have found to clarify these distinctions is to talk about what folklore is *not*.

Folklore is not necessarily untrue or old fashioned. Have you ever eaten *pan de muerto* on the Day of the Dead? Sent an email chain letter to everyone in your address book? Carried a special object or worn a particular article of clothing to bring you luck? Made a wish before blowing out candles on your birthday cake? These are all examples of folklore. Some have been around for many generations; some are relatively new. Some are meaningful to large groups of people; some are relevant only to a few people. First, whether or not these examples are true isn't relevant. In what way could a loaf of sweet bread be true? And it doesn't have to be true that special clothing will help someone win a race for a track star to wear the same socks to every meet. Second, these examples are not possessed or performed only by simple, primitive people, nor are they quaint or old fashioned. The fact that you recognize the above examples—or know other similar examples—illustrates that folklore is not simply the historical behaviors of other cultures; folklore is alive, developing, and changing in our lifetimes. Every one of us experiences and shares folklore.

Folklorists avoid the use of terminology such as "true," "primitive," or "simple" when they talk about folklore. These terms imply that folklore is fake or exists only in old-fashioned, nonliterate cultures. For example, some people might see quilts made by hand rather than by machine as simple, or they might consider paintings and sculptures by poor, rural, unschooled artists as primitive, but these labels assume a hierarchical value related to formal education systems. When we don't evaluate it by outside standards, we can see that this kind of art is simply the creation of artists who have ideas and values they wish to express within (or about) their own group or community. Folklorists go into the field in contemporary societies to observe, record, and write about people and what we do, what we believe, and how we communicate *right now*—the culture of our lives.

Folklore is not just another form of anthropology or literary study. The study of folklore touches on every dimension of human experience and artistic expression. It has grown out of the study of literature, has roots in anthropology, and contains elements of psychology and sociology. In many ways, it is the study of culture—visual and performing arts, sculpture, architecture, music, theater, literature, linguistics, and history rolled into one. The discipline of folklore has evolved into a way of thinking about how people learn, share knowledge, and form their identity. Studying folklore is a way of learning about people, of thinking about how we communicate and make meaning. It is different from its related disciplines in its approach and focus. As Richard Dorson explains, folklorists

> are concerned with the study of traditional culture, or the unofficial cul-
> ture, or the folk culture, as opposed to the elite culture, not for the sake
> of proving a thesis but to learn about the mass of [humanity] overlooked
> by the conventional disciplines. Historians write histories of the elite, the
> successful, the visible; literary scholars study elitist writings; and the crit-
> ics of the arts confine their attention to the fine arts. Anthropologists
> venture far off the beaten track, and sociologists look at people statisti-
> cally. (1976, 117)

While the field borrows, both theoretically and in practice, from the disciplines of history, literary study, anthropology, and sociology, folklorists use a different lens. Folklore differs from these fields in the way in which it looks at everyday, unofficial, expressive communication. Folklorists study how members of a group communicate creatively with each other, as well as what—and to whom—they communicate.

Folklore is not high art or part of official culture. "High" or "elite" art or culture is part of the formally acknowledged canon that we learn about in institutions such as schools, churches, or state organizations. A composition by Mozart, for instance, and a painting by Picasso are clearly part of high culture. Students study the work of Mozart and Picasso in school and are usually taught about these works by experts or professionals; likewise, professionally trained artists perform Mozart in concert halls, and Picasso's works hang in major museums around the world. The term *folklore* refers to the knowledge we have about our world and ourselves that we don't learn in school or textbooks—we learn folklore from each other. It's the informally learned, unofficial knowledge we share with our peers, families, and other groups we belong to.

Folklore is not popular culture. But popular culture shares a few more features with folklore than elite culture does: it is usually not considered part of the

3

canon of works or ideas taught formally in schools or other institutions, and it often appeals to groups of people who sometimes become linked through that artistic expression. However, popular culture includes many items that are in high demand, usually by large groups of people and usually for a fairly short, definable period of time. Pop culture is usually created or produced in large quantities for large audiences and is usually shared or transmitted through mass media such as television, radio, magazines, and the Internet. This category would include a television show that dominates people's conversations and captures intense interest as long as it is running but loses relevance over time once it is no longer broadcast. Other examples include the pet rock and mood ring fads of the 1970s or the poodle skirt and bobby sox fashions of the 1950s, which resurface now and then in nostalgic styles but rarely, if ever, attract the same level of original interest.

But is it—or isn't it? Unfortunately for those of us trying to come up with clear definitions, the lines between high, pop, and folk can be very blurry. Suppose, for instance, that a group of Mozart fanatics travel around the country together to view every performance of *The Magic Flute* they can find. Their love of the opera and the related rituals and behaviors they participate in are part of their group's tradition, part of what makes them a group. In that sense, the high art of opera is part of this group's folklore. Suppose a rural fiddler went to a performance of *The Magic Flute*, incorporated a few measures of the score into a variation of an Appalachian tune, and then shared the tune with his fellow fiddlers at a weekly jam session at his friend's barn. Although he's a member of a folk group that plays music shared in a traditional way, part of a canonized high art composition has now been folded into his group's own traditions. As for pop culture, the distinctions can be even less clear. While the television show *Glee* is not itself a folk performance, what about a weekly *Glee*-viewing party where friends gather to watch the new episodes?

Or consider Elvis Presley, a pop culture figure from the 1950s through the 1970s whose music, appearance, and image have been incorporated into everything from movies to paintings to wedding chapels. So many Elvis impersonators exist that they themselves could be considered a folk group. Stories exist about Elvis sightings across the world, rumors persist that he did not die in 1977, and contemporary legends about things Elvis said and did (or continues to do, if you believe he is still with us) continue to circulate. People have reported seeing Elvis pumping gas at a local 7-11, buying pastries in a London sweet shop, even posing as a Mafia boss in Los Angeles. Some mysterious events associated with Elvis have been reported—his face has appeared on a tortilla (subsequently put up for sale on eBay); his voice has been recorded in the background of an audiotape made long after his death. In what category, then, should we place Elvis and all the types of expression that surround him?

The main distinguishing difference between folklore and other types of cultural expression is in what we *do* with the stuff—how we learn about it and hear about it, and how (or whether) we incorporate it into our daily experience and lives. The differences are also clear in how we pass around different kinds of objects, verbal expressions, and behaviors with other people. As we've said, we learn official, elite ideas in school, church, or other official organized settings. We usually learn about pop culture through less formal means, such as television and entertainment websites. But we learn folklore informally through our interactions with other people. Elite art and culture are intended to reach, usually, those who are officially and formally educated or trained within official, formal settings. Pop culture and art are for everybody, whether connected to each other in any special way or not. Folklore reaches groups of people who share personal connections, values, traditions, beliefs—and other forms of lore—that in part define them as a group.

So is Elvis folklore? As a recording artist in the 1960s, probably not. But as a gas station employee in a contemporary legend or as a face on a tortilla, yes, he is.

Children's games offer another example of how we might sort out the differences. In the last decade or so, Pokémon and Yu-Gi-Oh! games and collectibles have been popular among elementary school children, especially boys. Children learn about these games through the media—cartoons, commercials, books, and ads all feature the characters from the games. They are meant to be enjoyed by almost any child, and because of the way these items are created and distributed, they themselves (and the general craze or fad they generate) are part of popular culture. But—suppose several fourth graders at a particular elementary school play the games every day at recess, in the same corner of the playground. They share the common experience of playing the games together. As a group, they may share stories, styles of play, nicknames, and so on, which are related to the pop phenomenon but are also personalized and localized by their interactions. Their daily game play becomes part of their identity as a group. It becomes how other people recognize them, as well as how they recognize themselves: they are "the kids at Gables Elementary School who play Yu-Gi-Oh! in the corner of the parking lot every day at recess." Again, the game figures themselves may not be folklore, but the process of daily interaction that has made the game play a feature of this group's tradition and identity is folklore.

Folklore is informally learned and unofficial, part of everyday experience. This type of unofficial learning is essential to folklore but is often difficult to pin

5

down in definite terms. Because folklore is expressive communication within a particular group, it is taught informally, through one's presence within that group. Therefore, the unofficial education of a young woman learning to quilt might involve her attending a gathering of more experienced women quilters, watching what they are doing, and being instructed in the art through that experience. She might even go online to read blogs from quilters, post comments or questions about techniques, or share photos of her own work in progress. She probably won't sit down with a book on quilting techniques and become a quilter just by reading about it, without any interaction with other quilters. Similarly, an artist may have taught himself to paint or carve. Perhaps as a child he whittled to create toys and as he grew older used that skill along with a love for nature and animals to create figurines of animals native to his home; and perhaps he worked with other carvers in his community to learn about different techniques. In any case, folklore comes to us through our experiences with others around us.

Folklorists often use the term *vernacular* to refer to the particular localized language, objects, and practices of groups within specific contexts; this term and concept can help us see the differences between what is considered official and formal and what is considered unofficial and informal. *Vernacular* is a more general term than *folklore* in that it can refer to anything that is locally or regionally defined, produced, or expressed. For example, most of us in the United States are familiar with the many carbonated soft drinks available in the supermarket. In some parts of the country, people may refer to these drinks as "soda" and in others, "pop" or "soda pop." In some regions of the South, people refer to all soft drinks as "coke," using the brand name of one kind of soft drink to refer to the whole category. Objects and practices, as well as verbal expressions, may be vernacular. Architectural styles may vary in different geographic areas, for example. In coastal areas of the United States, houses on or near the beach may be built on elevated platforms or stilts, without underground foundations, to suit the climate and shifting nature of the soil. Local materials may also influence building decisions: in regions where clay is plentiful and bricks can be easily manufactured, many houses may be built of brick. Where people live sometimes affects what they say, do, and make.

Like folklore, vernacular materials, behaviors, and expressions are created by and for people in everyday, local contexts, as opposed to those materials, behaviors, and expressions created by governments, schools, or other institutions. The term *vernacular* can distinguish between the things we do as part of society and the informal things that are still part of that formal structure. A group of people may celebrate Arbor Day, for example, by performing the officially

6

designated ritual of planting trees. But in conjunction with this act, a particular neighborhood group may hold a community tree festival in which children decorate trees with colorful handmade crafts and residents congregate under trees for picnics. The day itself is designated as a special holiday to honor and care for trees, but these residents have added their own spin to the day by creating community traditions and rituals that express their local interpretation of the official holiday. Vernacular beliefs and practices exist alongside mainstream or sanctioned beliefs or practices, not as lesser or deviant variants (particular local, vernacular, or individual versions) but as added or connected concepts.

Not everything that is vernacular is folklore, but all folklore is vernacular. Regional labels for objects or local variations in building styles in and of themselves are vernacular; but when they are considered in terms of how and when people use the names or change building styles, or how and why people express, teach, or share those vernacular concepts with others, they become items of folklore study.

Folklore has artistic, creative, or expressive dimensions. Although we have said folklore occurs in everyday settings, the process of creating and sharing folklore is by nature set off from the ordinary. People recognize it as different from ordinary conversation, for example, when in the middle of a discussion about the ten-page essay due for English class next week, someone starts to tell a story she heard about a particular professor who drops papers from the top of his staircase and assigns grades based on where they fall: papers closer to the top of the stairs get As and Bs, those in the middle get Cs, and those at the bottom, Fs. The rest of the group will most likely react with laughter, surprise, or varying degrees of belief or disbelief. The group may return to the conversation or may keep swapping stories about professors or other campus characters. For a few minutes, the sharing of the nuts-and-bolts information about the assignment has been interrupted by something more entertaining and creative.

Sometimes, the artistic, creative part of folklore is obvious, consciously highlighted, even arranged. A singer may sit in front of an assembled group and sing ballads, share songs with another performer one-on-one, or perform a song as part of another event. The artistic components may also be more subtly presented or be less apparent because they are inherent within the item of folklore itself. All folklore, though, is expressive; it conveys ideas, values, and traditions creatively even when it is not overtly artistic. A carved wooden spoon, even if it is plain and simple, can be a folk object if it is made with certain materials or with certain special techniques that are specific to a particular group. These artistic, creative expressions invite others to evaluate them in terms of what we might call artistic or creative quality and also in terms

7

of their skillfulness and appropriateness for the setting. (In the "Aesthetics" section of the Performance chapter, we'll present a more detailed discussion of these ideas.)

So, while we first want to acknowledge that folklore is difficult to define, we offer the following working definition:

> Folklore is informally learned, unofficial knowledge about the world, our-selves, our communities, our beliefs, our cultures, and our traditions that is expressed creatively through words, music, customs, actions, behaviors, and materials. It is also the interactive, dynamic process of creating, communicating, and performing as we share that knowledge with other people.

Scholarly Definitions of Folklore

Scholars have defined folklore both according to its components and according to theories that help us understand how it works. We'll take a look at some of these scholarly definitions and analyze how they clarify and extend our working understanding of folklore.

Among those who have focused on the items that folklorists study are Alan Dundes and Mary Hufford. Dundes provides a lengthy list that, while impressive, is not exhaustive (as Dundes himself acknowledges):

> Folklore includes myths, legends, folktales, jokes, proverbs, riddles, chants, charms, blessings, curses, oaths, insults, retorts, taunts, teases, toasts, tongue-twisters, and greeting and leave-taking formulas (e.g., See you later, alligator). It also includes folk costume, folk dance, folk drama (and mime), folk art, folk belief (or superstition), folk medicine, folk instrumental music (e.g., fiddle tunes), folksongs (e.g., lullabies, ballads), folk speech (e.g., slang), folk similes (e.g., blind as a bat), folk metaphors (e.g., to paint the town red), and names (e.g., nicknames and place names). Folk poetry ranges from oral epics to autograph-book verse, epitaphs, latrinalia (writings on the walls of public bathrooms), limericks, ball-bouncing rhymes, jump-rope rhymes, finger and toe rhymes, dandling rhymes (to bounce children on the knee), counting out rhymes (to determine who will be "it" in games), and nursery rhymes. The list of folklore forms also contains games; gestures; symbols; prayers (e.g., graces); practical jokes; folk etymologies; food recipes; quilt and embroidery designs; house, barn, and fence types; street vendor's cries; and even the traditional conventional sounds used to summon animals or give

8

them commands. There are such minor forms as mnemonic devices (e.g, the name "Roy G. Biv" to remember the colors of the spectrum in order), envelope sealers (e.g., "SWAK"—Sealed With A Kiss), and the traditional comments made after body emissions (e.g., after burps or sneezes). There are such major forms as festivals and special day (or holiday) customs (e.g., Christmas, Halloween, and birthday).

This list provides a sampling of the forms of folklore. It does not include all the forms. (1965, 1–3)

In the same vein, Mary Hufford defines American *folklife* (another term used in conjunction with, or sometimes interchangeably with, folklore) this way:

Like Edgar Allan Poe's purloined letter, folklife is often hidden in full view, lodged in the various ways we have of discovering and expressing who we are and how we fit into the world. Folklife is reflected in the names we bear from birth, invoking affinities with saints, ancestors, or cultural heroes. Folklife is the secret languages of children, the codenames of CB operators, and the working slang of watermen and doctors. It is the shaping of everyday experiences in stories swapped around kitchen tables or parables told from pulpits. It is the African American rhythms embedded in gospel hymns, bluegrass music, and hip hop, and the Lakota flutist rendering anew his people's ancient courtship songs.

Folklife is the sung parodies of the "Battle Hymn of the Republic" and the variety of ways there are to skin a muskrat, preserve string beans, or join two pieces of wood. Folklife is the society welcoming new members at *bris* and christening, and keeping the dead incorporated on All Saints Day. It is the marking of the Jewish New Year at Rosh Hashanah and the Persian New Year at Noruz. It is the evolution of *vaqueros* into *buckaroos*, and the riderless horse, its stirrups backward, in the funeral processions of high military commanders.

Folklife is the thundering of foxhunters across the rolling Rappahannock countryside and the listening of hilltoppers to hounds crying fox in the Tennessee mountains. It is the twirling of lariats at western rodeos, and the spinning of double-dutch jump-ropes in West Philadelphia. It is scattered across the landscape in Finnish saunas and Italian vineyards; engraved in the split-rail boundaries of Appalachian "hollers" and the stone fences around Catskill "cloves"; scrawled on urban streetscapes by graffiti artists; and projected onto skylines by the tapering steeples of churches, mosques, and temples.

9

Folklife is community life and values, artfully expressed in myriad forms and interactions. Universal, diverse, and enduring, it enriches the nation and makes us a commonwealth of cultures. (1991)

The preceding definitions illustrate the variety of things folklore can be and the detailed attention folklorists give to their subject; other, broader definitions consider what folklore does and what it means to the groups that share it. William Wilson stresses the humanistic aspects of folklore, which lead us to explore what it means "to be human." Wilson says, "It is this attempt to discover the basis of our common humanity, the imperatives of our human existence, that puts folklore study at the very center of humanistic study" (1988, 157–58). Dan Ben-Amos offers another simple definition: "Folklore is artistic communication in small groups" (1971, 13), which implies the aesthetic qualities of folklore and the importance of group interaction in observing and defining it.[2] Many other folklorists discuss the ways people learn, create, and share folklore and emphasize that folklore is a process people actively engage in. Barre Toelken describes this process as the main defining feature of folklore: "All folklore participates in a distinctive, dynamic process" (1996, 7). Toelken says the process of folklore is a combination of both changing ("dynamic") and static ("conservative") elements that connect with a group's past *and* present in ways that evolve and change through sharing, communication, and performance.[3] In 1938, Benjamin Botkin, folklore editor for the Works Progress Administration's Federal Writers' Project, offered the following forward-thinking definition:

Folklore is a body of traditional belief, custom, and expression, handed down largely by word of mouth and circulating chiefly outside of commercial and academic means of communication and instruction. Every group bound together by common interests and purposes, whether educated or uneducated, rural or urban, possesses a body of traditions which may be called its folklore. Into these traditions enter many elements, individual, popular, and even "literary," but all are absorbed and assimilated through repetition and variation into a pattern which has value and continuity for the group as a whole. (1938)

These kinds of definitions emphasize the fact that the expressions, customs, and objects folklorists study do not exist in a vacuum apart from the people who create and share them.

Several definitions highlight the ways that folklore is part of unofficial, non-institutional knowledge and experience. According to Jan Harold Brunvand,

"Folklore is the traditional, unofficial, non-institutional part of culture. It encompasses all knowledge, understandings, values, attitudes, assumptions, feelings, and beliefs transmitted in traditional forms by word of mouth or by customary examples" (1998, 4). Richard Dorson notes the contrast between unofficial culture and "the high, the visible, the institutional culture of church, state, the universities, the professions, the corporations, the fine arts, the sciences" and explains that unofficial knowledge is communicated through such channels as "folk religion, folk medicine, folk literature, the folk arts, and folk philosophy" (1976, 46). In other words, folklore is, again, connected with day-to-day experiences we share with people in our schools, neighborhoods, peer groups, and families. It isn't something we are officially taught through organizations or textbooks.

There are many more definitions, and new ones emerge as the discipline grows. None of these definitions is really wrong, yet none is absolutely definitive. Folklorists continue to define and redefine the term frequently because folklore itself changes, as does our understanding of it. Still, most of the current definitions share common features that help us develop a clear understanding of folklore. First of all, as we have said, it is commonly acknowledged by scholars that *folklore is informal, not formal; unofficial, not official.* Second, *folklore is considered to be both the "items" people share and study and the active process of communicating folklore to and with others.* Other components that folklorists frequently mention are communication, performance, art, group identity, shared beliefs and values, and tradition.

The American Folklore Society (AFS) notes that most definitions of folklore "challenge the notion of folklore as something that is simply 'old,' 'old-fashioned,' 'exotic,' 'rural,' 'peasant,' 'uneducated,' 'untrue,' or 'dying out'" and explains that although "folklore connects people to their past, it is a central part of life in the present, and is at the heart of all cultures—including our own—throughout the world" (AFS website). In all the definitions, several features remain constant: folklore is an active part of human existence and expression, involving art, communication, process, culture, and identity.

We'll restate our working definition again so you might consider it in terms of the other definitions we have presented:

Folklore is informally learned, unofficial knowledge about the world, ourselves, our communities, our beliefs, our cultures, and our traditions that is expressed creatively through words, music, customs, actions, behaviors, and materials. It is also the interactive, dynamic process of creating, communicating, and performing as we share that knowledge with other people.

As our discussion progresses throughout the rest of this book, we will develop terms, concepts, and examples that expand and support this suggested definition. We invite you to develop your own definition, one that expresses your understanding of the field, as your study continues.

Genres of Folklore

Although broad definitions of folklore don't always specifically name the "stuff" that constitutes folklore, folklorists have developed labels that organize and categorize types of folklore into *genres*. You may recognize the term *genre* from your art or literature classes as another term for classification. Barre Toelken says, "Just as doctors do not talk about the body without knowing all the principal parts, just as a linguist cannot talk about language without a vocabulary of terms that describe words, sounds, and meaning, so the folklorist does not discuss folklore without a sound knowledge of its genres. . . . Without a generic terminology, we would have little hope of understanding each other" (1996, 183). Using generic labels in discussing folklore offers a straightforward way of categorizing what folklorists study. It gives us a common language so we can share and discuss ideas and interpretations. Having a vocabulary that helps us conceptualize the qualities of items of folklore allows us to discuss it more easily.

Folklore can be categorized in many ways, based on its particular characteristics and how it is expressed. Three broad categories often used to describe folklore are verbal, material, and customary.[4] Within these genres, there are numerous types or subtypes of lore. You are likely to be familiar with at least a few examples of each of these genres.

Verbal folklore includes any kind of lore involving words, whether set to music, organized in chronological story form, or simply labeling an activity or expressing a belief with a word or phrase. Some of the most recognizable forms of verbal lore studied by folklorists are folk songs, myths, and folktales. The ballad "Barbara Allen," a knock-knock joke, or the folktale "The Tortoise and the Hare" may come to mind when you think about verbal texts you are familiar with. Along these same lines are contemporary or urban legends. These are stories about seemingly true events—for example, a report that a psychic appearing on a late-night talk show predicted that nine students from a midwestern university would be killed on Halloween by a person dressed as Little Bo Peep. There are numerous other verbal expressions of folklore, such as jokes, jump-rope rhymes, proverbs, and riddles. Even individuals' own stories about their lives, their personal narratives, are considered to be folklore (Stahl 1977). These may be entertaining, informative, or both. They may arise within everyday conversation or within an event or situation that includes other folk expressions or that is specifically marked as an expressive event. Regardless of whether the audience responds with laughter, tears, or rapt attention, this verbal lore expresses beliefs and values and may even educate members of the folk group that hear it.

Material folklore takes a number of different forms, some of it more or less permanent, such as architectural structures or functional tools, and some of it ephemeral, such as food, body painting, or paper ornaments. Permanent or not, material culture is tangible—it can be touched, seen, eaten, or lived in. In many cases, these material objects are handcrafted, but they may also be mass-produced items, such as holiday decorations, toys, or artifacts, that are used in expressive ways. A dreidel may have been manufactured rather than created by a craftsman, yet it can still be used by Jewish children in traditional Hanukkah games and therefore considered an item of folklore—playing the dreidel game involves both material and customary folklore (see below). Often, though, the material culture that folklorists study is created by members of a folk group, whether to function within a belief-oriented customary practice or an everyday folk event. Quilts are a type of material culture you may already identify as folklore. Folklorists have studied the artistry of quilts, examining the designs and colors used by different individual quilters and groups of quilters. In addition to analyzing the material objects themselves, folklorists have studied the informal learning processes by which quilters have taught each other techniques of quilting and elements of design. Extending the community's interactions further shows how the practice of quilting can be an opportunity for social interaction, with the women who are quilting sharing values and cultural knowledge while they stuff and stitch.

Several dreidels in the collection of Joyce Hersh, Bexley, Ohio

Dreidels in Joyce Hersh's collection range from elaborate, handcrafted, one-of-a-kind decorative art pieces to mass-produced toys meant for children to use in playing the dreidel game. The dreidels in the collection come from Ukraine, Italy, Israel, eastern Europe, and the United States. When Joyce's children were young, they received dreidels every year from friends and family members during Hanukkah. After her children grew up, Joyce decided she wanted dreidels of her own.

Many of the toy dreidels in Joyce's collection originally belonged to her children. Joyce and her husband, Alan, describe how they used to fill some of the plastic ones with chocolate gelt (wrapped, coin-shaped chocolate candy) to give the kids as gifts. Joyce tells of finding two painted ceramic dreidels while shopping on a family trip and then discovering when she returned that they were actually a set of salt and pepper shakers. They are impractical as shakers, though, since their shape makes it impossible for them to stay upright, but they are brightly painted and humorous examples of mass-produced, culturally significant material folklore. Another similarly amusing example is a plush keychain dreidel with a smiling face embroidered on one side, which she found in a local department store. Joyce collects these varied types and styles of dreidels, she says, to "counterbalance the Christmas hoopla" and to express her Judaism.

High-art and pop-art dreidels

The mass-produced or less serious-looking dreidels may seem on the surface to be less valuable or important than those that are handmade or artistically designed, but both Joyce and Alan believe that all the dreidels in the collection are meaningful because they express their Jewish heritage and reflect their own family's traditions.

As we looked at the collection together, Alan shared his memories of his Lithuanian-born grandfather, who, he said, "would never have used a dreidel that wasn't handcrafted." Alan's grandfather worked in the garment industry, and he and others in the family would carve dreidels from the wooden spools used to hold thread. The children in his family each received a new dreidel every year, and Alan remembers that "they

Assortment of hand crafted and mass produced dreidels

would spin beautifully." He also recounted the story of how Jews had used dreidels and the children's dreidel game to conceal the study of Hebrew and Jewish customs during the Greek-Syrian occupation. When groups of young boys who were studying the Torah saw the authorities coming, they would take out dreidels and spin them, so the Greeks would believe they were only gathered to play a game.

Taken together, these three elements—personal, family, and cultural narratives; the objects themselves; and the customary game—illustrate the complexity of folklore and communicate group values and shared identity to the Hersh family, the Jewish community, and anyone who views the collection.

Customary lore, of the three broad genres, is perhaps the most difficult to characterize. A custom is a repeated, habitual action, a usual way of doing something. For folklorists, custom refers to patterned, repeated behavior in which a person's participation indicates involved membership.[5] These practices may be stylized and/or framed by special words, gestures, or actions that set them apart from everyday behaviors, or they may be as simple as gestures used in everyday communication within an intimate group of friends.[6] A fraternity's secret handshake is a customary gesture that indicates membership in the group and also expresses to other brothers the significance of maintaining the closed society and adhering to its values. Teenage girls' attempts to conjure up "Bloody Mary" during slumber parties are customary behavior as well. Many belief behaviors, such as crossing fingers for good luck, are examples of broadly practiced customary folklore.

Even in this brief discussion of genres, it may be apparent to you that many communicative expressions are made up of more than one genre of folklore. Toelken describes the genres as "the forms and kinds" of folklore and says they "fall into a number of partially overlapping categories" (1996, 8). In the example above, the game children play with the dreidel is customary lore, yet this custom involves a meaningful cultural material artifact. Classifications of genre, while helpful in discussing the types of folklore studied, are limiting in that they suggest that individual texts are self-contained, not dependent on or related to other items of folklore. Another point to consider is that different "kinds of folk expression" (Toelken 1996, 184) may very well express the same beliefs or attitudes as another genre or subgenre.

Often, celebrations include folklore from each of the genres, and frequently the many forms of texts present in a celebration express important group values and beliefs. You are probably familiar with the variety of lore associated with many North American wedding ceremonies. Ceremonies contain such verbal texts as "With this ring, I thee wed" or "Is there any person here who has cause to believe this couple should not be wed?" Many ceremonies include certain pieces of instrumental music, such as Bach's "Jesu, Joy of Man's Desiring," the traditional "Bridal March" ("Here Comes the Bride") by Richard Wagner or Felix Mendelssohn's "Wedding March" (often used as the recessional). Brides, grooms, and their families often rely on customary practices to express belief in the marriage vows and share the hope that the marriage will last. A bride often searches for "something old, something new, something borrowed, and something blue" to wear or carry on her wedding day for luck. And of course there are many other significant, sometimes symbolic, texts of material culture. The white color of a bridal gown symbolizes the purity of the bride. Some ceremonies include the lighting of a unity candle by the bride and groom. And most receptions, big or small, include a cake from which the bride and groom share the first piece. A variety of post-wedding customs involve the cake, from the bride and groom eating the top layer on their one-year anniversary to unmarried women sleeping with slices of cake under their pillows so they will dream of their future husbands. In one wedding divination ritual, the bride throws her bouquet to the single women in attendance, and whoever catches it is believed to be the next to get married. The many elements of the rituals, verbal

17

expressions, and material objects that appear in wedding celebrations show the value of marriage to all those participating in the ceremony and reception.

Looking at genres used to be the main way folklorists approached and analyzed folklore. Now, although it's still part of the language of folklore studies, classifying by genre is no longer considered to be a primary goal of folklore study. Most folklorists now feel that in addition to the fact that items of folklore may bridge many categories, the whole idea of genre itself can be relative. What a folklorist might call a "tall tale" a performer might call a "big lie." What the performer would call it might also be relative, since he or she might place it in a different category than would someone in another group. Another example that illustrates the problem of absolute genre classification is Hmong story cloths. Some Hmong immigrants to the United States create elaborate, three-dimensional cloth sculptures called story cloths, which tell the story of their journey to their new country (and other stories as well). The cloths are material objects, they follow artistic and organizational patterns that are traditional for the group, and they also have a verbal component: the images depicted tell a story, and the maker may recite the story to others as she points out the features of the sculpture. In addition to all of these considerations, we may view the cloth itself as an example of folk art. Thus, the genre into which we place an item frequently depends on which elements we emphasize when we analyze it.

Yet, as contestable as the term may be, here we are—talking about genre. So what are the main reasons we sometimes still find genre a useful tool in looking at folklore? One reason, as we said at the beginning of this section, is that it gives folklorists a common language to use as a reference point. As folklorists study new and evolving folklore, they need to have ways to talk about those new types. The loose classifications of genre provide a foundation for identifying, discussing, and analyzing the qualities of items of folklore. Another reason is that folklorists sometimes focus their careers in the study of one particular type of folklore, and the genre labels help them locate and communicate with others studying the same type. Genre labels may also be helpful when members of a folk group perform only a certain type of folklore, or, perhaps more likely, a particular folk performer or artist specializes in a particular area. Having a name or label gives us a place to start in understanding artists' and performers' work.

Defining Folklore Beyond Genre Labels: Texts and Contexts

Throughout this book we use genre labels in examples to help us anchor our discussions of interpretation and theory. Genre classifications are not, however, the focus of our approach to understanding folklore. Our focus is on the *expressive ways people communicate*. While the use of genre labels is still a very handy way for us to talk about folklore, we want to introduce here a concept that goes beyond genre classifications and instead looks at folklore as a complex, interconnected act of communication. In this book, we frequently use the term *text* to refer to many kinds of folklore, including things we don't often think of as texts—performances, objects, and rituals, for instance. We use the term *context* to mean everything that surrounds the text—the setting, people, situation—anything in addition to the expressions, item, idea, or objects being shared. As part of our development of the definition of folklore, we want to broaden the idea of folklore types in order to give you more than one way to understand and talk about the verbal expressions, customs, and materials that folklore comprises. This will enable you to think about it conceptually, not just categorically. In later chapters, we will expand on these terms in much more detail, but for now we want simply to present them for you to consider.

You may be familiar with the idea of a text as something that is written: textbooks, works of literature (short or long), or subtitles that run along the bottom of a movie or television screen. However, the etymological definition of text is much broader. Specifically, *text* is derived from the Latin *texere,* which means "to weave." This aspect of the definition suggests that text is like a cloth, a material object, woven of many different threads, all combined to create a coherent whole. The word also figuratively suggests the "theme or subject on which anyone speaks; the starting point of a discussion" (*Shorter Oxford English Dictionary*). So in its most encompassing sense, *text* can refer to words, objects, ideas, and behaviors. Frequently, when we use the word *text,* either on its own or in conjunction with the words *folklore* or *folk,* we intend it to mean all these complex possibilities, as well as the particular content of a particular item of folklore.

Significant developments in recent folklore scholarship concern the type of texts that folklorists study, as well as the way they study them. Early folklorists focused on oral texts, examining the narratives of cultures, looking for beliefs articulated in them and connections between them. Those who studied written texts might have looked at a text as an example of a particular type of verbal lore, searched for the oldest version of a text, or sought remnants of oral narratives in literary novels or traditional beliefs referred to in a short story. Oral narratives are still studied by folklorists, but now a folklorist might consider social relationships between tellers and listeners or look at the circumstances in which a particular narrative emerges within a particular setting. Folklorists still study written texts, too—even what might be considered fine or elite literature.

19

But while in the past literary scholars who studied folklore might be interested in literature as a repository of folklore (Barnes 1979), scholars now explore folklore *and* literature, rather than folklore *in* literature (12). They might, for example, look at how understanding traditions helps readers interpret characters or story lines in a play, how a film presents a cultural view, or how a particular novel subverts our assumptions about a group or culture.[7] (One of the examples we include in Chapter 8, for instance, considers how foodways express and define gender roles in Zora Neale Hurston's *Their Eyes Were Watching God*.) In any case, folklorists are interested in oral and written verbal texts not as static objects but as an aid to learning about people, tradition, and expressive culture. And while oral and written narratives of all forms continue to interest folklorists, the field has broadened to encompass the study of a wide variety of "texts"—verbal, material, behavioral—that cultures use to express themselves.

Digital technology has further broadened the field by opening an additional venue for cultural expression. Many people, of all ages, genders, and races, interact on the Internet regularly, reading, responding to, and creating a variety of digital texts. Sometimes these texts are familiar, having been presented in other forms, media, or contexts. For example, verbal jokes may be passed along to friends and family simply through forwarding (Frank, 2009). Other times individuals more actively create texts that are shared via the Internet. Verbal lore—narratives, especially jokes—may be what comes to mind most readily as the type of text shared on the Internet, but these texts may be verbal, behavioral, or material (visual jokes or digital artwork, for example). It is easy to understand how material texts are created and shared digitally. Users' profile pictures, other images, and icons presented on social networks, in blogs, and on chat sites serve as material representations of users and communicate users' identity within the groups they are in contact with.

Shared material texts include visual jokes, such as political figures photoshopped into controversial locations, and more interactive shared play, such as *lolcats*, photos of cats accompanied by brief related captions in *lolspeak*, which users can both create and rate. Rating lolcats has become a behavior shared by many Internet users, who may or may not know the others who are rating the cats. In addition to interacting with online texts, some people perform personal or individualized online rituals. Examples would be checking one's horoscope every day or having a joke, Buddhist thought of the day, or other meaningful item sent to one's email. Others may be members of virtual groups or organizations that share and perform verbal-behavioral texts. Members of the Flyladies, for example, a virtual group dedicated to helping members clean and organize their homes, follow informal guidelines presented on the organization's website, Flylady.com. Members receive emails daily (according to the site, an average of 10 emails a day), containing cleaning tips, essays about orderly living, and "missions"—testimonials and challenges to guide members in accomplishing their daily Flylady tasks.

Regardless of the type of text, or whether people interact with it in the physical or online world, folklorists believe that in order to best understand cultural expression, they must study it *in context*. Folklorists care about where and when people interact with folklore, and what roles group members play in creating and sharing texts. Without considering these contextual factors, an urban legend is just another story, and a *tsoureki* is just a loaf of bread with eggs on top. Knowing who has told the legend, to whom, and in what situation provides the folklorist with much more opportunity to interpret what the legend means to the members of the community. Likewise, knowing who has baked the bread, for whom, and for what meal or event also permits deeper understanding. Sometimes, there will be a particular person within the culture whose role it is to perform a certain function. For example, only certain people may tell a particular story under particular conditions. There may be an "expert" (sometimes labeled by folklorists as a tradition bearer) who will create and/or teach others to create a certain item. Or it may be that *any* member of a group may perform or create texts.

It's important to note that the text being studied in a single event or performance may be different, depending on the context—the situation, the people present, and even the folklorists studying it. For example, if a folklorist is studying a ritual, he or she could be examining the significance of items such as the oral text recited during the ritual, a material object that is presented to a member being initiated into the group in the particular ritual, or dance steps performed during the event. Any of these could be considered texts within that event and could be studied as an element of the ritual. Certainly, some folklorists might choose to study all three texts together, looking at the ritual itself as the text. Regardless, any one of them is considered a text of folklore and is one of the wide variety of behaviors or tangible items that fall within the bounds of folklore study. This multiplicity of texts illustrates another important aspect of the study of folklore: the breadth of expressive communication that it includes.

A Brief History of Folklore Study

To understand how folklore came to encompass so many types of expression, it is useful to consider the history of the field.

Tsoureki bread.

The history of the study of folklore has been thoroughly discussed and can be found in a number of sources. Depending on the academic department in which you are being introduced to folklore—anthropology, English, folklore, humanities, or comparative studies, for instance—the instructor may emphasize different trends, movements, and people in the history of the field. So, rather than go into every detail of the history here, we want to provide a brief overview that is by no means exhaustive but that points out the major developments in the discipline that have influenced the way we currently approach folklore studies. (You may encounter some of the terms and names we mention here later in this book in expanded discussions.) Keep a few things in mind as you read the following section: while the structure we follow is loosely chronological, be aware that many of the movements and trends we mention were occurring at roughly the same time, with much overlap. This overlap illustrates the fluidity of the field, as well as its multidisciplinary and international flavor. Along those lines, scholars from interrelated fields, from a variety of countries, have contributed to the development of folklore study. We mention here only a very few of the important and influential scholars who have shaped the field in order to provide some signposts as you navigate its history. As you read this section, you will notice that many of the examples refer to verbal lore; this is not because nobody was looking at material or customary lore but because the focus for much of the twentieth century, especially in the United States, was on verbal texts.

In the early years of folklore scholarship, scholars studied lore of people who were unlike them. The romantic concept of "the folk" grew in the eighteenth century out of a sense that civilization separated humans from the natural world and that we had lost something pure and spiritual in the process. The Romantics thought that those who lived farther away from "civilized society"—that is, those in rural areas and small villages—were closer to humanity's natural, and therefore, better, state. Scholars traveled to these more remote areas to collect the remaining fragments of pristine "folk culture," reinforcing the dichotomy between the educated scholars who studied folklore and the uneducated folk who created and maintained it (see Oring 1986c, 4–6). The desire of these scholars was to redeem humanity by reconnecting us with our lost, more natural state of existence. These Romantic interpretations of the folk influenced the direction of folklore study for many years.

German scholars in the eighteenth and nineteenth centuries believed that members of the rural, lower-class communities of Germany held the knowledge of the country's ancient Teutonic past, and they feared that this culture and knowledge were disappearing as these groups were being wiped out, gentrified, or educated (Oring 1986c, 5). Scholars decided that they needed to collect and document this diminishing knowledge from those they deemed folk, so that Germany's cultural history wouldn't be lost. They saw their job as different from that of historians who were called on to record the significant events of the past. You might recognize two of the early scholars of the field in Germany— the Brothers Grimm. Jacob and Wilhelm Grimm's *Grimm's Fairy Tales*, written from 1812 to 1852, is a collection of stories shared by the rural folk of Germany Folklore was considered to be the cultural trappings of the country—its stories, beliefs, traditions, and rituals—not the wars won, paintings and music created, or churches built. This *nationalist approach* to folklore studies placed the emphasis on examining a dying culture, a culture scholars assumed was being displaced by the educated people of Germany, in order to reinforce a sense of shared identity. The Germans were the first to look at folklore studies in this way, but these nationalistic impulses extended to other countries as well. The German method of collecting lore was a forerunner of folklore collection and interpretation methods in other nations. One goal of this approach was to find the essence of the stories, beliefs, customs, and traditions that connected all the people of a given country to a common cultural past.

The term *folklore* was first used in 1846 by an English scholar, William John Thoms, who modeled his ideas for studying expressive culture on the work of the Grimm brothers (Oring 1986c, 6). In England, scholars of literature and history focused on collecting material and verbal texts and customary behaviors

23

of people in the British countryside; these texts were frequently referred to as "popular antiquities." As in Germany and Britain, in the latter part of the 1800s intellectuals in the United States began collecting folklore as a means of preserving the history of rural, preindustrial people. Bronner summarizes the transition from Americans' early interest in the study of "popular antiquities" to the collection of "folk lore" as indicating scholars were beginning to recognize that the lore they studied had relevance in people's daily lives and that folklore was more than merely old-fashioned historical objects or practices (1986). Use of the term "folk" rather than "popular" underscored the examination of groups *of people* within the larger population (20).

Another development around this time was the search to find the original text or the definitive, most accurate version against which to compare all the later (often with the implication of "lesser") variants.[8] Regional differences in folk texts and objects could also be studied this way. Folklorists looked for references to traditions and beliefs in order to locate folklore within a particular cultural, ethnic, or social framework and to trace the migration of texts as people moved from one geographic region to another and transmitted texts within and across generations or social groups. Identifying the meanings of words, references, or symbols, as well as looking for literary patterns in oral and written texts, anchored this approach in academic traditions of literary study, which reinforced the idea of the text as an object that could be studied separately from its setting or the people who shared and created it. Most scholars still assumed that folklore texts were remnants or artifacts from a fading past that needed to be preserved. This approach was part of the historic-geographic study of folk texts, which focused on comparing and analyzing the ways texts evolved through time and across geographic regions.

Related to the search for origins of folk narratives and beliefs was Solar Mythology Theory, which also appeared in the nineteenth century. Proponents of this theory saw connections between myths and mythological characters as expressions of beliefs about the sun and moon. This theory, developed by German linguist Max Müller, held that European folktales all derived from these solar myths and contained similar symbols related to night and day. Solar mythologists even applied this theory to non-European texts (Brunvand 1998, 188) and found that it also helped to explain the appearance of similar texts in different cultures or different parts of the world. This theory, while interesting when applied to the study of myth, did not help folklorists talk about things other than myths or about how folklore changed and adapted to the groups of people who shared it.

Around the turn of the twentieth century, many scholars throughout the United States and Europe were interested in how people shared and learned folklore. Franz Boas, a German-born anthropologist who was a leader in American anthropological and folklore scholarship in the late nineteenth and early twentieth centuries, examined *diffusion*, the way texts move and change from culture to culture, and he encouraged students to perform fieldwork. He focused on the differences and similarities between cultures and asserted that culture influences everything we know and experience. Whatever the influences, each cultural group is complete in and of itself, a phenomenon Boas and his colleagues referred to as *cultural relativism*. As Simon Bronner says, for Boas "cultural relativism stressed the integrity of individual cultures and, often, the individual within the culture" (1986, 69). This emphasis on culture and the ways culture shapes groups' and individuals' views of the world encouraged the later understanding of folklore as something that expresses, reinforces, and sometimes challenges people's values and beliefs.

Also at about this time, scholars were still working on cataloging related types of folklore, particularly verbal texts. In order to trace the transmission of texts, scholars such as Stith Thompson and Antti Aarne categorized tales based on their narrative elements or thematic features, such as types of characters, plotlines, details, or recurring motifs. Aarne and Thompson's *The Types of the Folktale* (1987) and Thompson's *Motif Index of Folk Literature* (1955) are still used by historic-geographic scholars who are interested in analyzing structural and narrative similarities among folktales and other forms of verbal lore.

Related to the study of transmission was the study of how folklore texts are organized and created. At this time, most folklore scholars still defined folklore as primarily verbal in nature and as being transmitted orally. These folklorists, including Stith Thompson, generated criteria that allowed them to track the transmission (and perhaps even the origin) of tales, songs, and other such verbal lore. Many scholars focused on narrative elements related to syntactic features that grew out of orally constructed narratives like epic poems and oratorical forms. Building on the work of Milman Parry, Albert B. Lord developed a complex system to describe the features of narrative folklore, called *oral formulaic theory*, sometimes referred to as Parry-Lord theory or analysis (1960). Scholars applied the principles of formal text analysis developed by Parry and Lord in the study of the structure and organization of a variety of texts from folktales to ballads to sermons.

In the 1930s, the US government established the Federal Writers' Project of the Works Progress (later Projects) Administration, in which thousands of unemployed writers participated in a vast project to collect the life stories, tales, songs, and verbal expressions of "ordinary Americans." Benjamin A. Botkin, national folklore editor of the Federal Writers' Project, supervised the collection of most of the life histories and urged the collector-writers to accurately record vernacular expressions, idioms, and dialects in their collections (Library of Congress 1998). Other important figures who participated in the Writers' Project as collectors or administrators include John and Alan Lomax, Zora Neale Hurston, and Ralph Ellison. Botkin and John Lomax, especially, influenced the direction of folklore collection through their emphasis on the process of interviewing individuals about their experiences and recording details of settings, situations, and cultural features.

Through much of the first half of the twentieth century, folklorists conducted in-depth studies within specific genres that in part formed the foundations of future theoretical investigations. Many important collections and discussions of the folklore genres came about. Among them, D. K. Wilgus's studies of folk songs, Wayland Hand's collections of proverbs and traditional expressions, George Korson's collections of occupational folklore, and the recorded song collections of the Lomaxes (John and Alan) continue to be important reference points for current folklorists who are interested in these genres. As folklorists began to examine those collections, they began to do more than just define or describe items—they asked questions about how people interacted with the texts. One interpretive method, *functionalism*, asked the question, what does the text mean to the group? *Structuralism*, another interpretive approach that followed on the heels of functionalism, broke the text down into parts and analyzed how those parts related to the whole in order to discover what was important about the item or text to the group. While folklore study has moved beyond these examinations that focus narrowly on a certain aspect of a text, the emphasis they brought to groups and people, rather than just texts and items, has remained.

Concurrently, linguists were developing theories about the ways we communicate and about how speakers and listeners interact with each other through verbal expression. Erving Goffman described and theorized about the ways utterances are usually framed or set off by words, gestures, or other markers that indicate when "speech events" begin, how they progress, and when they end (1974).

In the 1960s and 1970s, an important convergence occurred between folklore scholarship and linguistic scholarship about performance in verbal art. People such as Dell Hymes, Joel Sherzer, Dan Ben-Amos, Roger Abrahams, and Richard Bauman extended their interests in the events and texts of spoken communication to the situations in which speech takes place. Analyzing the act of speaking beyond the actual structure of the language or of individual utterances, these scholars looked at *how* we communicate—at language

26

as something we participate in, within clearly defined settings and situations (Kapchan 1995, 479–80). These developments encouraged a move away from a primary focus on products or texts, toward a focus on the *performance of texts in context*. Scholars began to look at the interactions among those involved in acts of communication, as well as the occasions and settings in which those acts take place. Looking at interactions between performers and audiences encouraged folklorists to see that performance is an artistic act; it sets off certain kinds of expression from the ordinary.

The focus on performance and artistic communication foregrounded *context*—the physical, cultural, and group settings in which folklore occurs—as central in understanding any expression of folklore. Scholars who looked at context, including Richard Bauman, mentioned above, and Barbara Kirshenblatt-Gimblett (1975), conducted detailed analyses of particular speech events that illustrated the value of careful contextual analysis.

As a result of this convergence of theories and disciplines, "a more symbolic view of performance" developed (Kapchan 1995, 480), which opened up exploration of the ways communication patterns reveal the beliefs, traditions, and values of speakers and listeners. Roger Abrahams conceived of performance as "cultural enactment" (cited in Kapchan 1995, 479), in which members of folk groups express and reinforce community identity. These more theoretical discussions extended to customary and material expression as well. Folklore scholars came to see that sharing folklore—verbal, customary, and material—is a lively activity that teaches individuals about the beliefs and values of the group and maintains identity through repeated enactments of ideas that are important to the group.

The performance approach helped to establish the core of the discipline as the study of artistic expression in groups and specific contexts. For folklorists, looking at performance provided the opportunity to expand the understanding of how people create, share, and relate with folklore texts. Some scholars, however, critiqued performance studies as not giving enough attention to the cultural, social, and emotional elements of folklore and as being too narrowly focused on specific speaking and performance contexts and not enough on wider social, political, or historical contexts (Limon and Young 1986; Sawin 2002). Limon and Young (1986) also pointed out that performance studies of the 1970s (and folklore studies in general) had neglected women's folklore and nonverbal texts.

These critics identified several areas that performance studies needed to include: structuralism and semiotics,[9] psychological and political perspectives, women's folklore and gender studies, material culture, and urban contexts (Limon and Young 1986, 448–54). They encouraged continued attention to work begun by "performance-oriented material culturalists"(453)[10] that explores how artists and other responding group members behave in relation to the objects they create. They identified some studies, like Michael Owen Jones's work with Chester Cornett, a woodworker and chairmaker from Kentucky, and Henry Glassie's seminal studies of Irish storytellers, as being attentive to how verbal artists and material artists connect with and relate to both the texts and objects they create and the people in their communities.

Several women folklorists in the 1970s had already begun to call for a new approach to folklore collection and study that focused on the expressive culture of women. Though folklorists had studied the culture of women throughout the history of the discipline, the focus had been primarily on the lives and lore of men, with the folklore of women—when studied—considered in relationship to men. The *Journal of American Folklore* recognized this with its focus on women's folklore in a special issue published in 1975. This issue, edited by Claire Farrer, included a number of articles that brought attention to the need for further focused research on the folklore of women, calling for approaches that weren't grounded in the male perspective. Other studies, such as those by Joan N. Radner and Susan Lanser (1987), Radner (1993), Elaine Lawless (1991, 1993, 1994), and Jeannie B. Thomas (2000, 2003) have continued the study of women and folklore. Their work has moved the study of performance, and folklore in general, toward a more *integrated approach* to understanding concepts of identity, group dynamics, and the wider contextual factors that influence performance situations.

In addition to the concern that the study of performance has overlooked key social and political perspectives, another criticism of the performance approach has been that its success depends on observers or analysts having intimate involvement within a performance community in order to be literate in its language and cultural systems. That kind of intimacy is difficult to achieve unless one is already a member of the group. Recognizing that interpretations of meanings without input from those expressing these texts was essentially an outsider-imposed interpretation, folklorists began to consult group members in order to incorporate group views into the analyses. This emphasis on collaborative interpretation, or reciprocal ethnography, continues to be relevant as folklorists strive to avoid elitist, ethnocentric interpretations of folklore that leave out the people who express and share the lore.[11] Performance is still at the center of the study of folklore, but the concept has been expanded along with the study of social dimensions—the examination of how our many roles and experiences influence our lives as well as our expressions about our experiences. The synthesis of these different approaches to folklore influences interpretation and provides opportunities for folklorists to consider the relationships among texts, performances, and people within local, intimate contexts as well as wider social and political contexts.

Conclusion

As we look at this long history of the discipline, we see how our understanding of folklore has developed to center on people and actions, rather than static artifacts. Groups of people have an expressive life they learn and share informally that helps them identify themselves as a group. Through fieldwork and careful collecting that records details of setting, group, and culture, folklorists study the importance of these expressive acts to the groups that share them. The folklore we share grows out of, and is performed in, particular specific contexts and is also situated within larger group, social, and cultural contexts. In order to understand what a particular folklore performance means within a group, it is important to involve members of the group in our fieldwork and interpretations. These assumptions underlie current approaches to the study of folklore.

Because of the fluid nature of the field and because it is built from so many influences, folklore continues to evolve and change. It's not just that people change but that our opportunities for expression change; the influence of the Internet, for instance, has had a profound impact on how people communicate, and new forms and adaptations of folklore have emerged as a result. This means that folklorists will have new things to say about performances and texts generated through these new means. Part of what we do as folklorists is to discuss these changes as they arise and continually examine our assumptions about groups of people and how they share folklore.

The study of folklore encompasses so many types of expression that it's almost impossible *not* to find something to enjoy within the field. Whether you are interested in literature, psychology, sociology, history, biology, or technology; whether you take a practical hands-on approach to your studies or prefer a more theoretical, philosophical approach, there is some aspect of folklore that touches on all those things. It's a matter of adjusting that lens we referred to earlier—the unique way of understanding people, art, expression, and communication that folklorists bring to their investigations.

CHAPTER 2

Groups

*I*f folklore is a way of learning and a way of communicating, then there must be a group of people who need to communicate something to each other. Defining a folk group by how and what it communicates allows us to look at groups formed and maintained by informal means—those not constructed formally as groups by founders with particular rules and guidelines, but held together by the practices and expressions of their members. This is one of the tenets of folklore scholarship: that informal or unofficial shared knowledge is a defining feature of a folk group.

The concept of folk group has evolved radically over time. The early assumptions that folk groups were somehow different from the rest of us and were primarily rural, uneducated, or primitive yielded to the understanding that all of us share folklore every day. Folklorists established that we all belong to folk groups and that groups also exist in urban, contemporary settings (see, for instance, Dundes 1980). Today, digital technology provides extended opportunities for groups to form and communicate in new ways. A great deal of folklore research in recent years has focused on how online communities form and communicate and how they share traditions. This research has opened up new understanding of what groups are and what constitutes informal shared knowledge—folklore itself. Most importantly, the ability of people to come together online as groups and the complexity of online interactions demonstrate the dynamic process of sharing and creating folklore.

As the innovations presented by the Internet show us, folklorists cannot always know how our understanding of groups, and the groups themselves, will evolve. But it is clear that once we let go of the notion that folk groups are quaint or old fashioned, we can see that *people* are the central component of all folklore. Folklore does not exist in a vacuum, nor does it only come to us out of a misty, idealized past. People share jokes, stories, games, traditions, beliefs, and customs every day, and those things help us to express and strengthen our groups' identities. Families, friends, coworkers, and others are all groups brought together by common interests and experiences. The idea of *folk* is problematic because of its connotations of simplicity and quaintness, so folklorists often replace the term *folk group* with the more generic term *group*. In either case, whether we refer to folk groups or use the broader, more expansive term *group*, the focus on people is clear. Folklore is lived, experienced, created, and shared by people. In the next sections, we look in depth at what folk groups are, and we provide examples of how they form, as well as how folklore can create, reinforce, and express group identity.

What is a Folk Group?

If anyone had ever asked you, "How did you learn to be a member of your family?" you probably would have laughed and replied, "It doesn't take any special skills or qualities to be a member of a family!" Yet, being a member of a family or any other folk group, no matter how loosely or informally defined, involves special knowledge of its language, behavior, and rules—spoken or unspoken. These types of communication convey and express the group's attitudes, beliefs, values, and worldview to other members of the group and often to outsiders. Folklore is learned informally as we grow up in a group or as we are introduced to or invited into a new group.

All of us, no matter how educated we become or how urban our lifestyles, express ourselves through folklore every day, and each individual holds membership within more than one folk group. A family, the first folk group in which most of us are active members, has its own folklore, often a subset of or conglomeration of different ethnic, religious, regional, or social group lore. In addition, families may even create—intentionally or unintentionally—their own folklore that is meaningful only to them. Each family has its own system of appropriate and inappropriate behavior, of narratives that illustrate and teach family values, of rituals that celebrate or even satirize its beliefs. There are shared jokes and gestures, and oral or gestural shorthand that only family members understand. There are objects that serve as repositories of family history, and objects used to convey certain family attitudes and beliefs, whether the objects would be perceived by outsiders as clearly connected to those values or not.

31

You are familiar with such folklore from your own early experiences. Whoever raised you had traditions, rituals, and stories that you learned simply by observing and practicing them—seeing them expressed or overhearing them and observing how other members of your family responded to them. Family mealtime customs are rarely explicitly taught to children, for example, but we pick them up by watching, listening to reactions when people do or don't observe the customs, and imitating and then practicing these customs regularly. In your family, you might have waited until all members of the family were seated and their plates filled before everyone began to eat. Perhaps someone said a prayer or blessing before the meal began or you all held hands while the blessing was spoken. There might have been customs you performed at the end or closing of the meal. In the Sims family, children had to thank their mother for the meal before excusing themselves from the table for the evening. And certainly no one was allowed to eat dessert without cleaning his or her plate! Rules such as these may have seemed silly to you when you were growing up, but they were everyday expressions of belief and acknowledgment of the family structure. These are some of the simplest yet most universal indications of membership in a group: seemingly uncomplicated, habitual practices that people learn—without knowing they're learning—that express the attitudes, beliefs, and values of a group.

Families also often share objects that represent significant relationships, values, and traditions. Artifacts of family culture may be anything from a handmade cedar chest passed down from one generation to the next to a jar of Nutella given each year at Christmas to a different family member. Two sisters in the Stephens family exchanged the same birthday card year after year. The recipient simply crossed out the signature at the bottom and added her own, then mailed the card on her sister's next birthday. After the sisters' deaths, family members kept the worn card and now tell stories about the exchange tradition and the sisters, even though the card itself is no longer in use.

The lessons learned at home weren't the only ones you learned as a child, though. At school, in after-school activities, at work, hanging out with friends and their families, unofficial knowledge was passed to you in many different situations. For instance, as you grew older and spent more time with your peers, you probably participated in discussions about holiday celebrations. If you've been at college, living with people your own age who come from different backgrounds, when Thanksgiving rolled around, undoubtedly you and your friends began talking about what you expected to eat when you got home or what you'd be eating if you went home with one of your friends. You might have assumed that everyone ate turkey and dressing for the holiday and discovered

32

that your roommate's family always has lasagna and a neighbor's family has ham, greens, and chitlins. Ethnic and regional backgrounds influence the way in which Americans celebrate this uniquely American day. Some of your peers may not even celebrate this holiday or may hold a day of remembrance instead of a celebration because their families are of Native American descent.

Confronted with different practices at the home of a friend, what did you do? Did you sit silent, absorbing that family's practices and wondering why what they did was different from what you did, or did you participate, following along ever so slightly behind their pace, imitating their behavior as well as you could? At your friends' homes, mealtime practices might have been remarkably similar or quite different. Perhaps you went to your friend's house for dinner

Women members of the Lovely family at the annual reunion.

Lovely Family

Each year at the Lovely family picnic, a visual record is made of who has attended. After everyone has eaten and before the first carload leaves, everyone gathers in one spot to pose for three photographs: one of all the females, one of all the males, and a photo that includes everyone. This ritual produces photos that chronicle the changes in the family from year to year. Many families participate in similar annual traditions and have their own unique ritual activities.

and assumed they would say grace before eating but were surprised when your friend's father said, "Good bread, good meat, good Lord, let's eat!" Maybe you thanked your friend's mom for the meal and your friends were surprised by your formality. Such activities were probably some of your very first encounters with the folklore of another group.

Definitions

Now that you know more about how to recognize some of the ways in which folk groups work and what they do that causes folklorists to identify them as folk, we want to introduce you to folklorists' attempts to define folk groups more precisely.

Many of our misconceptions about folk groups and folklore stem from the assumption that human society develops in a linear progression from one state or stage of civilization to another, in a process called cultural evolution. In the eighteenth century, philosophers saw the state of society as a step down, a devolution, from a purer, higher state. Beginning around the nineteenth century, the concept of cultural evolution began to be looked at from the opposite perspective. The assumption was that human society developed in a linear progression from a simple, uneducated, primitive state to a complex, educated, sophisticated state. Recognizing that urbanization and industrialization, even in their rudimentary stages, had influenced the ways humans experience the world and communicate their ideas, some scholars began to be concerned that we might be losing a sense of our history, or our connections to that history, as we progressed. They feared that progress, while inevitable, was in a sense wiping out or trampling down older, less sophisticated cultures. As a result, many scholars focused on collecting and analyzing the stories, beliefs, and practices of what they were convinced were "dying cultures" in hopes of preserving those cultures' traditions, or perhaps of capturing their own culture's roots or preserving their own culture's past.

However, while such approaches can be valuable in tracing and analyzing changes in societies over time, a linear model implies uniformity across cultures—that all groups develop in the same way—and suggests that wherever we are on the cultural timeline is always better than where we have been or where anyone else is or has been. That's where some get the idea that folklore is untrue, old-fashioned "nonsense," that it comes from a time when people were too uneducated to know better or exists only in backward or less advanced societies. This is also where the idea of folk groups as primitive, old fashioned, and rural came from.

Decades of folklore scholarship (and scholarship in other academic disciplines) have shown that the concept of a straight line of improvement is not the most accurate way to describe how cultural changes occur. Certainly, human societies and cultures continually change and develop, but not according to any preset path. Along with the understanding that cultural development is complex and not linear have come changes in the methods folklorists have used to observe and describe culture and in the interpretive frames they use to study the cultural information they gather. The changing definitions of folk group are key in these interpretive and analytical refinements.

In "Who Are the Folk?" Alan Dundes narrows the definition of folk group to something remarkably simple and, in doing so, establishes the idea that it is the perspective we take on a group that allows us to define it as a folk group. Essentially, he says, any group of two or more people who share a common factor are "folk" (1980, 6). This simple clarification highlights the important notion that "the folk" are not quaint, old-fashioned people sitting around a cracker barrel telling stories of the old days, nor are they living in exotic or primitive communities in far-off places. All of us are members of folk groups. Dundes also says, "It is in folklore that folk groups are defined" (12). This definition brings the idea of "lore" back in. Basically, it suggests that the very act of having and performing folklore means a group is a folk group, and it also implies that by studying the folklore of a group we can know more about how that group defines itself.

Barre Toelken defines a folk group similarly to Dundes but emphasizes the shared informal contacts between people, which form "the basis for expressive, culture-based communications." He describes what he calls the "dynamics" within a group that hold it together through shared traditions that move and evolve with the group as the group itself changes. These shared dynamics, which we might think of as continually evolving interactions among people, allow a whole system of "expressive communications" to develop, which maintain the group as a group and which are conveyed to children or newcomers as a way of bringing them into the group (1996, 56).

Like Dundes, Toelken says that a folk group may be as small as two people who share a close, ongoing relationship. He calls such a pair a *dyad*. Examples of dyads are longtime friends, life partners, and others who "express their relationship with words, phrases, gestures, insults, and facial expressions which they share more intensely with each other than with anyone else" (1996, 57). This is why even after many years and long separations, just the mention of someone's childhood nickname, for instance, can re-create the intensity of the connection between people and remind us of our identity (who we are) in relation to that other person.

35

In the 1970s, a number of articles examined definitions of the folk and folk groups through a wider lens than the discipline had used before. Richard Bauman's 1971 article "Differential Identity and the Social Base of Folklore" challenged existing definitions of the field. Bauman's examination of identity moves the concept of group to a more complex definition that underlies the premise of the definition we're getting at here: that folklore is a way of learning, in addition to being, on some level, what is learned.

Bauman (1971a) attempts to illustrate the social matrix of folk groups more directly. By integrating the ideas of *performance theory* into the definition, Bauman demonstrates that the lore of a group functions more obviously as an active transmission, a performed communication that allows members of a group to share and understand its identity. He argues that the "focus on the doing of folklore, that is, on folklore performance, is the key to the real integration between people and lore on the empirical level. This is to conceptualize the social base of folklore in terms of the actual place of the lore in social relationships and its use in communicative interaction" (33). (You'll read more about performance theory in chapter 5, "Performance.") Bauman's analysis paved the way for a broader concept of "group" in all its social, political, and theoretical meanings. His focus on performance allowed folklorists to consider the relationships between groups and between audiences and performers, leading to an awareness of the ways we construct the whole idea of "folk group."

Group identity depends not only on shared communication within the group but also on interaction with other groups, which helps define and reinforce a sense of "groupness." Both insiders and outsiders define or delineate a group. The *esoteric-exoteric* factors (Jansen 1965) are important in understanding groups, because sometimes groups base a lot of their folklore (and thus their identity) on presenting themselves to others or on defining themselves in relation to other groups. This may occur in order to combat stereotypes or, in a negative way, to further extend a group's own stereotypes of others, thereby defining itself more clearly by what it is not. Certainly, communicating *esoterically* (inside the group, sharing what we know about ourselves) is part of the reason for the lore, but its communication may not be only esoteric. Folklore and folklore performances also work *exoterically* (that is, to, for, with, and about those outside the group) to communicate between groups, with awareness or recognition of other groups' folklore, identities, values, and so on. Therefore, though folklore is essential to seeing the parameters or existence of a group, that group may not be the only forum in which the folklore is shared. Sometimes this group intercommunication—the transition of a folklore text that communicates esoterically into one that communicates exoterically—indicates a change in cultural attitudes, perhaps a sign of assimilation. For instance, wearing dreadlocks initially was associated with a particular ethnic and spiritual tradition, but now many people wear their hair in this style as a fashion statement.

Going beyond that, there can even be "a folklore form which derives its fundamental meaning from its direction towards outsiders, people of different identity" (Bauman 1971a, 36), something not necessary to communicate within the group but only as an expression of intergroup values. An example of this form of folklore would be punk rockers in the 1970s and 1980s whose dress and makeup styles were purposely confrontational, directed toward mainstream society. Black clothing and lipstick or safety pins stuck through the cheek or lips may have been a way to say, "You think I'm scary? Then I'll be scary." Similarly, hippies who grew their hair long and wore sandals and frayed jeans were expressing the rebelliousness and disrespect "the establishment" assumed their generation possessed. In other words, groups communicate through folklore within their own boundaries and also communicate with other groups about themselves.

Bauman's (1971a) examination of this "social matrix" of group formation, as well as Jansen's (1965) examination of esoteric and exoteric factors, contributes to Dorothy Noyes's expanded definition of "group." Noyes considers the way folklorists have dealt with the term and claims that "ideas about group are the most powerful and the most dangerous in folkloristics" (2003, 7). Historically, folklorists have expressed conflicting and confusing ideas about what a folk group is. At times, Noyes says, folklorists argued that only small groups could be folk groups; at other times, they talked about whole countries, or huge groups, almost globally defined (such as children, women, or students). Even many of the fairly broad definitions of the concept incorporated the idea of ethnic, racial, gender, and class connections between group members and among groups. Noyes does not disagree that such characteristics can be part of group identity but says that we have tended to look at folk groups as being at least partly socially constructed; that is, we assume some folk groups are defined *before they become a group* by an outside connection like race, ethnicity, gender, age, common interest, or class. We then assume that it is that outside, preexisting characteristic that makes the group a folk group. But if we always see a group as preexisting in some sense, then we risk falling into the us/them trap, in which "our" group is always different from "their" group. And often when we perceive other people or things as different, we perceive them as inferior to us.

To avoid this kind of trap, Noyes and other folklorists[12] emphasize the importance of proximity and interaction in creating and maintaining groups.

In this way of thinking, certainly groups may share characteristics related to culture, class, gender, ethnicity, or age, and certainly they may come together because these characteristics exist. But the factors that make a group of people a folk group are regular contact (proximity) and shared experience (interaction). People who interact tend to create folklore. That gets us back to Dundes's idea that "it is in folklore that folk groups are defined" (1980, 12). We like Dundes's rather circular definition, because it acknowledges the "doing of folklore" (Bauman 1971a, 33) as a key component of a folk group. Basically, if a group has folklore, it's a folk group. Folk groups express and share folklore that conveys to themselves and to others their understanding of the group's values, interests, and sense of identity.

How Folk Groups Form

Depending on a person's association with other people, folk groups form out of proximity; necessity, obligation, or circumstance; regular interaction; and shared interests or skills. These categories overlap a great deal. For example, some people might meet through circumstances and then discover shared interests or form traditions that connect them beyond the initial circumstances that brought them together. We'll discuss below some of the initial factors that bring groups together in order to explain ways in which folk groups form.

Proximity. One of the stereotypically recognizable differentiators of a folk group is ethnicity, especially when it is *someone else's* ethnicity. Usually, we notice these groups because of the differences in the way "they" celebrate holidays from the way "we" celebrate holidays or because "they" dress differently or eat noticeably different types of food than we do. For our purposes, we will talk about these as groups formed by proximity. Though all members of particular ethnic groups do not always live near each other, their origins are geographically defined. In ethnic groups, traditions, costumes, customs, and material culture (food included) may derive from the terrain and climate of the group's homeland. For example, Scottish sheepherders work outdoors in chilly, damp weather, so tightly woven, warm, heavy wool sweaters that resist moisture became part of the local knitting craft.

Of course, less markedly distinct groups can be defined by local tradition and can even be intermingled with ethnic groups that have settled in a particular region. Consider New Year's Day food traditions of different communities in the United States. Midwesterners often celebrate with sauerkraut and pork for luck, traditions that were brought to the United States by the Germans who settled in Pennsylvania, Ohio, and Indiana. Southerners may celebrate with black-eyed peas and other foods that have come from southern agriculture, and some Texans eat tamales on New Year's Day. Not all the people who follow these traditions are of German or Mexican descent or originally from the South, but because the people who live around them eat these kinds of foods, they do, too. The tradition is no longer associated with a particular ethnic or national group but with a local, geographically bounded group.

The ability of groups to share and build traditions in digitally based communities further complicates understanding of the ways groups form through proximity. Online settings can create a kind of virtual proximity that allows members from distant locations and diverse backgrounds to come together. The digital world creates spaces where people can meet virtually; group members are always as close as the nearest web-enabled digital device. Groups of friends and family members who may be scattered around the world can meet regularly in an online space, continue to share traditions, and build community and identity. In some cases, online communication offers opportunities for groups to strengthen beliefs and find camaraderie in ways they couldn't before because they are separated by physical distance. Robert Glenn Howard (2009) describes religious groups, for example, whose members use their online community spaces to reinforce their beliefs even when they are unable to meet in brick-and-mortar places of worship.

Necessity, obligation, or circumstance. Just as proximity may automatically gain a person membership in a folk group, so may necessity, obligation, or circumstance. Each of us is born or adopted into a family from whom we learn beliefs, values, and traditions. The family is generally the first folk group of which each of us is a member. Within that family, we may learn ways of expressing ourselves and our values that are proximity driven (through ethnic family traditions, for example), but a core is likely to remain that is purely defined by family practice and belief. Though an individual may not feel that he or she identifies with his or her family of origin, there are still values and expressions a person learns through the family that establish membership in the group. Equally circumstantial membership may be gained through peer groups. Whether we choose to or not, we pick up behaviors, values, and ways of communicating from our peers. Beyond the simple physical proximity of school or neighborhood, necessity or circumstance also distinguishes these age-defined groups. Along with popular culture knowledge, folklore may be shared along generational lines. Contemporary legends are frequently shared within peer groups and across regional or geographic boundaries while communicating meaningful concerns or values. Jokes, too, may be shared within generations, especially those jokes that deal with the particular concerns of an age group: for example, some dirty jokes allow preadolescents to publicly talk about bodily functions, and jokes and riddles that play on words can help younger children learn about language.

Regular interaction. Demarcations among groups are formed as we develop our own personal identities, distinct from our families and neighbors. Such groups are usually established first by proximity, but they are reinforced through regular interaction. Our lives become intertwined with the people with whom we repeatedly associate. Official groups of which we are members, or to which we turn for support, are places where we may also form more intimate connections; work groups are officially created by the fact that members all work together, but within that group a smaller group of coworkers who regularly lunch together, for instance, may form. These groups probably share actual or virtual proximity but may be created primarily through shared experiences that establish common values, behaviors, and attitudes. They may form because members share a common interest or come together to fulfill a particular purpose.

The Internet has become a powerful channel that offers people with common interests the opportunity to connect and interact in complex ways that reinforce a group's sense of community. While the online sharing of tradition is not necessarily a face-to-face process in virtual settings, regular person-to-person interaction certainly occurs (McNeill 2009). For example, those who have certain hobbies may find others who share those interests online, and through their online encounters, they can develop connections with the larger group of hobbyists and with smaller online groups, as well as connect physically with local hobby groups within their geographic areas. A yo-yo enthusiast, for instance, might search the Internet for new product evaluations or yo-yo tricks to perform and in the process decide to join a forum for people who share an interest in a particular type of yo-yo or performance style. The more the yo-yoers interacted online, the more elaborate and focused their connections would become. Within the forum, members would likely develop shared traditions, such as in-jokes, jargon, etiquette, or rules about who had the authority to comment first or last about a topic. They might create Facebook pages to keep in touch daily and to reach others who shared their interests. Members of the group might also share information about upcoming performances or conventions and arrange to meet at these events, reinforcing their virtual group connections, building on them to form communities outside the online world, and providing opportunities for complex, multidirectional interactions among group members (e.g., virtual with real world, or small local group with large online community).

40

Smaller groups might connect and form their own bonds through regular interaction within larger, more codified official groups—for yo-yoers, that might be the American Yo-Yo Association or National Yo-Yo League. As another example, one might be a member of a local neighborhood chapter of a group such as Alcoholics Anonymous that has its own narrative forms, rituals, and values, yet exists for essentially the same reasons as other AA chapters around the country. Or, in a college classroom, in which proximity is often created by the registrar's office and distinctions in age and cultural background may be great or small, students may still share lore developed through their interaction with classmates. In some ways, these groups may be what Dundes has referred to as "part-time" (1980, 8), but they still generate their own lore and experiences that can be shared among group members. While group members initially come together because of shared purposes, skills, and interests, they are more than likely bound to each other by regular interaction that unifies and reinforces their identity as a group.

Shared interests or skills. Often, particularly distinctive types of groups are those derived from shared interests or skills. These groups may begin in places such as classrooms or offices and expand outward, taking a shape generated by their members. Sometimes, individuals may come together seeking others with common skills or interests and form a group based on those commonalities. In other cases, these groups may be preexisting, with members moving into (and out of) them somewhat fluidly. A group brought together by skill or interest becomes a folk group as it incorporates more elements of communication.

Quilting circles are one type of the skill and interest groups typically seen as a folk group. Quilters, usually groups of women who create quilts together for their own use or to donate to charity, have met and worked together as long as quilts have been made, yet these groups don't remain static through time. For instance, quilters communicate with each other and learn about new patterns and project ideas through crafters' blogs, the Quilting Network online, the National Quilting Association website, or similar sites, and they share the new ideas they learn there with the face-to-face groups they belong to. Members talk when they meet about where to get supplies and about local shows that are coming up, and they share advice about where and how to sell their artwork or which online and local fabric shops have the biggest inventories or best prices. They may even decide to create blogs of their own or to open a local shop, and they advise and support each other in these individual or collaborative efforts. Groups of women quilting together or sharing patterns and tips in an online setting may also share stories about their lives, pass along recipes, debate about political issues, express their values and beliefs, and create a community that goes beyond just a utilitarian

41

collaboration (that is, to make quilts). What unifies the members, then, is not necessarily practicing the skill together in a room or simply sharing patterns or techniques; it's practicing the skill and communicating new ideas about it along with sharing other communications. Through this sharing, the group develops an identity that reflects more than just the members' interest in quilting. The group grows and evolves through its sharing of innovations in quilt technique and design, building on its own tradition of quilt making as well as developing within the larger tradition of quilting and quilting circles, taking this skill-based group to another level of intensity and interdependence.

Another type of skill-based group is an occupational group, though not all occupational groups are skill based. In some situations, occupational groups may be proximity based, at least initially. A retail or fast-food job that can be obtained without necessarily having any particular set of skills would be an example of this. However, occupational groups such as auto mechanics, computer programmers, chefs, and firefighters may come together because they have a certain skill and create their own lore for members, often related specifically to the skills of the job. Joe Ringler, one of the contributors to this book, did an ethnographic project with a specific group of firefighters that illustrates some occupational traits of this folk group. (The write-up of his ethnographic research appears in chapter 8, "Examples of Folklore Projects.") Automobile muffler mechanics in some small shops utilize their welding and repair skills to create figures from old auto parts. (We'll talk more about muffler men later in chapter 6, "Approaches to Interpreting Folklore.") Creative work such as this, performed through the techniques specific to the job, is an example of job-related behavior that defines subgroups within larger occupational folk groups. Some lore is related to teaching on-the-job skills necessitated by work conditions. Workers in some noisy factories, for example, wear earplugs to drown out the noise and often cannot communicate orally with their coworkers, so they develop hand gestures to "talk" with their fellow employees. This informal workplace sign language has to be taught to new workers. While the newcomer is learning, however, the "old-timers" may trick the new worker by sharing visual jokes about the newcomer, since he or she can't yet read the hand gestures fluently.

Self-Identification and Group Membership

The preceding explanations can provide useful starting points for analyzing how groups come to exist and how we become members of groups. But in many cases, more complicated factors influence group membership. Sometimes, we choose groups that express the identity we want to create for ourselves rather than find groups that express the identity (or perhaps, identities) we already have. We may seek new groups or reject groups that we belong to due to proximity or circumstance in order to express an identity that is closer to our own concept of who we are. Tad Tuleja describes a type of group that he calls "intentional" or "consciously chosen" in *Usable Pasts* (1997), and this is certainly a distinct manner of shaping a group that fits into our taxonomy of groups. As we would caution against too much hair-splitting in the separation between group categories, he too reminds us that such typing is more suggestive than precise, and he clarifies that "social identity is a patchwork affair, a process of making and remaking not only our 'selves,' but also the communal matrices from which they emerge" (7).

Self-identification is a complex process that cannot be overlooked in defining or establishing folk groups. Choosing to identify with a group often involves or requires deliberately expressing a clear sense of connection to the values, practices, and beliefs of a particular group. This process is a bit different than simply joining a group because one shares an interest or skill with other group members. It means taking a position that says "this is who I am" rather than "this is what I like to do." For instance, we know of a small group of fifth-grade girls who formed a "Weird Club." To belong, girls had to first declare themselves "weird" and request membership from the two founding members. Once granted permission, newcomers performed an initiation ritual to prove their weirdness that involved fairly innocent, silly behaviors like wearing mismatched shoes to school or climbing a tree at recess and singing a song. Initiates received a "certificate of weirdness" along with a weirdness level ranking, depending on how weird other members deemed them to be, and girls could move up in weirdness ranks during their membership in the group. These girls, who were already friends or who became friends through the group, chose to see themselves as "weird" and then joined and maintained the group as a kind of showcase for their performance of weirdness as they defined it.

Adding a layer of complexity to this process is the ability to connect with groups virtually. People might use the Internet to locate and link up with others who share similar ways of thinking and then form a group, or they might more deliberately seek an existing group to connect with. The Internet offers opportunities for people to communicate and express their identities in ways they could not otherwise, particularly when members might be seen by those outside the group as unusual. One such group would be those who identify themselves as furries. Members of this group express their appreciation for the anthropomorphic qualities of certain animal characters in science fiction and fantasy films, cartoons, and anime by adopting qualities and traits of the

From the collection of Martha Sims and Brian Lovely.

Stoneware face jug with salamander, approximately 11 inches tall, signed Matthew Hewell, 1996; inscription on the bottom reads "John 3:16."

Hewell Face Jug
Occupational, Family Art
Matthew Hewell, 1996

This jug is an example of a "face jug," made and fired in Gillsville, Georgia. Hewell's Pottery, in Gillsville, produces commercial pottery (terra-cotta pots and other garden pottery), but family members also create these "face jugs." These artistic pieces are fired in a wood-burning kiln toward the back of the Hewell's Pottery property. The firing process, glazes, and designs are obviously different from those of most terra-cotta garden pots, yet the principles of creating and firing these jugs are related to the commercial process. As with the work of muffler mechanics who use their occupational skills and techniques to create sculpture, the process for creating these stoneware pieces is related to the family's commercial enterprise. The Hewells hold an annual "Turning and Burning" in October, during which the public is invited to see the pottery "turned" by hand and "burned" in the kiln.

characters they identify with. They might behave as they believe their animal counterparts might behave and, occasionally, wear animal costumes that represent their adopted *fursonas*. Because they anticipate judgmental, exoteric attitudes from others who might not understand or might find their behavior off-putting, they are sometimes reluctant to express their fursonas openly. The Internet allows them to connect with each other and find out about local events, arrange meetings (*furry meets* or *furmeets*), share stories and costume-making tips, and interact as their fursonas online. Virtual communities can become realistic-seeming worlds, where members create identities based on the types of individuals and value systems they choose to embody. These communities share traditions, rituals, texts, and beliefs, as do communities in the offline world.

Another way in which defining groups becomes complicated is in members' *unwillingness* to identify themselves as members of a particular group. Sometimes, members are hesitant to identify themselves with a particular group because they fear outsiders will stereotype them or treat them differently because of their affiliation with the group. In other cases, members of one group may identify themselves in opposition to another group and thus, in a sense, change the manner by which they—as well as others—identify themselves. Such behavior can be attributed in part to esoteric and exoteric attitudes.

All of us know someone who could be assumed to be a member of a particular group but either passively does not choose to be identified as such or more adamantly refuses the label. This could be someone who is unwilling to accept an ethnic or religious label or someone who no longer shares the particular family beliefs with which he or she was raised. A person might adopt a system of belief different from the one he or she was raised in; for example, perhaps a person born and raised in a Jewish family in Israel moves to the United States and becomes a practicing Hare Krishna. In this case, ethnicity, religion, and geography are no longer linked. Other choices may be based less on changes in beliefs or values and more on conscious adoption (or rejection) of customs or behaviors associated with a particular group. For example, one Indian woman living in the United States might choose to wear a sari as her daily attire in order to express her connection to Indian customs, but another might choose to wear jeans and t-shirts as her daily dress. Class may also be an issue. Members of working-class families who have moved into a higher socioeconomic class may reject their humbler beginnings or, conversely, may continue to identify with their original group and reject the privileges of the social and economic milieu in which they now reside.

There are those who identify themselves as part of a tradition or heritage that their families have not been a part of for long because it suits their personal

45

interests and the way they wish to express their own self-identity. An example is Cynthia Taylor, a white oak basketmaker in the tradition of the Appalachian Mountains, a first-generation Appalachian American, born and raised in the Blue Ridge Mountains of Virginia. Though she identifies herself as working in a traditional art form that reflects her heritage, she acknowledges that her father moved to the area when he was in his twenties, so there is no generations-long connection to the mountains. Taylor's position is an interesting one in that she learned white oak basketmaking from Rachel Law, a West Virginian with many years working in the traditional art form. White oak basketmaking fit so perfectly with Taylor's identity—her love of nature and traditional arts, including her own previous work as a weaver—that she is now one of the few artisans practicing the craft and identifies her basketmaking as work that reflects her heritage as an Appalachian.

Taylor is, then, by virtue of the tradition in which she participates, a member of a group of artists and craftspeople who share a common Appalachian heritage. Distinctly tied to the land of the mountains, the tradition not only requires weaving skills but also involves hiking the mountains to find a straight, young white oak and then felling, splitting, and weaving the wood into the basket for which the particular tree is most suited. As such, the process reinforces a heritage of mountain life with which Taylor clearly identifies, even though her family has not lived for generations in the mountains.[13]

Family, School, and Occupational Groups

No matter how groups form or how we become members of them, they share a variety of types of lore—verbal, customary, and material. In the following detailed examples of family, school, and occupational group lore, we illustrate many ways that informal expressive communication works to connect members and to express identity both within and outside the group.

Family

An essential part of family life is the repertoire of stories we share that reinforce our memories and connections as family members. A family story may change over time, expressing one meaning originally and taking on another as time and tellings continue.

Stories about family members and shared family experiences often communicate a sense of family identity, showing that family (insiders) share a past, as well as values and beliefs that can be communicated through the family story repertoire. Since narratives are retellings of events, they may communicate different messages depending on the teller, the version of the story, and the context in which it is told. Family members who are gathered at the dinner table for a holiday meal may recount a story about an earlier family meal that is now part of the family's history. At this earlier meal, a young girl knew she wouldn't be allowed dessert if she didn't clean her plate. Everyone saw her clean her plate, but at first they didn't notice that she hadn't *eaten* all her food. When she left the table and ran to the backyard to spit it out, they realized she had been holding her peas in her cheek. This story could have a number of different meanings within the family. It might simply be told to pass along information: Laura doesn't like vegetables. Or family members might tell it to show a personality trait—for example, that Laura is sneaky or resourceful. As the story evolves, it may become a comment on how the girl has changed: "You mean, she didn't like vegetables when she was a kid, and now she's a vegetarian?!" Even a change in who tells the tale—or the frequency with which one member tells it—may affect what it communicates. If each time a particular family member tells it, the story becomes more exaggerated (so that, for example, instead of Laura filling a single cheek with peas, she fills both cheeks or she hides more than just her vegetables), then it could become a reference to its typical teller's gift for exaggeration. The story, or even a shorthand version of it ("the time when Laura hid the peas"), takes on many different meanings in the family. An outsider might not get the reference, but the family will understand its message and value it as communication specific to themselves and their family identity.

At mealtimes in the Stephens family, members might exclaim "I'm pancaked!" as a signal that they are too full to eat another bite of food. This expression is the punch line of a story about the father in the family, who had a big appetite and could eat more food than many people twice his size. Every now and then he would get a craving for pancakes and would eat pile after pile, with tons of butter and syrup. Once he had his fill, he might not eat pancakes for months, until he got another craving. One day, after at least a second helping of a stack of three or four pancakes, he stopped suddenly, pushed his plate away, and groaned, "That's it! I'm pancaked!" His wife and the children who were present were amused by his obvious physical discomfort and the way he expressed his feeling of being stuffed, so they told the other brothers and sisters the story and repeated it frequently. At family meals, members began to tell the story, leading up to the "I'm pancaked" punch line, even if there was nothing resembling pancakes on the table. When the father was living, members might say, "Hey dad, remember the time you . . ." and then tell the story. But over time,

47

members came to use just the tagline as a shorthand reference to the story, and the phrase itself became part of the family's communication. Family members now often use this expression at big family meals and holiday gatherings, where younger members have picked it up, even though some of them have never heard the story in which it originated.

The phrase and the story became so associated with the family that as the children grew and married, their spouses and children learned the saying, and they could use it as way to show their belonging in this new community. After forty years or so, the expression has become so well known in the family that younger members have been known to use it outside the family context. One family member used the line at college, unaware it wasn't a common expression for having overeaten, with amusing results among his confused friends.

In this family, this simple saying serves the purpose of announcing that members are satisfied and full at the dinner table, expresses the family's sense of humor and interest in language play, and connects the members to each other and to the original hero of the story, the father who ate the pancakes. Even members who never met him know about him through this and many other stories, all of which exemplify him as a character who often said and did funny things, sometimes on purpose, sometimes not. He was a highly respected member of the family as well, so it makes sense that an expression he created became an honored part of the family's personal language.

This phrase also shows how folklore evolves over time and with changes in folk groups. Over the years, the story evolved into a family saying that became all that was needed to convey the content of the longer narrative. Eventually, while the father was alive, the story became the explanation for the saying, rather than the saying being just the punch line for a family story. After he died, the story and the saying remained part of a family repertoire of stories about him that members tell, with the father as the central player in a series of character legends that define this important family figure. The saying itself is still frequently used, and it continues to express the idea that the people who use that phrase in that way are connected. New family members who marry into or join the family learn the phrase and can signal their connection by using it, indicating their intimacy and comfort level. Close friends of family members, like the young person's college friends, might also use the phrase. But in that case, the friends might use the "pancaked" saying as part of their group's folklore about their friend, as a member of their circle. This expression, like much family lore, is a part of a complex system of expressive communication—a communicative code, in a way—for belonging.

School Groups

In elementary and secondary school, groups abound. Whether they are informally established folk groups or groups established by the school system for extracurricular activities, we all learn many social lessons through our interactions and relationships in such groups. Elementary school groups often seem defined more by neighborhood than by personal interests, because we're all just learning how to go to school and how to associate in the world. The more specialized groups of middle school and high school tend to stem more from common interests, and because of this they are more likely to incorporate a variety of specific lore.

Elementary school, a time when everyone is exposed to new people, new ideas, and new experiences, coincides with the years during which the human brain most easily and quickly learns and develops language skills. It is no coincidence, then, that children's folklore includes much playing with language. Nicknames are a major feature of children's lore. One of the simplest types of nicknames may be derived from lack of linguistic development: an abbreviated form of a complicated name—for example, "Boo" for someone whose last name is Bouchel. Alternatively, "Boo," recognizable to children as a nonsense word, may be heard as the heart of such a name and then pulled out from it. More complex nicknames are developed through children's experimentation with language. Often, children create nicknames that use rhyme patterns and/or alliteration (beginning with the same letter) to mock or tease other children—whether friends or enemies. Particularly creative are those children who can also incorporate some deprecating term about a child's physical or emotional characteristics into these names.

Another way in which these names are created is by incorporating popular culture into them. This particular knowledge-generating process is another way we see school *culture*, not school *education* itself, broadening children's awareness of the world around them. For example, an outstanding player on the high school basketball team might be given the nickname "M.J." by his teammates. This label could be used respectfully, to acknowledge the player's skill on the court, associating him with sports star Michael Jordan. Or, if the teammates think the player is acting too much like a star, they might sarcastically call him "Mr. Jordan."

School extracurricular activities often create communities for students. Initially, these communities are formally established—for example, athletic teams or musical ensembles. On one level, these groups are defined by the school administration and follow specific guidelines set by the schools and their coaches and administrators, yet folk groups are formed within these formal

49

boundaries. The student members of these groups often shape them informally, in response to both esoteric and exoteric cues. As in elementary school groups, nicknames continue to be significant markers of such folk groups.

Equally significant are activities, attitudes, and labels that designate membership in meaningful ways, serving as identity markers in adolescent years, when searching for one's identity is so important. For football players on one Florida team, the mere mention of "the sled" was enough to spur them to work harder. The phrase was used as a warning: one person might say to another, "If coach sees you, you're going to have to run with the sled." The coach required a player who fell behind or misbehaved to run with the sled. It meant pushing extra weight while running uphill, so the thought of it was often enough to keep a player on his toes. Though the action of running the sled stemmed from a formal punitive measure instituted by the coach, using the phrase became a part of the team's oral lore that served to keep team members' behavior in check. No matter where they were, all the team members knew what this expression meant, so it served as a shorthand way of addressing the accumulated incidents of discipline. Calling on this particular punishment reinforced the work ethic that was important to that group and may have been a way to manage, or at least influence, team members' behavior both on and off the field.

Other teams may keep individual players or groups of players in line with hierarchy-defining folklore. Because a team's success often depends on everyone working together, establishing informal rules that condemn individuating—or lone wolf—behavior is central to team function. Often, this type of control begins with hazing new members. Whether experienced players hide others' practice uniforms, toss new members fully clothed into the showers, or come up with derogatory nicknames, breaking new players' egos and attitudes is often part of the process. These activities are controlled and maintained as much by the students within the groups as the formal rules are by the coaches and teachers who officially monitor and supervise the groups.

In middle school, high school, and college, instrumental and vocal music groups often function in ways similar to athletic teams. Bands, orchestras, choirs, and smaller ensembles formed and led by directors still maintain their own student-led power structures and guidelines. Concerts and other performances may seem similar on the surface from year to year, but the actual workings of the groups are likely to be driven by their changing membership. One of the groups most markedly different behind the scenes and in performance is a marching band. High school marching bands are often modeled after military bands, with crisp step-work and formations and uniforms consisting of dark colored blazers, cummerbunds, and hats with plumes. Rigorous training to teach members how to march in precisely measured steps combines with hours of music rehearsals for the group and more hours spent by individuals in music memorization. Strict adherence to uniform policies, attendance policies, and the dictates of each squad leader make for a show-stopping band.

Behind the scenes, behavior may be controlled in unofficial ways by groups and individuals other than the band director. Squad leaders, the officially recognized heads of each section of instruments, must follow particular rules to maintain the expertise and readiness of their squads, but they may also devise underground rules—not approved or even known about by the director—to keep the members of their individual squads in tip-top form. These rules may require, for instance, that a member who does not have her music memorized by a particular date polish the shoes or instruments of all the squad members on the afternoon before the show. A squad leader may also demand that a player who has not learned the marching formation for a show run laps after the day's practice.

Directors may respond in several ways to this vigilante squad leading. They may tacitly support the behavior by looking the other way, realizing such behavior works. (Chances are, the directors suffered or meted out the same during their band years.) They may vocally support whatever means their squad leaders take to get good results from the band members—each section for itself. Most unfortunate for individuals may be the director who does not tolerate these underground strategies within a band's ranks. If an individual player complains and a squad leader is reprimanded for such assignments or punishments, the pain may be even greater for the squad member than before.

Squad leaders and other band officers do not concentrate all of their efforts on punitive actions. Often, both officially and unofficially, band members are rewarded for their expertise. Official material rewards may consist of medals, braids, or stripes added to a member's uniform after a year's tenure in the group. Being named a squad leader is an honor in and of itself, indicating the respect the director and fellow band members feel for an individual. Then there are the unofficial accolades that in many ways indicate a member's acceptance by the old guard, the heart of the folk group. These awards may comprise both nicknames and material artifacts. In addition, these awards may be serious or ironic, depending on those bestowing them or receiving them. A superlative—for example, "best turns in the show"—may be awarded at the after-show debriefing to a musician for his precise formation marching. For a hard-working musician who takes the whole process seriously, this reward reinforces his hard work and shows how much fellow band members appreciate that work. Conversely, for the musician who works hard and rarely makes a mistake but makes one with confidence when she does, a "space cadet" helmet passed on from an older member indicates acceptance of this player despite a dramatic flub. This type of award may also be made at the debriefing after the show, but since it is made by another member and not the director and follows a tradition running through the ranks of years past, it stands as a form of the band's folklore, reinforcing the power of the members of the band to establish an inner circle, a core membership.

Occupational Groups

Along with family and friends, one of the types of group most people are members of at some time in their life is an occupational group. As with friendship groups or clubs, membership in an occupational group may be short term, part time, or temporary.[14] One might be a member for only a few months or for several years, or one might be a member for decades. For some individuals, though, an occupational group may be one of the primary groups they identify with throughout their lifetimes. Of course, occupational groups may be formally or informally constructed, so perhaps not everyone will be a member of an occupational *folk* group, though chances are most will. We're sure you've heard of professional organizations: Engineers' Unions, Actors' Guilds, Pipefitters, and other labor unions. These organizations have formal bylaws and rules for membership established by the members. Within these groups we may indeed find a folk group or even numerous folk groups, but those will be determined not because the members all have membership cards and pay union dues but because they share with each other informal means of communication that help them express their feelings about their jobs and their positions within their workplaces.

You might not think that a group derived from occupational connections would have attitudes, beliefs, and values to express. Who chooses a career or part-time job because they believe in something, right? But beyond those people who take jobs on principle, "for the good of humanity," there are many ideas that coworkers and even members of professions who may not have face-to-face contact with each other share. Some of the most common types of folklore shared in occupational situations are related to hierarchy, membership, job skills, and risk. Numerous studies of occupations that involve risk indicate that members may rely on verbal, customary, or material lore to express their feelings about risk.[15] Jack Santino (1988) writes about his work with airline employees who shared with each other narratives about a ghost who appeared on board to warn flight attendants that something was amiss on their planes. Attendants believed these ghosts to be crew members from recently crashed flights. Santino asserts that these narratives were shared among the crews in part because of the potential risk in air travel. Flight attendants have no control over their lives in their jobs, and belief in the ability to be warned by others within the airline industry may help provide them a sense of comfort in their jobs. Similarly, Patrick Mullen's (1988) study of Texas Gulf Coast fishermen suggests some of their narratives may have similar applications. Again, the lives of fishermen are often at risk because of changeable weather patterns or other unpredictable circumstances, and their stories may serve not only to wile away the hours waiting for their catch but also to allow them to express anxiety and even call on luck to see them through. Firefighters and police officers also share narratives that may be related to risk and fear, at least to events and experiences out of their control.

Emergency room nurses and doctors and police have their own narratives related to belief. A phenomenon often referred to by members of these groups called on to take care of the well-being of the public is the amount of extreme or unusual activity that takes place on nights when the moon is full. Interestingly, the full moon factors into the lore of many groups, both contemporary and historical, who are often considered to be superstitious, uneducated, or in other ways, backward in comparison to mainstream culture. Yet some members of these contemporary service professions refer to these full-moon evenings as more mysterious and dramatic than their typical work nights.

Occupational folklore is not only studied within serious, risky, or lifesaving professions; there is plenty of other group-defining lore to be found in other professions and occupations. Some groups may share narratives told to indicate membership, hierarchy within that membership, and other kinds of insider status. Retail and food services are occupations in which narratives and other verbal lore are shared. Because both of these occupations involve contact with the public, the lore of these folk groups often contains narratives about customers, whether specific regular customers or whole categories of customers. If you have worked in retail or food service, you are certainly aware of this behavior, even if until now you didn't realize it was folklore.

In an urban downtown bookstore, where one of us used to work, coworkers created insider language, including names for regular customers. One of those was "the *New York Times* Guy," who bought a *Times* every weekday morning around the same time. The employees didn't know his real name, but he, along with other regular customers, was a topic of conversation, and this label allowed them to refer specifically to him. "The Book Licker" was as easy to name as "the *New York Times* Guy," but his moniker served as a descriptor of his behavior, not his purchasing habits. He would come into the store, go into the art book

53

section, pick up a book, and open it to a picture. Once he had found his picture (at least, the workers assumed he was making a choice of pictures; they never knew for sure), he would look around to see if anyone was paying attention to him, and then he would lick the page, from bottom to top. Obviously, this was not desired behavior in the bookstore, so new workers learned about him fairly quickly. However, he wasn't just a customer with an identifying name. He was a customer about whom there were stories, and those stories were shared for different reasons.

During training for newly hired employees at this bookstore, there were many formal training-manual rules that had to be learned. However, important employee information was also disseminated at other times, such as during lunch hour, a time of heavy activity in the store, since it was located in a metropolitan downtown. During this hour, all the employees had to set aside their individual tasks and gather at the front register to keep an eye on the front area of the store, greeting customers and ringing them up. When there wasn't any register activity, workers passed the time by telling stories, and often an experienced employee would tell a story about the Book Licker. The stories about him generally followed the same pattern, beginning with, "Have you ever heard about the Book Licker?" and continuing to describe not only his behavior but also his physical characteristics.

Some might see this story as merely entertainment about an unusual character (which it could have been had an employee been telling the story to her friends after hours), but in the store, it also taught new employees—and perhaps reminded the old—to keep an eye on the merchandise and customers as they moved throughout the store carrying out their assigned duties or as they stood behind the register waiting to ring up customers. Detailed elements of physical description are important in determining this narrative's function as more than entertainment: it wasn't just an entertaining story, but a teaching story, because the individual was described for identification purposes. No doubt about it, the stories were entertainment as well (even if slightly disgusting entertainment), and they also served to help bring employees into the fold.

Interestingly, the employees at this bookstore were part of an occupational group that included workers at another downtown bookstore, because the Book Licker made the rounds. With the discovery of stories about him at another store, the narratives take on another meaning, expanding the bookstore employee community and incorporating another layer into the analysis.

Within the single store, the story entertains workers in downtime and teaches appropriate work behavior. When acknowledged and shared between the two bookstores, it expresses a sense of belonging to the book retail community and also communicates an attitude of "weird people populate downtown." These are all examples of esoteric folklore, lore that exists within a group and is understood only by members of that group, serving for them as identifiers of group membership in the downtown bookstore employees folk group. The workers at the bookstore were members of an occupational group because they shared insider language and narratives about people and events specific to their workplace.

Example: Folklore in Bounded Spaces

The above example illustrates how verbal lore can work to unify a group. In addition to verbal lore, groups also share material and customary lore that defines them esoterically and exoterically. In the following examples, we'll focus on folklore and groups in bounded spaces—that is, settings with distinct locations in real or virtual space—in order to highlight some distinctive features of the ways groups express their identities in relation to other groups.

Dressing in the Record Store

Most people identify themselves as fans of particular types of music or of particular performers. We learn about music in many different ways, from our friends and fellow fans and from those who promote and sell music.

We'll focus here on brick-and-mortar music stores, specifically independently owned shops that sell new and used CDs and records. You may be familiar with these kinds of stores, especially used CD/record shops, since they are commonly found near college campuses.[16] Employees of these kinds of stores, who are usually—although of course, not exclusively—white, middle-class males, often dress in certain ways, share stories and customs, and express beliefs about themselves and other groups that indicate their tastes and values about the music they listen to and sell. Frequently, these employees, because of the nature of their business and the kinds of music they sell, identify themselves as part of the counterculture. Their fashion choices often indicate to both insiders and outsiders their membership in a community outside mainstream culture. Those choices fall into two broad categories: the dressed-up and the non-dressed-up. The non-dressed-up are choosing to identify themselves with a single, generic anti-mainstream culture; the dressed-up employees choose to identify themselves with one particular subgenre of music.

The basic non-dressed-up employee tends to be interested in a variety of kinds of music, not one particular genre, and usually wears jeans, loose-fitting pocket tees, light jackets or overshirts, and work boots or "Chucks" (Converse Chuck Taylor vintage-style basketball shoes). The simplest uniform (at least to the outsider reading the employee's identity) for the non-dressed-up employee is the rock t-shirt statement. Jeans and a t-shirt promoting an individual's favorite band is all it takes to create this look. In spite of changes in musical styles and tastes, this general non-dressed-up look has been popular for decades.

A subcategory of this style that became popular in the 1990s is more of an alternative rock look that illustrates how the non-dressed-up look has varied and been adopted outside record-store culture. Many employees selected their t-shirts and jeans specifically to reshape the basic workaday look, taking the frame of the jeans, t-shirt, and jacket or overshirt and refining it in combination with that era's aesthetic. In contrast, in the 1980s, the jacket or overshirt was likely to have been a work shirt or military jacket. (Pulled out of context, this military wear was not an obvious mainstream fashion choice, but neither was it a statement against the military, as it might have been in the late 1960s.) T-shirts were extra large or larger, and shoes may have been thrift store dress shoes, though shoes weren't a big marker of the look during that time. For most 1990s non-dressed-up employees, the flannel shirt, rather than military attire, became almost exclusively the preferred style. T-shirts, formerly baggy and shapeless, became smaller and closer fitting. Because the popular Seattle bands of the time dressed that way, the small t-shirt and flannel shirt look was adopted by mainstream culture, even though this had been a type of overshirt worn by the generic, non-dressed-up rock 'n' roller for years.

The non-dressed-up style continues to evolve, but regardless of minor adjustments, the look in general is crafted to express nonchalance about corporate and mainstream culture, as the heart of the rock 'n' roll attitude is against corporate culture. At first it might seem that the look is so uncrafted that it is not intended to communicate with others; however, in reality it is expressive of these group members' shared feeling that clothing doesn't matter. Because rock 'n' roll's roots are in a time (1940s–1950s) when people usually perceived only culture and counterculture, these non-dressed-up employees vividly communicate (at least to themselves and those who read the style in this way) their membership in the counterculture.

Dressed-up store employees, in contrast, choose to identify themselves within a particular subculture rather than directly in opposition to the mainstream. Employees at these stores are often crystallizations of groups, embodying the persona of musical genres more intensely than other fans might; they are often people who have taken membership in a group to the highest extreme. Some employees might adopt the hair and clothing styles of particular performers or emulate the style associated with particular genres or subgenres of music. Employees given the power of ordering merchandise for the store can make sure that rings, makeup, hair dye, t-shirts, and belts similar to those they wear are available; the presence of those employees in the stores often creates a community of shoppers who are like those employees. Frequently, each employee will have a lot of visitors, an entourage. Often, customers come in as much to talk with an employee who is the epitome of one of these groups as they do to buy CDs. In these instances, customers may look to the employee as a conduit into the whole culture. Such employees serve as role models who offer makeup and fashion tips as well as inform shoppers with similar musical interests about what is currently the best CD to buy or band to go see. For customers who choose to identify themselves with a particular music world or seek a deeper connection with that music and the culture that surrounds it, these employees can be positive mentors and friends who offer models of a desired, adopted identity or lifestyle.

Strong responses by customers frequently are good for business; a charismatic employee often draws in clientele. But strong exoteric responses by customers to clerks in these stores may also work against the business, pushing customers away from particular stores because of the personalities, music interests, or clothing styles of those clerks. Their fashion statements extend beyond readings by their occupational group and related fan groups to the larger folk group of music listeners. People outside this group may have a different reaction to an employee than members of the employees' entourage.

For some who shop in these independent stores, listening to music may not mean the same thing as it does to these employees, it is not always the customers' greatest interest or hobby. For other customers, a particular clerk may be the wrong type, someone who's interested in music that doesn't interest the customer. Either way, tension may be created between a customer and the employees, either because of perceived differences related to the clothing statement made by one or the other (or both) or because of an interaction that occurs in the store. Many narratives exist about the attitude or behavior of clerks in particular music stores, which are shared by disgruntled or sensitive customers who may not return because of the way they were treated. Most of the standard narratives revolve around an employee's behavior at the register when a customer is making a purchase or when a customer inquires about a particular product. Sometimes the employee is described as smirking when a customer brings a selection to the register; maybe he shows the purchase not so surreptitiously to a fellow employee as he's ringing it up. Or the story may include a more blatant form of dismissal: a customer asks for a particular item and the employee responds, "Why would you want to listen to that piece of crap?" Whatever the variation, such narratives suggest that some customers see the clerks as elitist or obnoxious, people to whom they'd rather not give their money. This type of folklore exoterically defines a group outside the employee occupational group, creating a group that, in a way, stands in opposition to those employees.

Another type of exoteric narrative is shared by employees about the shoppers. Customers who hold up two unrelated CDs from completely different musical genres, for example, and ask "Which one is better?" figure in many stories, as do customers who buy the latest pop version of a classic and don't take the employee's advice to listen to the original. In these cases, the employees are defining a distinct group of customers who are outside their own music-oriented world based on their assumptions about how in-group music lovers should behave. Such exoteric interpretations are as much a part of group identity as the fashions that members wear and the stories they tell.

Anime/Manga Fan Groups and Cosplay

Like fans of particular types of music, fans of other popular entertainments seek out spaces where they can share and express their interests. Those interested in music can still visit the record stores, but often they turn to the Internet to listen to and learn about the music and performers they enjoy. Similarly, many other fan groups meet, grow, and evolve almost exclusively online, and their in-person interaction is secondary to their online identities, if it occurs at all. One group of fans with a strong online presence as well as a visible real-world existence is that of Japanese *anime* and *manga* fans, or those who self-identify as *otaku*.

Otaku are fans, especially obsessive fans, of anime (Japanese animated cartoons), manga (Japanese comic books, print cartoons, and graphic novels), and video games that utilize manga and anime-inspired graphics. The term *otaku* was originally a pejorative exoteric term in Japan, but it is now seen as positive, especially in the United States, where it has become a somewhat self-deprecating esoteric term adopted by fans who embrace the label to express their connection and devotion to the styles of art they love. While the anime and manga styles of cartooning, graphic art, and video began in Japan, the styles have become popular worldwide, with fans across the globe, and particularly vocal and active fan groups in the United States. Anime fan groups exist at most universities and colleges in the United States, and while otaku do meet in person to watch videos and share manga books and graphic novels, and they enjoy interacting with others who share common interests, certainly many of them first connected and continue to connect online.

Fan sites like the Anime Network draw fans together and allow them to link with others who are interested in specialized subgenres, with links to videos, news about upcoming events, and information about where to acquire costumes and other merchandise. Forums on this and related sites attract anime and manga fans of all ages and genders from many countries.

Even without direct face-to-face contact, fans build and share community and identity through regular interaction within the bounded space of the online fan forum. Fans who may otherwise feel separated from other fans because few people near them share their interest in anime can find a home online, where they debate fine points of plots and characters, speculate about upcoming story lines, and express their enthusiasm. Fans can post messages that contain specialized terms and references to characters and titles with confidence, knowing other fans will understand what they are saying. These uses of esoteric terminology permit members to show their credentials as group members—they legitimize their membership and active participation and serve as esoteric markers of identity for other group members. The forums also have rules of participation and recognized limits on what can be shared within the forum space. Fans feel comfortable within the forum, aware that their status as members affords them freedom to express group values and traditions without concern about interference or disapproval from exoteric groups.

As we have noted in comments about other groups, online anime groups also cross over into offline physical settings. Notable among anime fan groups are the regular meetings of fans at conventions in cities all over the world. Fans frequently learn of these events first on fan site spaces, where they share excited anticipation of the event and watch for details about registering and program schedules. Those who can attend a convention may arrange to meet up with online friends, reinforcing the group identity and creating even stronger connections when the convention ends and they return to their interaction within the virtual space.

Conventions have their own rituals and traditions that unite anime fan groups. While waiting in line for particular events, groups may "call out" a particular subgroup to see who else is there with similar interests. A waiting fan may shout out the name of a character of a popular video, for example, and others who like that character may call back in response or cheer to acknowledge their fellow fans and show their identification with that group. Crossover genres and texts also make their appearance; for instance, spontaneous performances of the "Time Warp," a dance popular with fans of the 1970s stage show and film *Rocky Horror Picture Show*, sometimes break out at conventions while fans wait in line for admission, uniting fans of both anime and *Rocky Horror* who may not have met in person before.

One form of convention behavior that unites groups in a vivid visual way through the material texts of clothing, wigs, makeup, and props, is cosplay (costume play), which is dressing up as characters from anime or manga series. Fans may don colorful wigs, oversized platform shoes, or contact lenses to make the eyes look larger and darker (or perhaps a particular color of lens to look like a particular character) and carry weapons, walking sticks, or other objects that represent the characters they emulate. Certain elaborate styles of cosplay identify the dressed-up person with a style—Hime or Gyaru girls, for instance—or with a certain look, such as baby doll gothic, for example, with cutesy short skirts and elaborately arranged curls. Cosplayers usually express a desire to be called by a character name while dressed up and may talk and behave in the persona of the character. Convention attendees understand and respect this tradition and reinforce the character illusion by playing along.

Frequently, complex sexual-social identities are expressed through the interplay of dressed-up fans. Characters may informally or spontaneously act out scenes at conventions, even if they didn't know each other prior to the convention. Characters who are rivals in their story lines may play-fight; lovers may embrace or kiss. Some cosplayers are acknowledged celebrities at conventions and may take part in formal scripted stage entertainments. Rival types and factions may call each other out and criticize or make fun of other groups; for example, those who prefer the harder-edged robotic style of *mecha* may tease those who gravitate toward softer, colorful, cutesy styles. Characters may recognize each other and briefly gather together at conventions, for fun or to pose for photos for other fans. Fans can distinguish subgenres fellow fans identify with based on the type of clothing, style of shoes, combinations of colors, and other elements of costumes. Sometimes subtle differences, such as eye color or a certain hairstyle (straight or curled, bright blue or pink, or dark black), represent entirely different characters.

A particular subgroup of otaku are fans of *Yaoi*, often referred to as Boys' Love or BL, which is a style of anime and manga featuring male-male romances; this genre is aimed at female teens and young women, but it has many male fans, too, as well as many older female fans. Fans are mostly straight, but many also are gay, bi, or questioning. Fans of this type of anime or manga may dress as characters from popular BL stories and act out scenes or perform in stage shows as their characters. Often girls dress as the male characters and perform BL scenes at conventions, or the players may be two boys, or boys and girls together. Dressing as Yaoi characters allows fans to play with the idea of identity, especially, in this case, sexual identity, within a safe, structured space that is recognized and supported by other accepting fans. All of these clothing and

60

prop choices are part of a subtle code of communication among members of the fan group.

Cosplay also affords members the chance to bond as a group in relation to outsider groups that may find their apparel and character roles strange, even off-putting. Groups of fans may go outside the convention space to get lunch at a local fast-food restaurant while still in costume, garnering confused or shocked looks, laughter, and sometimes, rude comments from those who are not part of the anime world. Cosplayers sometimes enjoy these encounters, seeing them as opportunities to communicate an important part of how they define themselves and to do so in the outside world, "in the light," so to speak, rather than hidden behind a video or computer screen. Dressed fans may maintain their character personas while outside or even exaggerate them in order to elicit responses from outsiders, reinforcing their sense of identity in opposition to nonfans.

When conventions end, fans return to online spaces with fresh connections, fueled by the interplay of traditions they shared in face-to-face settings at the conventions. Fans who couldn't make it to the conventions or who aren't ready or able to participate in the cosplay and other kinds of expressive activities in the physical convention setting can still share in the fun of the meetings. They can read postings containing personal narratives about fans' experiences and look at photographs of the events posted by attendees. Fans can even rate and comment on photos of cosplayers' outfits or share evaluations of the speakers and activities that took place during the convention. This back-and-forth sharing of expressions, customs, materials, and narratives strengthens the groups' identities and the identities of all the subgroups of anime and manga fans belong to. Without having the virtual space within which to make the initial connections, many of these groups could not communicate and reinforce their shared traditions as effectively as they do.

Groups and Belief

One of the types of cultural information most often communicated within groups is *belief*. Belief may be expressed in a multitude of ways, and it is likely to be present in almost every folk group—and across cultures—regardless of whether or not we identify those groups as having separate, particular belief systems. For example, we all recognize that religion involves belief; thus, it seems logical that a study of religious groups would include numerous belief-related texts. However, religious groups aren't the only groups who practice belief-related behaviors or express beliefs in tangible, noticeable ways. Another common type of belief expression is something we may speak of commonly as *superstition*. Folklorists prefer not to use that term because it implies a judgment from outside the group. But thinking about actions that you would label superstitious, yet that you perform yourself, might help you see one of the different types of belief behaviors. Why might you avoid walking under a ladder, for example? Do you fear the ladder will fall on you, or are you trying to avoid bad luck? Even if you don't believe walking under a ladder will bring bad luck, you might still take part in the practice. What is important to folklorists, regardless of your reasons for avoiding the ladder, is that you are taking part in a belief behavior that you share with other members of your community.

The term *belief* refers to both the things we believe in and the act of believing (see O'Connor 1995). Beliefs range from customary actions or behaviors that bring about a desired outcome, like practical advice or a home remedy or cure (e.g., eating horseradish to clear a head cold), to fundamental concepts, perhaps religious or supernatural, that we learn through verbal narratives such as myth (e.g., the earth is supported on the back of a giant turtle) or through observation and interaction within our particular communities. Another category of belief expresses our worldview and our understanding of the ideas and principles that matter to us. We don't always think of these things as beliefs, per se, but often refer to them as things we "believe in." For instance, we might say we believe in giving everyone a fair chance or helping our friends when they are in trouble or giving children time-outs instead of spanking them. We may express these beliefs through verbal texts like proverbs or personal narratives or through behaviors and objects. For example, placing a pineapple design above the front doorway of a house or on a gate is a sign of welcome and expresses an underlying belief in providing hospitality. These kinds of beliefs are based on our values, core guidelines that shape and direct our attitudes and assumptions about the world and other people. Both categories of belief may differ from group to group, and sometimes from person to person; our beliefs develop through complex, dynamic interactions of history, geography, gender, politics, ethnicity, and basically all the features and experiences that surround and are contained within the groups we belong to.

The question of belief—that is, *the act of believing or expressing belief* in something—is one of the most powerful elements of many kinds of folklore. Performers or creators of texts may express complete belief ("this is true; this really happened"), some doubt or skepticism ("well, I don't know for sure, but they say this really happened; now take this with a grain of salt"), or outright dismissal ("this is just an old story; everyone knows this is all made up"). They may experience these feelings even if they don't state them explicitly. Listeners or audience members, even scholars such as anthropologists and folklorists, may also hold varying degrees of belief in the expressions they observe and take part in. It is not the place of any outsider to make judgments or assumptions about whether any group's or person's beliefs are inherently true or whether they are good or bad. In other words, figuring out whether a text is actually true is not the most important thing to folklorists. What is important to the folklorist is how members of the group who participate in a particular expression connect and interact with, as well as comment on or respond to, the beliefs stated or implied in the text (verbal, customary, or material).[17]

Often we recognize and label our own beliefs as *knowledge* and others' beliefs as *belief*, in the sense of ideas that are unsubstantiated by Western scientific practice (see O'Connor 1995; Motz 1998; Mullen 2000). Therefore, our own beliefs and belief behaviors may be more difficult, even impossible, for us to identify and, especially, to discuss or analyze objectively (see D. Hufford 1995). We may not see our beliefs easily except in religious or spiritual contexts or within other clearly or formally defined practices. We also sometimes mistakenly assume that only other groups have beliefs that are associated with folklore, when in truth we all take part in belief-related activities.

Much of the basis for this assumption rests in early concepts of the folk as being unsophisticated and essentially different from those who study folklore. Patrick B. Mullen, in his article "Belief and the American Folk" (2000), provides an overview of the way in which the term *folk*, as well as the whole concept of who the folk are, is *constructed* by scholars' attitudes about belief. In order to see why and how concepts of belief influence our definition of the folk, it is useful to think about *social construction theory*. This theory suggests that we build our judgments—we socially construct them—from the concepts, values, and experiences that our own groups take for granted (see Berger and Luckmann 1966). The concept of worldview, that is, the way a particular group or individual defines and interprets experience, is obviously at play. What this complex theory boils down to, for our purposes here, is that ideas like "folk," "ritual," "belief," and even "lore" are in many ways social constructs. It's important to understand that social constructs do not necessarily describe or reflect the way things actually are but rather define things the way we think they are. Since constructs stem from our interpretations of the world, we have to examine these constructs as *constructs* in order to understand how our particular cultural and social experiences—perhaps biases—have affected our definitions of and reactions to the people around us.

In the early days of folklore scholarship, hierarchical constructs of the folk influenced the way in which belief was defined and perceived. Early folklorists, intent on their study of the *other*—those perceived as less sophisticated, less educated, and on the low end of what they believed to be a scale of cultural evolution—judged as inaccurate and incorrect much of what the folk believed to be fact.[18] Some scholars were quick to label such beliefs superstitions or relegate them to the realm of mysticism and magic. In fact, many considered the existence of so-called superstitions or magic-based practices to be one of the signs of an unsophisticated or primitive—that is, folk—society. They received support for these attitudes from their peers and other intellectuals who studied what they assumed were disappearing cultural groups. Mullen points out (2000) that these earlier scholarly interpretations of folk belief reinforced the position of the folk as *other* and of belief in particular as a facet of otherness. However, by the 1960s, folklorists were beginning to reflect more on the work of their discipline past and present and to consider ways to ensure objectivity and equity in their analyses by avoiding this kind of us/them thinking.

One of the first steps in this process was to start to disentangle definitions of folk belief. For instance, in the 1960s, Alan Dundes developed a definition of folk belief, specifically superstitions, as traditional expressions that have conditions and results, signs and causes.[19] He pointed out that in many belief behaviors (superstitions), a stated or implied if/then condition exists in the structure of the expression: *if* you walk under a ladder, *then* you will have bad luck. One of the signs here is the ladder; walking under it causes the resulting bad luck. Sometimes a third condition exists that allows us to avoid the result: if you break a mirror (cause), then you will have seven years of bad luck (result), unless you bury all the shards deep underground. This last condition is called a *conversion ritual*, because it allows a person to convert or neutralize the bad luck by taking a particular action that contradicts it. These behaviors may allow someone to feel a stronger measure of control over events. Mullen suggests that Dundes's "structural pattern could easily be applied to religious and scientific beliefs as well" and that "the structural definition does not distinguish superstition from other kinds of cultural beliefs or the folk from other groups" (2000, 126). The significance of this structural definition is that it blurs the line between religious and secular belief and establishes belief as an underlying feature of most folklore. According to Mullen, "belief exists at every level and in every context of society—official and unofficial, institutional and noninstitutional, enfranchised and disenfranchised, the center and the margins, and small and large groups" (139). Belief is no longer seen as a defining element of the folk or as a separate category of study as much as an element of study within any group—and potentially all groups.

The question of belief is often most apparent in studying religious elements in folklore. An important figure in the study of belief, Don Yoder, challenges the scholarly separation of definitions of religious belief and folk belief. Many scholars have lumped any form of folk belief, whether religious or secular, together as superstition. Yoder, however, points out that religious belief and folk belief are part of a "unified organic system of belief" in which all beliefs occur in particular contexts (1974, 13). Yoder's theory, in conjunction with Dundes's structural approach, helps us see that it doesn't matter for the purposes of scholarly study if a belief is true; what really matters is how it fits with the group's practices and traditions.

Another scholar, Leonard Primiano, explains that the academic distinction between folk religion and other, mainstream, forms of religion is artificial and is created by assumptions scholars have made in the past about the kinds of religious expression practiced in everyday life, as opposed to religious expression practiced through official or institutional channels (1995). Using the term *folk* to label certain kinds of religious practices and beliefs implies a separation between organized religion and personal, more intimate expressions of religious belief. The separation tends to privilege one type of expression over the other.

Primiano prefers the less loaded term *vernacular* to describe local and personal expressions of religious beliefs and practices, since it reduces the tendency to see folk and mainstream religion as being in opposition (or even separate from each other). Rather, Primiano says, vernacular religion "represents organized practices and ideas that have a dynamic relationship to official religion" (1995, 39). In other words, people may follow the rules, guidelines, and practices determined by the church or denomination they belong to, and they may also come up with their own ways to express their belief. Both types of expression are equally meaningful to those who practice them, and the personal or local expressions do not necessarily contradict or exist outside the codified practices. They may, in fact, support or enrich the official practices; they're just different ways to express the same values or beliefs. Using the term *vernacular* allows us to identify one way groups express their belief but doesn't evaluate or judge belief or its expression.

People work out their particular personal and cultural relationships with religion based on a mixture of influences. These influences come from everyday life, family experiences, and structured religious rituals, texts, and practices. In this sense, all belief—religious and otherwise—is vernacular.

Example: Belief and Contemporary Legends

You may have heard the term *urban legend* before, as the title of the 1998 movie incorporating well-known legends into the story line. Or you may have heard it used dismissively after you recounted a story you were told by a friend: "Oh, you *believe* that story? That's an urban legend!" Urban, or contemporary, legends usually have a very high belief component, with the tellers or listeners expressing, even insisting on, the veracity of the tales.[20] It rarely matters whether they can be disproved or whether concrete evidence for their truth exists. A major focus of folklorists' interest has been the "negotiation of belief" in the sharing of contemporary legends. In other words, those who tell and share contemporary legends work out for themselves or within the group whether or not they believe the story, think it might have happened, find it plausible, or dismiss it. Negotiating belief is about the interplay of listeners, tellers, and communities; the different levels and types of answers to the question of belief are all part of forming and expressing group identity.

Gary Alan Fine defines contemporary legend as "an account of a happening in which the narrator or an immediate personal contact was not directly involved, and [that] is presented as a *proposition for belief;* it is not always believed by speaker or audience, but it is presented as something that *could* have occurred and is told *as if* it happened" (1992; italics original). Likewise, belief is a consideration in Gillian Bennett and Paul Smith's claim that contemporary legends are seen "as untrue stories which are nevertheless believed by the community which transmits them because they resonate with their life circumstances and address their social and/or moral causes" (1996, xxiv). While it isn't always the folklorist's job to prove whether the events told in an urban legend are true, it is the folklorist's job to consider how, or if, tellers' and listeners' belief in the events affects the sharing of the story.

Sometimes belief in the events of a contemporary legend is more important for some groups than for others, because of real-world experience and context. For instance, in the late 1970s one of us observed how urban legends circulated while living in a small town in southwestern Pennsylvania where a series of murders of young women occurred. The first victim was found in the trunk of a car in the parking lot of a local shopping mall. Groups of high school students, most of them female, regularly shared contemporary legends, such as the story about a male killer disguised as a feeble old lady who convinces an unsuspecting young woman to give "her" a ride, then tries to kill the driver. Details of this particular story included references to the local shopping mall, the name of the store the young woman was shopping in, and a description of the fake old woman's clothing. In this and other tales, the killer's potential victim found a way to escape. The members of this group believed so completely in the events of the tales that they shared them as good advice to help protect each other from harm. The stakes of belief were very high for those who shared these tales because the stories gave them what they perceived to be life-saving tools. In this case, the believability of the legends was affected by the situation, an environment in which real events lent value to the cautions.

In addition to the effect such a context or situation can have on the general nature of belief in contemporary legends, groups of people may share a set of attitudes or assumptions derived from historical experience, which influences their belief, making some contemporary legends more potent, according to Patricia Turner (1992). The history of oppression and bigotry against African Americans has contributed to the plausibility of such legends, so the sharer's belief is more intense; the legends reinforce the group's identity and what they believe to be true about the world and their place in it. Such belief is often based on exoteric assumptions, both of what *we* think of others and what we think *they* think about us. This strong belief causes the legend to take on different qualities. For example, the legend of the Kentucky Fried Rat, in which a person notices his or her carryout chicken has a strange taste, then examines it to find a rat's tail sticking out of the batter, is related to uncertainty about the mass-produced nature of food preparation in fast-food restaurants.[21] But Turner suggests that unlike the kind of "accidental and usually unintentional contamination" (1992, 428) that occurs in such general food related legends, many of the legends she has studied deal with belief in *deliberate* product tampering, *not* by mysterious or unaware culprits but by known predators.

Often, Turner says, the culprit is believed to be the Ku Klux Klan or a white-owned corporation. If not a business owned by the KKK, it may be a company rumored to have made a large campaign contribution to a KKK grand wizard. In one story, tellers claim that a fast-food chain that locates many of its stores in African American neighborhoods is owned by the KKK and injects its food with some unknown drug that causes consumers to become sterile if they eat enough of it. The targeted victims are usually said to be African American males. Specific real world details contributing to the believability of such a story include the fact that the corporate offices of Popeye's and Church's Chicken (which was bought by Popeye's in 1989) were located in Louisiana in 1990. In that year, David Duke, former grand wizard of the KKK, was running for one of Louisiana's seats in the US Senate, and there was a rumor that the company's owner made a large contribution to Duke's campaign. Because groups like the KKK have targeted African Americans in the past, their involvement in such a scheme appears reasonable, and the legends may then "seem so plausible

67

that consumers alter their purchasing habits" (1992, 426). Turner asserts that "even when African-American informants claim not to believe the items they hear, the possibility that they might be true is often sufficient cause for those consumers to abandon the products" (427). Turner's work illustrates that it is crucial for folklorists to consider how the negotiation of belief that takes place between tellers and group members—*not* necessarily the factual truth of the content—influences the sharing of legends, as well as the behaviors of those who share them.

Conclusion

The idea of group is central in the definition of folklore because it is only within groups that folklore has meaning. All of us belong to groups that form for different reasons and in different ways, through circumstances or by choice, and we move fluidly in and out of those groups throughout our lifetimes. Every folklore text is created and shared by people who are connected to that text and to each other. And it is through those texts or expressions that members learn how to be a part of a group and teach others what it means to be part of that group. Folklore both forms and expresses group identity, through the interaction of group members and interaction with other groups. Understanding the formation and expressive culture of groups allows us to recognize that folklore is not simply objects, behaviors, or stories. It is an active process that allows groups of people to express their values and beliefs, form and convey their identities, and even test the limits of what a group accepts. Without understanding groups, we can't interpret folklore—it is groups that bring folklore to life.

CHAPTER 3

Tradition

In the approximately 150 years since the discipline began, folklore has been based on the study of tradition. To folklorists the concept of tradition has a much broader conceptual framework than the conventional idea of tradition. Mainstream definitions bring to mind something generations old, passed down from an elder to a youth, who then becomes an elder and passes the tradition down to a youth, who then passes it down, and so on. Certainly much folklore is shared in this way, but tradition for folklorists entails a cultural understanding of a process or text that is shared within the community, perhaps from generation to generation, but is more likely shared among those who are current members of a folk group. Traditions may perhaps even be invented within a group as a way to convey and express beliefs to other members of the group or other groups. The concept of tradition and the ways our understanding of it has evolved are central to the study of folklore. The term appears throughout this book as one of the signposts that guides how we see folklore expressing and building group identity. For introductory purposes, we will begin with the idea that tradition is simply the sharing of something of cultural significance from group member to group member. In the following sections, we consider some of the theoretical underpinnings of the concept of tradition and discuss what traditions are, how they come to be, and what they can mean to the groups who share them.

What is Tradition?

Whether we are studying a specific item of folklore or the way in which group members communicate and learn that text, tradition is a vital, dynamic feature of the culture of a folk group. In fact, tradition is often the first word to come to mind when people consider the definition of folklore itself. Age-old traditions are considered to *be* folklore by many. Because the idea of tradition is so familiar, there are often questions about how folklorists' interpretation fits with a general understanding of the term. These questions show an interest in how traditions are passed along and a clear connection to the idea of learning and continuing traditions within a particular group.

The way folklorists look at tradition often differs from familiar assumptions, so here we address a few concepts one by one, using them as a framework to develop a better understanding of the current approach to studying tradition. For folklorists, tradition

- is both lore and process
- helps to create and confirm a sense of identity
- is identified as a tradition by the community.

Tradition is Both Lore and Process

The idea of tradition is essential to the process of folklore and investigations of folklore studies; however, as the discipline has grown and changed, the way in which folklorists perceive tradition has changed along with it. No longer does tradition suggest merely a relic passed down within a community, from generation to generation. This evolution has occurred, in part, because folklorists no longer see themselves as gathering the remnants of an illiterate or unsophisticated group in order to preserve the group's cultural history. Instead, we foreground as elements of tradition those features that groups rely on to maintain their current sense of group identity.

The term *tradition*, like *folklore*, refers to several related concepts. It indicates the *lore* of folk groups as well as the *process* of communicating that lore. The term also extends to everything that goes into the process of making a tradition a tradition. For example, a story, the act of storytelling, and the ways that stories and storytelling come to be meaningful within a group all matter when we talk about tradition. This definition of tradition implies a sense of continuity and of shared materials, customs, and verbal expressions that continue to be practiced within and among certain groups.

The concept of *continuity* suggests the importance of time and repetition in the process of tradition, but it is also used to acknowledge that traditions do not always come to us from generations past. Traditions may be repeated through time, but as Toelken points out (1996), time may be a matter of "years" or of "moments." Repetition is important in establishing continuity, since a group repeats something because it matters to the group; if it isn't meaningful, it won't be repeated, and if it isn't repeated, it won't become a tradition. Continuity doesn't mean sameness or exactness, either, because traditions are not always duplicated exactly every time they are repeated; rather, the term *continuity* refers to the threads of meaning and significance that connect traditions with groups. *Sharing* describes one-to-one teaching and learning of traditions (for example, by a recognized storyteller) but also helps us conceptualize transmission within a group, among its members, as well as between groups. It helps us see that tradition doesn't always move in a straight line from past to present, one generation to the next. Tradition incorporates space as well as time: we share traditions from group to group, person to person, place to place—*in the present*—across and within groups.

Tradition Helps to Create and Confirm a Sense of Identity

Some folklorists theorize that groups select traditions, choosing events and heroes from their cultural past that shape that past to match their present conception of themselves (Ben-Amos 1984, 114–15, with reference to Hobsbawm and Ranger, 1983). Selecting traditions reinforces the values and beliefs of the current group's makeup. Once we can understand that there is a process of "selective tradition" (Raymond Williams, quoted in Ben-Amos 1984, 115), the ways in which tradition helps create or confirm a group's sense of identity become much clearer.

Participating and sharing in a particular group's traditions allows members of the group to feel they are a part of it. You might recognize this in your own group of friends when you share jokes, stories, or practices that make sense only within that group. By sharing these things, you tell yourselves and others that you have a special connection to that group of people. Often, we are unaware of how we form connections or how we come to share traditions. As we discussed in the "Groups" chapter, we are simply born into some groups, like families and regional or ethnic groups, and we naturally become or choose to become part of other groups based on the work we do or interests we share. As members of these kinds of groups, we participate in traditions as a matter of course, learning about them almost without thinking about it. In some cases, though, we actively choose to take part in a group's traditions in order to create or confirm our own sense of identity within the group.

Sometimes, we consciously decide to join a group because its traditions appeal to us. These kinds of groups often can be joined or entered publicly— for instance, an Irish American club, or other cultural heritage groups that gather with the express purpose of sharing certain traditions. To join, a person

71

would either need to possess Irish heritage or be interested in Irish culture. Another example would be the very lively and often publicly visible groups associated with television programs, movies, or other elements of popular culture. Suppose, for example, you see some *Star Trek* episodes and enjoy the characters and storylines. Because of that interest, you watch more shows and learn about the characters and creators of the series by reading magazines or searching online. Later you find out a *Star Trek* fan convention will be happening nearby, so you go. There, you meet others who share your interest, you enjoy spending time with them, and you agree to meet them at the next convention. Within a fairly short time, you have begun to learn about in-jokes, special insider jargon—maybe you have even adopted a Klingon nickname or created an alternate Star Fleet persona—and voilà, you're a Trekker. The point is, you have sought out a group that allows you to express certain aspects of your own interests and identity that you have chosen to develop by participating in the traditions of the group.

At other times, group members who share more than just the main interest or characteristic of their group might decide to form another group based on that different interest. A few members of a book club who also enjoy gourmet cooking, for example, might decide to get together once a week to prepare new recipes, or a group of friends might decide to form a gardening club and invite others from around the neighborhood to join. Each of these groups can then exist and grow, forming new kinds of traditions as they emerge into their own kind of identity.

In other situations, we may find that we have become part of a group through association with its members. The most obvious example here would be when people become part of new families through marriage. A new spouse, for instance, knowing that a special family party was coming up, might volunteer to cook a favorite traditional dish or make a traditional costume. New step-siblings might arrange a holiday ritual that combines aspects of both their families' traditions. By consciously organizing our own participation within the traditions of a new group, we announce our desire to be a part of it, which helps to ease our acceptance. Recognizing traditions validates the identity of the existing group and signals our willingness to be identified as one of its members.

Tradition is Identified as Tradition by the Community

The flip side of creating or confirming identity through participating in tradition is that *groups must identify traditions as meaningful.* The key to understanding the role of tradition is to examine what a tradition means within a particular group. Along with that comes the idea that folk groups claim as tradition and participate in those activities that allow them to share values and beliefs that are important to them. For example, one of the central dishes of an American Thanksgiving meal is the turkey. Many other foods accompany the turkey—dressing, macaroni and cheese, greens, lasagna—based on the regional, ethnic, and/or family customs of those dining together. Those variations allow group members to identify not only as Americans but also as Americans with some specific ethnic or regional identity. However, consider those who choose to celebrate the tradition with a vegetarian "turkey." Made of some vegetable product (often tofu—or Tofurky—or some other non-meat-based protein) and molded to resemble or represent a turkey breast, this item is created to connect vegetarians to their folk group's customary behavior and serves as part of their Thanksgiving tradition. The same protein could be processed into sausage or beeflike products, but to allow for identification as part of a larger folk tradition, it is presented in the form of "turkey." Groups who incorporate vegetarian turkey into their Thanksgiving dinner may do so because they see the *idea* of turkey as somehow central to the whole concept of a traditional Thanksgiving dinner. Turkey, for some people, is what Thanksgiving dinner is all about, even if they don't eat it.

As the pseudoturkey example suggests, in order for a tradition to be passed along within a group and earn the internal status or longevity deemed necessary for a tradition, it must be relevant and meaningful to the group. However, that doesn't necessarily mean it will always be performed in exactly the same way or be exactly the same lore.

How do People Learn and Share Traditions?

Henry Glassie (1995) describes the most esoteric form of learning a tra ditional art as a kind of osmosis; simply sharing the same air with an artistic mentor teaches us what we need to know and allows us to take in the essence of the art form. A Turkish potter Glassie consulted described the process this way: "In youth, while learning, you breathe in the air of experience. The air circulates within, mingling with the breath of your own soul. Then in creation you exhale and your works emit a certain *hava*, an air that they inevitably share with works created by others who inhale and exhale within the same atmosphere" (408). This rather poetic description illustrates the main idea at the heart of current concepts of how we learn and share tradition; examples from fieldwork (such as Glassie's) and those we consult in the field have helped us to "understand tradition as a process, an integrated style of creation" (408).

Following that line of thinking, it becomes clear that the idea of passing down a tradition no longer describes the way we understand the process of learning and adapting traditions. Traditions originate in many ways, and although sometimes they certainly originate in groups that came before us, the idea that something is passed *down* suggests that the sharing of traditions is *only* linear and chronological. Anthropologist Clifford Geertz writes about the idea of culture as a web (1973, 5).[22] Thinking about tradition as part of a web of behaviors and texts helps establish a clearer idea of the way in which traditions are shared, built on, and influenced by the cultural behaviors of folk groups and their individual members.

Visualizing culture as a web and tradition as something that is actively transmitted and circulated across that web helps us to see that the past is only one part of a very fluid, complex process. This concept acknowledges that tradition is, on one level, "the creation of the future out of the past" (Glassie 1995, 395) yet also shows that the past is only one avenue through which we share and continue tradition. Yes, we learn from past groups, but we also learn from people and groups that exist now; we form and adapt tradition in the present to suit groups' current interests and experiences.

This idea can be illustrated through a few examples. A simple transmission of an item of folklore might occur when a child in New Hampshire learns a jump-rope rhyme from her mother and teaches it to her best friend. Not long after, her friend moves to Chicago. She gets together with a few girls to jump rope and recites the rhyme—new to them—and it becomes a part of their local rope-jumping tradition. Perhaps another group of girls jumping rope nearby hears this new rhyme and learns it by watching and listening as the other group performs it. Even though this tradition has been passed from one generation to another, it has also been shared among peers and has moved into a new geographical community as well.

In another hypothetical situation, a folk art tradition may be changed when people come together from two different folk groups. Two women sit next to each other working on a quilt. One, an experienced quilter, shows the other a design stitch to work into a certain part of the quilt. As they work, the younger of the two women tells a story, told by members of her family, of a mythical animal believed to confer good luck. The next time they get together to work on a quilt, the experienced quilter shows the younger woman a design for a quilt for her daughter, who is going away to college. To wish her daughter luck, she has included in it a figure that looks like the animal the young woman recently described.

These two examples of transmission of lore between members of different folk groups demonstrate how Geertz's web concept allows us to visualize the

74

larger connections and how an individual may influence the traditions and behaviors of several groups. Equally important is recognizing the intermingling of group lore, the manner in which groups shape and contribute to the lore of other groups.

When we think about who passes traditions along and who will learn a tradition and keep it going, often a single individual comes to mind. Folklorists have used the term *tradition bearer* to indicate a specific member of a group who carries out a tradition for other members of the group and sometimes actively and consciously teaches or shares it with others. This label may effectively identify an individual the group recognizes as, for example, a master craftsperson or skillful storyteller; however, not all folklore is communicated by a single individual with the specific *role* of tradition bearer in his or her folk group. Consider the rope jumpers in the example above. Three individuals—the girl in New Hampshire, her mother, and the friend who moved to Chicago—all taught the same rhyme to others. One girl taught her friend (one-to-one sharing), but then the friend taught all the members of a group in Chicago. Then, many members of a different group learned this new rhyme by watching and listening to the friend's group. No single individual owned this particular tradition or had a greater or lesser right—or ability—to share it.

As Dorothy Noyes has argued, the concept of a tradition bearer exists as part of "an old paradigm that understood the people as bearers, not makers, of tradition" (2003, 11). It suggests, then, a "sanctified" text, merely moved along by a particular person, rather than used by people to communicate. It also implies a more conscious performer, communicating in a standardized context, much like a professor lecturing in a classroom or a piano teacher guiding a student's fingers over the keys. Noyes points out that in his earlier definition, only those noted individuals who formally pass on traditions have an active role in sharing and continuing a group's traditions; the other group members are, then, always passive recipients of those traditions. This is an outmoded, elitist way of looking at folklore and how groups operate, because it suggests a "specialist folk" who have more power over tradition transmission than other group members. However, while all members of a group can and do share traditions, there are sometimes master craftspeople or skilled performers whose acknowledged roles in the group involve passing along an item or performing a process. These people may know a specific text better than others or may be elders or people especially experienced in a particular type of performance. We recognize the value of the term *tradition bearer* to describe this type of teaching or sharing by a performer, because it can help folklorists talk about the people they work with as consultants. But it is important to acknowledge that such examples illustrate

75

only one way in which traditions are maintained and learned. All members of a group participate in an ongoing process of sharing and remaking their own lore.

In most situations, the informal nature of folklore does not require only a single individual with a specific role to express a given tradition. Adolescents tell each other about the friend of a friend who saw the *Oprah* episode in which a famous designer confessed to not wanting African Americans buying and wearing his label's clothing. Children in their elementary school classrooms teach their desk-neighbors how to fold cootie catchers. In most cases, there is no nine-year-old "master folder" teaching everyone else the techniques during recess. Often, every member of a folk group has the authority or ability to communicate traditions. The process or lore is repeated in informal settings by many group members, and that continues the tradition. Folklore concerns the identity of groups as defined by the group, not by any individual inside (or outside) it; we share traditions in many different ways, in many different contexts, across the whole web of culture.

Especially important to note is the vitality of tradition. Traditions are behaviors *we do right now* that connect us to other people in a group and may also connect us to another culture, provide us a sense of ethnicity, or help us make other connections. Traditions are those informally shared behaviors, customs, and verbal expressions that circulate within and among groups. We share and continue them because they help us tell other members of the group and those in other groups (that esoteric/exoteric idea) who we are and what matters to us. That is *why* we pass traditions across the web of community. When we mentioned the web of tradition above, we noted how complex and varied the passing along of tradition can be. Group members can teach each other, they can learn by observing, or sometimes they simply begin participating as they become interested in joining a group or establishing an identity within it.

Example: Tradition in Our Daily Lives

In the following essay, college student Patrick Blake reflects on how traditions related to food have affected his sense of group belonging and personal identity as well as provided a cross-cultural bridge for understanding groups different from those he belonged to.

In my family, food has played a paramount role in forming and maintaining traditions. Until I was age 17, my dad made a squash and marshmallow casserole for Thanksgiving, a dish which is surprisingly appealing to everyone in my very large, extended family. However, problems developed when my sister transitioned her diet from nearly carnivorous to vegetarian to vegan over the course of a year. As the big day approached, my sister became genuinely despondent because she would not be able to enjoy our traditional Thanksgiving fare (marshmallows are non-vegan), and felt left out. To ameliorate the situation, my dad prepared a vegan squash casserole and a tofu turkey. My sister was satisfied, but my grandmother was irritated that her son's cooking had been compromised, that our family tradition was weakened. What ensued was a quick-forming rift between my sister and my grandma because of a disagreement on a seemingly petty issue: the ideal meal for one day out of the year. However, all was forgiven and as a family, we accepted vegan Thanksgiving.

By assisting in long meal preparations at Thanksgiving and many other meals, I have become both enthusiastic and adept at cooking. Cooking is interesting to me because it involves creation, it gives an opportunity to form something greater than what one starts with. When living with three foreign students one summer, I noticed the differences, large and small, in the way people prepare food. I began to explore cooking with foods I had never eaten, like plantains and okra. Although some meals I cooked were far from delicious, others were unforgettable. Every Friday my roommates and I created a potluck meal, and designated ourselves as specialists with aprons that read things like "Mr. Meat Man." Throughout the week, the four of us never interacted as a group, except on Fridays. But while cooking, over the sounds of our eclectic music collection, we talked. Inevitably, the conversation reverted to tales of how we learned to prepare some uncommon food, like squash and marshmallow casserole. Without a common activity like cooking or eating, I could have never established the relationships I did with my roommates. Food became a synonym for conversation, it meant it was time to enjoy each other as people and forget about everything else.

Conversely, my last Thanksgiving meal preparation brought me to withdrawal and depression. My dad passed away on November 1st, and I went into a state of shock, rather than sadness. Even leaving school for Thanksgiving break did not bring reality into focus, as I continued life as though nothing had happened. Returning from a trip on Thanksgiving

Day, I arrived barely in time for dinner. As the meal wore on, I became increasingly anxious and antisocial. When the pumpkin pie came out, and we had not yet had any squash and marshmallow casserole, I asked to be excused from the table, all the while irritated with myself that the absence of a squash and marshmallow casserole could have such an impact on me. At the time, I was still learning to appreciate food for what it is.

I have learned a great deal from others through food. For me, food has been the avenue that can lead to enlightenment. On a trip to Mexico, I lunched at a dilapidated café. Although the food was excellent, I was disturbed by the smell of sewage emanating from a nearby river. Eventually, I asked another nearby patron if the smell was always so putrid. She indicated that it was, and also told me that I was to blame, because I had just eaten beef from cattle raised upstream on the Santa Cruz River. I jokingly asked if there was anything I could do to correct my wrongdoing, and, to my surprise, she invited me to spend Memorial Day weekend working to repair the river. I agreed. On a lunch break one afternoon, I sat down for some time alone, only to be invited to try some *menudo* by two Mexican high school teachers. Without hesitation, I slurped the cilantro-garnished soup, to their amazement. The men explained that the soup was made with *el estómago de vaca,* the cow's stomach. The men chuckled at my initial repulsion, but became truly satisfied when I continued eating. Over the course of our semantically strained conversation, the men told me about Mexican politics, education, and economical worries. They also invited me to a salsa dance in the plaza, which made for one of the best foreign comedic acts many locals had ever seen: a 6'5" Caucasian with no sense of rhythm attempting to learn salsa in one night. This is one of a host of situations in which my experience with food has led to something grander.

Food experiences are important to everyone, though many people may be unaware of it. My own interest in and experience with food is merely an introduction into the role food plays in our lives. Food serves to make traditions, to communicate emotions, to teach us, and to connect us with others.

Do Traditions Disappear?

We claim our identities, in part, through our traditions, so the more invested we are in defining ourselves as members of a particular group, the more invested we may become in maintaining the traditions of that group. Because traditions provide us a sense of belonging, we become attached to them and concerned about losing them. Traditions can connect us to past generations (or our own pasts), link us to ethnic and religious identity, and tie us to particular people and cultural behaviors that are important to us. Sometimes we simply get caught up in nostalgia for things past, and that shapes our attitudes and expectations about tradition. Our individual lives are short, so it may be comforting to feel that sense of connection with the past. We often look backward to see who we are or to see how secure our identities are as a way of seeking assurance that our lives will continue to have relevance into the future. For all these reasons, it is natural to wonder what may happen if our traditions disappear.

We acknowledge that there are situations in which traditions do indeed end—or are forcibly changed or put to an end. For instance, history records examples of several native groups in North and South America that almost disappeared due to disease carried by European settlers. Territorial wars between settlers and native groups, sometimes even deliberate acts of genocide, wiped out entire native communities. Several groups converted to religions introduced by the colonists, and in the process they stopped practicing their original traditions—sometimes under threat. These groups were radically altered and, in some cases, were destroyed entirely, so that many of their traditions were, in a very real sense, lost. For folklorists, these kinds of situations present a host of difficult questions and research challenges. The discussion of the ways tradition itself can contribute to such destructive acts is uppermost among them. What esoteric and exoteric assumptions play into the kinds of attitudes that lead one group to force such influence on another, for instance? Such questions reflect the complexity of tradition and the ways groups interact, and they frequently have no easy answers.

Most of the time, though, traditions change and evolve naturally, and what appears to be an ending is really an adaptation, part of the process of folklore. Our discussion focuses on these more natural, evolutionary kinds of changes that typically occur in our everyday experience.

Since traditions exist because they are meaningful for groups, they rarely ever end outright. For example, suppose you and your group of high school friends always got together and ate pizza at one person's house every Friday night. After graduation, the group scattered to different colleges or occupations,

79

some moved away, and the Friday night pizza tradition ended. However, during spring break a few of you manage to get together on a Wednesday afternoon at a local pizza place and catch up on each other's lives. Perhaps you reminisce about some of the silly things your high school group said and did during your Friday night pizza fests. Following that reunion, you and your friends might decide to create a group on Facebook where you can stay connected and perhaps reconnect with others in the original group you had lost touch with. When the group meets again the next spring break there are more members present with more memories to share. The group has changed, and the specific behaviors and contexts have changed, but there is still that sense of continuity in the shared experience, as well as the important central features of the tradition the group has identified: getting together and eating pizza. That sense of continuity marks the new pizza gathering as traditional.

A change of day, time, or venue may seem insignificant, yet some people become concerned that to change tradition is to corrupt it. But performing a traditional practice in a new, slightly different way does not mean it's wrong or disrespectful of tradition. If there's a new way, it's likely that the group members have, consciously or unconsciously, adapted the tradition to be more meaningful or effective for them, as *current* group members. In the example above, you and your friends may never again be able to see each other every Friday night, but maybe you will plan spring break pizza lunches or will one day share Friday night pizzas with your children and their friends as a way of continuing the central elements of the tradition that meant so much to your teenage friendship group. If a verbal expression, object, or custom continues to have meaning for a group, it will most likely continue in some form.

Sometimes traditions may change or appear to end because of convenience or changes in taste. For example, to make a pumpkin pie, a cook used to have to first find a pumpkin of suitable size, cut it, peel it, cook it, and mash it, all before combining it with other ingredients and pouring the mixture into a crust. Now, cooks may choose to use canned pumpkin from the supermarket and cut out a great deal of labor and time. Another changing food tradition is that many families no longer make refried beans by cooking them in lard and choose instead to use vegetable shortening. Perhaps this change came about because the family has come to prefer the taste of beans without lard, because concepts of healthy cooking have changed, or because someone in the family has heart disease or high cholesterol. These kinds of changes may come about by necessity.

Much of our concern about losing or corrupting tradition is a holdover from the misconceived idea that folklore is a relic of a dying, pure past and that

80

tradition is something that comes to us from distant ancestors, so it can never change. We have seen that folklore and tradition are far more complex than that. Our concern may also arise from confusion between tradition and history, which are not the same things. While historically, certain practices may end, traditions evolve, adapt, and merge as groups share and continue them. The Pony Express is no longer delivering mail, for example—that's a historical fact—but a group of historians who study the Pony Express days may get together at a yearly conference and share artifacts and memorabilia that relate to their interest—that's their tradition. Traditions rarely end completely unless they cease to have meaning for the group that performs them, or the group reaches a natural or logical end. Groups are as variable as individuals. So while some people are happily growing and cooking pumpkins and some are frying their beans in sizzling lard, others are sharing vegetarian beans or pies made from canned pumpkin—and all of them are taking part in traditions that matter to them.

Dynamic and Conservative Elements of Tradition

Once we recognize the idea that traditions rarely die but instead are adapted to be meaningful to the groups practicing them, we can move on to approach those changes more theoretically. For something to be considered a tradition, it must contain the features *the group identifies as essential* in defining tradition. At the same time, to remain relevant, a tradition *must continually adapt* as groups develop and change. In *The Dynamics of Folklore* (1996), Barre Toelken presents a clear way in which we can consider tradition as a balance of elements that change and elements that stay the same. Toelken suggests that folklore possesses both "dynamic" (changing) and "conservative" (static) features that allow it to be adaptable yet still preserve a sense of continuity. Toelken maintains that the conservative side of tradition is all the factors within such a performance that are defined by the community, those that are more powerful than the individual's preferences. It is the creativity of expression in any given situation that Toelken characterizes as dynamic, the factors that keep the tradition vital (37–38). While Toelken focuses primarily on the nature of verbal art and the changes individuals make through their creative choices, these concepts are also relevant to nonverbal art and the process of change brought about by groups.

Pulling together these two pieces—the conservative and the dynamic, or "the twin laws of folklore process"—provides an explanation of how variation can exist within folklore while remaining true to the basic ideas of folklore. Toelken suggests that certain elements of a text's characteristics or structure are less likely to change than others and that verbal lore may remain the most conservative by nature, as its structure and meaning may be dependent on rhyme and wordplay. Even so, the situations in which these kinds of expressions are shared create the sense of dynamism. Some of the possible variations of a folk text are in how, when, and by whom it is shared; even when the text is consistent, the setting in which it is shared may not be. You might ask a group of your friends a riddle your brother shared at a family gathering, for example, but the people present and the situation may influence how the riddle is answered or even received. The importance placed on a tradition by an individual or particular group may be the primary dynamic element, whether the variation is intentional or not. The Friday night pizza tradition changed because the group members decided deliberately it needed to change, but sometimes people may not even be aware that changes are happening because they occur naturally as traditions are shared. Contemporary legends offer great examples. For instance, a legend told in the 1950s about wealthy carmaker Henry Ford rewarding an unsuspecting Good Samaritan who stops to help when Ford's car breaks down might not have much relevance in the twenty-first century. With a slight variation—replacing Ford with a current wealthy business person like Bill Gates or Donald Trump—the legend continues to be contemporary and believable (at least in the sense that its believability can still be negotiated and not immediately denied) and communicates meaning within the group that tells it. In other cases, the dynamic elements may be consciously changed to adapt to the perceived taste of a particular audience or context. For example, you might have heard a great joke, but in order to tell it to your grandmother, you decide the language needs to be altered—cleaned up a bit. Yet the essence of the joke—its narrative structure, concept, and the punch line—remains essentially the same.

When we look at such dynamic and conservative features in nonverbal traditions, we can see variations and adaptations taking place in them as well. High school and college marching bands, for example, accumulate several layers of tradition within them. There are officially sanctioned traditions that are carried out in many different bands over long reaches of time and space, yet there are also other traditions that are unique to each school's particular band members in any given generation.

The bands march in straight rows with measured steps (some steps are high and bent kneed, while others are performed with toy-soldier-straight legs), breaking out of their rows and moving in formation to create designs, images, and even words as seen from the bleachers. When The Ohio State University's band, for example, performs the "Script Ohio"—in which band members march into a complex formation of the word *Ohio*—the *i* is traditionally dotted by a fourth- or fifth-year sousaphone player. This tradition began in the 1930s and has evolved in response to changes in the group as well as audience reaction. Now, when the sousaphone player dots the *i*, he or she kicks, turns, and bows toward the stands, an innovation that came about when a sousaphone player performed these actions to help cover up a musical timing problem. The crowd reacted with cheers, and *i*-dotters have kicked, turned, and bowed since then. This embellishment illustrates the influence of both individual choices (in this case, a creative solution to an external problem) and audience response in shaping traditions.

Marching bands also have their own more specific traditions; each band has unique steps and vocabulary that only members of that band will understand. Most members will recognize traditional steps, styles, and language used by other bands, but each band's interior world will be different. The formal training of the bands most likely will occur at preseason band camps, but throughout the band's season, informal interactions will teach band members certain ways to approach routines and music as well as certain ways to interact within the band, on the field and off. As in many other groups, seniority is important and an individual band's traditions will show this in different ways: for example, the new row members will be required to polish the squad leader's shoes, or a more experienced member will automatically have a spot, but less experienced members will have to challenge another musician for a spot.

Variations in recipes serve as useful metaphors for the variations in traditions, highlighting the conservative and dynamic elements of material texts, as well as customary and cultural expression. Timothy Lloyd examines the tradition of Cincinnati Chili, a regional food developed in the Cincinnati, Ohio, area in 1922, and then adapted by several restaurants that expanded in the 1940s and 1950s (1981, 30). One element of Cincinnati Chili that sets it apart from other chili is its presentation. The chili is not merely a thick soup; it is served over spaghetti and then, depending on the diner's preference, topped with cheese, onions, and/or beans.

On one level, we can see Cincinnati Chili simply as a regional food tradition identified with this southwestern Ohio city and a means by which many Cincinnatians identify themselves. Those who have moved away from the area may consume a traditional feast of Cincinnati Chili on return visits— some even going so far as to take some frozen chili home with them. In regard to dynamism and conservatism in tradition, we can expand our analysis to the way in which this regional food tradition becomes even more significant locally through the dynamic differences in the secret recipes of neighborhood chili parlors. The secret recipes themselves add to the distinctions between the chili served by the major parlors but also lend themselves to the mystique and pride involved in one's loyalty to a certain brand. Several major chili parlors thrive in the Cincinnati area: Dixie Chili, Empress, Gold Star, and Skyline. (We have listed them in alphabetical order so as not to play favorites.) A number of single, independent parlors are sprinkled throughout the city. Ask a Cincinnatian which she or he prefers, and it is unlikely you will receive an indifferent response. Transplants might even exclaim, "You call that chili?" Many residents of the city identify themselves by showing their loyalty to the parlor located in their home neighborhood and may go so far as to model their own home recipes for chili on a particular parlor's recipe. This tradition of consumption and creation of chili indicates regional pride (Lloyd 1981, 31), and the ongoing adaptations show the significance of this *foodway* to the identity of many Cincinnatians.

As with the analysis of many American foodways, the study of Cincinnati Chili is not limited to examining a neighborhood's devotion to a certain restaurant's recipe. Though Lloyd does not categorize the chili as an ethnic food, he traces some of its ingredients to several eastern Mediterranean dishes, in particular citing the presence of cinnamon (as found in Greek, Bulgarian, and Arabic dishes) and a general tendency to contrast sweet spices with hot ones. This spice balance along with tomato, pasta, and beef or lamb often is tasted in Greek and Italian foods (Lloyd 1981, 35). Again, the variations indicate the dynamic nature of folklore.

Yet another level of dynamic process in folklore has to do with the way people perform and share texts. Early in folklore study, folklorists assumed all folklore was shared through face-to-face interaction in small groups. The growth of technology changed that understanding. For instance, in the 1970s and '80s, folklorists studied what some termed office lore or Xerox lore, which involved coworkers photocopying jokes, cartoons, and amusing sayings to post at their workstations or share with their colleagues. Now people use the Internet to do some of these same things. People use email to share contemporary legends, jokes, narratives, and other lore, and websites, blogs, social media networks, and interlinked electronic devices like smartphones and e-tablets offer countless varied opportunities to connect with other people and share, develop, and maintain tradition. As often happens when technology becomes part of mainstream interactions, there are those who have concerns that subsequent changes to the way people communicate will have a negative effect on traditional values and behaviors. But as you can see from the list above, the method of transmission is a dynamic element of the equation and the texts shared may be considered the more conservative elements. These innovations have influenced the ways we define and understand the nature of folklore, groups, and performance, vividly demonstrating the dynamic processes of tradition.

As you can see from these discussions, dynamic changes may be subtle or dramatic. A group's choices may be made consciously, either for creative or aesthetic reasons or because of audience awareness and the need to adapt to tastes, or changes may happen without conscious awareness or control, in relation to groups' or individuals' experiences. But changes do need to be relevant, meaningful, and appropriate to the group in which the folklore is shared. Toelken's theories about the twin laws of folklore show that a central feature of folklore is that it is variable and always responsive to the external and internal changes that influence groups.

From the collection of Barb and Art Vogel. Photo by Earl Vogel.

Traditional Quilt, Carrousel *[sic], Mary Porter Borkowski.*

Borkowski's first experiment with narrative elements in quilting, Chasing Rainbows, *Mary Porter Borkowski.*

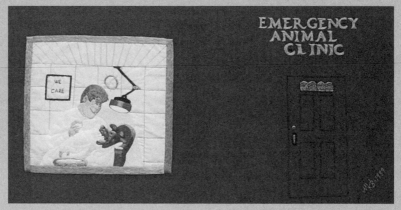

Silk Thread Painting, Animal Clinic, *Mary Porter Borkowski.*

Quilts and Silk Thread Painting by Mary Porter Borkowski

The three pieces shown were created by Mary Porter Borkowski, who began her creative work making traditional quilts (though her quilts were often based on the principle and techniques of traditional quilting, not necessarily on existing traditional patterns for quilts). Borkowski was taught to quilt by her mother and grandmother and made her first quilt at age fourteen.

After some thirty years of quilt making, Borkowski's work changed. Her quilts began taking on more narrative qualities, with images representative of narratives central to the structure of the quilts, as in the quilt depicting the journey of Christopher Columbus (see preceding page). She continued to develop this inventive work in narrative thread painting throughout her life (Borkowski died in 2008). Borkowski became more interested in these narratives and began creating what she called "silk thread paintings" as discrete texts, no longer as elements of her quilts. Unlike much embroidery, Borkowski's thread paintings are multi-textured, creating complex illustrations for narratives of her own life. Borkowski was a storyteller, and these thread paintings allowed her to bring together her skill with thread and fabric and her desire to express the important, sometimes dark and sometimes darkly funny events she observed and experienced.

Mary Borkowski's work exemplifies the development from traditional, vernacular art to a new, innovative form of expressive material text.

Some of Borkowski's quilts are part of the permanent collection at the Smithsonian, and some of her silk thread paintings are in the collection of the American Folk Art Museum in New York City.

(Photos and biographical information courtesy of Barb Vogel)

Inventing Tradition

Among the most dynamic processes groups take part in is the invention of tradition. Since historians Eric Hobsbawm and Terence Ranger brought attention to the idea and coined the term "inventing tradition" in 1983, folklorists have been exploring and expanding on the concept. As Hobsbawm and Ranger explain, invented traditions may be entirely invented, created, and put in place for particular reasons, or they may be more subtly emergent and take hold quickly (1).[23]

Because we have already considered how dynamic and conservative elements of folklore work together to keep a tradition relevant and meaningful to those who share it, the idea of inventing tradition may not seem so farfetched. Clearly, if a tradition can be adapted to suit a slightly different audience or if it can be altered to maintain its meaning or significance within the community practicing it, *invention* can't be too far behind. Different ways of inventing traditions allow them to emerge in a variety of situations. In some cases, a new group may invent traditions that it assumes will be carried out in its future. Other cases may include the creation of a tradition by an existing group, again with the assumption that this tradition will maintain its existence. A group might even invent a tradition it doesn't intend to continue forever, with the expectation that other traditions may replace it as the group's needs change.

Jay Mechling's fieldwork on the Boy Scouts of America illustrates a great deal about the process and basis of tradition, "especially in reminding [us] how dynamic and changeable a 'traditional' activity can be" (2001, 79). The basic structures of Boy Scout verbal and customary lore are officially sanctioned, yet each troop makes them its own in the particular way it acts out them out. Mechling points out that some members of the scouting troop he worked with have recognized the importance of creating traditions that express the unique characteristics of their troop. One person talked of the act of creating new customs and traditions ("C&Ts") and said "of all our C&Ts at camp, our most important C&T is always to invent new C&Ts" (86). Mechling sees this as "a lovely paradox that describes well the dynamic tension between creativity and tradition, between invention and convention, in folklore" (29).

The Boy Scouts, whether inventing or adapting, work within an existing group to create traditions that instill meaning in their interactions. In less formally defined groups, we can see how inventing tradition also works to establish and identify the parameters of the group itself. For example, one of our former students wrote of an experience in which she and a friend went out to get ice cream and commiserate about their boyfriends. They began writing a "Why I Hate Boys" list on a napkin. The activity had no specific precedent in their experience, but when another friend called on them with "boy trouble," they decided it was time to go out, get ice cream, and write up another list. Since then, whenever a friend of theirs has problems with a boyfriend, the group goes out for ice cream and creates a new list. The activity has become a regular one—an event that they identify as a tradition—for these women and their friends. Their invented tradition maintains a bond between members of the group of friends and allows them to express and explore their relationship values.

The ability of groups to invent traditions and, in the process, possibly invent themselves connects with wider cultural and social implications. Handler and Linnekin suggest that tradition is about cultural interpretation and challenge earlier perceptions of tradition as existing in a dichotomy with modernity—as somehow apart from or in conflict with people's current experience (1984, 273). While they focus on tradition as maintaining continuity with the past, they also assert that the crucial feature of tradition is that it is "a process of thought—an ongoing interpretation of the past" (274). We would go further and suggest that tradition is also about our ongoing interpretation of identity and how we make our identities understood to each other. Ultimately, as Handler and Linnekin argue, "invention of tradition" exists, and this "ongoing reconstruction of tradition is a facet of all social life" (276).

If inventing tradition is a constant process of cultural interpretation and reconstruction, it is clear that it can also be a socially and politically empowering activity. Tad Tuleja states the necessity for the politically powerless to invent their own traditions, "creatively utilizing 'past practices'—both inherently aged ones and deliberately aged ones—as manipulable markers of a common identity" (1997, 3). He points out that groups can be in control of their own identity through this process. One example would be the winter holiday Kwanzaa, a celebration of spiritual and cultural unity that incorporates traditions, values, and principles from countries across Africa. This holiday was deliberately created in the 1960s to promote a sense of a shared heritage and identity among African Americans. Tuleja weighs in on the debate about tradition not by suggesting a categorical definition but by confirming that the term "does not necessarily imply a venerable lineage" (3). He breaks down the term *invention* as well, examining the etymology and noting that in every sense, "invention suggests the creative impulse," not the negative connotations of fakery or falseness (4).

The Question of Authenticity

Tuleja's passage works well to move us into discussion of a key debate in folklore studies: the question of authenticity. As his comments imply, a concern that is likely to surface when considering the ability of groups to invent traditions is how we will know whether a tradition is authentic if there is no history that identifies it as such.

In some ways, once we've argued and accepted that tradition can be invented, arguing what makes it authentic is unnecessary. First of all, folklorists used to be more worried about authenticity when we thought of tradition as only texts that were old, quaint or rural, and pure. Those terms have been successfully reexamined and, for the most part, rejected, as we have seen. Second, once we shift our interest from isolated texts to the groups that share those texts and the ways they share them, the notion of authenticity is less of a concern. This shift allows us to see that tradition is primarily about people, communication, and identity. Authenticity depends on how a group defines its own traditions. The requirement for "authentic" tradition to have a long-standing history may be more relevant for some groups than others; and some groups may stress duplication in extreme detail, while others may accept broad variations. In other words, authenticity is best understood in terms of communication within a group; if a group is sharing a particular tradition, communicating through it, and giving it meaning, the tradition is authentic. Authenticity is a relative term and depends entirely on who is determining the authenticity and for what reasons.

Still, the debate continues, primarily in three contexts: the commodification, or marketing, of folklore; the political and social uses of texts; and the scholarly study of texts. Usually, the question of authenticity arises in these contexts in reference to exoteric definitions of traditional texts and materials or exoteric definitions of authenticity.

Commodification is the process by which something becomes a commodity—something that is bought, sold, or traded. Familiar examples of the commodification of folklore are easy to find, from the popularization of so-called country arts like quilting or tole painting to the adoption of fairy-tale themes in the creation and selling of new Barbie dolls.[24] Many raise the concern that folklore manipulated in this way—to make money—devalues the expressive and communicative qualities of folklore texts, turning them into meaningless objects. Many scholars believe the marketplace approach to folklore texts and themes is potentially damaging to the intimate, perhaps emotional, connections such items in their original contexts create for group members that share them. The story of Cinderella, for instance, exists in many forms and in many cultural groups. But when it is first retold and marketed by a major corporation as a movie and is then further repackaged and marketed as a story that features a doll as the main character, the potential for local flavor or individual variations is reduced. The commodified, homogenized version created by movie makers and toy companies may supersede or obscure authentic local versions. Political or social uses of folklore are also familiar, although they may be hidden more successfully within accepted organizations or institutions like schools, governments, or special interest groups. These manipulations may be part of marketing efforts or may come from a desire to preserve or protect so-called traditional culture; or they may be motivated by the desire to celebrate or uphold a group's founding values or history. The question of authenticity becomes highly politicized in the deliberate construction or manipulation of traditions to influence people's values or behaviors. In its most extreme form this kind of manipulation approaches propaganda.

Early in his career, Richard Dorson introduced the term *fakelore* to describe these kinds of purposefully directed, created texts, first with reference to collections of fabricated folktales written and sold as popular entertainment. In the 1970s, he revisited the idea and looked at it more theoretically, in terms of political and social institutions and also in terms of the way the lore is collected and interpreted. One of Dorson's main concerns was the possibility of political manipulation through fakelore. Whether through intentional dissemination of actual folklore or through the more likely creation of tales and songs espousing particular political values, these uses of folklore are built on the nationalist (and nostalgic) aspects of tradition, with people—usually a dominant political, governmental, or commercial organization—creating or co-opting lore for political and popular means. In some cases, the intention was to impose particular "values and misinformation" upon a population (1976, 17). Dorson mentions such practices by North Vietnamese agents in Laos, and also by the Soviets, Bulgarians, and Hungarians, where themes prevalent in local traditions were either built on or manipulated in order to convert local inhabitants to communism. Of course, communist countries are not the only ones to practice such manipulations. A good example from the United States would be the use of the image of Uncle Sam, a patriotic figure meant to personify the United States, as a recruiting tool during World War I.

Folklorists have discussed Dorson's ideas about fakelore for decades and have disagreed over whether it even really exists. The conscious creation and misuse of tradition certainly occurs, often for deliberately persuasive purposes. But in some cases deliberately manufactured texts become part of the authentic— that is, informally shared and expressive—tradition of groups. An often-cited example is Paul Bunyan, a figure created from a conflation of characters that appeared in legends told by American lumbermen and loggers in the nineteenth century. A lumber company used Paul Bunyan as a marketing tool, reproducing tales about him and printing his image on their marketing materials. Now, though, so many Americans have heard the stories and learned about the legend of Paul Bunyan that the character has become an accepted part of folklore about the American frontier period. (In fact, it has almost become traditional in introductory folklore classes to tell the story about Paul Bunyan's true origins to illustrate how institutions can manufacture or manipulate folklore themes!)

Scholarly examinations of authenticity often center on the reasons that texts, like the Paul Bunyan tales, are commodified or manipulated, as well as on what happens after the texts are introduced. Another scholarly concern is with the very fact that authenticity is such a loaded term for some groups; it means so much to many people, for a variety of sometimes conflicting reasons. The main interest of folklore scholars is not necessarily whether traditions are authentic or not but rather the ways groups perceive authenticity. Some investigate the ways groups (particularly government and corporate groups) use their positions of power to influence the traditions of others. Many scholars who study the public and institutional presentations of folklore investigate the ways some groups manipulate others' perceptions of what is authentic in order to trick people into accepting a certain tradition. It is fascinating to consider the interrelationships among market forces, educational institutions, governments, special interest organizations, and folk groups with regard to how they all define and present their own concepts of authentic tradition. Once again, the most important idea is that the determination of authenticity, or the evaluation of the relative "folkness" or "fakeness" of a tradition, depends upon the group of people examining the text.

Example: Traditions in Folk Art

As we delve into the subject of tradition, we want to keep in mind that traditions exist because they mean something to those who partake in them. In this section, we will look at how two different self-taught artists,[25] creating work in similar cultural surroundings, are part of larger traditions; each created pieces in his own individual style but drew from similar influences to express ideas and values he found meaningful. The work of R. A. Miller and Howard Finster provides an illustration of the way in which a tradition exists as a core from which group members, in this case artists, can draw but still bring in their own creative identities.

The work of both Miller and Finster belongs to an artistic tradition common to the southern United States that is tightly interconnected with and supported by religious beliefs and religious communities. Both were born in the South, and both spent time as preachers. In addition to incorporating religious messages and symbols in their art, both include images and materials from other artistic traditions. Figures from popular culture and patriotic images take their place alongside Christian icons and verbal expressions in their work. All of these images were created with recycled materials like those used in the work of other self-taught American artists.

From the collection of Marita Sims and Brian Lovely.

Whirligig, *R. A. Miller.*

Often self-taught artists work with the materials at hand, whether creating multidimensional collages or simply recycling found materials (Greenfield 1986). Both Finster and Miller began their creative careers painting on found materials, such as plywood or tin, and continued to utilize similar materials. Finster created elaborate sculptures and three-dimensional collages, or *assemblages,*[26] whereas Miller's three-dimensional work primarily takes the form of "whirligigs" (small windmill-like constructions) In Finster's backyard environment *Paradise Garden,* for instance, the artist combined boards and planks of wood and tin, old bicycle frames, discarded television screens, rocks, and other objects into complex two- and three-dimensional recycled texts. Sides of buildings and walls—whatever surfaces or materials are available—are painted with figures of people and animals, or covered with hand-lettered Bible verses or religious phrases. Miller's three-dimensional works, on the other hand, are less complex and utilize mainly painted scraps of wood or metal, fixed to a pole or rod. Miller went further than using only old, discarded, or recycled materials and adapted the *idea* of work with found materials to keep up with the demand for his work. For example, a collector of Miller's art may have brought him an old door to paint, or he himself may have purchased vinyl shutters on which to paint when he ran out of scrap aluminum, plywood, or architectural cast-offs.

Traditional rural southern life and American popular culture influence the artwork of both men whether constructing objects and decorating them or simply painting on flat tin or wooden surfaces. In addition to the whirligigs

From the collection of Martha Sims and Brian Lovely.

Painting on tin, Lord Love You, R. A. Miller.

designed to catch the wind in rural yards, Miller created cutouts of chickens and pigs, a connection to his farming days. His patriotism shows in the American flags he painted on scraps of aluminum siding and Uncle Sam outfits appearing on Blow Oskar, one of his most popular images.[27] Of course, the requisite southern icon Elvis is depicted in both Miller's and Finster's work. Miller's Elvis consists of two cutouts, a silhouetted male figure and a guitar, while Finster often painted portrait-style images of the early Elvis. Another American icon, the Coca-Cola bottle, figured into Finster's art. His work with such American images gained public attention and is recognized as characteristic of folk artists, which brought him the opportunity to create the ultimate Coke bottle: an eight-foot bottle painted for the "Coca-Cola Olympic Salute to Folk Art."

In their home communities, the artists' whirligigs, paintings, and other artwork have drawn the attention of neighbors and outsiders. Residents of Gainesville, Georgia, where Miller lived until his death in 2006, may be proud of the notice he received and be glad of the business brought to the Rabbittown area by people who came to visit Miller and buy work from him. Requests in a local convenience store for directions to his home would receive a quick response. The musicians of the Georgia band R.E.M.—both insiders and outsiders, in a way—have incorporated Miller's work, as well as Finster's, into their videos. Finster's work is even more widely known than Miller's, both inside and outside his community, and has appeared on covers of CDs and in other highly visible locations. Finster's daughter Thelma Finster Bradshaw tells of the attention locals paid to her father's art, including the special interest shown

Painted wood cut out, Howard with the Weight of the World
(front), Howard Finster.

by a woman named Edith Wilson, whom Finster had converted when he was
a preacher. She contacted art galleries; as a result, according to Bradshaw, the
Atlanta Council for the Arts got word of his talent, and interest in his work from
outside his community grew (Bradshaw 2001, 130).

Public recognition, whether local, national, or global, has given voice to both
of these artists' beliefs and values. Sharing religious messages in the images,
symbols, and narrative elements of their religious experiences and traditions

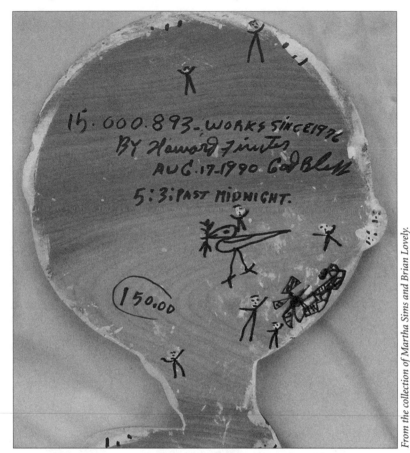

From the collection of Martha Sims and Brian Lovely.

Painted wood cut out, Howard with the Weight of the World *(back of globe),* Howard Finster.

was integral to their belief systems. Angels, spirits, saints, and devils populate their works, communicating spiritual values from their Baptist tradition. Each placed a high value on religion, Finster having served as a preacher at Chelsea Baptist Church and as a traveling preacher (Bradshaw 2001), and Miller having preached at tent revivals and the Free Will Baptist Church (*The New Georgia Encyclopedia* online). Miller's stock religious images are devils, angels, and crosses, and even some of Miller's paintings of nonreligious figures include simple religious phrases, most often "Lord Love You." In conversation at his home where he exhibited and sold his work, Miller spoke about his faith and the idea that his art—and hence his message—is accessible to those who want it.

Like Miller, Finster concretely and directly incorporated religious narrative traditions, telling stories of his sins and of being "saved" by his faith in

Jesus. These paintings often include images of himself as a character named Howard. Experts and those close to him agree about the importance of religion in Finster's work. A past director of the American Folk Art Museum suggests that Finster "cannot be understood fully except within the context of Southern evangelical religion. His work is replete with images from biblical narrative and the popular piety of a thousand Southern road signs" (Wertkin 1998, 16). Finster's daughter Thelma explains how central his religious beliefs are in his work: "If you're not personally acquainted with God, my father hopes his paintings will introduce you to Him. With his art, he tries to show each of you a little piece of Heaven that could be yours if you'd only let God walk into those empty spaces in your heart" (Bradshaw 2001, 8). The longstanding oral tradition of testifying—talking about one's religious experiences to convince others of the religion's power—is apparent in Finster's and Miller's interactions with those who spoke with them about their art, and perhaps more importantly, in the verbal features of their work. The art of both Finster and Miller, then, exists within and illustrates the Christian evangelical tradition of a calling to share the word of their God with others.

R. A. Miller and Howard Finster both presented traditional messages in traditional forms, yet they articulated them differently. As small-town southern artists with strong religious values, Finster and Miller drew from a palette of religious images and narratives, but their lives included more than religion. Their American patriotism and exposure to popular culture appear in their work as well, a part of the everyday life of their communities. Built from the values of the artists' religion and everyday life, the work of Finster and Miller is part of a strong artistic tradition, too.

Conclusion

Traditions do far more than connect us to the past. They link us to family, friends, neighbors, and other groups we belong to; they are part of who we are and how we define ourselves. Whether we consciously create them, join those that already exist, or ease into them when we are born, we engage in an active process of building and sharing identity every time we take part in traditions. Studying tradition allows us to understand not just what we care about but also how we express ourselves across the complex web of communication we share with those around us.

CHAPTER 4

Ritual

*G*roups frequently devise ceremonies or performances that enact deeply held beliefs or values. These are rituals, and they make our inner experiences of traditions visible and observable to members of the group and often to outsiders. Have you been initiated into a club or other organization in an elaborate ceremony? That's a ritual, one that marks your status as a full-fledged member of the group and tells the rest of the group as well as outsiders that membership is important—it makes you special, different from others who don't belong to the group. If you have ever taken part in or seen a court trial, you have probably seen witnesses place their left hand on a Bible and raise their right and swear to tell the truth. That, too, is a ritual, which makes it clear to all involved that truth is both a sacred and secular principle that the US legal system venerates. Participating in that ritual implies that the witness, too, recognizes that truth is a founding principle of the law and agrees to uphold it, regardless of the witness's faith or belief in the binding power of the oath. This ritual and the principle it symbolizes are so powerful that if a witness refuses to take part, his or her testimony may not be accepted, and if it is discovered that a witness has lied, he or she may be punished.

Some rituals are long-standing parts of group behavior, but—as with traditions—it is possible for groups to *create* rituals that express important ideas. Rituals signify changes in state or status and frequently signal or celebrate important stages of life. Rituals are associated with birth, puberty, marriage, and death, and rituals establish our entry to or exit from different parts of life or group experience. Because they are sometimes so ceremonial, rituals are often filled with costumes, pageantry, and mystery. During a ritual, the world changes, reality can be suspended, and traditions become real, tangible experiences that we can actively take part in.

Folklorists study rituals because their complexity and dramatic qualities make them dense with meaning: they are significant expressions of a group's traditions, beliefs, values, and identity. Because rituals are so important in making the process of folklore visible, we want to focus in depth on this complex category.

In the following sections, we discuss how rituals reflect and create meaningful experiences for groups and we provide extended examples of a variety of rituals.

What is Ritual?

A ritual is a particular type of tradition that many folklorists study as a distinct category of folklore. Rituals are habitual actions, but they are more purposeful than customs; rituals are frequently highly organized and controlled, often meant to indicate or announce membership in a group. Most rituals bring together many types of folklore: verbal, such as chants, recitations, poems, or songs; customary, such as gestures, dances, or movements; and material, such as food, books, awards, clothing, and costumes. For example, one of our contributors, Mickey Weems, in "Gay Rituals: Outing, Biking, and Sewing" (see chapter 8, "Examples of Folklore Projects"), describes some of the ways that ritual actions, verbal expressions, behaviors, and objects help to define groups within the gay community.

Generally, rituals are performances that are repeated and patterned and frequently include ceremonial symbols and actions. Perhaps most significant to our recognition of rituals is a frame that indicates when the ritual begins and ends (Myerhoff 1977, 200). Most rituals are stylized, highly contextualized, deeply symbolic activities that enable groups to acknowledge, exemplify, and/or act out certain traditional ideas, values, and beliefs. Family and community celebrations, sacred and secular ceremonies, and a variety of other structured performances include rituals. Rituals, then, require a set of beliefs and values that group members accept and want to have reinforced. The ritual works to teach their importance by emphasizing—even acting out—these values or beliefs. Like tradition in general, most rituals are simultaneously static and dynamic, with core features that are typically repeated and recognizable but with room for great variation, depending on the group. Rituals frequently employ symbols and metaphors to represent important concepts. Moving the tassel on the graduation mortarboard after a student receives a diploma, for example, symbolizes the graduate's change in status. This small ritual acknowledges the emphasis that the group places on education and growing up and shows the appreciation of successfully completing the various stages of life and formal education.

Rituals occur in many settings. Sometimes they take place in more formalized settings, or the ritual itself creates its own space. For instance, in the baptism ritual we'll describe later, participants frequently gather at a church at a pre-established time to observe and take part in baptism ceremonies. However, in some groups, baptisms can also take place when the opportunity arises at random times, not just predesignated times. For instance, a preacher at a church camp might hold an impromptu baptism at a lake when several adolescent campers express a desire to join the church. In this less structured setting, rituals emerge from situations when the necessary elements are present. Usually we think people need to be together in one physical place for a ritual to take place, but people are stretching that assumption and finding creative ways to meet to practice rituals together through technology in virtual settings. A pagan group, for example, might create and share YouTube videos of ritual performances so members can follow along at home on their own, when they are separated from the rest of the group. More specific ritual meetings can take place online on celebratory days when members can't meet physically; for example, on the summer solstice, groups of pagans from all around the world log onto website forums to honor the solstice by staying up all night and exchanging inspirational thoughts and poems throughout the sacred event. The online gathering stands in for and enacts through different methods of expression what the group would do if members could all be together—stay up all night celebrating the solstice.

It is important to understand that regardless of where and when they take place, rituals are outward expressions or enactments of inwardly experienced values, beliefs, and attitudes. In other words, we can't look at a person and automatically know he belongs to a group that values education; we can, however, see him cross the stage at graduation and move the tassel on his mortarboard. We can observe and discuss that outward expression, that ritual action. That's one reason rituals are so important to groups and to folklorists: they make intangible values, beliefs, and attitudes—which are frequently hidden—concrete and visible.

While many rituals are infused with a sense of seriousness and deliberateness and others are less serious, existing as much for entertainment as for any other purpose, they are all typically important to the participants. In many parts of the United States, for example, Groundhog Day, February 2, is celebrated with an elaborate public ritual in which a groundhog is prodded out of its (supposed) hibernation place and held aloft by a local official. The official then announces whether the groundhog has seen its shadow and, if so, declares that six more weeks of winter are on the way. If the groundhog does not see its shadow, the official declares that an early spring is on the way. Some communities hold parades and celebrations on this day. One community in Pennsylvania has so completely associated itself with the ritual held on this day that its eponymous representative groundhog, Punxsutawney Phil, is regarded in the eastern United States as the authentic seasonal prognosticator. News media usually report on this popular ritual as an amusing highlight during local weather reports or as part of the light news of the day. Still, even though it is typically a lighthearted event, the ritual forms part of the Punxsutawney community's identity that others outside the community readily take part in.

Because rituals work on so many different levels and in so many different ways, the concept of ritual is at once simple and highly complicated to define. Its simplicity rests in the fact that it requires a structure based on the forms that rituals have taken in the past. Its complexity is based on the fact that it may occur in a multitude of situations, within any group imaginable, and relate to or convey the significance of group beliefs, attitudes, or practices of greater or lesser importance. But no matter what it conveys, an idea big or small, sacred or secular, a ritual is a particular type of action-driven tradition.

The idea of ritual as action-driven tradition is clearly described in Barbara G. Myerhoff's definition (1977). One of her key claims is that ritual "defines a portion of reality" (199). By performing (and sometimes creating) a ritual, a group is in essence designating a moment in time during which its members are required to pay attention to some of the rules and/or beliefs held or promoted by the group. And the goal of the ritual isn't that members simply pay attention to these ideas. Often the more important objective is that they are persuaded to believe that the values portrayed or referred to during the ritual are indeed *real, true* values the group holds. The act of ritual is often an act of *convincing*. Myerhoff also contends, then, that one of the important purposes of a ritual is to *persuade*, and she says that "action is indicated because rituals persuade the body first; behaviors precede emotions in the participants" (199). The phrase "fake it 'til you make it," a popular psychological dictum adopted from twelve-step programs, applies to rituals. The doing of the ritual, participating in an event that acknowledges the significance of a cultural transformation, trains the participants to feel the event's worth.

Rituals can feature numerous special event markers: oral performances (songs, dramatic readings, or recitations); dances; special foods (perhaps foods requiring time-consuming preparation); and dramatic lighting (dim light, candlelight, or spotlights of some sort). Often, rituals involve dressing in ceremonial attire (or at least attire different from the everyday), and material objects frequently are incorporated into the activities performed by leaders of the group and its members. These items of material culture add weight to the process and reinforce the sense of the ritual's being *real*. These paraphernalia of ritual envelop participants in an environment that suggests that everyone understands that these special events and the ideas behind them are important to the group's identity.

Along with these tangible factors is the intangible *frame*. The frame is what sets apart ritual from ordinary events, even those rituals that seem commonplace to us. This frame may be gestural, oral, or time oriented, and its function is to alert people to the significance of the action sandwiched within it. In other words, some utterance or behavior introduces the ritual so participants know it is beginning, and another utterance or behavior brings the ritual to a conclusion. It often involves some sort of oral component, whether it's a song, a narrative, or incantation that draws participants' (and sometimes observers') attention to the transition being made. At many wedding receptions, the best man stands and raises his glass, gives a toast wishing a long and happy married life to the couple, and then all the guests clink glasses. A common birthday ritual occurs in many families when the birthday cake is presented and served. In one family, an adult might call everyone to the table and announce that it's time for the cake. That announcement alerts everyone that it is time for the ritual of blowing out the candles. In another family, someone will carry the cake into the room, candles lit, and place it in front of the birthday person. Usually, the group sings the birthday song, someone will say, "make a wish," and the birthday person blows out the candles, all in one breath. Many families clap or cheer for the birthday person, and then the cake is cut. The birthday person receives the first piece. For many groups, cutting and serving the first piece of cake ends the formal frame of the birthday cake presentation ritual.

Low-Context and High-Context Rituals

Low-context rituals are those that are less formally designated and usually not announced or planned in advance. For example, the conversion ritual of throwing salt over your shoulder when you spill salt is fairly low context. It occurs for a specific reason in response to a particular event (spilling salt) but isn't planned in advance and doesn't involve elaborate, thought-out performances or verbal expression. It may be performed when others are present or when one is alone and does not require a particular setting. In contrast, most high-context rituals are very stylized and occur at set times for specific, announced purposes. These are often public events, such as weddings or christenings.

Boy blowing out the birthday candles.

In high-context rituals, there are likely to be particular dress codes participants must follow, and/or designated ceremonial clothing or jewelry they must wear. In some kinds of rituals, officials' or leaders' attire may be different from that of celebrants or participants, but each person who plays a specific role in the ritual is likely to wear special clothing. These differences in clothing indicate who's who in the group: who's a novice, who's an official, who's merely an observer. In a formal Christian christening, for instance, the baby wears a white, lacy gown, the parents wear their best clothes, and the officiator—usually a priest or minister—wears religious robes. Secular ceremonies often incorporate clothing, too—Girl Scouts in the United States perform a "crossover" or "fly-up" in which younger girls may walk across a bridge (a real one or one constructed temporarily for the occasion). Once across the bridge, they exchange their old hats or sashes (sometimes both) for the type of hat or sash worn by girls who are at the new level. Girls also typically are given pins or badges that indicate their membership in the higher level of the group. Such attire provides a visual representation of the group's hierarchy.

High-context rituals are typically conducted by someone. Usually the experienced members of the group, sometimes even specially selected members, run the ritual and make sure it happens in the right way. Participants, too, may have specific actions to perform or words to recite. In a Girl Scout troop, the leader usually plans the ceremony and instructs participants in the correct behaviors; there might even be a rehearsal. Leaders may get their ideas from books provided by the organization or may learn from other experienced leaders, and many local variations exist, depending on the group's interest. One group may sing songs or perform skits, and another may light candles, for example. But the core elements, the crossing of the bridge and the presentation of sashes or pins, must be there, and it is the leader's job to ensure those events happen smoothly and correctly.

Invented Ritual

Just as there are invented traditions, there are invented rituals. The two are similar in that both express and reinforce identity. Invented traditions, though, may primarily reflect awareness that a group needs traditions that individuals can regularly participate in and that can identify them esoterically—and perhaps exoterically—as members. An invented ritual, however, is more of a *consciously constructed event* that may signify transition and/or change in membership or position. Rituals mark and announce changes in state, status, or role, and we continually create rituals that we find meaningful. Invented rituals can make the changes even more meaningful through pageantry and performance and perhaps even add an air of mystery. Rituals can at the same time lend a sense of conscious control over the boundaries between one state or role and another—or at least indicate conscious awareness of the boundaries. In general, rituals deepen and enrich the meaning of a particular tradition.

Many families, for example, create rituals that celebrate or acknowledge certain firsts in a child's life. A baby's first steps might be marked with a shopping trip with the parents, siblings, and grandparents to buy the child's first pair of shoes, and when they return home they hold a short ritual in which the shoes are placed on the child's feet for the first time. The loss of a first tooth might be celebrated by reading a story about the tooth fairy at bedtime, and the child may then be presented with a special box to place the tooth in before tucking it under his or her pillow. Each child in the family will take part in these events, perhaps throughout the extended family and for many generations, or they may be limited to only the children of a particular family unit.

We know of a family that celebrated an important "last" in their children's lives, complete with a formalized ritual to acknowledge the occasion. When a child grew too big to be carried by his or her parents (perhaps around age ten, or earlier or later, depending on the child's size), this family invited family members and friends over for a "last carry" party. After everyone arrived, the father announced that the child would now be carried for the last time. He would pick up the child and then pass him or her to the mother, and then other guests would take turns carrying the child around the house. When everyone had had a chance, they all congratulated the child for having become a big kid who no longer needed to be carried (or could no longer be carried comfortably) and presented small gifts in honor of this milestone. This family consciously decided to invent a ritual that recognized this significant passage because the members believed such moments often went by unnoticed: first-time events stand out, but parents seldom realize they have carried a child for the last time, given a baby the last bottle, or changed the last diaper. They created a tradition that highlights these bittersweet moments by calling together people important in the child's life to celebrate the "last carry" at a party; then they enriched the tradition by inviting the partygoers to take part in a ritual that formally acted out the significance of this sign of maturity.

Groups can invent rituals to acknowledge events or traditions that their wider society or culture does not acknowledge or does not acknowledge to the degree their group wishes. As Myerhoff, Camino, and Turner suggest, it is crucial to understand that all rituals (particularly those associated with rites of passage) are "constructed—fabricated, built, created—for that indicates that we may then be able to create and provide them for ourselves if they are not already bestowed upon us by our society" (1986, 387). For instance, in most Protestant groups in the United States, the date of a person's death is not formally commemorated, as it may be in other traditions or cultural groups. While many informally acknowledge the date of a person's death by visiting the grave or by preparing the person's favorite meal for the family dinner that day, Protestants do not possess any codified, preexisting sacred or secular rituals that memorialize a deceased one on the anniversary of his or her death. If a group, family, or work group, for example, wanted to mark such a day in some special way, they might decide to hold a candlelight service or sing songs that person enjoyed, in a formal, structured way. They may create an entirely unique ritual or borrow aspects of other groups' rituals—burning incense, for instance, or writing prayers on scrolls to ensure the person's eternal contentment. They may repeat this event each year or hold the same kind of event on the death dates of many honored friends and family members. This invented ritual would then become a heightened part of that group's tradition of commemorating a person's death.

105

The Question of Belief in Sacred and Secular Rituals

Many people associate the term *ritual* primarily with religion; sacred activities often define religious group practice. Often, sacred rituals, such as a seder or a communion, embody the most deeply held principles of a particular religious group and may enact noted events in the history of the religion. Sacred rituals are associated with nearly every group that has beliefs about spiritual or supernatural worlds or phenomena. These kinds of rituals typically take place in the presence of a group—other congregants or a family, for instance—but some sacred rituals are less public and may be performed privately, even secretly. Not all sacred rituals are connected with mainstream religious groups, but all make belief visible.

This is not to say that participants have to be true or fervent believers to take part in a ritual but rather that because these rituals illustrate core beliefs, participants must at least acknowledge and understand the beliefs to be a part of the group. For some, belief is the most important fact, and some say that those who do not believe are "just going through the motions" or are diminishing the power of the activity, dismissing the behavior as just a ritual without any sacred or deeper significance. In some cases, belief may be the whole point of the ritual. Appalachian snake handlers, for instance, believe that if the participant is not a true, sincere believer in God's transformative and protective power, he or she will not be able to safely handle the deadly snakes that figure into the group's religious services. Similarly, some sacred healers claim that if the person seeking treatment does not really believe in the efficacy of the treatment, he or she will not receive the curative benefits of it. On the other hand, some healers say it doesn't matter if the patient believes, but it does matter if the healer believes. One healer explains that even if the patient doesn't believe in the cure, "it does take something to heal somebody else" (Babb and Little Dog 1994, 28). This healer believes being a "good person" is necessary in order for the healer to be able to cure. The question of belief is clearly relevant, but the ways participants approach the issue of belief are of greater interest to the folklorist than assessing the validity or veracity of the beliefs expressed through the ritual.

Secular rituals, those not overtly associated with any sacred or spiritual beliefs, can also have great significance for participants, and the question of belief may have just as much relevance. In many cases, secular rituals teach us some of the rules, beliefs, and attitudes necessary to our functioning in the society in which we live. We learn about how to behave in different situations and different types of relationships through our participation in rituals. Many adolescent rituals, for example, surround divination of future mates or lovers.

A young woman might be instructed to peel an apple without breaking the peel, then to throw it over her shoulder without looking behind her. She then turns around, and the letter the peel forms on the ground predicts the letter of the first name of her future spouse. While a slight supernatural component exists here, most of these kinds of secular divination rituals don't involve spiritual components but do involve belief in the connection between certain predictive actions and their outcomes. The stakes are not too high for belief here, though; a girl won't lose anything if she performs the ritual without believing in it or if she does it incorrectly. It might not work, but no harm will come to her.

Some secular rituals do have higher stakes because they directly and strongly express a group's values and beliefs. Participants in a retirement dinner ritual, for example, in which the retiree formally receives a gift or award that commemorates the end of his or her working life, clearly *believe* that finishing one's career is a significant life event that deserves public acknowledgment. There is no religious or sacred content inherent in this ritual, but it is infused with the group's beliefs about the value of work. As another example, athletes, even those at the highest level of competition, participate in rituals, whether as individuals or as an entire team. These behaviors may be as simple as a golfer eating the same breakfast every day she competes or members of the hockey team touching a plaque inscribed with an inspirational phrase on their way from the locker room to the rink. Athletes who practice these rituals (which some might label superstitions) may perform an action because they did it at a previous competition in which they were successful, or they might practice it simply *because*, having no discernible or traceable reason supporting the behavior. Athletes, no matter how skilled, realize that they are not guaranteed a win simply because they participate in the ritual, but there is clearly an investment of belief in the process—even if athletes take part in it just in case.

Many rituals combine both sacred and secular elements. Such interwoven types of rituals express complex connections between a group's sacred principles and the familial, social, and community values by which it conducts its secular life. Weddings and funerals, for instance, often incorporate both sacred and secular aspects; many weddings incorporate traditional secular as well as sacred music, prayers at designated times, religious blessings, and secular traditions such as the white gown or the "something borrowed" tradition. Funerals often are complex interplays of the sacred and secular. One small-town funeral ritual we have participated in involves a ceremonial drive behind the hearse to tour the deceased person's neighborhood before attending the full mass at the local Catholic church. Both of these types of ritualized events are celebrated by the religious as well as the nonreligious and by

107

members of many different faiths and can be either completely or mostly sacred or entirely secular.

Seasonal celebrations also often combine sacred and secular features. Springtime celebrations of renewal, for example, are more than just indications of significant beliefs within a particular religion's practice. Formal sacred rituals surrounding seasonal holidays may happen in places of worship; however, in members' homes, informal, more secularized rituals may also occur, marking the date as personally significant to the member as well as to the entire congregation of their church or religious group. Such distinctions take the holiday to a new level, allowing members to make their commitment and belief more personal, more integral to their own daily lives, as well as part of a larger system with which they may have only weekly (or sometimes less frequent) contact. For some, this personal or more distinctly family- or community-based ritual may involve a special food that grandmother cooks only on that holiday, or a special family event, like getting up early on the day after Christmas to go shopping.

The power of ritual to define a group according to its sacred and secular beliefs can have dramatic consequences, particularly if the ritual expresses ideas another group finds unfamiliar or even threatening. A well-known example from US history is the Native American Ghost Dance religion of the nineteenth century. The religion was based on a belief that the performance of a particular dance—the ghost dance—would help to heal the earth and end the white European expansion in the American West. The dance developed as a way to embody this belief and to literally bring about those hoped-for consequences. Dancers believed that performing the dance called up the spirits of the ancestors (ghosts) to join with the living and generated great power that could hasten the return of the land to its rightful occupants. White government officials, understanding the resentment of white occupation as well as the strong spiritual and cultural beliefs the dance expressed, feared the potential power of the dance ritual to unify and strengthen native groups, so they outlawed the practice of the religion. Groups continued to perform the dance, though, and eventually its practice spread from the Northern Paiutes to groups within the Arapaho, Sioux, Cheyenne, and other tribes. In 1890, the dance was performed near Wounded Knee, South Dakota. US soldiers rounded up hundreds of participants in the dance ritual, and the conflict soon escalated into the infamous Wounded Knee massacre of Native Americans by government troops. The white government and settlers believed the ritual could strengthen the Native American resistance, and as a result, fear of the Ghost Dance (and the attitudes and beliefs it enacted) figured prominently in the continued white suppression of Native American communities throughout the West.

Liminality and Ritual Space

The nature of ritual, the way it is framed as a separate time and experience outside the everyday world, allows the participants to enter a space that is different from their real world environment. By carving out that moment from other moments, it can be transformed into something different. Through altering such things as their clothing, language, and behavior (at least in high-context rituals), the participants create a liminal space.[28] *Liminal* comes from the word *limen*, which means "on the threshold." When we experience a liminal state or are in a liminal space, we are on the edge of something new, a transitional place and time where what we were (our role or status before the ritual began) and what we will be after the ritual ends are mixed and blended; or, in another way of thinking about it, we are neither what we were nor what we will be. For the duration of the ritual, the participants can change identity, become something other than what they typically are. Experiences are heightened and sometimes aided by consumption of special, perhaps intoxicating, foods or other substances. Some rituals surround experiences and events that are themselves liminal. Puberty, for example, a time when we are not quite children and not quite adults, is itself a kind of liminal state, frequently marked in many cultures with elaborate sacred and secular rituals. For some, liminal spaces created through ritual are magical or mystical realms where literal and symbolic transformation can take place. The purpose of ritual is to create this altered, in-between space so that beliefs may become real and possible and transformations can more readily occur.

The transformative power of the ritual space is sometimes easiest to see in rituals that take place in sacred belief systems. In the Apache Sunrise Ceremony, for instance a puberty rite that celebrates a young woman's coming of age—the young woman is believed to embody the powers of Changing Woman, the first woman, according to Apache systems of belief. During the ritual and for a few days after, the young woman is believed to have healing powers, and members of the community visit her during this time to be cured by her. The ritual that celebrates and marks her physical change leads to a symbolic change, and the symbolic change is then made real and is reflected in her new position in the community as a young adult. The Sunrise Ceremony rituals are both deeply sacred and of high importance in the secular, social world, where young women undergoing the transformations literally emerge as new members of adult society. Extended family members gather during this time, strengthening bonds and reinforcing family connections as they welcome the young woman into adulthood. The Sunrise Ceremony expresses and reinforces sacred beliefs and secular ideals that are meaningful for the group.

109

Another ritual that illustrates the concept of ritual space is the full immersion baptism practiced in some evangelical Christian denominations. Prayers that invoke the Holy Spirit at the start of the baptism ceremony open up the ritual space and close it off from the world outside the ritual. In some churches this ritual requires that people being baptized be aware and completely accepting of the transformation they are about to undergo, so they are able to understand the importance of the ritual and can make a deliberate choice to join the church.[29] The opening prayers ask God to listen to and accept candidates' pledges to live as a Christians. The preacher asks each of the baptism candidates in turn if they intend to join the church and devote their lives to God, each answers yes, and then the officiant, a preacher or minister in most cases, eases each of the candidates down, immersing each in a pool of water, or in some cases, a river, lake, or pond. The preacher helps each participant out of the water, then typically congratulates and welcomes the newly baptized church member into the congregation. Final prayers then close the ritual and signal the return to the world outside.[30]

This baptism ritual creates a sacred context in which the plain, literal water that can cleanse only the body becomes divinely blessed water that can symbolically cleanse the soul, or "wash the sins away." The immersion also signals, more concretely, that the person has become a recognized, official member of the family of Christian believers. After the ritual, those baptized are considered full members and in many cases can then take official responsibilities within the church, such as collecting offerings and assisting with the preparation and distribution of communion wafers and wine (or grape juice).

Because ritual spaces are different from ordinary life, people can do and say things in a ritual that in their daily experience would be unusual, perhaps even inappropriate or unacceptable. Amy Shuman describes social and religious inversions that occur during the ritual exchange of gifts of food during Purim, a celebration that commemorates the Jews' victory over destruction and oppression (2000). During Purim, families and friends traditionally exchange food gifts, usually baked goods and other sweets, with unspoken rules of exchange governing them. For this holiday, the rules of giving are slightly different from the usual social concept of "downward giving," in which people give gifts to those of lesser status—to younger people, the elderly, the poor, or from boss to employee or teacher to student—with no expectation of reciprocity (Shuman 2000, 499 [referring to Nancy F. Joffe 1953, 386]). The tradition of Purim gift giving, Shuman explains, "does imply reciprocity" (499).[31] Furthermore, the food shared is exempt from a few important religious and social rules. The food is not strictly monitored, as it is throughout the rest of the year (to ensure that it is kosher—ritually proper), and the source of the food is not always openly known. It is delivered by children dressed as biblical figures to adhere to the admonition that third parties must deliver the food gifts; those who prepare the food are not supposed to deliver it. The disguises symbolically hide the giver and the source of the food (498). Beyond the ways the food is prepared and delivered is a larger social inversion: women largely control the entire process of this public ritual, and men serve only a token role as messengers. This is in opposition to the usual control of public life by men in orthodox Jewish communities. Shuman suggests that because the rules of food production and exchange are suspended during the Purim gift exchange, the ritual allows participants to cross the boundaries of ordinary life (503).

After Purim, households typically have more sweet food than they can possibly consume. The food and the complex play with social relationships it generates become "excesses"—too much sweet, nonnutritious food, too much destabilization of usual roles (Shuman 2000, 506). As Shuman puts it, the ritual food exchange "symbolically disturb[s] the very centers of household order in Orthodox Jewish life" (506). If the community were to remain within the space of the ritual, social rules could be questioned and potentially overturned, or contaminated (not kosher) food could be consumed. The excesses of meaning created by the ritual of the gift exchange, Shuman says, can only be managed "by the return to ordinary life" (506). The food is shared with non-Jewish coworkers the day after Purim, and the children who had disguised themselves as figures from the Bible to deliver the gifts return to being just children. As Shuman explains about the nature of this ritual, "If gift exchanges involve a transformation, in which food, in this example, stands for social relationships, the trick is to effect the transformation in both directions, first from food into ritual, symbolic of, among other things, social relationships, and then back to the ordinary" (506–7). In other words, the ritual space must open to allow the transformations to occur, but then, to control the possibly destabilizing forces that those transformations generate, the ritual space must close.

Kathy Neustadt (1992) describes a community clambake that illustrates a different kind of liminality from that presented in Amy Shuman's discussion of the Purim ritual food exchange. Whereas the Purim food exchange creates a type of ritual space that breaks, almost chaotically, from the usual order of orthodox Jewish life, the clambake in Allen's Neck, Massachusetts, creates a particular type of order that stands outside the typical behavior of the community.

The clambake has been a tradition in the Allen's Neck community since August 1888, when it was first held by the Allen's Neck Friends (Quaker) Meeting as a Sunday school outing. Soon after, it became so popular that it turned into a fundraiser for the Friends Meeting (Neustadt 1992, 14). The clambake itself

111

requires the Friends—and some "friendly but unconverted neighbors" (79)—
to work together to create this seasonal rite of passage marking the end of
summer, which reflects the agricultural and environmental rhythm of the area
(145). The preparation for the clambake requires that community members
seek out supplies and foodstuffs in both nature and their own stores, and in
so doing, they observe changes in their physical environment effected by the
change in season (145).

Changes in the natural resources of the area have occurred since the clambake tradition began, yet the menu is more or less the same. One of the original
seasonal items no longer served is mackerel, a "timed fish," one that appeared
and could be caught during the particular time of year the clambake was held
(Neustadt 1992, 118). In general, fishing has grown much less possible as a voca-
tion, and even the clams are now imported from Maine (80). Other regional
foods, like brown bread, are found most often at meals such as clambakes and
are rarely served at home. Brown bread is cooked by steaming for three hours,
and women today don't have the time to prepare it on a regular basis (128–29).
Along with fishing, the community's roots are in farming, with poultry farms
part of their past, and more recently dairy farming has come to predominate
(79). These seasonal bases of the area's economic history are important to the
timing of this late summer gathering.

The traditional foods and methods of preparation are important in defining
and shaping the clambake, but the social interaction of the Friends, other residents of Allen's Neck, and even the area's summer residents—all those who put
on and attend the feast—create the liminal space that alters the community for
a time. The ritual activities give them the opportunity to reevaluate their community through interactions with their neighbors at the same time that they are
assessing their physical environment (Neustadt 1992, 146). It is this social and
cultural reassessment that forms the basis of the ritual liminality.

The liminal space created by the clambake allows for a number of changes
in status in the community. The Allen's Neck Clambake is no longer simply a
local celebration; this small community has gained national attention on the
strength of its "traditional New England clambake" (Neustadt 1992, 8), and that
may contribute to the changes the liminal period might offer. Summer residents
and those from outside New England attend; the Smithsonian Institution's
1988 Festival of American Folklife presented an Allen's Neck Clambake (8).
Neustadt thinks it's possible this notice may elevate the community in the eyes
of outsiders based on the success of the feast and the pride the clambakers feel.
In contrast, however, this temporary transformation may be awkward for some
of them; they are sometimes stressed by the effects of the popularity on their

local event. More likely, Neustadt proposes, the change may be in the "internal" status of the residents, "striving to elevate themselves as clambakers or, perhaps, to achieve greater perfection as a community" (147).

The reiteration of the community through this seasonal ritual seems a predominant theme in the voices of the community members themselves. The stories that community members share about their common experiences and attitudes add meaning and value to the clambake: a conversation about the correct materials to use for the bake may turn into a discussion of the importance of hard work, or comments about favorite recipes can lead to reminiscences about childhood and to larger questions of "moral and aesthetic judgment" (Neustadt 1992, 72). Just by participating in and lending their skills to the clambake, members of the group express their understanding that they are "part of a larger, integrated, seamless whole" (132).

Each member of the core group of the Quaker community finds he or she has a role to play in putting together the clambake, even though those roles may never be stated outright. Several Friends with whom Neustadt spoke recounted how the Clambake Committee always stays the same (89); one community member stressed the importance of taking part: "'You're not sure you've ever been on a committee, but you go . . . just go and do what needs to be done . . . it's as simple as that'" (91). In creating a space and time during which people rely on each other, taking on particular roles and doing what needs to be done, the ritual of the preparation and presentation of the clambake emphasizes Quaker values, such as lack of social hierarchy, a belief in human goodness, and the sacredness of life (78). Most importantly, Neustadt concludes, the "clambake is much more a form of symbolic intensification of the group's identity, in which a communal activity communicates through its process the everyday experience of the group" (158).

Neustadt's and Shuman's studies show two distinct ways in which liminality created through ritual allows important cultural experiences to happen. Both situations require that the ritual space open, providing an opportunity for a transformation to occur, but the transformations are of different types, one challenging cultural order and hierarchy and another reinforcing cultural values by establishing a certain cultural order.

Types of Rituals

Some of the most common and widely held rituals include those related to important events such as birth, puberty, marriage, and death. Some rituals are practiced by an entire community or within a large geographic region, and many are identified with a particular culture or ethnicity. An Irish wake, for example, is a particular postfuneral ritual celebration that is practiced both inside and outside Ireland and among groups that do not necessarily have identifiable Irish heritage. A similar ritual is the New Orleans jazz funeral procession, in which musicians follow the casket through the streets playing upbeat tunes. That ritual, though, is more closely associated with New Orleans than the Irish wake is with Ireland and is not performed as frequently by outside groups. To the participants in these and related events, these rituals are central to the expression of the group's attitudes and beliefs about how the living should respond to the end of life. These are powerful and valued concepts, even if the rituals involve some entertaining or light-hearted elements.

Following are some examples of categories of rituals that may be familiar. Keep in mind that as with other folklore texts, categories overlap, and elements of each kind of ritual may be related to elements of other kinds. The labels we suggest are meant to help illustrate and describe the many situations in which rituals are performed and have meaning.

Rites of Passage

Rites of passage mark notable dates or stages in a person's life. Most rites of passage occur at times of change or transition: birth, puberty, entering adulthood or coming of age, marriage, and death, for example. In some groups, rites of passage involve fasting, body modifications, or ingestion of ceremonial foods or substances; in others, ceremonies are not as elaborate and are embedded within ordinary group interactions. According to van Gennep, these kinds of rituals have three stages: separation (preliminal), transition (liminal), and reincorporation (postliminal), when a person who has gone through a ritual returns to society with a new status ([1908] 1960, 11). Rites of passage are practiced in all cultures, but the events celebrated vary from culture to culture.

Folklorist Bill Ellis has studied a phenomenon of contemporary adolescence that has been labeled "legend-tripping," examining not just single instances of it but looking at legend-tripping as a common age-related rite of passage (1982–83).[32] Chances are good that if you were raised in the United States, whether in a rural or urban community, you have participated in a legend-trip or have certainly heard about one from some of your peers. The basic structure of such a trip involves traveling with a group of friends to a particular location—often one that is considered by adults to be off limits. Setting is always central in a legend-trip narrative and its variants, and details that specify local features are prominent: for example, the big white house on Walhalla Ravine is haunted, and if you go there at night you can hear the screams of the ghost of a person who threw herself from the bridge in front of the house. Sometimes the legends involve materials or objects present at the site or specific actions the legend-trippers must perform (or are warned not to perform). Whether the location is an isolated piece of property outside a small town's limits, a home on a city street—usually a street that appears more rural than urban—a cemetery or old church, or a dangerous curve on a rural road, the participants of the ritual must travel there together. Ellis characterizes legend-trips, in general, as sharing a number of qualities. The most common element of these legend-trips is the method of transportation: the automobile, an important connection to the time of life at which most trippers participate (1982–83).

Ellis suggests that because these events occur between ages sixteen and eighteen, the activities are "linked to the coming-of-age crisis among white small-town or suburban adolescents" (1982–83, 61). His study draws parallels between the adolescent "ritual of rebellion," the freedom afforded to adolescents by use of the automobile, and the opportunity to escape adult supervision and rules (64–66). Risk and often fear are important ingredients, too. Such risks add to the excitement of the adventure and can also be used to increase one's status as a person who has survived the trip. This accomplishment is part of what marks legend-trips as rites of passage, experiences that indicate one has moved into another stage of life.

S. Elizabeth Bird studied legend-trips involving the Black Angel—a graveside monument of an angel with outstretched wings, oxidized and therefore black—in Iowa City (1994). One story told of the Black Angel says that if a visitor makes physical contact with or bothers the angel, "the offender will die within 24 hours, seven years, or at an unspecified time" (199). Of course, there are rumors that support these claims. Bird suggests that Black Angel legend-trips and similar events are, of course, about having fun, but that if we consider how tightly interwoven our culture and expressive communication are, we can see there is a lot more going on than just an exciting game. Stories about the Black Angel and what will happen if she is disturbed are, Bird explains, "intimately concerned with death, sex, morality, and the texts provide a narrative frame for the event itself" (202). Those who go on legend-trips to see the Black Angel may be "confronting the anxieties that accompany maturity and approaching adulthood" (202). Going to visit the angel is a part of adolescent life in Iowa City in spite of the rumored dangers involved. Taking a legend-trip to the Black Angel is such a big rite of passage that one person Bird talked with said, "'You can't graduate from City (High School) unless you know about the Black Angel'" (203).

115

Cry Baby Bridge, Groveport, Ohio.

Cry Baby Bridge

In many cities and rural communities, there is a "Cry Baby Bridge" about which scary legends are told. At many of these bridges, it is believed that there has been a death—often, though not always, the drowning of a baby or young child. Perhaps the dead child is heard crying late at night, or its mother may cry over its loss. Sometimes the story involves the death of a member of a young loving couple. The spirit of the young lover may cause cars to stall late at night on the bridge. Headlights may move rapidly toward those visiting the bridge—and then mysteriously disappear. The exact legends may differ, but the basic activity of telling the story and traveling to the bridge to experience the haunting is often part of growing up in the particular communities in which the bridges are found.

Camp Chase Cemetery.

Camp Chase Cemetery: Legend of the Lady in Gray

In this cemetery, located on part of the grounds of a former Civil War military prison for Confederate soldiers, legend has it that there is a young woman, wearing gray, who walks the cemetery, crying, and may leave fresh flowers on one of the graves. (A couple of graves have been named as the recipients.) When we went to investigate, we saw no fresh flowers, but there was a bouquet of artificial flowers at the base of the main marking stone within the cemetery grounds.

Coming-of-Age Rituals

Coming-of-age rituals are a particular type of rite of passage that acknowledges the transition from childhood to adulthood. These rituals occur around the time of puberty and frequently involve extended community participation.

Many groups celebrate coming-of-age birthdays, often gender related. Many Jewish families give their male and female children Bar Mitzvah and Bat Mitzvah celebrations, at age thirteen for boys and twelve for girls.[33] The child's reaching the designated age indicates he or she is fully responsible for abiding by the commandments of the Jewish holy scriptures. (As children, they are not required to follow them but are encouraged to learn them.) A boy becomes a

117

Bar Mitzvah and participates in Shabbat services soon after turning thirteen, at the least, reciting a blessing over the weekly Torah reading. Vernacular rituals differ, though most contemporary practices include the boy's making a speech beginning with the phrase "today I am a man." In more conservative groups, women are not allowed to participate so fully in religious services, so the Bat Mitzvah celebration is likely to be only a low-key party.

A search on the Internet can show just how elaborate contemporary Bar and Bat Mitzvahs have become, bringing up a number of sites for companies that arrange celebratory receptions. Celebrations discussed on such sites clearly rival wedding celebrations, with some sites even promising help with such issues as how to pick the right Bar Mitzvah DJ. Other sites promise parents help with writing a poem for the child's Bar or Bat Mitzvah candle lighting ceremony.

Some Latino families in the United States also celebrate a significant birthday for their adolescent daughters; this secular ceremony for her fifteenth birthday is called a quinceañera. This custom is primarily secular yet often involves a Catholic mass and/or blessing by a priest. Some believe this celebration used to indicate a young woman was ready to be courted and married, but it is now more readily acknowledged as a marker of the transition from adolescent girl to woman. Although scholars aren't sure exactly how or where the custom began, most assume it "has origins in pre-Columbian cultures, as a coming-of-age ritual for young women" (Castro 2001, 194). However, not all celebrants take part in this ritual because of its ancient connections. Folklorist Katherine Borland points out that the quinceañera may be as much about establishing contemporary community as maintaining historical cultural roots. Borland says that in the state of Delaware, many Puerto Rican girls celebrated the quinceañera, not because their mothers did but because their friends did (Borland, 2003). Regardless of what it may have originally symbolized, "much of the research on quinceañeras shows that families want to maintain a cultural historical tradition, and the celebration of a daughter's fifteenth birthday is a means of continuing cultural ties to a Latino heritage" (Castro 2001, 195).

Quinceañera

> *Here, Adriana Mancillas shares some photographs from her quinceañera. She comments, "I was raised in South Texas, and although you would think traditions would be the same in South Texas as in Mexico because they're only a few minutes apart they're actually not. You go to Mexico and quinceañeras somehow have more meaning beyond the pretty dress and the big party." But as she tells us, her own celebration ultimately was very meaningful for her. She describes her experience and feelings about the event below.*

This picture shows me with my "damas" and "chambelanes." All of these children in the picture I am somehow connected to, whether by blood or by friendship. As you can see, the total number of children is 15. I don't know exactly how many children originally walked down the aisle of the church with the quinceañera, but as far as I can remember, the total has always been 15, symbolizing the magic number where you all of a sudden stop being a girl and become a woman.

Seeing this picture reminds me of so many things that happened that day, and before that day. My mom, the coordinator of my quinceañera, was constantly making phone calls to these kids' parents making sure they had their outfits ready, and that the oufits matched, that the boys' shoes were black, that the girls' hair was done nicely, that the kids wouldn't chicken out. It was such a hectic experience before we got to this point of smiling at ease in front of a camera.

Of course, everything is expected to be perfect or the girl and her family will never hear the end of it. Somewhere along the line word will come back to a girl that so and so was saying this or that about her big "coming of age" party. Fortunately, this never happened to me. But a quinceañera celebration has to be perfect. This was one of the main reasons I didn't want one in the first place. Aside from that, I consider myself to be extremely Americanized so having a quinceañera or not at first was close to meaningless. I have never been girly, I have never taken proper etiquette classes or been taught to be polite at all times. I'm a tomboy at heart. But after it happened I thought it was the greatest thing ever. I'm not the only one who thinks this way. But the typical girly-girl would be planning her quinceañera for years. It's like a fairy tale dream she gets to fulfill and I understand that now.

A huge part of this picture reminds me so much of my mother and how important my quinceañera was to her. She got all of her brothers and sisters together, as the custom usually requires, and assigned to them things to buy or money to pitch in so that it all could end up this way: perfect. She physically went out and bought all this stuff: the decorations, the cake, the food, my crown, my dress. And she hired the band and the photographer. She's a perfectionist, so everything she could do herself she did. Her efforts made me appreciate this experience so much more. Underneath all the commotion of getting this right, through a year of intricate planning, I knew what she cared most about was making this memorable for me and living her dream of having a quinceañera through me. This is why I appreciate this occasion the way I do. It's not at all an easy thing to put together. When someone goes all out to do this for you, you can't help but feel loved and special.

This following picture shows the "religious" portion of my quinceañera. This part of my quinceañera actually was prior to the big celebration. It was really great for me to walk down the aisle of my church and have everyone that cares for me be there. It's definitely exciting because well, I've been to so many quinceañera ceremonies in the past and it's really a special moment because everyone sees you in your dress for the first time. It's very similar to a bride walking down the aisle. So when I was doing that it was just so amazing.

In the picture, I am kneeling before the altar. The majority of Mexicans or Mexican-Americans are predominantly Catholic. A few of us, like myself, are raised Protestant. As a result, I believe my quinceañera had a few differences. The man shown speaking in the pulpit is my pastor. They have me kneel on beautiful handmade pillows with my name and the occasion sewn on them. My parents sit beside me at my right. My chambelan [male attendant] sits to my left.

My pastor gave me a ton of advice for the future. He knew I would give in to adulthood and that things would change for me henceforth. He's been my pastor since I was about 9 or 10. He's seen me and he knows me. He knows where I struggle spiritually. He's a very loving pastor. So when he was speaking to me one-on-one in front of a whole crowd I couldn't help but get all emotional. I began to cry. I began to remember meaningful moments from my childhood. Responsibility was so minimal in my past and now things were going to change.

Traditionally, when you turn 15 it means you're ready to be exposed to dating, even the possibility of being wed. But times have changed and many women have changed their priorities in life. Marriage isn't something we look forward to at 15 or 16 anymore. Today it's more like a quinceañera is more a sign that a young woman is ready to become responsible for her own actions, that somehow responsibility and maturity will be expected from her from that point on.

After the big "tearfest" at the altar, another speaker gave me advice. She was my parents' and grandparents' pastor in Mexico at one time. She knows my parents thoroughly so she gives them advice as well. Then she did something unexpected. I had never seen it happen at other quinceañeras. She handed me a clear glass vase. One by one, each of my damas and chambelanes brought me a rose and placed it in the vase I was holding. As they came up, the speaker recited Bible verses that spoke about wisdom, happiness, and promises of God. At this point I felt more than loved: I felt humbled and blessed by my loved ones and by God.

Finally, I got a song. A professional singer sang a song to me from behind the altar. It was a song that tied in perfectly with what I was feeling at that point. I felt honored, loved, special, and yet so humbled. As soon as she was finished, my chambelan took my hand and we walked down the aisle together. The sweet melody my father composed for me on his piano resounded from the speakers. My parents followed me down the aisle, then the rest of the damas and chambelanes, then the public.

Most quinceañeras define the religious part of the ceremony as lifeless and boring. I guess it would be if spirituality doesn't play a big role in their lives. This certainly wasn't the case for me. This was probably one of the most amazing experiences I will ever have in my lifetime.

Initiation Rituals

Initiation rituals express a person's entrance into membership in a group. Groups with initiation rituals are usually well defined, with clear hierarchies and structures, perhaps even laws or rules of conduct. Some initiation ceremonies and rituals are private and secret; others are open to the public. Examples include sorority and fraternity initiations or ceremonies, and inductions into occupational or honorary societies. Rituals may include reciting promises or pledges, performing humiliating acts to prove one is willing to do anything to belong, or being presented with ceremonial artifacts or clothing that show others one is a member.

Initiation rituals can be very elaborate. Initiations involve activities that an individual initiate or group of initiates perform to prove their worthiness or to bond them to each other and/or to the group. Some formal ceremonies publicly announce that the members now fully belong (induction). In some cases, initiates might take part in complex scavenger hunts or riddling games that require them to learn information or locate objects associated with the group they are about to join. Initiates might also be asked to perform actions that humiliate or degrade them, such as being a lackey to a higher-ranking group member for a period of time or eating disgusting foods or even being deprived of food. In the extreme, such activities amount to hazing, a questionable, sometimes dangerous practice, which has been officially banned by college Greek organizations and most college and high school administrations. Hazing is most often associated with fraternities and sororities, but it has also occurred in other groups such as athletic teams. Some rituals involve lighting candles, wearing robes, displaying special colors, or exhibiting symbolic materials that represent the group's values and history. Individual groups may follow fairly prescribed procedures and rules for the initiations or create their own new rituals for initiating members, or they may combine official activities with local touches.

The men's varsity swim team at a small midwestern university, for example, once designed several humorous, embarrassing activities for its new freshmen members. On one day, the new swimmers had to carry a brick everywhere they went on campus and acquire the signature of each of their professors on a piece of paper attached to the brick. Another day, they had to wear an article of brightly colored women's clothing. Other students and faculty looked forward to seeing each day's requirement and, by the end of the week, could easily identify the new swimmers. This was likely to have been a desired outcome of the initiation ritual: new swimmers stood out because of their membership on the team and became clearly identified with the group. Another effect was that outsiders responded to the activities and the initiates: some offered encouragement, some playfully teased the initiates, and some made fun of them. The interaction between the outsiders and the initiates confirmed the sense of unity among the new swimmers as well as highlighted their collective identity as members of the team. Initiations are intended to strengthen the bond the initiates feel, to make their membership, at least for a time, one of the most significant features of their lives. Also, such rituals create a sense of a unique, shared experience with a particular group, setting them apart from others who haven't had that experience.

Naming Rituals

There are many rituals associated with naming that range from a public presentation of an infant within an informal gathering of a family group to elaborate ceremonies in which names are bestowed by religious or community leaders. In some groups, a child's name might be the same as or a variation of a respected elder's or might be chosen to convey aspects of a particular ethnicity or culture, and rituals might exist to solidify those traditions. A seemingly simple act like giving a baby a name may be a crucial element in forming identity and taking one's place in society and may be so important that groups express the value of the naming process through formal procedures.

While names and traditions associated with them are important in most groups, some groups have developed rituals that concretize their importance through actions and performances. Well-known examples of sacred Western rituals are christening or dedication ceremonies in which the child's name is publicly announced to a group of family and friends, and confirmation ceremonies in which celebrants choose names that express their spiritual identities. In some Nigerian communities, elaborate ceremonies take place during naming, in which many names—some of them silly or ridiculous—are offered and rejected, until the father whispers the child's "true" name to the mother, who then formally announces the name to the whole family. Naming rituals such as this tell the family and larger community who a child is and where he or she belongs, as an announcement and confirmation of that child's identity and membership.

Example: Rituals and Private and Public Identity

The curtains draw away from the center of the stage as dry-ice smoke billows out from between them. Bass beats throb through the audience and ten college-aged African American men, dressed in their fraternity's colors, strut onto the stage, each carrying a cane. The music stops and the group of young men halt in position and create a pyramid formation, four in the front row, three in a row staggered between them, a row of two behind them, and a single figure in the back. They pause for a moment, each resting both hands atop his cane, while the crowd applauds. A few members of the fraternity in the audience shout out their fraternity's Greek name. Then one of the men in the front row taps his cane solidly and rhythmically on the floor, three times. The other nine men join him, performing dramatic moves with their canes—a combination of baton twirling and juggling—and intricate dance steps. At times, music spun by a DJ accompanies the stepping, and at other times the only sound (other

124

than applause, supportive shouts, or occasional catcalls—or "cracking") is the tapping of the canes or hand-clap games between members.

African-American Greek organizations across the United States participate in step shows, performing "soul stepping" in a variety of different venues and for a variety of different reasons. At The Ohio State University, the Divine Nine[34] hold an annual step show competition as one of the central entertainments of the African American Heritage Festival, and the annual tradition draws large and boisterous crowds every year. The competition is fierce and each participating sorority and fraternity choreographs, designs costumes (incorporating their organization's colors), and selects music to impress the crowds and outdo their performance from the previous year. African-American Greek organizations use stepping performances like these to reflect ritual initiation (since the public performance isn't the ritual initiation itself) and present identity.

Folklorist Elizabeth C. Fine illustrates the ways that the rituals enacted during the step show help to express, form, and strengthen the group's identity (2003). Stepping is connected to some of the more hidden or secret initiation rituals that occur during the fraternity or sorority pledging process and that may have evolved from college student rites of passage (151). For example, in some shows, members of a pledge class march or perform "on line," a direct reenactment of their time spent lined up with their fellow initiates during the initiation process (151). The step show provides an arena for new members to publicly announce their new status as full members of the group (4). Just as importantly, stepping is a visible expression of the group's identity and serves as outward indication of the group's "spirit, style, icons, and unity" (3).

Through the step shows, participants share with each other and their audiences who they are and what their groups stand for; stepping "creates, perpetuates and comments on the worldviews of participants and embodies the social drama from which worldviews arise" (E. Fine 2003, 59). For example, the complex choreography and the skill needed to accomplish the steps require cooperation and discipline, two key values the group may possess and may wish to express to others. One particularly challenging piece of choreography is performing steps while blindfolded—a real crowd energizer when the performers are tossing canes. The coordination required, but perhaps more importantly for the brothers themselves, the sense of awareness of each other on stage, clearly makes visible the fraternity's unity. As Fine explains,

> stepping is an expressive performance art that also functions as a ritual of
> group identity. Whether it celebrates the rite of passage to brotherhood or

125

Photos by Christopher Southard.

Iota Phi Theta Fraternity, Inc., Beta Mu Chapter (The Ohio State University). The 17th Annual Pan-Hellenic Black Greek Step Show, 2004.

sisterhood, enacts the social drama of group maintenance in black Greek-letter organizations, or celebrates African American cultural identity at annual festivals such as the Philadelphia Greek Picnic, stepping stimulates communitas among spectators and participants alike. (2003, 74)[35]

In addition to providing particular rituals and traditions for members of the black Greek community, these step shows also demonstrate social and cultural connections with non-Greek members of college communities.

Step shows illustrate and reinforce a shared identity within the Divine Nine and also allow for the individual fraternities and sororities to engage in public, ritualized competition and differentiate themselves from each other. Such competition is both verbal and physical and may challenge or recognize the skills (or perceived identity) of another group. Frequently, the imitation of a step or verbal phrase or gesture may mock the performances of another group. This kind of playful, competitive mockery generates strong responses from the audience, either in recognition and support of the jibes or in defense of the fraternity or sorority being mocked. At times, groups may also acknowledge others' expertise by incorporating steps identified with a particular group. The introduction of an innovative step or sequence—such as jumping "rope," with a tall, thin man serving as the rope—can bring down the house and set a high bar for subsequent shows. Establishing these distinctions through performance is an ongoing element of each group's identity that, as Fine states, gives Greeks the opportunity to "negotiat[e] the status of each group within the social order" (2003, 61).

For African American fraternity and sorority members and their audiences, many of whom are familiar with these performances, the ritual elements offer an opportunity to express their values and beliefs and receive responses to them. They are able to make public their identities and redefine those identities, both through the unifying elements of their performances and the responses to those performances.

The public nature and growing popularity of these ritual performances also opens up the fraternities and sororities to evaluation and judgment by groups who may misinterpret their performances. Recognizing the potential for rituals to allow outsiders to make judgments, leaders of the African-American Greek community have attempted to guard against divisiveness by urging groups to focus on positive themes and avoid inappropriate behaviors or language that degrades or belittles any other Greek groups (National Pan-Hellenic Council [NPHC] 2011). The groups are thereby urged to think about their actions within the organization as well as experience another level of redefinition and presentation of identity, an exoteric awareness of the way the Greek organization is perceived. The NPHC, the group that has historically overseen African-American Greek society activities and administration, recognizes this power, asserting that cultural expressions such as the step shows "may . . . also have the potential for individuals to form opinions about the values and beliefs of local fraternities and sororities, as language, behavior, and symbols send strong messages" (National Pan-Hellenic Council 2011).

The awareness of outsider perceptions can be used to the advantage of the groups insofar as it allows them to consciously shape the message they send and influence outsiders' opinions of them. Again, the Greek organization administration recognizes this fact: "Step shows provide students, parents, faculty members, college and university officials, and the public a forum to better understand the unique culture (e.g., history and traditions) of African American fraternities and sororities" (National Pan-Hellenic Council 2011). Some have gone so far as to suggest that the conscious shaping of the message can be used to attract and recruit new members or even market the organizations (National Pan-Hellenic Council 2011). These are examples of conscious actions taken to control the public identity of the performing groups through the regulation or adaptation of their rituals. The group's decision to consciously seek ways to manipulate the ritual in order to control public identity is motivated by an awareness of public perception and of how ritual can make people think positively or negatively about the performers.

Conclusion

Ritual, because it makes beliefs visible, opens up a group's beliefs to evaluation and judgment by those outside the group. Interpreting the power and/or meaning of a ritual is often difficult, even for experienced folklorists, because it often involves making assumptions about a group's beliefs. Relying on assumptions based on an outsider perception can result in reductive or generic analyses, which suggest all rituals of a certain type have the same meaning for all groups. For example, one might mistakenly assume that an initiation ritual in Mexico would have essentially the same purposes and effects as an initiation ritual in Denmark. Scholars have questioned this functionalist approach toward belief and ritual, because it privileges the presumed knowledge of the scholar over the actual meaning held by those practicing the ritual.

Where does this leave us in studying ritual? How do we examine the rituals of others without making ethnocentric (or other sorts of outsider) assumptions? Sensitivity to the group's own understanding of the importance and meaning of its rituals must be maintained in order to ethically interpret the practice of the ritual. Such study requires an awareness of the principles of reciprocal ethnography as practiced by Elaine Lawless (1992), in which the folklorist returns to the group being studied, bringing her analysis to discuss with the group and to ascertain their response to the interpretation. It is the folklorist's responsibility to respect the beliefs and meanings rituals embody by consulting group members about their perceptions of and relationships with the rituals they perform.

Rituals are important—and are almost always spoken of as being important; they mark events, values, beliefs, and experiences that are considered valuable

enough to merit an outward expression. Some rituals may be big, grand performances, complete with costumes, music, and choreography, and others may be
simple, small actions, frequently unnoticed by anyone outside the group. The
elaborateness, complexity, or level of detail is not necessarily connected to the
significance of a ritual to a group or individual. It depends on the group, case by
case, in context—we must consider a ritual within a particular group and context before making assumptions or judgments about its general significance.
Whether rituals are entertaining, exciting, and full of drama and pageantry,
or quiet, private ceremonies, they matter—they have meaning—to those who
participate in them.

CHAPTER 5

Performance

*T*hink of the last time you attended a musical performance. It doesn't matter whether you were listening to a punk band or a country singer or attending the symphony or the opera. How were people in the audience dressed? Was there an abundance of black clothing? Cowboy hats? Did the lead singer introduce the other band members? Did the crowd sit quietly or stand and sing along? Did any of the performers say "you're a great audience," and did the audience cheer? Maybe you took part in a tradition associated with this kind of event or a particular performer—held up a match, lighter, or cell phone to bring on an encore, wore evening clothes on opening night of an opera run. Was it a good show or not, and how did you know?

The point is that you (as a part of the audience) and the performers created a kind of event together in which you all became part of the others' experience. Wearing a cowboy hat that matched the lead singer's could have encouraged a connection between the performers and audience that added to the performers' desire to put on a good show. Wearing your best clothes to the opera on opening night showed that you were part of the group and understood its rules, and it also may have implied a certain social status.

These features of the show you attended have little to do with the songs the singers or bands performed, but everything to do with your experience. There are many performances going on in our example: the performers on the stage, in their official role as performers, and the many activities you and your fellow audience members engaged in that allowed you to express the traditions, values, and beliefs of the fan group you belonged to. It is this experience of performance and what it means to performers and audiences that matters, beyond what we might think of as entertainment value. In essence, the notion

130

of explicit and implicit relationships between performers and audiences and the complex dynamics that lead to or stem from these relationships are at the heart of contemporary folklorists' approach to performance. In the following discussions of performance, we will illustrate how folklorists consider performance in context and think about the relationships among audiences, texts, and means of expression.

What is Performance?

So far, we've been talking about people, texts, behavior, and the many ways that folklore communicates, and now we want to consider in depth the moments in which all these pieces come together, enacted through *performance*. Some performances are easy to spot. Many rituals, for example, begin at a predetermined time and place, and an announcement or other signal opens and closes the performance (think of the processional music at the beginning of a formal wedding and the "I now pronounce you . . ." proclamation at the end of the ceremony). Frequently, performances have clear settings and recognizable structures that indicate to participants that the performance is taking place. Barre Toelken (1996) writes of Native American storytelling sessions, for instance, which take place at specified times (some tales can only be told at certain times of the year) and for defined purposes. A group gathers to hear the tales, and the storyteller takes center stage, so to speak, and narrates story after story, sometimes in a set order.

Most often, though, performances of folklore happen naturally within daily conversations and situations. That may make them less readily apparent, but all expressions of folklore are performances, nonetheless. Suppose, for example, two friends are talking about their classes on the first day of the semester and one brags to the other, "I just know I'm going to get all As this term." The other shakes her head and says in a teasing tone, "Be careful—don't count your chickens before they're hatched." The first speaker chuckles and agrees to be a little more realistic. These two have just taken part in the performance of a proverb.

Performance is an expressive activity that requires participation, heightens our enjoyment of an experience, and invites response. In order for a performance to happen, a recognized setting must exist (participants have to know a performance is taking place) and participants (performers and audience) must be present. The details of the setting and relationships between participants can be quite complex and fluid, but all participants understand that they are engaged in some kind of performance activity. Each of us interprets the performances

131

of people in our own folk groups naturally as part of our group's communication process. If group members and audiences are not able to understand and interpret someone's performance, it may not be a successful expression of the performer's ideas. As folklorists, our interpretations may be more complex, breaking down the elements of a performance and using certain language to talk and write about our analysis; however, the roots of these interpretations can be seen in everyday responses to folk performances.

Example: A Proverbial Performance

The proverb example above illustrates one of those familiar, everyday performance events, and here we will look at it in more depth to introduce important terms and ideas that we expand on later in the chapter.

Proverbs, like most other folk genres, can be defined in many ways. Most folklorists agree that a proverb is a short traditional statement, phrase, or saying that conveys some philosophical or wise observation about a situation or about life or human nature in general.[36] Proverbs or proverbial sayings are not performed in the sense that a person stands up in front of others in order to recite them; rather, they are most often performed within an ordinary, everyday situation, usually as part of a conversation.

In the example, the speaker prepared her friend for the warning when she shook her head and said in a teasing way, "Be careful." Her recitation of the proverb, with its carefully chosen text, delivered the message. The laughter and agreement to be realistic showed recognition of the performance and understanding of its content and intention. These actions, or markers—the teasing tone, the delivery of proverbial content, the laughter and comment on the message—all signaled the beginning and end of this performance. (We'll discuss markers in more depth later in this chapter.) The very fact that both participants performed and reacted to the proverb and each other in the way they did reveals a lot about their understanding of the performance contexts and of proverbs in general. So for this example, let's think about what the performance of the proverb means in terms of the text (content), context, cultural elements, and the effectiveness of the performance itself.

Most of us enjoy considering what proverbs mean and how they differ from one another or how they are similar or different from proverbs from other cultures. The text of a proverb is fixed; that is, it doesn't change much from one performance to another, so it occupies the conservative end of Toelken's conservative-dynamic continuum. For this reason, when we talk about proverbs we often begin with the content of the saying and what it means. The verbal content of a proverb has to be fairly limited in order for it to work; the words have to be so familiar we have no doubt about why the expression is being used in a particular situation. We typically hear proverbs repeated by others in our community, within the folk groups we belong to.

Proverbs are rarely meant to be taken literally. The warning above, of course, has nothing to do with actual chickens. The proverb performer was cautioning her friend to remember that we shouldn't assume something will happen before it actually takes place or that we can't expect to have something until we actually have it. We don't need any immediate or direct contact with the origins of a proverb in order to use and understand it, although the explanations of origins usually make sense to us when we learn them. Most of us have little or no experience with hatching chickens. Yet, this saying is repeated so often that we can use it appropriately even if we know nothing about chicken farming. Some proverbs come from tales or stories that we know so well we don't have to recite the whole story for the proverbial saying to make sense. The phrase "crying wolf" is a good example. The whole story, even if we aren't sure of every detail, is implied in the short familiar phrase (Abrahams 1983, 20–21). In any case, we usually understand the meanings of proverbs because of the many times we have heard them performed and applied. This is why we say the texts of proverbs are usually fixed. What is not fixed, however, is the manner in which we use or perform proverbs. So even though the words themselves don't change, every proverb is essentially new every time we perform it.

The "counting chickens" proverb might be applied in many cases where someone appears to be "jumping the gun" or maybe even "putting the cart before the horse." These are similar sayings that have related meanings. Wise farmers know that seeing a dozen eggs in the henhouse does not mean they will end up with a dozen new chicks in a few weeks. The eggs may not be fertilized, or a fox may invade the henhouse and eat them. To "jump the gun" means to start doing something before you should, or before the time is right. It comes from track events, in which runners crouch down at the starting line and wait for the starter to fire a gun before they can jump up and sprint away. Starting before the gun goes off may result in disqualification. So if you "jump the gun" you are acting hastily and risk getting into some trouble. If you "put the cart before the horse" you are doing things out of order and will probably not accomplish what you set out to do. You might not even be able to start; a horse-drawn cart won't go anywhere if the horse is behind it.

All three of the sayings we have been talking about comment in a slightly different way on the dangers of making hasty assumptions or jumping to the end of a process before going through the first steps. The friend had to sort through these and many other related sayings to select just the right one to issue her advice. Clearly, however, her choice of proverb to perform at that moment depended on a lot more than the words themselves. Most important may be her decision to use a proverb rather than issue a simple statement such as "you can't be sure of that" or to use a more direct proverbial warning such as "don't get your hopes up." Perhaps she wanted to save her friend from possible disappointment. Using a proverb allows her to soften the blow a bit, shortens the number of words she needs to use, and draws on the wise observations of generations who have come before to add weight to her advice. It also allows her to draw on a shared personal history, perhaps, in which the two had joked with each other before. It may be that the braggart sometimes tends to have unrealistic expectations, and the two friends have talked about this problem before. Perhaps the proverb speaker thought it would be gentler, and probably more fun, to instruct through a proverb than to admonish outright. The acceptance of her advice, signaled by amusement and assent, shows that the message is clear, and no one is offended by the warning.

Expressing all of this important information in a fun, artistic way telescopes the communication without a lot of discussion and shows their close connection as friends and as members of a group that understands a particular set of proverbs. The performer had to think beyond the content to select a proverb that was culturally appropriate as well as textually appropriate.

Every culture has proverbs that express in verbal shorthand important traditional ideas and knowledge based on common sense and experience. Proverbs are frequently culture specific—meaning that they express this knowledge in terms that people from that culture or group will understand. Many proverbs, such as the European American "don't count your chickens" example, come from agriculture, so they are familiar to most people around the world. But that proverb would not make sense in a culture where no one had ever raised or even heard of chickens. Similarly, "jumping the gun" would not be meaningful to a group that does not hold footraces or does not use guns. Yet proverbs from across the world comment on the same kinds of experiences and express the same kinds of wise observations. A proverb from Guyana, for example, is "Not every crab hole contains a crab." Crabs are a far cry from chickens, but this proverb makes it obvious that people from rather diverse cultures have developed wise sayings to caution that things don't always turn out the way we expect or assume they will. In her performance, the friend obviously selected a proverb that had resonance for both people in order to be sure she would communicate her feelings.

Analyzing texts and performances of proverbs in this way, in relation to how members of folk groups use them, allows us to make observations about what concepts and attitudes are important to the group members in this particular setting. We can also think about how members incorporate specific, local elements of experience into particular expressions of group identity. Looking at proverbs within a context enables us to consider how group members are different and the same, analyze the effects of those differences and similarities, and consider who performs proverbs, where and when, and for what reasons.

We can also consider aspects of the relationships between friends in this example. We know, for instance, that they are friends. That point is significant in understanding why the performer felt comfortable enough in the relationship to choose a proverb. We also know (or have established in this example) that the performer is female. That may have significance, depending on the other person's sex—think for a moment of the different dynamics that might exist in this example if one is male and one is female. Age might also be a factor. We might assume the two are of similar age since it appears they are taking classes together, but perhaps the performer has returned to school after working and raising a family for twenty years and is twenty-five years older than her friend. Now switch it—suppose the performer is twenty years younger than the other. Would the younger person have the right to criticize the older person? Do certain groups have a code of social etiquette that permits a younger person to express criticism of an elder? Does friendship always allow for such flexible roles? Would the nature of performing proverbs permit someone to express attitudes of authority playfully or in a way that would not be acceptable in a more formal situation?

In this description of the use of a single proverb, we can see many of the complex elements that folklorists consider when analyzing performance. The specific words used are certainly important, to a greater or lesser degree, depending on the type of folk genre we are studying (for proverbs, as we have said, the verbal text is central). But the words form just one part of this act of performance. We must consider the conditions or context in which a performance occurs, including its participants. Also important are the relationships between the people involved. Our ability to employ proverbs accurately, clearly, and wittily may identify us as effective performers enacting a lively tradition that expresses and reinforces our understanding of the group's knowledge, values, beliefs, and experiences. We can look at the success of the performance by considering how the participants reacted to it and to the other people present and by looking at the aesthetic dimensions of the event.

135

The Study of Performance

In the nineteenth century and first half or so of the twentieth, folklorists were usually more concerned with the products or outcomes of performance than the performance itself. In the 1970s, Richard Bauman's *Verbal Art As Performance* (1984)[37] solidified the framework for future studies of performance in folklore. Bauman drew together scholarship from the fields of linguistics, anthropology, literary study, and folklore to create a more unified, theorized understanding of performance in verbal art. His main theme is that verbal communication carries an artistic or "esthetic dimension" (3) that is connected to the specific setting and culture of those participating in the communication. Bauman conceives of performance as "a unifying thread tying together the marked, segregated esthetic genres and other spheres of verbal behavior into a general unified conception of verbal art as a way of speaking" (5). Verbal art encompasses narration of myths, stories, and related genres as well as speech; performance "brings them together in culture-specific and variable ways, ways that are to be discovered ethnographically within each culture and community" (5). And because performance carries an artistic dimension and is perceived to be different from everyday, routine kinds of speech or behavior, it is "marked as subject to evaluation for the way it is done, for the relative skill and effectiveness of the performer's display of competence" as well as being "available for the enhancement of experience" (11).

What all this means, basically, is that people communicate within specific situations and settings, and these communications are performed for certain reasons and in certain ways that have meaning to the members of folk groups and communities. Performances are usually set off from everyday experience by certain *markers*—words or gestures that signal when a performance is about to take place and when it ends. This marking off or "framing" (see Goffman 1974) implies the artistic nature of such expressive communication, heightens our enjoyment, and invites critique or evaluation.

Folklorists pay attention to the performed act of expressive, artistic communication—the when, where, with whom, how, and why people communicate. In addition to actual content, words, or actions (texts), folklorists consider literary, linguistic, or physical nuances of those texts (texture); and they study these elements within specific groups and settings (contexts).[38] Performance is easy to see when we look at verbal art, especially oral verbal performances like songs, stories, or sayings, but theories related to performance have been extended to other kinds of folklore, like ritual, custom, and even material objects. As we talk about all these dimensions of performance and performance theory, it is important to keep in mind that folklore is something we *do*, not just something we possess. Performance study foregrounds this perspective on the active sharing of contemporary folklore.

Performance Texts

We talked earlier about the concept of *text* in relationship to many types of folklore beyond just verbal types. Here we will develop that idea in connection with performance and consider how performances themselves form a complex text that we can take part in, observe, and analyze.

It is, of course, undeniable that texts exist, but not in isolation. They exist within groups. People sing songs, tell stories, and share jokes, for example, and the physical properties of those items are certainly real—they have words, sentences, and sounds. But the specific content of those items varies depending on the performer, the setting, the region, and of course the group in which they are shared. Folklorists often collect texts of related items in order to compare how different groups shape and express similar material. Variants of jokes are a good example. In some northern US states, for example, people tell rather inappropriate jokes about "hillbillies" from "the hills" or "hick towns." The same jokes may be told in southern states with the words "Yankees" and "cities" substituted for the derogatory labels. Analyzing performance enables folklorists to see how and why groups shape and share their traditional forms of expression.

We usually think of stories and songs and other verbal expressions when we think of texts, but as we said in the first chapter, folklorists frequently use the term to refer to nonverbal art and objects, even behaviors, such as rituals or foodways. Performance analysis, as folklorists have used it, examines material and visual arts and practices as well as verbal lore. These items may be what we typically think of as folk objects, like quilts, baskets, or friendship bracelets and can also be common material objects with practical uses, like food, clothing, and buildings. Even connections between objects and their creators can be thought of as a kind of performance.

In some rural communities in Pennsylvania, for instance, many farmers, particularly those of German descent, decorate their barns with colorful designs called "hex signs." These circular designs incorporate traditional features that symbolize prosperity, health, and protection. For example, many designs show a six-pointed star, which are thought to ensure protection from fire, or the stylized image of birds called "distelfinks" that may bring good luck and happiness. These designs are often prominent in the eaves of the barn roofs or are placed in a series of large circles on the front of the barn, sometimes evenly spaced between the loft doors and windows. The hex signs that decorate the eaves are symbols of luck and good fortune but are also expressions of tradition, common decorations that express group identity regardless of the degree of belief that having a hex sign on a barn brings good fortune. Farmers in local communities develop their own ways of communicating through these traditional representations on their barns. We could say we "read" these meanings from looking at the barns.[39]

To get even a little more abstract, consider how we might read an activity or symbols of activities. Think of a horseshoe, for example, suspended over a doorway—a common rural North American good luck charm. The horseshoe itself is not a performance, but the placement of the object is a marker of the idea that a horseshoe hung with its ends up (so it looks like a *U*) brings and holds good luck inside the home. At least, the fact that the horseshoe is there indicates knowledge of that tradition. Another example is *feng shui,* a traditional practice from Asia of arranging furnishings and objects inside a house in such a way as to bring harmony, energy, and spiritual goodwill to inhabitants and visitors. For example, beds may be aligned north to south, with the head at the north. As with the good luck horseshoe, someone who understands the text can read the placement of the furnishings and understand the ideas the home dweller is trying to convey. Even if the person who arranged the objects within the space isn't there to explain, someone who knows the system will be able to interpret it.

When we read an object or practice in this way, we are in a sense analyzing its performance—what it communicates actively to the world, both within and outside the folk groups that created it (esoterically and exoterically). Through performance we can describe and discuss how such texts evolve and communicate within a group and how groups express their identity through them. The performance approach establishes folklore as current, evolving, and always expressive, regardless of the type of text we analyze.

Texture

Texture includes the literary, linguistic, and/or physical characteristics of an item of folklore, as well as the features of the performers' presentation or style that affect the performance of a text and the audience's reactions to it. In verbal texts, rhyme, alliteration, metaphor, and other kinds of figurative devices—basically, anything connected to the way words relate to each other and convey their meanings—are included in texture. Many paralinguistic features—that is, features connected to language but not actually language—also shape the texture. These would include, for example, a performer's gestures, particular emphasis, winks, sounds, and facial expressions.

As the description above suggests, the concept of texture was originally identified in and applied to mostly verbal texts. Dundes (1964) acknowledges that texture could be described in other forms of folklore, but little has been done to extend the discussion of texture to customary and material folklore. However, understanding texts as more than verbal performances allows us to see how the idea makes sense. For material objects, texture could be literal texture—the way something feels—rough, smooth, hard, lumpy. We might also think about the textural features of a material object that are related to its creation and the artist who created it. A doll made from corn husks, for instance, may look much like other similar dolls, but suppose one artist uses scraps of her daughter's clothing to fashion dresses for her creations or tucks a cloth heart under the folds of the dress. These could be interpreted as special textural touches that make these cornhusk dolls unique to that creator (performer) and to a certain group, such as her family or neighborhood. Customary folklore, too, has texture. The performance of "The Star Spangled Banner" at most American sporting events is a recognizable tradition in which the same text, performed in very similar contexts, can change noticeably depending on the creativity of the performer. Someone might sing it in the style of a gospel hymn, an operatic aria, or a pop song. These variations could be seen as details of texture that influence the performance and make this particular text unique.

A challenge folklorists face when considering texture is that it is difficult to separate from text and context. Are rhymed words more part of the texture or text? Is a storyteller's decision to stress or repeat a phrase part of the texture or are her choices influenced by the context? Is the shade of green in a piece of folk art a detail of texture or text? Because it is so difficult to separate texture from text and context, folklorists are likely to discuss features of performance without labeling the features separately, simply describing and analyzing the entire performance: text, texture, and context all wrapped together.

Context

The physical settings and social situations in which members of folk groups share folklore, as well as the relationships among audience members and performers, make up the *context* of the performance. Basically, as we discussed earlier, context refers to anything and everything that surrounds a text and performance. In studying a certain folk text we cannot simply lift it from its context and begin to accurately understand its importance to a particular group. It must be seen within a larger context, as part of a cultural system. In addition, it is necessary to understand that the folklorist's interpretation of its significance should not be the final word. As the text is an element of a group's folklore, the group members are the experts on what those items or practices mean, so the folklorist shouldn't just walk away with a set interpretation and consider her work complete. Folklorists consult extensively with group members throughout the process of fieldwork and analysis in order to understand as clearly as possible the significance of texts within specific contexts. This kind of approach emphasizes the shared, community-based nature of folklore; it is a process that people create and participate in together.

Scholars have described context in many ways. Dundes described it as the observable setting in which a performance occurs (1964). Dell Hymes added a psychological dimension in his description of performance (which he calls "communicative event") as taking place both within a physical "setting" and a "scene" defined by the psychological and social circumstances surrounding the performance (1974, 55). Dan Ben-Amos identifies two types of context (1993). One is the "context of situation" and the other is the "context of culture." The context of situation is "the narrowest, most direct context" for folklore (216) and comprises the specific time period in which the performance occurs as well as the details of the place and circumstances in which the event takes place. Ben-Amos describes the context of culture as "the broadest contextual circle which embraces all possible contexts . . . the reference to, and the representation of, the broad shared knowledge of speakers, their conventions of conduct, belief systems, language metaphors and speech genres, their historical awareness and ethical and judicial principles" (215–16).

Ben-Amos's distinction between these narrow and broad perspectives demonstrates many overlapping contextual spheres: the setting in which the performance takes place, the events and interrelationships between group members and performers that occur during the performance, and the situation within the narrated or performed text itself. Beyond these situational contexts is the larger context in which the entire experience occurs, which has to do with cultural and social factors that shape the group's experience outside that particular performance.

So understanding context involves more than identifying or recovering texts within particular settings or even analyzing what takes place between performers and audiences during a performance. It also requires "the investigation of how participants, including 'investigators,' weave together what they encounter in a situation with what they bring to it through acts of memory and imagination" (M. Hufford 1995, 531). In other words, when we consider context, we need to think about what we know before the performance begins, as well as what we learn while the performance takes place.

Physical Context

When folklorists analyze context, they typically begin by observing and describing the physical environment of the performance event. It is important to know where the performance takes place, both in terms of geography and the specific setting. The physical environment also includes who is present—performers and audience members as well as any observers (including, of course, the folklorist). Details of the physical appearance of those present or of the setting (for example, sitting at the kitchen table, frilly white curtains on the windows) may also be important. Some folklorists consider online contexts as types of virtual physical settings that can be observed and described in the same ways as physical offline contexts. In any case, folklorists are interested in the details of where and in what circumstances folklore performances occur.

The physical elements of the performance itself can also be part of the context. These include gestures, changes in tone of voice, shifts in pitch, and rhythm. Frequently, we can record performances digitally or on tape and film, but sometimes we are unable to capture performances on tape, particularly those that are not preset in time or place as a performance or are not recreated for the purposes of collection. In these cases, it is important to observe carefully and take accurate notes on the physical elements in order to describe in writing the details of a performance as precisely as possible.

Folklorists need to be aware of anything going on at the time of a performance that may shape or affect it. This may, for example, include the occasion of the performance—that is, why it occurs at a particular time in a particular place. It would certainly be significant to know that a particular ritual is being performed at a designated time during a graduation party, or that a ghost story–telling session takes place on a snowy evening during a power failure, or that cooks are sharing traditional recipes while a family is planning the Thanksgiving Day menu. Family stories recounted about a beloved matriarch might be performed or interpreted differently if the stories are told at her birthday than if they are told at her funeral.

Describing what happens during a performance not only gives us an idea of the action taking place but also gives us some idea of why the actions occur. It is this interpretive dimension of performance, as well as performer and audience responses, that we consider when we observe relationships and interactions among performers and audience members.

The reactions of performers and audience members convey details related to performance, beyond the description of a statement or movement. For example, laughter is a physical activity, so we would report someone laughed. But laughter might also signify a particular psychological state: the person who laughed may be amused, which we typically interpret as a pleasant state, or may be expressing discomfort through nervous laughter. Boos or hisses suggest a different psychological response, as does squirming in a chair or storming out of a room. Elements such as these may suggest the types of relationships that exist between audience members and performers.

Social Context

Broad elements of the performance context include those things that relate to the group, community, and culture within which the communicative expression takes place. In a family situation, for example, part of this wider social context would be the family itself and all of the interactions between family members. Likewise, ethnic background, religious affiliations, occupation, regional connections, culture—all these are social aspects of performers, audiences, and settings that influence the events taking place during a performance. These kinds of social components influence how those present interact and may reflect assumed roles or expectations within the group or community.

As the study of performance has grown more complex, the concept of context as more than just the physical settings or internal characteristics of performance has also become more complex. Inherent in any performance, especially those that are observed, recorded, and analyzed by folklorists (or any scholars), is the reality that relationships among listeners and performers may reflect long-standing socially defined roles or expectations that influence the performance and its interpretation.

Status within the group affects how performers and audiences interact and who gets to perform what kinds of material. In the telling of a dirty joke, for example, adults frequently have a different status from children by virtue of their age. Children might try out such jokes on each other, but in any situation where adults are present, they would most likely be reprimanded for attempting an off-color joke. Teenagers might or might not be permitted to tell an adult-oriented joke in some mixed-age settings, again depending on who is present. Adults can tell jokes among coworkers, friends, or adult family members but avoid off-color material when children are present. An adult has a greater range of options than a child does in recounting such material, but age is still a determining factor—these jokes are for mature tellers and audiences.

Jokes like this are often based on social assumptions about gender, race, and class. To better understand this, consider different environments in which you have heard or shared jokes. Have you ever been in a situation in which someone made a remark or told a joke that made you feel uncomfortable? How did you react? Did your age, gender, or status within the group affect your reaction? If a boss told an off-color joke to a group of employees, for example, the relative power positions within the workplace would be a factor in understanding the performance, as would the gender, ethnicity, age, and perhaps other characteristics of those present. Perhaps some listeners felt offended by the joke, but because the teller was their employer, they didn't express their feelings openly—but they didn't laugh, either. Perhaps older (or younger) members of the group laughed, and perhaps males reacted differently from females.

To a folklorist who collected and studied that joke in its context, your reaction and the reactions of the others present would be important in analyzing the joke's performance and could reveal details about the relationship(s) between the teller and the listener(s). Learning about the nature of those relationships through careful observation and consultation with the members of this occupational group would help the folklorist contextualize and comprehend the performance. The folklorist would try to note facial expressions, comments, gestures, and other sorts of reactions and ideally would ask those present why they did or didn't laugh or what they thought of the joke. It would also be important to talk with the teller about his or her choices: Why did the boss tell the joke at that moment? What did he or she find funny about the joke? There are many ways to approach this performance, but in this context, the power and status relationships among the group members would obviously be crucial in understanding the place of dirty jokes in this group's interactions.

Folklorists typically try not to assess the "rightness" or "wrongness" of the performed materials (either verbal or nonverbal), apart from analyzing how group members use, share, and react to them within their physical and social contexts. It may be appropriate to talk about a particular group's social mores and customs and to consider how certain items of folklore or performances may deviate from or reinforce them, but not in a way that judges those items or performances according to preconceived assumptions or ethnocentric concepts. Because our own worldview influences the way we perceive social situations, such judgments are frequently exoteric (outsider) interpretations. Any evaluations of the propriety of a performed text need to be considered within the group's broad context, as well as the specific performance contexts, and need to be developed in consultation with performers and other group members.

143

Recognizing Texts in Context: Performance Markers and Framing

When Bauman says that performance links "marked, segregated esthetic genres" with "other spheres of verbal behavior" (1984, 5), he is touching on another crucial element of context: those actions, words, or other signs that let us know a performance is about to take place, is taking place, and is finished. We often call these signs *markers,* and they are an important part of describing and analyzing performance. They are the signals that tell the participants to pay attention—something important is happening, something that is set apart from (segregated from) the ordinary (Bauman 1984). These markers "frame" performance in much the same way we would frame a picture and hang it on a wall. The frame creates a social space with clear boundaries in which performers and audiences take part in the artistic and evaluative process. Within that space, fiction, history, story, tradition, art, teaching, all exist within the narrated or performed expressive event outside the normal realms and constraints of reality or time. The frame itself calls attention to and allows us to interpret what happens within the frames, both the text that is performed (narrated event) and the entire performance (the narrative event) (M. Hufford 1995).

Sometimes certain language devices or actions mark the beginnings and ends of performances. Familiar formulaic phrasings, such as "Once upon a time," often used to start a fairy tale or bedtime story, might be used to signal the beginning of structured performances and conversational performances. The fairy tale ending "and they lived happily ever after" might be used at the end of a spoken or written fairy tale to let readers know the story is finished. Some African folktales, for example, begin with the phrase "A story, a story let it go, let it come" or "Another story is coming. Stop talking and listen" and might end with "And so ends my story" (Abrahams 1983, 14–15; see also specific folk tales, 297, 312, 313, 331). Clearly stated verbal markers generally signal to performers and listeners that it is time to pay attention, guide them through the performance, and let them know when it is time to relax or perhaps comment on the performance they have just seen. These kinds of markers are clearly announced and intended to purposely draw attention to the events within the frame. They occur within a situation that is already heightened—that is, different from everyday experience.

Verbal performances also occur within and throughout ordinary experience, and these encounters include clearly marked expressive acts of communication. Even verbal folklore that is not narrative in nature (that is, not a story with a beginning, middle, and end) is typically signaled, or marked, with words or gestures. A proverb, for example, might be introduced with the phrase "You know what they say . . ." or a joke by the phrase "Did you hear the one about . . . ?" The beginning of a narrative of importance might be indicated by the teller's looking around the group, being sure to catch each person's eye, then leaning forward and lowering her voice to a stage whisper. But markers are not always direct or static; we all recognize and use more seamless markers in our everyday experiences. Not all of them are fixed; their form depends on the structure of the performance, not on the structure of the narrative.

As an example of a more conversational performance, imagine a situation in which a group of coworkers is complaining about heavy rush hour traffic. As they gripe about the grinding commute, one person says, "You know what, last Tuesday morning, just as I was getting on the highway, I saw this guy in a red pickup truck who . . ." Because she has gained the listeners' attention by including a direct address ("You know what"), given localizing details ("last Tuesday morning"), and referred to a sequence of events that involved her ("just as I was," "I saw this guy"), the others perk up their ears and start listening to their friend's words in a new way. They now expect to hear a personal narrative about her experience, with a beginning, middle, and end, perhaps with some vivid descriptive details, which somehow comments on the problem of fighting rush hour traffic congestion. The listeners also are invited, by virtue of the fact that the performer has announced a narrative with artistic dimensions, to judge how well the teller recounts her story and whether or not it fits the conversation context and to comment, if they choose, on the narrative. They might gasp in amazement or look puzzled or invite more details, depending on their judgment of the performance.

Performances like the personal experience narrative described above are not always marked by a particular well-known phrase or sentence that tells the listeners explicitly that the story is over, and the signals may not be verbal at all. The signal may be gestural, physical, or tonal—a certain expression on the performer's face, a wave of a hand, a long pause, or raising or lowering the voice. Performers may also use their own unique signals that are usually phrased or placed in such a way that the listeners understand the frame. These personal markers, even if they do have an idiosyncratic spin, resemble traditional folktale endings that comment on the story, such as "And that's a true story" or "And so the story goes." They are recognizable as framing devices that set the narrative performance outside everyday conversation.

Some evaluative markers—like laughter at a particular point or at the end of a tale, in which both the performer and listeners announce their agreement that the story (or its performance) was humorous—provide performers with feedback they can use to decide what to say or do next. If audience members

145

laugh at the end of a story, it may signal both their understanding that the anecdote is finished and their appreciation of the story. The laughter may also signal a kind of approval of the message as well as the skill with which the teller performed the tale: imitated voices, dramatic pauses, the creation of tension and suspense. Their encouragement could give the teller an opening to begin another story ("they like that one; here's another they'll like," he may think) or, if tellers are taking turns, allow a new teller to begin a story she hopes will be as well received.

Most of our discussion of framing and performance markers has focused on verbal texts, but framing is an important concept in all types of folklore performances. Rituals, as we have already discussed, are frequently marked off or framed by behavioral and verbal cues. Customary behaviors are often framed within everyday experience in much the same way as personal narrative. For example, if someone boasts or makes a claim, he or she may then knock on wood to avoid tempting fate into causing the opposite to happen: "I've never failed an exam in my life—knock on wood!" This custom arises in response to something that may be said in ordinary conversation, and it has a clear beginning and end.

No matter the type of item being performed, good listeners know how to pick up on the signals that begin and end performances so they know what they should do: pay attention, clap, laugh, get ready to listen to the next story, or perhaps just go home. Good performers, likewise, know how to frame their performances successfully so audiences will be ready to fulfill their active roles as listeners, judges, and perhaps commentators. The frame creates the artistic context that enhances enjoyment and invites evaluation and interpretation.

Reflexivity

An astute folklorist would apply careful *reflexive analysis* to uncover, to the best of her ability, the impact of her own shifting roles as a performance unfolds. The term *reflexivity* refers to anything in the performance and surrounding contexts that reflects, looks back upon, or comments upon *itself* (Berger and Del Negro 2002a, 63). The reflexive dimension of folklore is part of its context.

Folklorists need to be aware of how their own presence during a performance might influence things. Merely having someone from the outside watching and recording or taking notes could affect how comfortable the performers and audience members feel with presenting material, for instance. Taking a reflexive approach in analysis means we need to be honest with ourselves and look critically at the interactions among performers, audiences, and folklorists.

For instance, if a narrative performance takes place within a setting where the performer(s) and audience are all family members, a certain level of openness and shared experience may exist between them that would allow fairly personal, familiar content to be shared without the participants fearing disapproval. However, in storytelling sessions where outsiders (folklorists, perhaps) are present, the teller may avoid content that would be hard to interpret outside the family context. When the folklorist analyzes the features of the performance, she has to incorporate her understanding of how the absence or presence of outsiders might have influenced the performer's choices. Not doing so will weaken the interpretation because it ignores a critical element that could have had significant impact on the performance.

If the folklorist is herself a member of the family group, it would be relevant to consider how her role as both collector and observer influenced the performance, and even the analysis. Might her family members have treated her differently, in subtle, perhaps unconscious ways that influenced the content or sequences of stories, for example? If she interrupted the performer to ask a question, was that question seen as an unwelcome intrusion by an outsider (in her role as observer) or accepted as a natural part of the flow of telling stories, as it had usually been? Might personal assumptions or biases based on exoteric experience be wrong, or at least incomplete? It is also important to think about the implied assumptions we bring to the analysis of any performance, rather than rely solely on insider knowledge, or even particular interpretations we have learned.

A reflexive perspective offers a critical and interpretive stance that incorporates the researcher's experience into the analysis. One contribution is the insight personal experience provides. Reflexive discussions from the researcher's personal point of view as both an observer and participant can enrich the overall interpretations. For instance, a folklorist who is also a member of the group he or she is working with, in a family, perhaps, could explain details that an outsider might miss or could provide clues based on experiences about why certain events occurred in a particular way. On the other hand, being part of a group may mean we are too close to the context to see clearly; that is, we may be so emotionally or personally connected to the group that it may be difficult to be objective or critical. Careful reflexive discussion of the insights, limitations, or problems that may result from our connections (or lack thereof) with the group add value to interpretations and provide an honest assessment of our own roles. This kind of interpretation also opens up possibilities for other folklorists, who may be able to add their own interpretations that fill in gaps or offer alternatives.

147

On a deeper level, reflexivity itself is an interpretation. Many folklorists study the ways the shifting roles of folklorists, performers, and group members interact to create a complex performance and lead to many layers of meaning and awareness. One such folklorist is David Hufford, who has considered the ways scholars employ personal observation and experience, consciously and unconsciously, in their interpretations of group beliefs and belief-centered practices (1995). Basically, reflexivity blurs the lines among performers, audiences, scholars, and group members and highlights the dynamics of performance.

The awareness of reflexive dimensions in folklore has contributed to methodological approaches to folklore study and ethnography known as reflexive or *reciprocal ethnography*. This methodology stresses the importance of collaboration in analyzing folklore performances and actively seeks to foreground the interpretations of group members and performers along with the scholarly interpretations of the folklorist. Reciprocal ethnography incorporates the voices of scholars, performers, and group members into published analyses, acknowledging the shared expressive and communicative qualities of folklore performance. (We will cover reciprocal ethnography in detail in chapter 7, "Fieldwork and Ethnography.")

Emergence

The term *emergence* as used in folklore studies can be looked at in several ways: in the sense of something new coming into existence; in the sense of something that arises out of (emerges from) a particular performance context; and in the sense that every performance differs from every other, that new texts emerge through performance even if the same material is being performed and the same people are always present.

One way to think about emergence, in the sense of something new forming, is to consider how folk groups form and evolve. We talked about the qualities of folk groups earlier and described the many ways they form, depending on the members' interests and the contexts in which they come together. In this way, we could say that groups emerge within contexts, just as performances do. The folklore groups share changes as the groups evolve together, and new traditions and customs may emerge over time and with members' interaction. High school sports teams, for example, often have traditions and rituals that each group of athletes shares with the team members that follow them. Even if teams do some of the same things from year to year, the specific members of the group continually change. As a result, a group might introduce a new custom or ritual that emerges as a new tradition.

New forms of folklore have also emerged as the ways people communicate have changed. Chain letters, in which one person sends a letter to a group of others and instructs them to make copies of the letter and do the same or a terrible tragedy will befall them, have been commonly circulated through the mail. Now, chain letters circulate frequently through email and have taken on their own special characteristics related to the method of transmission. Email itself has created or influenced entire categories of expression: emoticons, contemporary legends about employees who accidentally send scathing complaints intended for coworkers to their bosses, and messages in which the sender receives a written or visual "reward," sometimes the punch line of a joke, only after he or she has forwarded the message to a certain number of people.

The Internet has generated what might be termed whole new emergent genres, which folklorists have begun to explore. Online user profiles, for instance, can be read as folklore texts that present user identities and personas (Westerman 2009). Monica Foote, in "Userpicks: Cyber Folk Art in the Early 21st Century" (2007), looks at avatars, which are icons that serve as conscious expressions of personal identity or moods and have developed into traditional means of establishing and sharing online personas. Another interesting topic is the popular Internet phenomenon of memes, which are ideas, texts, and images that are passed around through websites, social media, and blogs and often rely on fixed structures to communicate complex jokes and commentary. One recent popular meme is "Tourist Guy," a visual text in which, initially, a figure was photoshopped into a photograph of the observation deck of the World Trade Center, presumably seconds before the plane hit the tower on September 11, 2001. Anonymous Internet users then copied the man's image into other photographs showing him in a variety of situations and locations all around the world. The series of images became a sort of absurdist joke, copied and adapted by thousands of people. According to Michael Dylan Foster (2010), an unsuccessful attempt to create a similar "Vacation Gal" meme featuring Michelle Obama failed presumably because people simply didn't like it, partly because it was too conscious an attempt to create a meme. The failure of "Vacation Gal" to catch on demonstrates that in this case emergence required people to accept the text in order to be willing to pass it along into the traditional joke cycle.

Another aspect of emergence is related to traditions that change form over time or have different meanings for different members of a group. Traditions associated with objects, customs, or rituals, for example, may sometimes emerge into narratives and form an important part of a group's identity. In the Stephens

149

Charlie Stephens's dinner bucket.

family, Martine's father's "dinner bucket," a metal pail in which he carried his lunch into the coal mine, held many meanings for family members. Her father used it as a utilitarian object that carried his food and water. Each day he saved a few pieces of food and a little water, and when he returned home from work, he gave these to his children. The children waited eagerly for these treats, and this family custom was part of the intimate link between them and their father. But the leftover food was also associated with a coal miners' belief that the children were not aware of: many miners said it was bad luck to finish all the food in the dinner bucket. Miners shared this belief and practice, perhaps as one way to make sure they would always have some food or water in the event that an accident or cave-in occurred and they needed to wait for rescue. Now, Martine's father's bucket is a reminder of the family connections as well as an example of a central element of her father's occupational group. The dinner bucket itself, the custom of sharing leftover food, and the expression of the belief about saving food all appear frequently in her family's stories about her father. Folklore about a single object (or the object itself as text) can transform as new meanings emerge, so that it may be associated with custom, belief, and narrative. In this case, these emergent meanings have become important features of the family's definition of itself as a coal mining family in relation to the father's occupation.

From the Stephens family photo collection.

Bill and Charlie Stephens on their way to work, 1936.

In many groups, folklore emerges in a response to an event. Americans experienced an example of new folklore emerging from experience when the space shuttle *Challenger* exploded in 1986. Not many hours had passed after the media reported news of the explosion before jokes began to circulate about the event. Many people were at first offended by the jokes and regarded them as being in poor taste; folklorists, however, understood the emergence of these jokes as a response to an experience we had difficulty comprehending. As tragic as the explosion was, Americans began to share jokes that may have helped to express the general discomfort, sadness, and anxiety they felt in the aftermath of the tragedy. Similar jokes emerged after the shuttle *Columbia* exploded in 2003. Interestingly, the structure of the jokes, as well, was often the same—frequently a question-answer format, with content adapted to suit the particular context.

Another national tragedy that engendered jokes and other forms of humor was, perhaps surprisingly, the September 11, 2001, attacks in New York, Washington DC, and Pennsylvania. Humor related to the events of September 11 focused on American pride and even the ability to recover from the shock

151

and pain of the events. For many, creating and telling the jokes was a kind of coping mechanism that allowed them to express their feeling of confusion and anger. Bill Ellis (2002) analyzes the verbal and visual jokes that began to circulate shortly after the disaster, discusses how they were shared, and describes how they evolved from expressions of defiance and anger to predictions of triumph over terrorism and assertions of hope and survival. Some were less clearly expressions of attitudes toward terrorism and fell into the sick joke category. The jokes differed from country to country and reflected each nation's own relationship to the United States as well as its take on the threat of terrorism. These and similar jokes commonly develop after tragic events, particularly, as Ellis points out, when those events are widely reported and heightened by the electronic media (2001, 2002).

These more general or obvious examples illustrate broad types of emergence, showing new folklore coming about as a result of large-scale changes, for example, a change in group membership, in medium of transmission, or in physical or psychological context. Yet, in a broader sense, we might say a text—whether a story, song, dance, ritual, or any other sort of folklore—doesn't really exist until it is performed. The specific text of that performance exists only for the time the performance lasts. If you have ever attended several showings of the same movie, this phenomenon is probably familiar: you see and hear new things in every viewing, and your experience of the event differs depending on the time of day, the people you go to the theater with, perhaps even your mood. Performers who repeat the same material again and again experience this quality of performance firsthand. Even if the content doesn't vary much (a play script, for example, or an aria in an opera), performers might emphasize a certain line differently each night or even forget a line and have to improvise. The audience might react with laughter during one performance and with silence at the same point another time. In essence, because the experiences of audiences and performers constantly change and evolve, both from performance to performance and during a single performance, a new text emerges with every performance.

Every performance differs from every other, depending on the context and the group in which the performance occurs (Bauman 1984, 37 [referring to Georges 1969, 319]). Bauman explains that this "emergent quality of performance resides in the interplay between communicative resources, individual competence, and the goals of the participants, within the context of particular situations" (38). In other words, everything that goes on during a performance, everything that surrounds it, affects the nature of the performance. The text itself may change, perhaps as a performer adapts material to suit the audience's needs or responses. If the audience is restless, a performer may shorten a story, for example, or if the audience's attention lags, the performer may insert a few spicy details to liven things up. Albert Lord (1960), in his study of oral epic poetry, said that "the length of the song depends on the audience" (in Bauman 1984, 17). The performance context affects the performer's choices, and those choices affect the text itself.

Folklore That Pushes the Boundaries

During performance, the relationships between audience members and performers can shift and change. Audiences become caught up in the performance and, for its duration, regard performers in a special way—as being outside the bounds of ordinary experience. In this sense, a new kind of social structure emerges from the performance (Bauman 1984, 42), and this shift in perspective gives the performer a temporary power over the audience. As Bauman says, "When the performer gains control in this way, the potential for transformation of the social structure may become available to him as well" (44). In other words, the usual rules of social interaction don't have to apply; the performer can say and do things during the performance that would be completely unacceptable outside the performance context.

This is why, Bauman suggests, we sometimes have such uneasy relationships with performers. We admire them, perhaps even revere them, but at the same time we regard them as being outside the mainstream, somehow set apart from the rest of us. As outsiders, they sometimes behave in ways that surprise and shock us. Think of the stories we read in entertainment magazines or see on television about celebrities who trash hotel rooms, steal merchandise from stores, or generally behave badly in public. Or they might be outspoken advocates of particular causes or might, perhaps outrageously or profanely, point out problems they see with the world. A late-night talk show host does a monologue about absurd things the president said or did that day, and while we are laughing, we might also be wondering about whether or not our president is such a good guy after all or whether our political system is really working. Performers show us what it looks like to break or change the rules: they can subvert (challenge and undermine) the accepted rules and limits and reveal the potential that all of us have to push against our group's standards. As Bauman puts it, "In the special emergent quality of performance, the capacity for change may be highlighted and made manifest to the community" (1984, 45).

On a basic level, this transformative power of performers and performances generates one of the most entertaining aspects of sharing folklore: it allows us to play, creatively and safely, with what is permissible or acceptable within our group's social and cultural contexts. Singing a parody of a religious hymn, for

153

instance, opens up an opportunity to have a little fun during what could be a boring church service, or creating an unflattering private nickname for an overly strict teacher may help students vent frustration while eluding punishment. In most ways, this potential for folklore to enable us to question society and authority is positive. As part of the process of forming and expressing identity, folklore frequently tests the limits of what groups accept and perceive as being appropriate and may allow us to question and challenge, even subvert, social norms. Many effective protests against oppressive or unethical organizations and institutions have been launched or supported through folklore. Songs written and sung by labor organizers in the 1930s, for instance, helped to bring issues related to the rights of industrial workers to the forefront of politics and social activist movements. Similarly, political jokes are a familiar way that members of democratic societies express their views, critique government policies and officials, and help to keep political dialogues open and ongoing.

On the other hand, this is one element of folklore and groups that is sometimes uncomfortable for us to consider. It is important to take care not to romanticize groups and folklore, assuming that they are always charming or reaffirming when, as a matter of fact, folklore can communicate negative messages. Folklore can, for instance, communicate negative assumptions about race, gender, and social class, or any group we identify as "other." Such negative messages are apparent in groups such as the Ku Klux Klan, which teaches members how to function in destructive ways both inside and outside mainstream society. Negative messages expressed in folklore may be more subtle and less formalized, too, such as when groups of children share rhymes or songs that make fun of people from other cultures. Such expressions can seem fairly innocuous—silly songs that poke fun at fans of a rival sports team, for example, or jokes about absentminded professors. But in the extreme, assumptions expressed through folklore about other groups can suggest or reinforce inappropriate and even dangerous attitudes. The belief that groups of young urban men who dress alike and listen to hip-hop must belong to street gangs promotes racist stereotypes about urban culture. "Blonde jokes," as innocent or funny as they may seem, can potentially reinforce the sexist notion that it's acceptable to ridicule women or that women aren't intelligent. The customary idea most Americans learn when they are children that boys shouldn't wear pink can play into more complex homophobic attitudes. Contemporary legends about Chinese restaurants serving dog meat instead of beef can engender fear and mistrust of Chinese Americans.

This aspect of folklore analysis can cut pretty deep: we have to consider race and gender prejudices and stereotypes, social inequities, hierarchies based on

154

economic power, and class distinctions as serious topics, certainly. Many of these assumptions are connected with the esoteric and exoteric elements of group identity and expression we discussed earlier. Unfortunately, folklore can have negative connotations mixed in with art, humor, and playfulness; folklore unifies a group and reinforces identity, but not all of a group's shared characteristics are necessarily positive. Some folklore reinforces uncomfortable stereotypes and attitudes that are so deeply entrenched we don't even recognize that they are part of the worldview of a group.

We are not saying that all folklore like this is inherently bad or always leads to such conclusions; nor are we suggesting that we should not study such texts or groups. All aspects of folklore are legitimate topics of study. But we do need to be aware that we express ideas about others through our folklore and we do, in part, define ourselves by those ideas. Folklore helps us form and express identity in the midst of an always complex, sometimes confusing, social context, in which our sense of who we are is frequently questioned and challenged. Some of the negative elements of folklore are part of this confusing, shifting social palette. Understanding the potentially negative elements in folklore allows us to analyze dynamics within and among groups, recognize the interplay of contextual influences, be aware of our own biases, and engage in more honest scholarly discussions. Astute folklorists incorporate their awareness of these complex challenges into their discussions, don't shy away from them, and deal with them openly.

Example: Performers that Transcend Roles and Rules

Simply being a performer of folklore may define someone as having an expanded role within a group, and performers often transcend limiting roles within their communities through their artistic roles. By pushing limits, performers can change their own status in a group. A familiar example of the ways performing folklore can change the power dynamic in a group is the case of a high school class clown. Frequently, the class clown is a person who is not considered popular in the usual sense of attractiveness, athletic skill, or economic status. The class clown makes just the right sarcastic remark during the world's most boring math class or teases the football star at lunch, somehow managing not to get beat up too badly. The clown tests the limits of what is acceptable by being funny or acting out in wild behavior what the rest of the group might not dare to try. While the clown may not be popular—that is, may never be elected class president or date the richest kid in school—he or she, at least while performing, changes status. No longer dismissed as a geek, a nerd, or a brain, by virtue of performing goofy imitations or telling a silly joke, the clown plays an accepted, perhaps valued, role in the group.

155

The class clown is an example of an important character in folklore studies: the *trickster*. Tricksters appear in the tales of many cultures, and their presence helps to illustrate how folklore performances and performers can challenge or even overturn existing social systems and structures. Some well-known examples of tricksters are Coyote, who appears in many Native American stories; Anansi the spider, who is central in much West African and Jamaican folklore; and Hermes, messenger to the gods in ancient Greek tales, who was also known for his ability to trick the gods. A couple of frequently discussed tricksters from popular culture are the American cartoon figures of the Road Runner and Bugs Bunny. Bugs sometimes gets into trouble and may be fooled occasionally but almost always manages to escape or triumph in the end, a major feature of trickster tales. No doubt you have encountered other tricksters in many familiar texts. What is most important to know about tricksters is that they constantly break rules, test the limits of authority, and push the boundaries of what is acceptable or even possible in society. Tricksters' antics are entertaining—we laugh at their mistakes and the way they fool or confuse others, and in the process we may learn to see ourselves and our societies more clearly.

In one Native American Coyote tale, for example, Coyote meets a young boy who is searching for a whip-poor-will he has been listening to, so he can watch it sing. Jealous of the boy's preference for the bird's song over his own, Coyote asks the boy to listen to his howl and tell him how he likes it. The boy covers his ears, says he still prefers the whip-poor-will, and sets off again in search of the bird. Coyote slyly offers to lead the boy there by a shortcut. The boy agrees, but then Coyote leads him over rough ground, where the boy falls in brush and trips in gopher holes. They reach the whip-poor-will's location, but by then it is morning, the boy is scratched and bruised (not to mention humiliated when he realizes he has been tricked), and both the whip-poor-will and Coyote are gone. The boy must make his way back home alone, having missed the whip-poor-will entirely. Coyote lies to the boy, fools him, allows him to get hurt, and then leaves him alone far from home—certainly not acceptable things to do to a child—all in the interest of teaching a lesson and getting revenge. Years later, when he is more mature, the boy realizes Coyote taught him important lessons—one of them, to watch out for tricksters like Coyote (see Magoulick 2000 for a discussion of the preceding tale).

Trickster tales like the Coyote story above are prime examples of the way that performances and performers of folklore can subvert or challenge social norms. Trickster performances in the tales playfully and irreverently break taboos or violate rules. Likewise, performing in and listening to performances of trickster tales may act as an entertaining escape valve that allows performers and listeners alike to laugh at social restrictions. Barbara Babcock-Abrahams (1975) explains that because the trickster behaves within stories in socially inappropriate or unacceptable ways, he makes it possible for us to imagine escaping the social rules and limitations we face in our real daily lives. And, as Lewis Hyde points out, in addition to crossing socially accepted or imposed boundaries, "there are cases in which trickster *creates* a boundary, or brings to the surface a distinction previously hidden from sight" (1998, 8). For instance, when Prometheus steals fire from the gods and gives it to humans, he recognizes that a barrier exists between the gods and humanity and then pushes through the barrier. When Anansi, a spider-god trickster in some West African tales, steals all the world's wisdom and then must release it back into the world after he realizes there is always more wisdom to possess, he first creates a distinction between the wise and the ignorant and then uses newfound wisdom to erase the line. In these kinds of stories, creating and crossing boundaries are certainly related activities, Hyde explains, and so "the best way to describe trickster is to say simply that the boundary is where he will be found—sometimes drawing the line, sometimes crossing it, sometimes erasing or moving it, but always there, the god of the threshold in all its forms" (9–10). Tricksters embody the creative, dynamic force inherent in folklore that allows groups to evolve and grow.

Trickster tales present us with dilemmas that may stretch our ability to accept people or behavior that falls outside our limits, may enable us to push those limits to a new standard of what's acceptable, or may, because we react strongly against something the trickster does, reinforce the standards. In the simple act of performance—whether telling, listening, or reading—we, too, can vicariously cross the line of socially acceptable behavior, break the rules, or rewrite the rules entirely.

Aesthetics

Because the text that emerges depends on the people present, folklorists emphasize the experiences of audiences and performers. This analysis extends to the ways in which people evaluate performance. As Bauman said, the marking off or framing of performance creates an expressive event that enhances our awareness and invites evaluation. As the text emerges through performance, the text itself and the overall performance become subject to evaluation. Audiences evaluate the performer's competence and skill, the text that emerges, the performance itself, and the overall aesthetic effects of the experience.

The study of folklore often involves consideration of embellishments and changes individual performers might make in texts and forms of delivery, as well as their reasons for making them. We can make observations about performers' voices, gestures, and expressions or consider their stage presence. We can observe audience members' reactions or responses and analyze what those responses say about their relationships to the performers, their traditions, each other, and their communities. We also might think about how effectively a performer accomplishes the goals of the performance, as performers, artists, and audiences understand them. What, for example, makes a particular performance of a song "good" or "bad"? What makes one painting better than another? What draws listeners into a story? What makes something beautiful?

These kinds of questions elicit responses from the audience to the creative elements, or *aesthetic* qualities, of a verbal, customary, or material expression or performance. One way of thinking about aesthetics is in terms of what Michael Owen Jones calls the "ohuli-ahhh/ugh-yuck complex" (1987, 173); in other words, when we see or hear an artistic work, we tend naturally to judge or evaluate it, so we react to it, usually with expressions of like or dislike. In his work, Bauman begins by acknowledging the "esthetic dimension of social and cultural life in human communities" (1984, 2) and describes the scholarly use of the term *performance* as a way "to convey a dual sense of artistic *action*—the doing of folklore—and artistic *event*—the performance situation, involving performer, art form, audience, and setting" (4). It is this artistic dimension that, as we have said, invites audiences to respond to and evaluate performances, performers, and creative texts and objects themselves. The artistic elements in folklore get our attention, they interest us, and so we respond to them.

According to Henry Glassie, if something "engages the senses, demanding and gaining the total involvement of the person, it meets aesthetic needs" (1992, 269). Glassie writes that the key to understanding aesthetics is in recognizing how we are affected by the term *anesthetic*. If we are anesthetized, we feel nothing (269). According to Glassie, "The aesthetic is the opposite. It enlivens the nerves, and when the nerves are excited, when the senses are seeking their own pleasure, leaving no room for boredom, preventing any feeling of alienation, an act is aesthetic and it has met the first requirement of art" (270). Most definitions of folklore refer to the artistic or creative elements of its forms, as in Dan Ben-Amos's simple definition of folklore as "artistic communication in small groups" (1971, 13). The artistic elements inherent in folklore necessitates a response.

Michael Owen Jones explains that "the aesthetic impulse—a feeling for form and a desire to perfect form—is apparent in dozens of subtle ways in the things we make and do during the course of daily interaction, problem solving, and the accomplishing of tasks" (1987, 81).[40] We study aesthetics in order to understand and evaluate artistic works, whether verbal, visual, material, or performing arts. Aesthetics is a constant part of the discussion of folklore, whether considering how aesthetics works to shape our ideas of folklore or considering what elements of art stand out most in a group's judgment or perception of it.

Clearly, there are many problems in evaluating folklore from a mainstream perspective. Applications of rigid rules or evaluative criteria created by mainstream scholars or critics that invite judgments about quality are frequently outsider definitions of what is considered good or pleasing to members of the group and so may create inaccurate or unfair standards that misdirect our analysis of folklore. In order to understand how and why we respond differently to fine arts and folklore and thus evaluate aesthetic qualities in different ways, folklorists have considered the artistic qualities in folklore that distinguish it from fine art. We can distinguish features of folklore that clarify ways that folk groups generally create and evaluate their own artistic expressions.

Living in an Aesthetic World

Step inside the home of Bruce Siple, and you'll immediately be introduced to the colors, shapes, and objects that Siple loves. As he explains, "I want to live in a house where I see things I like." Siple displays found objects, made mostly of bright, intensely colored plastic, in patterned installations inside his home. First-time visitors to his home express the kind of "ohhh-ahhh/ugh-yuck" reactions described by Michael Owen Jones (1987) in his work on aesthetics. While Siple says his home rarely elicits obvious ugh-yuck reactions, visitors do sometimes say they could never imagine living in a house like his. In any case, visitors are never neutral—because the place itself is not neutral by any definition or description.

Siple's work is untraditional in many ways: it's not decoration; it's not art hanging on a wall, contained within a frame. It's art that spills outside the boundaries of our expectations, covering walls and furniture, tables and shelves.

Most of the living room and an entire side room are given to Siple's displays. In the living room, the coffee table consists of a stack of glass disks of graduated sizes sitting on a silver metal base. On each layer of glass rest precisely arranged, solid-colored red, blue, yellow, and green plastic objects. On the lowest level of the table, tiny cars, buses, and trucks appear to be stalled in traffic behind each other as they circle the table

While this black-and-white photograph cannot capture the exuberant colors in the mantel display, it shows the symmetry, repetition, and form in Siple's work.

Photo by Randall L. Schieber, © 2011.

rim. Moving higher up the piece, motor vehicles alternate with toy rockets. Oversized, opaque yellow, red, and green whistles intermingle with repetitions of the table itself: clear plastic rings topped with stacked plastic disks and finished off with yellow-orange pen barrels. Items on the small top tiers are more shape and color than identifiable object, until reaching the very top of the work, where a foot-tall orange sippy cup is guarded by a pair of plastic Shriners and a guitar-wielding Godzilla.

This coffee table (which doesn't really function as a table in the usual sense) is the physical centerpiece of the room, but it's not the single most dramatic piece in the room. That would be the fireplace mantel, covered with a symmetrically organized array of plastic plates and tumblers, hamster tubes, a variety of animal figures, and other bright items. The side room adjoining the living room is devoted entirely to such visually stunning displays. This room is filled with tall shelves, vertical cases, and other pieces of furniture covered with even more symmetrical collections of bright objects, including toys, pieces of medical equipment, tools, utensils—a nearly endless list of items both familiar and strange to the viewer.

Singling out any theme or category as a focus wouldn't do the work justice, nor would it bring the viewer a better sense of the meaning of the

The familiar plastic utensils and objects in this portion of one installation take on an abstract aesthetic rhythm and form that transcend their utilitarian functions.

art Siple creates. Visually, Siple doesn't intend that each piece be seen as a discrete item but rather as an element in a larger composition, echoing qualities of *bricolage*, a process of combining a variety of found items and available materials into a holistic design that means more than the sum of the individual parts. In the act of collecting together bits and pieces of objects from many sources, Siple reflects the spirit of the *bricoleur* in a literal sense; in addition, his combining of elements of art and function by mixing the pedestrian flotsam and jetsam of ordinary life with aesthetic elements like the interplay of color, light, and line fits closely with the Lévi-Straussian concept of cultural bricolage (1971). As Kapchan and Strong (1999) explain, the cultural bricoleur "unhinges forms from their rootedness in history and recombines them in novel ways" (240).

The objects have identities and histories within the social, commercial world; they are recognizable parts of popular culture, mass-produced bits of the visitors' and artist's social environments—lunchboxes, pill bottles, curlers, cups, and spoons. Yet these objects are aligned and arranged in ways that form new identities. The concrete *things* in the displays are decontextualized from their original, traditional uses or settings and are recontextualized by the artist—and his guests—as abstract parts of aesthetic compositions, with new identities and histories.

The work is not strictly what most would call fine art or even home decor, nor is it based on entirely mainstream principles, and Siple is not what some would call an outsider artist. Yet like many traditional outsider artists who create visionary environments, Siple expresses an obsessive need to collect, display, and arrange objects inside his home that reflects a fervor similar to that of artists who devote their creations to expressing religious or spiritual values. (See, for example, the work of R. A. Miller and Howard Finster, which we discuss in chapter 3.) Unlike most visionary artists, though, Siple, an avowed atheist, does not conceive a higher purpose (at least not in the religious sense) for his work. But he does, he says, have a strong desire to communicate his ideal of aesthetic form through his art and his dwelling space. When asked about his vision, Siple explained that he sees and creates in some of the displays what he calls a kind of "secular mandala," an artistic expression of the perfect world—in this case, one based on color, light, form, symmetry, and a sense of whimsy and surprise.

Ultimately, what impresses the visitor most is that Siple's work is playful, accessible, and open to view and interpret or simply to enjoy as attractive, colorful, arranged collections. The artist is a trickster, playing with, interacting with, and interpreting these familiar items in order to encourage the viewer to do the same, but in new, unexpected ways. The trickster's role is to act outside the boundaries of accepted taste and decorum in such a way that we react to what the trickster does. As a trickster, Siple does not break serious taboos or challenge ideas of ethical or moral behavior, but his work suggests he intends to catch us off guard, maybe knock us off our sure footing with regard to our concepts of beauty, utility, home decoration, and art. Visitors to Siple's house contact and cross the boundary between what we label home and exhibit. The marriage of styles, ideas, social assumptions, pop/fine/folk, high class, and lowbrow brings about a new understanding of living room and gallery, art and decoration, play and seriousness and so comments on and challenges traditional assumptions about taste, propriety, and art.

Bruce Siple's unique perception of the world challenges us to view the things around us differently. In his view, the leftovers of our consumer culture move through our lives like a "constantly flowing river of incidental, overlooked, cast-off" commercial stuff that we just allow to slip away, from objects we don't use anymore to the packaging that envelops and contains the things we buy. He thinks we see and touch so many ordinary, mundane things every day that we often fail to notice them and even less often perceive their implicit forms and colors. "Most people look at a cap from a bottle of laundry detergent, and see a cap," he says, "but I look at it and see something different"—the aesthetic possibilities within and around the cap. He looks at a hamster tube and sees not a part of a pet's playground, but "a beautiful gesture." By re-presenting such ordinary, everyday objects as beautiful gestures, by pulling pure light, color, and balance out of our society's river of castoffs, Siple creates a complex cultural environment based on his vision of the entire world as an aesthetic realm, inviting a response from every person who walks through his front door.

Critic versus Group Consensus

For mainstream or popular arts, we often make judgments about a work's quality based on the rules or values imposed by a particular school or artistic movement. Fine art is typically evaluated by critics who are acknowledged as the arbiters of taste. Folklore, though, by definition, is evaluated by community consensus, not by an individual with some privileged understanding of what makes art good. In the fine arts, one artist's new or completely radical expression of a particular idea may often be heralded as a new school or direction in that particular field of art. On the other hand, Barre Toelken says that the artist who creates folklore tends to "reinforce past group aesthetic." He explains that art can be seen as "a field of tension between conservation of tradition and experimentation, between the solid maintenance of older ideas and the dynamism of new ones." Artists try to resolve this tension in two different ways, he says. The folk artist, who is "usually allied to culture by ethnic, religious, family, or occupational ties, will tend to resolve the tension in the direction of group consensus." The fine artist, on the other hand, "will follow the impulse to resolve [the tension] by doing something new and dynamic" (Toelken 1996, 203). Fine art seems to go against the grain, and folklore reflects the group's values and identity. Toelken makes it clear that neither type of art, fine or folk, is better than the other; they are simply different, with different sets of aesthetics.

Traditionality

Because folklore incorporates traditional ideas and values, one of the ways we can view the aesthetics of folklore is in its connection to traditions. In order to be considered good, examples of folklore need to successfully execute the tradition; that is, they have to express what is lasting and immutable about

163

that particular genre—its conservative aspects. Food and traditional recipes illustrate this principle well. For example, many families have a special family recipe for meat loaf. Most American meat loaf recipes contain a mix of ground meat, bread crumbs, egg, and herbs, often topped with tomatoes or ketchup and baked in a loaf-shaped pan. If this is what you think of as meat loaf, and a friend served something different that he called meat loaf, you would probably still recognize the dish even if it did not contain exactly the same ingredients in the same proportions. However, what if the loaf were shaped like a dome? Or it did not contain meat, or was made of tuna? Or it had a filling of melted cheese? How far may a meat loaf deviate from a particular structure and still be a meat loaf or still be judged *good* meat loaf? The quality of your friend's loaf would have to be evaluated against the standards of the community—in this case, your family's recipe and preferences. If something doesn't fulfill the group's definition of a tradition, the group may not consider it a successful example of that tradition. Your friend's food may be delicious, but it may also be a lousy meat loaf.

Skill

Skill includes individual expressive details created by artists and performers, within limits agreed upon by artists and audiences, within given folk groups. According to Gerald Pocius, skill is a defining characteristic of art in general, but skill itself is culturally determined and depends on the audience's or viewer's determination of how much talent the artist has to have to create a particular work (1995, 423). Skill may also be judged by how complicated the work is and how difficult it was to create (423). Performers themselves define skill based on their understanding of their audiences and their application of their own performance standards (Tallman 1974; K. Goldstein 1991). Audiences judge performers based on how effectively their performances meet the standards of the particular audience or folk group, and the emergent qualities within performance allow performers to place their individual creative skills in front of audiences, inviting evaluation (Bauman 1984).

Skill is crucial in understanding the aesthetics of folklore, but like quality, it cannot be measured in absolute terms. Because folklore arises from and exists within a particular context, it embodies the traditions of the communities that create it. Certainly, then, one way to understand skill is to look at how specific groups evaluate specific objects, verbal expressions, performances, and performers.

Richard S. Tallman's (1974) work with a Nova Scotia storyteller illustrates how folklorists have approached the study of aesthetics in general and skill in particular. Tallman first of all emphasizes that we can't consider aesthetics

Recipe Box

When is a meat loaf not a meat loaf? Do these recipes resemble your family's traditional recipes?

My Meat Loaf

  2 lbs. hamburger

  2 eggs

  1 1/2 cups bread crumbs

  3/4 cup ketchup

  1 medium onion, chopped fine

  2 strips bacon

  1 can (8 oz.) tomato sauce

  1/2 tsp. salt

  Mix meat, eggs, bread crumbs, ketchup, salt, and onion. Put into loaf pan. Cover with bacon. Pour tomato sauce over the top. Bake one hour at 350 degrees.

Meat Loaf Italiano

  1 egg, beaten

  1/2 cup cracker crumbs

  1/2 cup minced onion

  2 cans (8 oz.) Italian tomato sauce

  1/2 tsp. oregano

  3 cups shredded mozzarella cheese

  1/2 tsp. basil

  1 tsp. salt

  1 clove minced garlic

  dash pepper

  1 1/2 lbs. ground beef

  Combine egg, bread crumbs, onion, 1/3 cup tomato sauce, 1 cup cheese, oregano, basil, salt, and pepper. Mix well and add meat. Mix and shape into a flat rectangle about 10" x 12" on waxed paper. Sprinkle remaining cheese over meat mixture. Roll like a jelly roll and seal ends. Place on rack in shallow pan. Bake one hour at 350 degrees. Remove from oven and drain fat. Pour on the rest of the tomato sauce. Return to oven and bake another 15 minutes.

Girl enjoying Cottage Tuna Loaf.

Cottage Tuna Loaf

    1 package (1 lb.) California style cottage cheese

    2 eggs, beaten

    1/2 tsp. salt

    2 cans (7 oz.) tuna

    1 cup packaged herb-seasoned bread stuffing

    1 cup tomato sauce

    1/2 cup chopped onion

    Blend cottage cheese, eggs, and salt. Place 1/2 cup mixture in greased 9" x
    5" x 3" loaf pan. Mash tuna smooth and blend thoroughly with remain-
    ing cottage cheese mixture and remaining ingredients. Place on top of
    cheese layer. Press down lightly. Bake at 375 degrees for 45–50 minutes.
    Allow to stand five minutes before unmolding.

without considering context. Because contexts change, it is important to realize, too, that the aesthetic can change and that "the concept of an aesthetic, particularly a folk aesthetic, is dynamic." In order to get a sense of that dynamic aesthetic, Tallman focuses on one storyteller within one community, because, according to Tallman, "the study of aesthetics is most fruitful when approached in terms of one person's aesthetic" (121).

Based on his observance of several storytelling sessions and conversations with Bob Coffil, the teller, Tallman identifies several factors that influence Coffil's selection of tales and his skill as a performer. One of these is his ability to select a repertoire through a process that reflects his "aesthetic response to the broader tradition" (1974, 122). Coffil considered all the tales he had heard and chose certain ones to tell based on his understanding of the communities' traditional assessment of good stories, and he could create new stories based on the traditional principles he learned from other stories. The performer also showed the ability to fit a story with the context; that is, he knew which story to tell when, based on the storytelling setting, on comments that others made, or on listeners' responses to his stories. Tallman asserts that a good storyteller in this context is one who helps the listener visualize moments in the story, but perhaps more importantly, he suggests that "in order to accomplish this, the performer must have a vivid picture in his mind to tell or describe." Coffil told Tallman that someone might say something that triggered his imagination, "'and then I'll picture it, and then I'll tell it" (127). This ability to create images is especially important when telling tall tales, because they are grounded in realism. Thus, if a tale is told as personal experience, set in the real world, its impact depends on the ability of listeners to imagine the incongruous details that help them recognize the fantastic, "untrue" elements of the tale (128).

From his assessment of Coffil's particular aesthetic sense as a performer, Tallman distinguishes some characteristics of the folk narrative aesthetic, which, he says, generally have to do with context, the type (genre) of folklore being performed, the explicitness of the aesthetic (as defined and expressed by the performer), and the degree of skill the community perceives in the performer (which Tallman calls "professionalism"; 122). Tallman's work with Bob Coffil underscores the importance of the performer in understanding, embodying, and articulating the aesthetic that grows out of the community. In a related analysis, Kenneth Goldstein emphasizes the need to consult with performers about their own criteria for defining a skillful performer (1991). He discusses the concept of "bigness" as a way the folk song performers he talked with evaluate a "good" folk song and a "good" performer. Bigness, as the singers describe it, refers to the size of the performer's repertoire—that is, how many songs the singer knows, how lengthy the songs are, how complete the lyrics are, and the forcefulness and expressive qualities of the performer's voice (168).

Obviously, the specific aesthetic criteria Tallman and Goldstein gathered from the performers they worked with may not necessarily apply to all genres or in all cultures or folk groups, but their approaches illustrate a framework for talking about aesthetic responses within a particular community. Because each group may have its own definition of what makes a performer or performance good, we should ask artists, performers, and audiences what criteria they use to evaluate the quality of their community's artistic expression, in order to enrich our interpretation.

Practicality

One distinguishing feature of some folklore texts is that they often (but not always) have a practical role in the community. In fact, as Gerald Pocius points out, art has often been defined as that which is not practical, and this has confused the idea of aesthetics, especially as applied to the study of folklore. Pocius explains, with reference to William Bascom, that "historically, the issue of whether items were useful or artistic was central to the concept of what constituted art. What was considered art was limited to those things 'with elaboration beyond point of utility'" (1995, 420). Since folklore, in many cases, combines the utilitarian and the artistic, the fine art concepts of aesthetics are not always applicable to the evaluation of folklore. Quilts, pots, bowls, pitchers, and baskets all perform obvious practical functions. A pitcher may be pretty to look at, but if it can't hold water, it isn't a very good pitcher. Sometimes, then, one important element in folk art is that it may have to be able to perform its job well. That practical aspect of the folk aesthetic can be considered along with the artistic merits of the piece.

Seeing practicality as a feature of folklore may be contested because it can't be applied in all cases. Woodcarvings in the form of animal shapes or intricate puzzles, for example, are often created for the enjoyment of creating them and for exhibiting an artist's skill or creativity. They aren't utilitarian objects and, in that sense, come closer to fitting the "art for art's sake" definition. And what about songs, stories, verbal folklore—do they have practical applications or uses? Not on the surface, perhaps, although many folklorists would say verbal lore may have certain purposes—to instruct or describe certain types of traditional behavior, for example. (Keep in mind, too, that even in the case of these more purely artistic items, elements of consensus, traditionality, and skill are evident.) Practicality is not a feature of *all* types of folklore, but it can be a useful way to understand how *some* kinds of folklore operate in a community, what makes folklore meaningful to the community in which it is expressed, and how it is different from mainstream forms of art.

The Nature of Aesthetic Response

Even with these very loose parameters of consensus, traditionality, skill, and practicality to guide us in considering evaluations of the art in folklore, it is clear that there is no single set of standards or characteristics that can be applied to all examples of a particular genre, and certainly not from the outside. What's more, as we have seen, standards differ from group to group and from performer to performer.

Diane E. Goldstein addresses these issues in her evaluation of testimony narratives based on her fieldwork in an American evangelical church (1995,

31). She identifies the significant characteristics that church members use to evaluate the competence and power of a particular narrative performance. She describes an aesthetic of storytelling for this group in this context that she calls a "competence continuum," which acknowledges a "complex system of variables" (32). The two ends of this continuum are marked by simple participation at one end and a moving spiritual impact on congregation members at the other end. In the middle lie "the rules and norms for genre performance which include the constraints and aesthetics of particular genres and events." These would include familiar elements of narrative and linguistic performance, such as the use of metaphor, rhythm, and other verbal devices. There is one higher category of competence, but it is reserved as beyond judgment: "speech which is believed to be directly inspired by God" (35).

In the church Goldstein studied, members call this kind of narrative expression *sharing*. According to Goldstein, sharing "is seen as an attitude, an experience, an ethic and aesthetic, and ultimately as the reason for all encounters . . . analogous to a sacrament" (1995, 32). Church members value the act of sharing more than they value a well-crafted performance. In this instance, the group's aesthetic has to do with belief and how effectively the narrative communicates spiritual experience. If the narrative doesn't guide listeners to powerful religious experience, it isn't as highly valued, regardless of how well it might fit an outsider concept of an effectively performed story.

Goldstein's example illustrates the connection in folklore between communication and artistic expression and shows the relative nature of art. The notion of relativity extends beyond the fairly simple understanding that what one group considers art may not be considered art by another group, although that is certainly part of the definition. Relativity in this case also relates to the definition of what art is and how it is defined in terms of aesthetic response. As Jones reminds us, our notion of art can encompass the everyday, as long as the aesthetic impulse is evident in viewers and audiences. If art is something we have an aesthetic response to, then anything we respond to aesthetically contains, by definition, artistic qualities.

The members of the evangelical church in Goldstein's study find art in— that is, they respond aesthetically to—the religious testimonies of their fellow members. As Goldstein puts it, the group determines competence "based on the congregation's knowledge of the individual speaker, the speaker's past and potential performances, indications of the grace of God in emergent performance, and perceived motives of narration" (1995, 32). Goldstein explains that members of the congregation know each other well and know how frequently individuals share their experiences and how actively they participate in the life of the church and community. They value a story by an experienced person, even if it is told clumsily, more than a story by a newer or less experienced person who tells a story with skill. Part of the group's evaluation of the art of spiritual sharing has to do with whether or not it communicates spiritual experience. In this sense, these verbal narratives have a practical application for church members: to enrich their connection to God. The response is to the teller as well as to the story.

So where does all this leave us in understanding the evaluation of goodness or effectiveness in folklore? Since we can't rely on a single, overarching standard, we need to look at texts and the group, as well as at the nature of aesthetics, for answers. Michael Owen Jones proposes that *the aesthetic* denotes "a system of philosophical discourse and articulated principles regarding form." In other words, aesthetics involves an understood set of standards and a way of talking about those standards as they relate to a text or performance. Aesthetics, not necessarily the artistic object, Jones says, "is the subject for consideration" (1987, 170). Jones approaches aesthetics in terms of *responses*—that is, the ways audiences and viewers react when they encounter a created object, text, or performance. He provides several useful terms that describe the nature of aesthetics:

- aesthetic attitude
- aesthetic response
- aesthetic judgment
- taste

Jones writes that an *aesthetic attitude* is a way in which people respond to or are willing to be affected by something artistic. In other words, when we encounter something artistic, we are willing and prepared to perceive it as having artistic qualities and to respond in some way. The concept of *aesthetic response* is closest to Glassie's suggestion that the aesthetic "engages the senses" (1992, 269). Jones reminds us that these responses can be either positive or negative. Either will elicit a reaction comprising an "intellectual state and physiological condition" (1987, 172) not expressed in relation to a formal *system* of criteria—the ohhh-ahhh/ugh-yuck reaction we talked about earlier. More sophisticated than aesthetic *response* is aesthetic *judgment*. Jones suggests judgment is evaluative, derived from one's response, and is actually the expression of that response. When we judge art, we think about how and why we respond and what in the work has led us to that response. As Bauman suggests, audiences judge performances based on the competence and skill of performers (1984). Skill and competence depend, in part, on how well the performer knows the conventions and expectations of the audience, in terms of what makes a good performance (11). The audience members' aesthetic reaction, then, grows out of their willingness to be affected by art, their heightened experience of that art, and their judgment of the work based on their group's criteria.

Underlying aesthetic reactions, Jones argues, is *taste*. We all recognize that taste is a major influence on one's response to a creative text. "I may not know art, but I know what I like" is a phrase people often use in prefacing their responses to a piece of art or music, the type of creative text most people readily judge. Those who have a response based on more than taste are often assumed to be critics or experts. Scholars are not immune to this elitist perception and often refer to taste as though it is a lesser form of critique. Jones cites two authors, James West and Dan Crowley, whose work tells us that "the matter of *taste* is crucial to understanding the nature of aesthetic response and aesthetic judgment. As such, taste should be the primary concern in discussions of *aesthetics*" (1987, 173).

Simply put, taste is about what we like and what we don't like. In some small towns and suburbs, for instance, lawn art is very popular. Some residents place life-size concrete or plastic geese on their porches or front lawns, and often they dress these geese in elaborate costumes, depending on the seasons or holidays. Some may be dressed in the uniforms of homeowners' favorite sports teams. Neighbors and commuters passing through the neighborhoods may look forward to the season when the baby geese begin to carry their schoolbooks and wear rain slickers and boots. These sculptures and their decorative clothing may not suit the taste of everyone in the neighborhood, and some neighbors may disapprove of them. But those who display the geese see them as artistic embellishments to their property and enjoy sharing ideas and patterns for goose accessories.

Personal preferences are obviously less global than aesthetics, but they affect individual expressions of aesthetic response and judgment. Therefore, it is important for folklorists to consider these personal expressions as part of their study of folklore. "What is required," Jones says, "and what all of us possess as a fundamental feature of our humanity, is a feeling for form affected by multiple experiences and expressed in various ways" (1987, 175). Jones urges us to see that the "high art" idea of *the aesthetic* is only one piece of the picture and that folklorists should concentrate on studying the "people factor" of aesthetic attitude, response, and judgment. Perceiving aesthetic quality is an activity that audiences and artists perform together. Basically, aesthetics reside in *us*.

171

Photo by Evan Schieber.

Costumed concrete goose.

Personal Narrative in Performance

It might be difficult to imagine that an ordinary person's ordinary story of his or her experiences might be deemed worthy of study. However, this type of story—a *personal narrative*—is the epitome of folklore in that it is such an everyday, human mode of expression yet is still a creative manifestation of one's

172

values, beliefs, and attitudes. Personal narratives are framed and performed artistic expressions, with both a recognizable structure of the *performance* and sometimes a familiar structure in the *narrative* itself.

Personal narratives surface during everyday conversations as well as in more distinct storytelling sessions, and their emergence is highly dependent on the context recognized by both the storyteller and audience. Listeners recognize storytelling performances as a mode of entertainment or communication; there is a "storytelling tradition" (Stahl 1977, 18). In addition to knowing that people tell stories, members of an audience recognize the performance markers that indicate or *frame* a story. When someone turns to you and says, "One time when . . . ," you know that a story is coming. Such opening markers are part of a typical performance by a storyteller, whether that teller is presenting a personal narrative or a narrative or legend that belongs to a larger cultural repertoire. Stahl suggests that "the tall tale or lie in particular could not be understood without the personal narrative tradition as a frame of reference" (18). In other words, without our familiarity with the markers that set up a personal story, a joke or tall tale begun in a similar fashion would not be effective. Part of the fun of these kinds of verbal performances is that they play with our expectations. We expect a personal narrative to follow such natural or conversational story openers, but the obviously fictional twists clue us into the fact that the teller is doing something different. Our awareness of how a personal experience narrative is set up is what allows us to understand the surprise and get the joke.

Not only does someone telling a story know how to cue the listening audience, a performer is frequently aware of *when* to tell a story and *which* story to tell. A person's awareness of when it is appropriate to share narratives may indicate membership in a group. An effective personal narrative shows a teller's awareness of performance structure and narrative structure and invites evaluation from its audience. The audience plays its part by evaluating the performance based in part on awareness of this appropriate time and content. The aesthetic response or evaluation allows us to see the appropriateness of the performance context. More simply, the audience's response to the story and the teller's own awareness of how well it fits the situation are part of the storytelling performance. Whether the evaluation is overtly expressed by those listening to the narrative or covertly conveyed as a cultural meaning or significance that the performer may be aware of, a story's "traditional attitude," according to Stahl's discussion of personal narratives, is an important feature (1977, 20).

The context in which a personal narrative is shared is an important element of its place in a group's folklore, and its structure is important, too. A personal narrative may have a clear and satisfying narrative structure that includes the same type of arc that appears in more literary types of narratives: a beginning, middle, and end; defined characters; and a story that builds to a climax and resolution. In addition to the narrative itself possessing a clear structure, the performance will include markers that frame it as both opened and closed.

A narrative *performance* can be traditional, and the narrative itself may also be traditional because of its content. Stories can express group and individual identity, one feature that establishes the traditionality of this kind of text. Individuals' beliefs and knowledge are affected by the people within their social and familial groups, so their stories often reflect these group attitudes. The collective nature of the attitudes and values illustrated in an individual's stories helps place the stories in a particular group's tradition. In other words, concepts important to the group are often expressed in personal narratives. An individual story may also become, over time, a part of its teller's own repertoire. Sandra Stahl explains that a narrative becomes part of a particular teller's repertoire because it reflects an attitude or concept significant to the teller; it doesn't simply relate to a single moment's conversation (1977, 24). Stories that express a teller's values and attitudes become part of an individual tradition of storytelling, emerging in different situations in which a teller can communicate by performing his or her narrative.

Personal narratives are unique in that they frequently arise within conversations, and this conversational setting creates a different type of evaluation. When these narratives appear as part of conversations, people often feel free to interject comments and interact with the text and performer. Evaluation of the whole performance depends on the group's aesthetic sense and the performer's understanding and expression of the group's aesthetics. The narrative structure and evaluative interjections must successfully follow the pattern, themes, and flow of a conversation. For example, someone tells a story about her bad day, beginning with losing her car in a crowded parking garage at a downtown shopping center. One listener might express sympathy by adding, "Oh, yeah! That mall parking lot is just so confusing." Another might tell a story about a time when she lost her car, and another might offer helpful hints about how to avoid losing a car in the parking lot in the future. Someone might even say, "A friend of a friend of mine had an even scarier experience than that. She got lost in a parking lot at Christmastime . . ." and then launch into a contemporary legend. This chorus of responses indicates the appropriateness of the original narrative. Such conversational evaluation is part of a personal narrative performance.

Personal narratives are part of group traditions and express traditional group attitudes. Unlike other types of narratives that are primarily characterized by traditional storylines, plots, and characters, the identifying elements within narratives of personal experience are found in the attitudes and concepts addressed in the story (Stahl 1977, 14). The group in the above example is taking part in a recognizable activity in which friends vent about lousy days or explain their bad moods by telling stories about their frustrations, big or small. Sometimes one person is the main teller and others pitch in with comments and support, perhaps even stories of their own. This activity is traditional for many groups, particularly friendship groups. As the telling of the bad day narratives continues, performers and listeners share their connections to each other through their stories, express common experiences that solidify their groupness, and express attitudes about those experiences: malls can be scary, Christmas shopping is annoying, and it's important to have friends to vent to. In this case, the activity of sitting around and sharing stories is valued by the group, and whatever attitudes the group expresses about the events of their lives are also significant.

The narrative itself, the storytelling context, community aesthetics, and the message communicated by the narrative are factors that help us see personal narratives as folklore. It is in the "components of the performance rather than in the stories themselves" (Stahl 1977, 17) that the personal narrative tradition is determined.

Example: A Personal Narrative Emerges

The following transcription of a personal narrative performance provides a detailed illustration of emergent narrative, context, and audience and teller interaction as a folklorist might interpret it. This discussion considers an actual recorded event and uses a more complex applied approach to understanding the performance of personal narrative in its context.

First, we need to understand the physical setting, part of the immediate situation of the performance context. The performance took place at the Washington, Pennsylvania, home of Charlie and Jerry Stephens, both in their sixties at the time. Seated at the kitchen table were Charlie and Jerry and their daughter Martine, a folklorist who had asked her parents about their experiences as members of a coal-mining family. Here is an excerpt from the transcript of their conversation, in which Charlie tells a story about a workday experience that occurred in the coal mine when he was much younger:[41]

Jerry: The closest group of workers that ever were, were the ones that were in the mine.

175

Charlie: (*interrupting, speaking quickly, with excitement*) Hey, Jerry, how about the time—

Jerry: (*talking over him*)—they'd stick together. They depended on each other for their safety, and they are like, uh, probably the closest group of workers I can think of, outside of, maybe, men in war.

Charlie: There are things . . . like you say . . . significant. (*glances at his wife, chuckles*) I didn't tell Jerry a lot of this. (*slight pause*) This happened. There are guys living could jump me for telling this. Dick Johnson was a—(*to Jerry*) remember him?—a great big overgrown guy, Jer?

Jerry: (*nods*) Yes, I do.

Charlie: He was always picking and stuff and I got tired of it—

Martine: (*interrupting*) He was always what?

Charlie: He was always just insulting you like, you know? He'd come up behind you and go like this (*hits the back of his head with the open palm of his right hand*)—on the back of your head. And I told him, I said, "Don't do that no more." So he done that one day, and man, I hit him and he went down—

Martine: Oh no!

Charlie: And Pete Chunko, Andy Gaynor, Jim Thomas, Steve Thomas, and I think Hal was there (*Jerry and Martine Chuckle.* [*Hal was Charlie's brother-in-law*])—And [Dick] jumped up, and I was ready for him. He knew not to come at me. He was bleeding. He said (*in a loud, angry tone*) "I'm gonna have you arrested! I'm gonna do this! How about that, Pete?" (*in a normal tone*) And I'll never forget (*laughs*), Pete Chunko said (*in a sing-song tone*), "What are you talking about? I didn't see anything happen." (*Jerry and Martine laugh*) "How about you?" Andy Gaynor said (*in an exaggerated tone of false concern*) "What the hell did you do to yourself, Dick? You're bleeding." (*chuckles*) And old Hal said, (*in a menacing, more serious tone*) "What are you trying to do to my brother-in-law?" (*pauses, then chuckles, then all three laugh*)

The italicized notes within the transcript indicate aspects of the performance that would not be apparent to those who had not been present. It is important to know some of the performance characteristics in order to "get" the situation in the story. For example, when Charlie imitates the voices of the others, he uses

176

tones of voice that suggest how insincere they were, which makes it clear to the listeners that the other coal miners all conspired to protect Charlie by pretending they didn't see him hit Dick.

We can also consider the framing signals that mark the performance within its conversational setting. The teller begins by saying, "This happened. There are guys living that could jump me for telling this." This opening may be Charlie's particular way of marking his tale, but it is clearly an announcement of his intention to tell a story, and it does sound to the listener like a familiar announcement that a narrated event will follow. His short narrative ends with a comment from a character, and it is the tone of Charlie's voice (stern and somewhat menacing, a shift from his earlier tone), followed quickly by his own laughter, that signals the end. The listeners are clearly aware the tale has ended (what more could be said?—all the characters have spoken, and the teller himself is laughing at his own story), and their laughter signals their involvement in bringing the story to its close. We know that this is a performance, because it is clearly framed and structured.

It is also important to understand the relationship between those present to understand their interaction—husband and wife confirm shared experience, and the family connections also help us understand the story's situation. (Hal, for example, was Charlie's brother-in-law, a notorious hell-raiser, who appeared in many family anecdotes.) The fact that the teller, the listeners, and the folklorist are all family members and that family members are also part of the narrated event make this as much a family story as an occupational narrative, and so the story could be analyzed within both contexts. The daughter's triple role as a family member, listener, and folklorist may have an impact on the performance—and on her—and certainly on its interpretation. In this context, reflexive analysis is crucial in order for the folklorist to be clear about any biases, special or hidden knowledge, or preconceived assumptions about meanings or significance that could influence her analysis, even unwittingly.

A significant part of this performance is the intersection of the occupational and family contexts. As a member of this family, the folklorist had heard many stories about incidents in the coal mine and at first assumed that Charlie's narrated event described the closing of the ranks by members of the group against an outsider who did not conform to the group's unspoken rules of conduct. But rather than assume she knew everything the story meant to the tellers and listeners, she asked questions about the character of Dick Johnson and learned that he was perceived as both an annoyance and a danger to his crew. While the outsider interpretation may have had relevance on one level, the performer *and* the performance event suggested another reason for telling the story as well as a more complex level of meaning for the events recounted within the narrative. As they talked about the story and the incident, Charlie explained that "guys like that [like Dick Johnson] got on your nerves, [so] you couldn't concentrate." Since underground coal mining involves heavy machinery and hard physical labor in an atmosphere of potentially explosive gases, any behavior that distracted workers from their jobs could result in serious, even fatal, accidents. Furthermore, during the conversation, Charlie's story follows a comment from his wife that the men in the mine "depended on each other for their safety." The performer's comments and the sequence of events in the physical performance context suggest that Charlie and his work crew valued safe behavior so much that they chose to ignore, even cover up, Charlie's aggressive act toward Dick. In that occupational context, we might interpret Charlie as a protector who kept the crew from potential harm.

In addition to interpreting the possible meaning of narrated and narrative events, we can evaluate the skill of the storyteller and the effectiveness of the performance—its creative, artistic, or aesthetic dimension. This performance is effective because it logically follows a point made in the conversation, it has a satisfying (if simple) narrative structure, and it pleases the audience. We noted before that the story follows a comment in the conversation about mine safety, which opens up the narrative space in which Charlie tells a story about maintaining safe behavior. Those listening appear to express approval of the tale as it goes on and at the end with laughter or expressions of surprise and involvement ("Oh, no!"). Their reactions could indicate they found the way Charlie handled the situation made a successful narrative because he administered a kind of poetic justice that was narratively appropriate. In other words, we usually expect villains in stories to get the punishment they deserve and appreciate it when they do; this teller fulfills that expectation, so the listeners find the story satisfying. The teller also amuses the audience by mimicking voices and emphasizing the exaggerated way the characters defend him while they mock Dick. Charlie's act works within the narrated event of the story and the narrative event of the performance as well as in the larger context of the occupational group.

Conclusion

The focus on performance in folklore allows us to locate artistic expressions within the groups that create and use them. It shifts us away from a limited examination of fixed, static, flat objects and encourages our attention to the lively communication that takes place through the sharing of folklore. In performance, we can describe activities that include dynamic changes and allow traditions to emerge. It enables us to understand ourselves as observers and participants, as part of the process of creating communicative art and making meaning from it. Most of all, studying performance helps us see people as an integral part of the folklore they share.

CHAPTER 6

Approaches to Interpreting Folklore

$\mathcal{A}$s we have emphasized, folklore communicates: it is an ongoing process of expressing information and beliefs within folk groups. As folklorists, we examine the verbal, customary, and material texts of folk groups to discover why and how they are important to the people sharing them. In the earlier days of the discipline, scholars began to seek deeper ways to interpret, rather than simply collect and describe, folklore. Our understanding of groups, tradition, ritual, performance, and the whole broad concept of text that underpins our discussions in this book grew from those deeper explorations.

As the discipline grew and the kinds of texts folklorists studied broadened, scholars developed theoretical and analytical frameworks that reflected prevailing concerns and interests. Many theoretical and analytical frameworks exist, and as with other aspects of the history and study of folklore, interpretive approaches may overlap and change in line with our ongoing explorations in the field. Some of these approaches have become limiting in that they reduced the potential interpretations of folklore to narrow, essential meanings. Current scholarship involves a multifaceted approach that draws on past theories in innovative, dynamic ways but also considers multiple levels of understanding and recognition of the interplay of texts, groups, performances, contexts, society, and culture. Folklorists may explore dimensions of function, structure, psychological or sociological influences, and theories related to gender, race, social position, and power.

To continue to develop your understanding of the history of the field and to provide a map of the path folklorists have traveled, we offer here a fairly detailed overview of several approaches taken by scholars in the last century and a half of folklore study. We'll discuss how folklorists have applied such approaches and look at ways in which they have contributed to and continue to inform the study of folklore.[42]

Functions: Purposes, Roles, and Meanings

Folklorists have always been interested in understanding meanings of folklore texts, and in the earlier days of folklore study, that meant looking at how the folklore *functioned* within the community of which it was a part. This approach was valuable in that it was one of the first to firmly attach interpretation of folklore to the very people who were using it to express their beliefs and values. One of the early proponents of functionalism was William R. Bascom, who identified what he called the "four functions of folklore" (1965). The four functions Bascom suggests folklore provides—informally teaching cultural attitudes (often to younger group members); escaping accepted limitations of our culture; maintaining cultural identity; and validating existing cultural norms—essentially boil down to one function, as Bascom himself claims: "Folklore is an important mechanism for maintaining the stability of culture" (1965, 298).

Bascom's approach established a framework to help folklorists consider the meaning of folklore and make sense of how folk groups employ it and what it might mean to them. It was a jumping-off point for people to think more concretely about what folklore does and means, rather than what it is. One value of Bascom's approach is that it does consider the folk group and acknowledges that folklore has meaning within the group. His approach looks at folklore as a way of communicating values and information among members of the group. This early, functionalist approach appealed to folklorists at the time. Many of them picked up on the work of anthropologists such as Bronislaw Malinowski and A. R. Radcliffe-Brown who looked at culture and society as an organic whole. Folklorists found this holistic model appealing because it suggested the natural or organic connection between people and their expressive culture.

But major problems with this organic view emerged as folklorists began to use it in more and more contexts and to analyze more kinds of performances. It became clear the functionalist approach was just too broad. Bascom claimed folklore acted as a mechanism to maintain cultural stability. Yet, if we assume that folklore only serves to reinforce the norm, there is no room for it to accommodate changes in beliefs and attitudes or for new forms of folklore to emerge. One obvious problem is that Bascom's system ignores "the way folklore questions, critiques, protests, and sometimes undermines stability" (Mullen 2003). For example, as we mentioned before, tall tales allow tellers to express humor

181

and play with the idea of deceitfulness in order to entertain and challenge listeners. As another example, children's parodies of well-known Christmas carols may annoy adults and express children's growing comprehension of appropriate and inappropriate language and behavior. The songs allow children to be a little rebellious and play with the traditional "sweetness and light" of the holiday season. If we assume folklore always maintains the stability of culture, we can miss the challenges to stability some folklore performances can present.

Reducing the analysis to one overarching function implies, further, that folklore always means the same thing to a folk group, no matter when or where it occurs, and all genres of folklore function in the same ways across entire cultures. That implies, for example, that superstitions are always about controlling the environment, cause and effect, or attempting to escape fate; or folktales always allow performers and audiences to escape from their mundane lives and teach important cultural values. We have come to realize that this kind of analysis of function presumes to provide a single, overarching interpretation of what folklore *means* and assumes that all similar texts function the same way in every group. And, of course, if the function does not change, that implies the group does not change. In addition to assuming that all groups work in the same way, functionalist interpretation implies that groups stay the same across time and changes in membership. The functional approach is always conservative; the functions themselves remain static and conservative. Functional analysis, then, is ahistorical, suggesting that the text has always been and always will be used or performed for the same reasons *regardless* of context. For instance, Patrick B. Mullen, in his work with Texas Gulf fishermen in the 1960s and 1970s, asserted that the fishermen's belief behaviors and expressions (or "superstitions") were primarily a means to predict and/or control the risks involved in their work ([1978] 1988). Later, Bonnie Blair O'Connor (1995) pointed out that the approach Mullen and others used was problematic because it reduced the complex systems of belief behaviors to a single purpose or function.[43]

Another problem with a focus on function is that it reinforces the elitist notion that the educated, trained folklorist understands the meanings of a group's folklore better than the members of the folk group (O'Connor 1995, 41–44). A functionalist framework requires us to make meaning of folklore, so if there's only one meaning, someone has to decide what that one meaning is. Because folklorists sometimes assumed they knew the meaning of everyone else's folklore, the practice of seeking a single meaning or function maintained the old us/them dichotomy, which lent itself to a view of the folk as uneducated and their culture as unsophisticated. The reasons for this attitude are rooted in the folklorists' desire to find a way to make folklore make sense in all situations.

Realizing that any search for a single meaning could become biased and ethnocentric led to an understanding that *any* approach that gave the folklorist total power over making or interpreting meaning was problematic. More recent approaches have incorporated *reflexive* and *reciprocal* dimensions of analysis and recognized folklorists as part of an *interpretive partnership* with their consultants. When folklorists first began using the functional approach, their interpretations were considered to answer definitively the question of what a particular kind of folklore means for the folk. It is still possible for us to consider what a text means within a folk group, as long as we do not look to a single interpretation of that text as the *only* way to understand its value *or* assume that its meaning is the same within different groups. The more generic definition of function—the role or purpose something or someone plays in a given setting—is a reasonable way to consider this interpretive strategy. Looking at an item from this perspective allows us to explore what the object, verbal expression, or practice communicates or signifies among the varying contexts in which it occurs within a group.

Bascom and other proponents of functionalism broadened our understanding of the idea that people communicate meaningfully through folklore. Analyzing the limitations of the functionalist approach helped us understand that meanings of texts depend on what a particular group of people does with a specific item of lore in a specific situation. It's always about what's happening in the group and the context. We can't isolate folklore meanings from folk groups just as we can't isolate folklore itself from people.

Example: Multiple Meanings in Context

Timothy Correll and Patrick Polk's study of "muffler men"—sculptures of people or animals created by muffler mechanics out of used auto parts—shows how an item's function can be meaningful in different ways, not only within a single group but also to more than one group (2000). Muffler men are material texts significant to the occupational culture of many muffler mechanics. Within this occupational folk group, the sculptures hold different meanings, depending on the specific mechanics creating and displaying them. For some mechanics, building the sculptures allows them the opportunity to be creative, to express an ability to see things artistically while still utilizing the welding and mechanical skills necessary to their jobs. For other mechanics, building (or taking part in building) a sculpture serves as a rite of passage, indicating a mechanic's membership in a group of skilled tradesmen or perhaps even his status as an employee at a particular shop. In still other cases, mechanics build these sculptures once they open their own shops or begin work at an independently owned shop (as

183

opposed to corporate shops). Other independents feel the sculptures look unprofessional (Correll and Polk 2000, 10). Many of these interpretations—and similar ones—relate to the mechanics' sense of occupational identity.

The sculptures are also significant to the public that lives in the neighborhood or city in which the sculptures are located. Some community members enjoy them and use them as identifiers; they become local landmarks, a unique way of recognizing or identifying a location within a certain neighborhood. Community members might use the muffler sculptures when they are giving directions, for example—turn left at the corner with the muffler man—and they "are frequently conceived of as intimate neighborhood fixtures." More importantly, they are "used to formulate and express notions of community and locale" (Correll and Polk 2000, 83).

Between mechanics and the public, muffler men often create a communicative bridge. The statues may have been designed as a form of advertisement, to draw attention to a shop's presence, but they are likely to grow into members of the community. Neighborhood residents may take ownership of the sculptures, as happened when one mechanic/artist "not only came up with a new idea for a sculpture, but he also began to solicit suggestions for additional works that would be particularly meaningful to members of his audience" (Correll and Polk 2000, 85). In this particular instance, a mechanic constructed a snake of muffler parts and placed it in front of his shop. Two neighborhood girls stopped to look at the sculpture, and one mimed a snake charmer. Drawing on the girl's interaction with the snake, the mechanic decided to sculpt a snake charmer. The next time he saw the girl, he asked her for suggestions for another sculpture; she suggested he make a rabbit, so he did (85). Correll and Polk point out that these "statues placed outside automotive repair shops may take on a multiplicity of meanings based upon any number of idiosyncratic factors associated with the processes of design, construction, and display" (95). Their work demonstrates that muffler men have *many* functions, not one single meaning that fits in every context.

Structure: Patterns, Themes, and Formal Relationships

Sometimes folklorists are intrigued by the ways texts relate to each other, or they might examine the parts of texts or performances in order to understand them fully. Consider, for instance, structure in the following story:

There once was a beautiful young girl who was mistreated by an evil, magical woman. The evil woman cast a dreadful spell upon the girl, and she fell into a long

184

deathlike sleep. One day, a handsome prince came along, saw the sleeping girl, and was so enchanted by her beauty that he kissed her. The girl woke up, married the prince, and they lived happily ever after.

Is this the story of Sleeping Beauty? Snow White? With a little tweaking, could this be the story of Cinderella? Maybe Rapunzel? How many other stories do you know that have characters like a beautiful girl, an evil female villain (usually a stepmother, queen, fairy, or witch), and a handsome prince, and how often does the villain try to harm the girl before the prince rescues her?

We recognize these tales because, yes, we have heard them many times (or have seen the popular movie versions), but also because the plots and characters are familiar and stable. We recognize the stories' *structure*. Structure is more than the plot; it includes the characters, the actions they perform, places, names, and repeated words and phrases—any basic elements that make the story recognizable. By focusing on structure, we can do more than describe one story; as F. A. de Caro explains, this kind of analysis attempts to identify the essential characteristics in every individual example within a given genre. He says that a "structuralist analysis should reveal a basic, underlying pattern which accounts for all the parts of the whole and how they relate to each other in forming the whole" (1986, 177–78).

This approach, while primarily applied to stories, works in many other genres, too. Among the most widely shared structure-dependent verbal expressions are jokes and riddles. Riddles are usually short verbal forms that ask or imply a question or puzzle that must be answered or solved. Robert Georges and Alan Dundes have pointed out that many riddles begin with a "descriptive element" that consists of a topic, or object described, and a comment, which gives more information about the topic (1963, 113). So, for example, in the riddle "It goes on four legs in the morning, two in the afternoon, and three in the evening," the topic is "it" (the thing that goes on different numbers of legs) and the comment includes those details that describe "it": the number of legs and the time of day. The topic and comment imply that "it" remains the same while the other things change. The answer, "a man," defines what "it" is. We then see the metaphors at the heart of the riddle: a baby crawls on all fours, an adult in the prime of life walks on two legs, and an elderly person uses (or may use) a cane. To "go" means to walk; the implied legs are sometimes literal legs but also mean hands, knees, and a cane; and the times of day are metaphors for periods of life.

Not all riddles fit this pattern. Others offer a conundrum, in which something possesses opposite, apparently paradoxical, characteristics: What has eyes but cannot see (a potato)? What gets wet as it dries (a towel)? The answers depend on metaphor and wordplay (in this case, puns and idioms) to make sense: *eyes* can have more than one meaning; the word *dry* can have the sense of "dry out" (become dry) or "dry off" (make something else dry). These kinds of structural classifications provide one way of describing folklore and of understanding what makes examples of folklore work the way they do.

Regardless of the exact form, many jokes and riddles rely on structure to work. If we don't understand that the structure of a conundrum, for example, demands that we think about different meanings or uses for words, we won't be able to participate in the game. To illustrate further, here's a familiar joke that demonstrates very clearly the power of structure:

Knock-knock.
Who's there?
Boo.
Boo who?
Aww, don't cry, it's just a joke!

The first line of a knock-knock joke always sets up a strict pattern of reply and response. The "knockee" (the person being set up by the knock-knock line) is obligated when he or she hears those words to ask "who's there?" if the joke performance is to continue. What follows is always a statement from the "knocker" (the person who started the joke), which is then questioned again in the "——— who?" line and revealed in the joke's final line as a pun, a misdirection, or some other verbal trick. Children, when learning about this kind of joke, get the structure down pretty easily. When someone says "knock knock," they readily respond "who's there?" and proceed to ask and answer questions in exactly the right order. It's harder for them to understand until they have developed more sophisticated cognitive skills that the last line has to play with a misunderstanding or verbal trick to resolve the mystery of who or what is knocking on the imaginary door. But even until they get the humor part, they quite happily repeat absurd, unfunny knock-knock jokes with perfectly organized structural patterns.

It doesn't take long for us to get the fairly broad puns and tricks knock-knock jokes involve, and once we put the elements of structure and wordplay together, the form is remarkably flexible. Knock-knock jokes work in various permutations and on many levels, mainly because they have very clear repeated structures, regardless of the content. In fact, playing with the structure itself is the foundation of the humor in some knock-knock jokes. For instance:

Knock-knock.
Who's there?
Banana.

Banana who?
Knock-knock.
Who's there?
Banana.
Banana who?
Knock-knock.
Who's there?
Orange.
Orange who?
Orange you glad I didn't say banana?

This joke typically delights children who have recently learned the structure of the knock-knock joke, understand verbal puns and sound-alikes, and can anticipate an unexpected, but structurally satisfying, outcome. The success of this joke depends on how familiar both participants are with the structure of this type of joke. The knockee must recognize after the second knock-knock that a game is afoot and that the knocker is playing with structure and our expectations about what should come next. The knockee's willingness to continue past the second knock-knock depends on his or her understanding of another element of knock-knock structure: the surprise or trick in the punch line. The success of the performance relies on the basic road map that structure provides, even if the exact route is unfamiliar.

A more sophisticated level of structural play occurs in one knock-knock joke that relies on the ability of the knockee to complete an entire knock-knock structure in his or her head, and more importantly, on the willingness of the knockee to play along:

Would you like to hear a new knock-knock joke?
Sure!
Okay. You start.

Like jokes and riddles, as we mentioned earlier, stories often contain recognizable structural patters. Early scholars studied the structure of myth, the fundamental stories shared within a culture that describe how the universe and things within it came to be created and how they operate. *Myths* are usually presented as existing outside time or before our own history, are usually believed to be true within the group they belong to, and may even be considered sacred. They typically present broad summaries of characters' actions within a set plot that defines a particular event. *Tales,* on the other hand, usually focus on a single story that does not obviously relate to big, universal themes and are generally understood to be fiction. In other words, the tale of Red Riding Hood is (on the surface, anyway) the story of one girl's encounter with an evil villain; it is not about how the gods (or other beings) came to introduce evil into the world, as in the Greek myth about Pandora. Both may reveal something about the nature of evil and how humans face it, but they do it on a different scale. Still, the similarities in structure prompted interest in the relationships between myths and tales.

The analysis of structure gave scholars a concrete way to talk about how stories are organically related to one another and to other narrative genres. In classifying verbal texts in *The Morphology of the Folktale* (1968), Vladimir Propp presented a system of describing tales according to patterns of story events, a "morphology" (a term borrowed from biology that means a study of the form and structure of an organism, and is applied to the study of language) that described the organic nature of tale structure. Propp proposed an approach based on the recognition that certain kinds of folktales (referred to as *Märchen*—a German term that means, loosely, "fairy story") shared remarkably similar internal features. In most of these stories, a young character must overcome hardship, has an adventure (or adventures), is helped and/or hindered by magical or supernatural beings, and eventually triumphs in the end. Frequently, these heroes and heroines leave home and go on journeys or quests that test their intelligence, wit, and physical stamina. Often they return home transformed by magic, marriage, or plain old experience. Many of these themes had been identified by other scholars and classified in an index to the elements and motifs (recurrent elements like events, characters, scenes, and objects) that appeared repeatedly in tales from around the world.[44] Propp's approach brought the thematic elements together with an examination of the ways those elements fit into one coherent whole, structurally and organically.

Proppian analysis has been broadly applied to many types of folklore in many different groups. In looking at a personal experience narrative, for example, we might examine how closely a story told by a man describing his adventures as he hitchhiked around the country in his youth resembles some of the classic *Märchen* plot elements described by Propp. Although he doesn't specifically address Propp's plot elements, Barre Toelken applies this kind of comparative, structural approach to the Native American tales recounted by a Navajo teller named Yellowman (1976).

Much of folklorists' interpretation of structure has been geared toward verbal genres; however, folklorists have also examined and analyzed the structure of material items. Henry Glassie provides detailed structural analysis of the rules and laws of vernacular architecture in *Folk Housing in Middle Virginia* (1975). As Glassie explains, "The set of rules, taken together, is the whole that is

greater than its parts; the rules structure the whole" (20). Glassie's close examination of the parts and their relationship to the whole provides one way to
determine the underlying principles that govern the whole and to help us recognize individual variations. His work provides an example of the applicability
of an examination of structure in nonverbal texts.

One major benefit of this approach is the emphasis on wholes, rather than
on parts, when describing and analyzing a text. First of all, analyzing structural
patterns has allowed genre classifications to be more than just labels for groups
of related items that share certain thematic features. We can, for example, say
that folk songs involve singing, are primarily shared face-to-face rather than
in print or through recordings, and have some connection to a group's traditions. These are thematic classifications, based on surface characteristics. But
if we look a little more deeply at structure, we see distinctions in the types of
stories the songs tell, or the use of certain verse and chorus structures, or many
other features that allow folk song scholars to distinguish among ballads, lyrics, and call-and-response songs (among many other subgenre classifications).
This approach makes *genre* not just a label or name for something, but a "real
form, which exists regardless of any interpretation or classification" (Ben-Amos
1976a, 220). Analyzing structure has helped to uncover basic elements that
form and clarify meaningful genre and subgenre classifications.

Related to the idea of genre flexibility, a focus on structure permitted folklorists to examine in more analytical detail those forms that are very structure
dependent, like jokes and riddles, or literary texts that incorporate folklore elements. Before the focus on structure, scholars had primarily dismissed riddles,
for example, as lesser forms of verbal folklore and often considered them to be
mostly in the realm of children's lore or games. Once forms were identified and
analyzed, scholars could see the relationships between those characteristics that
revealed deeper linguistic and cognitive patterns. The forms of riddles create
frameworks for the clash between the real and the metaphoric content that
leads most of us to laugh. In part, the structure both supports and leads to the
answer to the puzzle, creating a complex, sophisticated performance.

From its foundations in folklore studies, the study of structure has integrated physical, formal structures of texts with larger structures of culture and
groups. Examining structure permits a wider view of folklore in relation to
culture, beyond geographical identification. Many of the plots and characters
in folktales seem almost interchangeable, or certainly very closely related. One
reason for this similarity, according to many who take this approach, is that
folktales center on broad strokes of plot rather than on innovation and unexpected twists and turns. In other words, one of the main identifying structural

189

features of a folktale is that it emphasizes plot structure and character types and deemphasizes unique, specific events and characters (Oring 1986b, 127–30). Many perceived the structural approach to folklore to be useful in analyzing certain universal elements in many kinds of verbal folklore. For instance, looking at structure allows us to see that many cultures share riddles that require mental agility and cleverness. Does this pattern suggest a human tendency toward puzzle solving and a cross-cultural value on wit? Does the fact that many of the world's stories include protagonists who must conquer villains in the face of apparently insurmountable odds reflect the universal battle between good and evil, as depicted in many of the world's myths? Looking at tale structure in this way enabled folklorists to study similarities and differences among different cultures' traditional stories, and ways in which the concept of genre can extend *beyond* the forms of those specific stories.

Within genres and cultures, the analysis of structure also demanded close attention to the details of oral texts and generated a complex system of describing and defining them. A system of *ethnopoetics* (Tedlock 1971 and 1992) originated to describe not just the structure of the narrative, for example, when someone laughed or gestured, but also the structure of the sound of the words and utterances and how they contributed to the overall narrative performance. For example, rising and falling inflections, stressed words, loudness or softness, tone, and pitch could be indicated by lines and notations, similar to the diacritical marks used in dictionaries to aid in pronunciation. Line breaks could indicate where phrases or clauses ended, similar to the way a poem is presented on a page. Because in many cases structural analysis requires close attention to *how* things were said as well as *what* was said, this system of notation has proved very useful for those studying structure in linguistic terms. It allows description of structural patterns as well as examination of performance styles and techniques. More importantly, scholars can use an ethnopoetic approach to discuss how expressive language works within particular groups and performances and can extend this discussion to the holistic analysis of meaning and culture. Many folklorists who analyze personal experience narratives find the use of ethnopoetic notation an effective way to describe speech and verbal performances within conversational genres and stories of life experience and to establish the artistic or expressive elements of those kinds of narratives.

Ironically, the major problems with the structural approach have to do with some of its perceived benefits. Overemphasis on genre resulted in much scholarly energy being spent on defining what things are, rather than analyzing how they operate within groups. This interest in classifying does make sense, because, as de Caro points out, one way, "perhaps *the* major way human beings create order and structure reality, is by creating categories and placing entities within those categories" (1986, 182). Categorization helps us to make sense of the world. When categories blur or break down, we tend to feel confused, maybe even anxious. "What is this thing?" we might wonder, or "How should I respond to it?" It may even be that one reason societies create taboos and other sorts of social restrictions is to prevent us from behaving in ways that might cause categories to break down (182). Taboos help to prevent or at least reduce the social confusion and anxiety that could result from confronting something that appears to be something else—or perhaps appears to be more than one thing at the same time.

We know, though(as we have discussed in the genre section), that categories do overlap. Strict adherence to structural categories like genre limits our ability to interpret individual items, or even the loose categories we use for the sake of discussion, within a context. As de Caro says, we have to "transcend categories in order to adapt, to learn and to innovate, however threatening that effort may sometimes be" (1986, 182). Breaking out of categories, examining the blurred areas, allows us to consider how folklore works within a group and to consider the effect of the blurring and overlapping that often takes place. An overemphasis on structure highlights what texts look or sound like, but not what texts—or even genres—mean to a group, or when, where, and why they exist. So while the focus on structure has been successful in expanding our concept of genre, one potential pitfall in the approach is a tendency to stop there, to see the ability to name something as the end of analysis rather than the beginning.

Thus, the structuralist approach suffers some of the same problems we've illustrated in our discussion of emphasizing functions: a search for universal themes and patterns that reveal absolute human characteristics or values can be reductionist and elitist. Making assumptions about all people that apply in all cases deemphasizes the importance of individuals and groups and ignores some of the dynamic processes of folklore. It focuses almost exclusively on constants, things that apply in all cases in any culture, rather than on the shifting aspects of meaning that depend on group dynamics and contexts. Structural analysis does illuminate similarities between groups and between texts that are shared in many different groups and reveals the many ways in which groups deal with and express their understanding of basic narrative themes (such as relationships, life, death, and growing up), but that doesn't mean we can say all people possess the same thoughts and feelings about those themes.

Because studies of structure at first focused almost exclusively on verbal folklore, the approach became associated for some time with only verbal genres. Furthermore, the heavy emphasis on genre classifications limited, for many,

191

the scope of structural studies, at least when it was used more for identifying than analyzing. And finally, the danger of relying too heavily on a reductive search for overarching meanings created concern that a focus only on identifying structural patterns, by itself, was too simplistic. For these reasons, a strict structuralist approach fell out of favor with many scholars. However, interest in structure has remained strong in folklore studies and in its many forms has proven to be useful from a variety of perspectives. Elements of this approach continue to inform integrated approaches to folklore studies.

In spite of some of the problems with this approach as mainly a method for classifying verbal texts, folklorists have found the principles of structural analysis to be very useful and adaptable. Early investigations focused on tales but employed structural analysis to look at how tales fit into larger structures of society, aesthetics, and symbolic meanings. Recent folktale scholars have continued this approach, advocating integrated interpretations of folktales that combine analysis of structure, social contexts, and symbolic meanings.[45]

Perhaps the most enduring application of the structural approach has been in performance analysis and contextual studies. Any consideration of frames or performance markers, for example, is by nature a consideration of structure: frames shape—that is, structure—the social and artistic spaces that surround and provide a venue for performance. Bill Ellis (2001 and 2002), for example, has studied jokes as part of a larger structure of social response to national or global disasters or tragedies. Many studies of rituals and other socially defined events include attention to structure both in terms of the sequence of events (verbal and nonverbal) and in terms of how those events fit into larger social and contextual patterns. Some folklorists also discuss material texts and how their physical or internal structures relate to larger principles of group aesthetics, performance, and communication. As part of a holistic approach to studying folklore, the principles and theoretical applications of structural analysis remain valuable tools for folklorists.

Psychoanalytic Interpretations: Symbols and Metaphors

Established by Sigmund Freud in the early twentieth century, psychoanalysis stresses broad themes of psychological, social, and sexual development as a way of understanding individuals and human behavior in general. As applied to expressive communication, *psychoanalytic analysis* involves the interpretation of symbolic meanings within texts that illuminate the shared developmental and life experiences of all humans. There has been a connection between psychoanalysis and folklore, as many psychoanalysts have thought a culture's folklore presents a look at its collective psychological concerns (G. Fine 1992, 45). Among these was Bruno Bettelheim, an Austrian-born psychologist and child development specialist who analyzed fairy tales as symbolic metaphors for puberty, sexual maturity, seduction, and death (1976).[46] Gary Alan Fine points out that psychoanalysts have also examined beliefs, rituals, and traditions to learn about child rearing, personality, and "national character" (1992, 45); the latter has certainly been a subject of interest for folklorists themselves, at least in the early years of the discipline

Is it reasonable, then, to assume folklorists can interpret psychological symbols? Other approaches folklorists have used, such as those based on functions and structures, have parallels with other fields that consider texts, groups, and societies, like sociology, anthropology, humanities, and literary studies. Psychology, though, considers interpretations of the human mind, or psyche, determining or attributing human behaviors in relation to how people feel and think. The question is: Folklorists are trained to look at texts and performances, but are they trained to look at human minds? This question is at the heart of objections to using psychological theory to interpret creative, expressive texts and performances—*in the field of folklore*. However, while some folklorists dismiss this approach for its problematic emphasis on interpreting human thoughts and psyches, others have made persuasive cases for the powerful insights psychoanalytical interpretations can offer.

One of the strongest proponents of the psychoanalytic approach to folklore study was Alan Dundes, who worked to illustrate the value of this approach through his own analysis of texts as well as through outright arguments about the power of this kind of interpretation. Dundes argued that psychoanalytic interpretation offers one of the most in-depth ways to go beyond mere collection of texts or artifacts and descriptions of context. The key Freudian ideas Dundes finds important to folklore study are "the range of concepts such as 'projection' and 'family romance'" (2002, xvi).[47] In a collection of his essays employing psychoanalytic interpretation of folklore (2002), Dundes writes about the ritual of calling on "Bloody Mary" (also known as Mary Worth and Mary Whales), usually practiced by preteen and teenage girls (rarely by boys). The basic components of the ritual involve a young girl, or girls, entering a bathroom (usually at night or in a darkened room) and chanting the name "Bloody Mary," "Mary Worth," or "Mary Whales," repeating it a certain number of times, often accompanied by particular gestures or movements. The chanting and movements are said to summon or conjure up the figure or face of a woman in the darkened mirror, frequently with blood on her face or clothing. As Dundes begins his inquiry into the meaning of the ritual, he calls for a more

193

thorough interpretation than any previous folklorists have provided for it.[48] His analysis refers not only to this earlier work—and ultimately presents interpretations of it—but also draws specifically on fieldwork collections performed primarily by his own undergraduate folklore students in 1996 (80). Dundes selects ten versions of retellings of the ritual and focuses his analysis on those ten representative retellings.

Based on the various accounts of the rituals Dundes examines, which include the components presented above, he finds it "abundantly clear that this girls' ritual has something to do with the onset of the first menses" (2002, 84). He argues that in American culture there is no formal ritual connected with a girl's first menstruation but "that the 'Bloody Mary' ritual serves an analogous function for prepubescent American girls" (84), and he provides several reasons for this interpretation. He discusses the *context*, or elements of the ritual related to its performance or practice, the specific *language* used during the event (primarily the name of the figure), and the *images* that the girls hope to conjure up by their actions.

The *context* of the ritual, both physical and psychological, is essential to Dundes's interpretation. The participants in the custom, according to the accounts he studied, are most often young girls between the ages of seven and twelve, and since the average age for an American girl's menarche is twelve and a half (according to a 1977 study Dundes cites), he claims the behavior is likely "to be an anticipatory ritual, essentially warning girls of what to expect upon attaining puberty." In addition, the location in which the ritual is performed, a bathroom, connects it to menstruation and adolescent girls' anxiety about dealing with it; several of the versions he addresses include flushing toilets (2002, 85).

The variations on "Mary's" name serve as linguistic clues to the custom's connection to young girls' physical changes. Dundes draws attention to the name "Mary," suggesting that it operates on several different levels. One possibility is as a reference to the Virgin Mary and the risk of pregnancy, a concern for adolescents during this time; another is a connection between the name "Mary" and the verb "marry" (2002, 85). He places even more weight on the possibility of the name "Mary Worth" suggesting that a young woman's *worth* is related to having menstrual periods that allow for her to bear children once she is married, thus fulfilling her role in society (86). This interpretation, he believes, explains why "'Mary Worth' was selected as an alternative name for 'Bloody Mary.' . . . In terms of symbol substitution, if we take the two names as synonymous, then 'Mary' is the constant, and 'Bloody' must be equivalent to 'Worth' which is precisely the argument here advanced." The term *Bloody*

Mary itself also holds possibly erotic implications in that it is the name for an alcoholic beverage with a nonalcoholic "virgin" version (86).

Obviously, the word *bloody* and images including blood are key to Dundes's interpretation of the ritual as related to prepubescent menstruation anxiety. In addition to the bloody images, though, the bathroom mirror creates—or reflects—images of these girls that are significant to their perception of sexuality. He mentions a number of popular cultural images of women, such as Barbie dolls and women in mass media advertisements, which affect adolescent girls' self-image and awareness of "looking good" (2002, 86). In addition to these contemporary factors, he refers to a number of beliefs from the past or from other cultures that caution against menstruating women looking in mirrors or that connect this action with witches or witching (86–87).

Based on his interpretation of the texts collected by his students, Dundes returns to several of the texts explored by other folklorists and applies a psychoanalytic interpretive approach. He examines a version of the ritual to which Simon Bronner referred that requires the participants to "prick their fingers with a pin to draw a drop of blood . . . [to induce] a young pale-faced girl to appear in the mirror with 'blood running down her face from a large cut in her forehead'" (Dundes 2002, 87). Freud would, Dundes states, term this "upwards displacement" of the blood in the young girl's body (87).

Another text and interpretation of interest to Dundes is Janet Langlois's study (1978) of variants of the "vanishing hitchhiker"; she collected a number of these that mention a spot of blood left on the backseat of a car by a female hitchhiking figure.[49] Dundes makes sense of this variant by claiming that this spotting refers to a pubescent girls' anxiety of "showing" (2002, 88). He goes on to say that the convergence of the "Bloody Mary" ritual and the "vanishing hitchhiker" legend actually provides an adequate interpretation for the legend, which Brunvand himself (according to Dundes) does not provide. Dundes posits that the hitchhiking legend works metaphorically as a cautionary tale, connecting an adolescent girl's sexuality with being "picked up": "With this reading of the legend, we can see how a 'Bloody Mary' ritual in which a girl bridges the transition from prepubescent girl to nubile nymph might be related to a story about the dangerous consequences of a girl's being picked up by a male driver with a hot rod" (89).

Dundes addressed potential critics of his analysis by reminding us that folklore, "a socially sanctioned outlet to permit individuals to do what is normally not permitted by society, superego, conscience, normative morality, and the like often needs the guise or disguise of fantasy" (2002, 89). To further ground his interpretation, he points out that it accounts for the details of the ritual: it is performed by girls (either an individual or a small group of girls together), it is carried out in a bathroom, and the outcome of the ritual is the appearance of a bloody image of a woman (or the girl's face) (91). The psychoanalytic interpretation of this ritual allows Dundes to connect its details with the broader psychological themes he uncovers and to explain them in terms of human psychological and sexual development.

The psychoanalytic approach to folklore interpretation is problematic for many folklorists. Among the major criticisms is that psychoanalytic theory is too broad, much like the reductionist emphasis on function: it assumes that all human beings share exactly the same experiences and that particular texts express that experience in the same way. For example, all tales about beautiful young girls oppressed by powerful, evil women are always about the psychosexual tension between adolescent girls and their mothers. As Dundes himself puts it in a discussion of the potential pitfalls of psychoanalytic analysis, psychoanalytic theory makes "the unwarranted assumption of pan-human universality" (2002, 5). This idea that one particular universal theory explains all texts conflicts with folklorists' understanding that texts are shaped by specific contexts. Another criticism is that this theory assumes it is possible for a researcher (or any outside interpreter) to determine what's going on in the minds of other people. The focus on reciprocal ethnography, in which the folklorists' consultants provide responses to the interpretation suggested by the folklorist (see the discussion of reciprocal ethnography in chapter 7, "Fieldwork and Ethnography"), stands in clear opposition to such an interpretive approach that assumes unconscious motives for sharing and creating folklore. Another limitation to the psychoanalytic approach is that it is most frequently applied to verbal texts and is difficult to apply to the study of groups, performance, materials, and customs.[50]

One specific scholarly criticism of this approach is of the way psychoanalytic analyses of texts have been carried out. In their critique of Dundes's work, Limon and Young say such analysis "remains too textually and etymologically oriented and consistently lacks the fieldwork, ethnographic analysis, and intense engagement of Freud that would lend legitimacy to, and serious consideration of, his provocative speculations" (1986, 448). Gary Alan Fine, too, claims that Dundes's work, and the psychoanalytic approach in general, while producing "considerable insight" (1992, 46), sometimes lack enough detailed data in the form of careful collecting (55). While a specific instance of analysis may apply effectively to a particular text, "often no corpus of data is presented," and "the issue of the representativeness of the material is not adequately addressed." Fine goes on to say that most "Freudian analyses are marred by a lack of interest in collecting" (55).

For some folklorists, psychoanalysis provides insight into the more symbolic, psychological aspects of folklore that other approaches may not address in as much depth. Such interpretations are difficult to uncover because the meanings and symbols are often hidden within the text. As Fine says, "Folklore provides a socially acceptable outlet for meaning that cannot be displayed otherwise. If the meaning was overt, the text would have to be repressed" (1992, 48). Psychoanalysis offers a way to open up the text, and folklorists like Fine see value in this approach if it is done thoroughly.

Fine suggests two specific criteria that he believes should be applied by folklorists to evaluate the effectiveness of psychoanalytic interpretations: "Is the analysis internally consistent? And is the analysis externally valid? Although neither question removes subjective judgment, they at least provide a more explicit basis for evaluation" (1992, 51). To illustrate these criteria, Fine examines Dundes's analysis of "The Hook," a contemporary legend that features a young woman and young man parked at a Lover's Lane, who are *almost* attacked by an escaped sex maniac. He finds that Dundes's analysis on the "ideal text" works but cautions that such "*interpretations must ultimately be based on empirical data*" (53–54; italics original). He also critiques Dundes's claims about the homosexual nature of football and says this argument does not hold up to the scrutiny of his criteria, even citing Dundes's own point that "'the interpretations should read out of the data rather than being read into the data!'" (in Fine 1992, 54–55).

This kind of analysis, to look at symbolic meaning, is compelling for many folklorists and in some cases seems to make sense. Fine has applied and critiqued Dundes's approach and agrees with Dundes that "the goal of folkloristics is not to understand the text, but to understand people" (1992, 47). Fine lists several topics (which he calls "themes"), besides sexuality, that can be addressed with such analysis: power, in particular gender based; racial or ethnic conflict; and the Oedipal complex (48). He asserts that folklore for psychoanalytic folklorists is "the reflection of the concerns and anxieties of those who are its creators, performers, and also its audience" (47).

If folklorists choose this approach, though, careful textual analysis and good fieldwork are important, as Fine asserts in his work. One avenue some have used is to explore a more hybrid form of analysis, combining different approaches that can create a system of checks and balances. Multidimensional analyses that integrate close textual examination, explorations of symbolic meanings, and contextual studies may offer ways to articulate feelings and attitudes that psychoanalytic study purports to uncover. Dundes's work has generated much discussion, and, despite the criticism, its provocative claims continue to challenge folklorists to explore deeply the texts they have collected and to recognize that considering symbolic content can be a valid perspective.

Social Dimensions: Texts and Performances in Complex Contexts

Interest in meanings, forms, and symbols informs folklore studies, but as we discussed in the chapter on performance, most folklore analyses currently focus primarily on the communicative aspects of folklore—on texts and groups as part of a complex process of communicating ideas that shape and reflect experience. Folklorists look at how, when, and why people share folklore and consider ways the relationships among people and their physical, social, and cultural contexts are expressed through acts of communication.[51] Growing out of this people-and-communication-oriented philosophy, folklore study incorporates theoretical and philosophical perspectives from cultural studies, gender theory, critical race theory, and other sociopolitical theories of culture. Combining discussions of physical and social contexts with analyses based on such theories, folklorists look deeply into the interconnections among communal, social, and political forces, along with personal, physical, psychological, and emotional characteristics that shape the underlying values and relationships we often express through folklore.

Dimensions of class, race, politics, ethnicity, gender, culture, religion, sexuality, ability or disability, and society overlap to influence worldview and our expressive communications. Think of your own experience as you read this book. You are a certain gender, a certain age and race, and those factors might influence how you react to the content—what material you question, what you seek more information about, what makes sense right away, what is unfamiliar. You draw on all the qualities that define you when you express ideas or respond to your experiences, just as all the things that define you shape those ideas and responses. In a very important sense, then, your concepts of who you are and the roles you play in the groups you belong to are constructed within—and by—these social contexts.

Many scholars who are interested in the social dimensions of folklore have focused on oppressed or underrepresented individuals or groups, those who have been excluded, ignored, or discriminated against by mainstream groups, in other words, those who have been pushed to the margins. In her analysis of the performances of Appalachian singer Bessie Eldreth, Patricia E. Sawin (2002) describes how Eldreth's age, gender, and social status define her role as a community member, a role with fairly stereotypical expectations for women.

As a singer, though, she can perform songs that covertly question authority, sex roles, and social hierarchies through the performance. As both performer and community member, Eldreth draws on all her roles and experiences in her artistic expression, and as she performs, she conveys attitudes, beliefs, and values that are, in turn, influenced by those roles and experiences—as well as by the performance context. Furthermore, those who analyze her performances and her role form responses, opinions, and expectations based on their own assumptions about poor, female, Appalachian singers; their analyses are also shaped by their direct experiences with her performances. Considering such complexities of social and cultural contexts provides a way to theorize about these kinds of interactions among the social dynamics of the performer, performance, audience, and observers.

This approach is particularly potent for folklorists. First of all, folklorists recognize how hard it is to separate out the many influences that surround us and the many roles we play; they recognize that each individual is a member of many groups and as such takes on many different roles and may express attitudes particular to those roles at certain times. In addition, an integrated approach that examines social dimensions offers folklorists a way to deepen the study of the interplay between specific performance contexts and the forces within larger social contexts that influence performances and texts. Folklorists look at vernacular or nonmainstream experiences and expression and investigate how those perspectives comment on, critique, or challenge mainstream social or cultural values while solidifying and communicating group identity. This approach broadens our understanding of how folklore can operate as a means of expression for sharing and revealing group values, beliefs, and attitudes—both esoteric and exoteric—as well as a means of influencing and reflecting experiences, and it provides a foundation for discussions of issues related to power, status, gender, race, ethnicity, and other social dynamics.

In the pages that follow, we will take a look at some of the ways folklorists have considered social dimensions. For the sake of discussion, and recognizing that emphasizing particular categories in many ways applies artificial distinctions that are themselves socially constructed, we'll focus on questions of gender, race, and social or political hierarchies.

Folklorists began paying more attention to gender when they realized that a relatively small number of studies and articles had been published about women's culture. In 1975, a special issue of the *Journal of American Folklore* published a series of articles that addressed women's folklore "by examining both the images of women and the genres through which women's creativity

199

has been viewed and by suggesting genres and approaches not previously recognized" (Farrer 1975b, xii). This collection was a concentrated attempt to
bring together the perspectives and analyses of a number of folklorists working
to understand the unique characteristics that set women's folklore apart from
male experience and culture. In addition, these essays reconsidered the assumptions about women's culture that had previously limited attention to the stereotypical genres usually attributed to women and went beyond witch stories,
home remedies, quaint beliefs, and women's domestic roles (v–vi).

A decade later, Rosan Jordan and Susan Kalcik (1985) focused more on specific genres of women's folklore and women performers and the contexts in
which they perform. Like the folklorists whose work is featured in the 1975 special issue, these folklorists looked at performances taking place in private and/
or domestic arenas. Jordan and Kalcik point out that both gender and experience can bias fieldworkers toward a certain perspective in their observations
and are likely even to affect what the researcher perceives as important or worth
noting. They direct our attention to the fact that such biases shape not only
the choices of which types of cultural expression folklorists consider (and have
access to) but also the interpretation of that lore (1985, x–xi). This collection
demonstrates that simply because women's roles may be seen through a male
cultural lens as subordinate or somehow marginalized, folklore allows women
power and control within their own environments (xii). Jordan and Kalcik note
that these "studies also yield new insights into the realm of men's folklore and
into the ways in which the two domains affect each other—whether the relationship be one of contrast or complementarity" (x). Their work acknowledges
the cultural, expressive connection between men's and women's folklore and
the way in which each shapes the other, rather than only looking at women's
creative expressions to describe how they "aren't male."

Recent studies of gender in folklore extend more broadly into cultural and
social dimensions of gender experience and expression beyond mainstream
contexts and conventions. One example is *Manly Traditions: The Folk Roots of
American Masculinities* (2005), a collection of essays edited by Simon Bronner
that explores aspects of American male identity through the lens of folklore
texts and performances usually associated with men. Although some of the
essays in this collection have been critiqued by some as presenting a rather
narrow definition of masculinity (see, for instance, Greenhill 2006 and Gilman
2011), it is one of the first comprehensive looks at masculinity in folklore studies and does begin to address the complex interactions of maleness and social
constructions of identity. Another work, *The Fierce Tribe* (2008), by Mickey
Weems, examines masculine expression performed in the Circuit, dance party

events for gay men in which participants engage in often stylized ritual enactments of nonviolent masculine interaction through dance and body display.
In the Circuit, Weems explains, men can play with the definitions of maleness and male power that are often defined in mainstream culture in terms
of war and violence. Works like these and promising studies of shifting interrelationships between males, females, cultures, societies, and politics expand
our understanding of folklore and the roles it plays in defining and expressing
concepts of who we are.

Among the greatest contributions of studies of gender in folklore is that
they uncover ways that socially and politically constructed assumptions can
marginalize some groups that don't conform to a dominant group's definition
of mainstream. Because it deepens the way we understand groups, such folklore
scholarship has led to investigations of the interplay of multiple factors, such
as gender, age, class, race, and other characteristics. It further deemphasizes
reliance on genre as the main way of understanding folklore and emphasizes
particular contexts and "modes of presentation" (Deemer 1975, 107) in folklore
analysis. Studies of gender and folklore led naturally to the insight that questions and definitions of identity reach beyond gender to questions of power
and dominance—who's in charge, who makes the rules, who defines what is the
norm. Folklorists have carried these questions into a wide range of topic areas,
among them, the following:

- personal experience narratives in terms of political or social resistance
  to dominant cultural narratives
- vernacular expressions and beliefs within the larger realm of mainstream religious practices or customs
- assumptions about and attitudes toward particular groups expressed
  through jokes and anecdotes
- customs and traditions as expressions of identity in opposition to or
  compliance with exoteric and esoteric assumptions about identity
- how studies of identity and social roles reflect and define folklorists'
  sense of their own shifting identities and roles

In the following section, we'll glance at a few recent studies to give a sense of
the breadth and depth of the social dimensions of folklore.

The potentially volatile topic of race has been an important focus of folklore study in recent decades, particularly discussions of how our interpretations and perceptions of race are shaped by our assumptions and experiences
of our own and others' racial identities. Folklore scholars have considered the
complex definitions of and responses to race by looking at performance and

201

texts in a wide range of contexts. A special issue of the *Journal of American Folklore* ("Africana Folklore" 2005), for example, presents several articles that "(1) reflect transnational perspectives; (2) explore new kinds of relationships between folklore and politics; (3) offer new perspectives on intra-racial issues among Africana people; (4) expand our ideas of "African American"; and (5) engage the impact of technology in processes of community maintenance and social identity" (Prahlad, 2005, 266). In *The Man Who Adores the Negro: Race and American Folklore* (2008), Patrick B. Mullen draws on critical race theory and his own past and current work in his discussions of social constructions of race and identity. He examines how folklorists' choices of texts as well as their interpretations can be influenced by their own particular socially constructed racial and cultural experiences and assumptions, and how those choices in turn influence images of blackness and whiteness in American folklore studies.

Multilayered studies allow folklorists to integrate discussions of the ways official, institutionalized texts and beliefs differ from vernacular, traditional texts and beliefs, as well as the ways those differing positions inform, conflict, and sometimes mesh with each other. For instance, in "Representing Trauma: Political Asylum Narrative," Amy Shuman and Carol Bohmer (2004) examine the ways power, politics, and culture intersect to affect the narratives of refugees who come to the United States seeking political asylum. Immigration lawyers frequently advise applicants for asylum to "reframe what they often understand as a personal trauma into an act of political aggression" (396). Applicants' success depends on how well they can shift their expression of their experiences to be in line with the ways others perceive or define political persecution. In this case, the government organization that decides whether to grant political asylum also decides what constitutes political persecution or aggression and plays a strong role in deliberately defining individual asylum seekers as members of "a persecuted group" (397). In other words, what gets said and the way it is said depend on the expectations of those who have the power to decide what happens to those who tell the stories.

This kind of condition in which one group has power or dominance over another in social, political, and/or economic contexts is termed *hegemony*. Hegemony can refer to obvious conditions in which one group controls another, such as in a country with a tyrannical political regime, or to less obvious situations, such as when the aesthetic tastes of members of one social or economic class determine what kinds of art or music become desirable within a particular community. It can also apply more generally to the relationships among those who perform and create expressive texts and those with the social and political power to control how those texts are used and shared.

Mario Montaño, in his article "Appropriation and Counterhegemony in South Texas: Food Slurs, Offal Meats, and Blood" (1997), argues that hegemonic influences affect the kinds of foods people cook and eat in South Texas. According to Montaño's research, the dominant, Anglo culture in South Texas took over the basic elements of several traditional Mexican foods and used them to create food that Anglos perceive as ethnic Mexican but that South Texas Mexicans do not label as truly Mexican in taste or origin. These foods have become favorites of Anglos, who believe them to be Mexican foods, and they have spread across the United States, being served in Tex-Mex eateries and even those labeled as simply Mexican. In fact, South Texas Mexicans believe that these foods, such as fajitas, have been adapted so much that they are not the same foods Mexicans label with those names. This hegemonic[52] influence has turned Mexican food into something Mexicans no longer recognize as part of their own culture. In a counterhegemonic[53] action against the predominance of what most Anglo-Americans perceive as Mexican food, many South Texas Mexicans insist on maintaining traditional foodways that Anglos find distasteful, for example, preparing cow's head barbecue. In response, some local government authorities, who are mainly Anglo, have established legal guidelines to control or prevent the preparation of such foods.

For folklorists, the kinds of esoteric and exoteric social dimensions we've been discussing are crucial, as are the ways particular groups influence the shaping of other groups' identities. The following discussion of an essay that recalls some of our earlier references to African American fraternity step shows (see chapter 4) demonstrates the fascinatingly intricate interconnections among groups that a multidimensional analysis of performance can reveal.

Tom Mould's "Running the Yard" (2005) examines African American fraternity step dancing as performance that helps express, form, and strengthen the group's identity. It also more thoroughly addresses the show as a "ritual space" (96) where African American college males can present and challenge stereotypes within the black Greek community and in American society generally. In this way, performers in the ritualized step shows play with exoteric and esoteric definitions of masculinity and race that can reduce black masculinity to narrow, stereotyped images. Ultimately, Mould claims, the fraternities' step routines present several versions of black masculinity, so "there is no single black masculinity constructed during step shows" (99).

One of the many interesting points Mould makes about the fraternity shows is that they deal with stereotyped images on a number of levels. On one level, the step shows themselves may portray common stereotypes of black males but mediate them through performances of those stereotypes. Performers can

negotiate their identities, in a sense acting out various roles that stretch definitions of their roles and images as black men, in ways that are accepted and
understood by the black community. While the images of black identity may
or may not be in some part derived from the ways *white* masculinity is viewed,
Mould says, the fact that black performers perform these roles for themselves
and for black audiences "is a liberating shift from past contexts that have risked
being hegemonic and alienating" (83). Mould claims that the performers "construct their steps whether consciously or unconsciously within a set of standards that are defined partly by what they inherently claim to be via national
stereotypes and partly by what they claim not to be" (98–99). However, in the
ritualized context of the step shows, as Mould points out, audience members'
and even performers' expectations can be exaggerated and overturned, allowing performers to present versions of identities that express and negotiate alternative images of African American masculinity.

On another level, the shows also present expected stereotypes of African
American *fraternity* men. And within these more narrowly focused esoteric
expressions, the performers and audiences can also encounter and challenge
yet more layers of the group's own definitions of black masculinity:

> For black fraternity men, the contestation of proscribed images of mas-
> culinity occurs firmly within the genre of stepping, regularly challenging
> the expectations, assumptions, and stereotypes of what it means to be an
> Alpha or Sigma, what it means to be in a black Greek organization, and
> what it means to be a black college man. It is here that fraternity stereo-
> types are upended, where the 'nasty' Ques dress up in tuxedos, where
> the distinguished Alphas become sexually charged, where the ladies' men
> Kappas become hard warriors. (Mould 2005, 100)

Performers also create exoteric identities by reversing the exoteric identities
of other fraternities through a process of differential identity (Bauman, 1971a)
where one group defines itself in contrast to another. Mould comments that
one way groups play with their own esoteric, sometimes stereotyped expectations of identity is to imitate and mock the particular steps and moves associated with specific fraternities that compete in the step shows.

The steps, styles, and demeanors are so recognizably associated with one
group or another that the imitation becomes a way to communicate identity
and awareness of others' definitions of identity. Finally, Mould further examines how the identities expressed and played with onstage connect indirectly
to life offstage, because the success of fraternities' and individual members'

performances in the shows accord recognition and reputation associated with the various images projected onstage. As Mould says, "Folklore often provides the means not merely for expressing values and attitudes about gender, but for defining and challenging them, with implications that extend beyond the performance event and into daily life" (2005, 79).

Conclusion

Current approaches to folklore study focus on people and how people communicate with each other within the particular contexts that shape their cultural expression. At the center of interpretive strategies in folklore are the texts and contexts, reflective thinking, and the complexities of the interactions and interplay of performers, audiences, groups, researchers, and society. Thinking about folklore from so many different perspectives has also provided a way to understand larger concepts related to social and cultural forces and how those forces mold and inform the ways we express ourselves informally, artistically, and creatively. Likewise, we can see that our expressions reinforce, extend, and sometimes challenge those forces. It's a constant give and take. Analyzing folklore allows us to share with others our own understanding of the complexities of how and why folklore conveys meanings.

CHAPTER 7

Fieldwork and Ethnography

$\mathcal{A}$s much fun as we find reading about folklore to be, nothing can compare to the opportunity to do one's own ethnographic research, exploring a group and the creative ways in which its members communicate with each other. Ethnography is the process of studying and learning about groups of people, as well as the written description and analysis of those observations. It is through ethnographic research and the written descriptions of their findings in the field that folklorists share their ideas.

From the early days of the discipline, folklorists have gone into the field to study the songs, stories, objects, behaviors, and beliefs of the cultural groups about which they have written. Folklorists don't necessarily have to go far away to gather information. Much contemporary folklore research takes place within local communities. The "field" is wherever folklore occurs: it could be a classroom, a locker room, or even your family's kitchen.

When a folklorist decides to go into the field, there are two levels of the fieldwork experience to think about. There are the *practical* elements of research—the who, what, where, when, and how. And there are the more *philosophical* aspects of research: What relationship should the researcher have with consultants? How should the folklorist work with consultants and the information collected from them? What will the folklorist do to recognize the collaborative nature of fieldwork and interpretation and ensure respect for folklorist-consultant relationships, as well as for the texts and those who share and perform them? Where and when will the interpretations be shared with the consultants and others? Finally, how can all of this be presented effectively in the written ethnography?

Many folklorists and other humanities professionals have written in detail about the fieldwork process, and you may find it useful to look at their more specific discussions if you plan to take on a large-scale fieldwork project. For our purposes, we want to present information about some of the larger issues of fieldwork research and data collection, though we may refer to some of the work those other researchers have written about the process as we go.

Fieldwork is a complicated process because it involves both practical and philosophical concerns. We want to start here by laying out the elements of the active practical research process—apart from the interpersonal, ethical, and interpretive issues—so you will have an overview of the basic steps of the process. After that, we will present some of the more complex ethical issues related to the process to provide you with an idea of the kinds of things you will want to consider as you begin researching and presenting your own ethnographic work.

Collecting Data: The Nuts and Bolts of Fieldwork

Finding Ideas

As you have read about the texts and folk groups in this book, you may have wondered how folklorists go about contacting the people and finding the folklore they write about. There are a couple of primary collecting situations, or ways to observe folklore in its natural context. Sometimes a folklorist just finds the study. Being aware of and open to folklore and catching it in the moment allow you to begin the search. Other times you may have to actively seek it. Perhaps you are aware that a person is a recognized artist or performer, and you decide to find out about the ways that person creates and communicates. Folklorists collect their material by *identifying folklore* within everyday situations, as well as by *seeking folklore out*.

Collection contexts can occur naturally or can be arranged by a folklorist and her consultant. Being able to observe a performance in its natural context does provide a perspective that can't be replicated; however, the work doesn't always have to be collected in action. In other words, collecting information from a consultant when you are not able to observe a performance is still valid. For example, you might see a wall hanging you admire, so you arrange to talk with the artist about her work. She might describe the work, how it was created and what it means to her, and show you the kinds of materials she uses. You don't have to see her actually sew the cloth to gather information about her traditional process and personal innovations.

Some Ways to Identify Folklore

- Think about groups you belong to or know about—family, school, and so forth—and about the traditions, behaviors, language (names, titles, expressions, stories), or special ways of selecting roles within the group. Examples: Do you always eat or prepare certain foods when you get together? Do you share a gift-giving tradition that involves handcrafted objects or particular artifacts? Do you share inside jokes? Who does the group acknowledge as leader and why?
- Think about your own personal traditions. For instance, maybe you are an athlete who wears a certain pair of socks for every game, so you decide to talk with other athletes you know and find out what kinds of things they do before or during games to ensure a good outcome.
- Identify patterns in people's behavior. Have you ever noticed that the same group of people always sits together during lunch breaks at work, for instance? Does the same person always bring the same kinds of foods to family gatherings?
- Consider local artists, performers, and craftspeople. Whose work have you seen or heard and admired?
- Ask friends or family members to talk about their own rituals and traditions and listen for interesting details that you can follow up on.

Some Ways to Seek Out Folklore

- Natural contexts

    Scheduled events where you know folklore performances take place or texts exist, even if you aren't sure exactly what it is you'll find. It's already organized for you; all you have to do is get there. Go, and take along video or audio equipment for recording. For example, perhaps you have heard from a musician friend that a group of fiddlers gets together once a week at a local farmer's barn to share and learn new tunes. You understand the context is traditional, so you ask your friend for details and arrange to sit in with the group during the next jam session.

    Found situations in which folklore just happens. For this type of discovery, you need to be able to recognize folklore in context and be able to collect it—for instance, as in the proverb example in chapter 5, "Performance." Or perhaps you are sitting with a group of coworkers sharing stories about your most annoying customers, and you recognize a traditional storytelling context. With the others' permission, you pull out your recorder and record your group's stories for analysis later.

Regardless of the collecting situation, you still have to go back to the people and talk with them about the folklore they're sharing and about how they learned it, why they shared it, and so forth.

Performances or events you regularly participate in. For example, say you belong to a group of video game enthusiasts. The next time you get together with the group, you might ask if you can record the activities. Or suppose you belong to a book club, so you ask to record the discussion at your next meeting.

Artists' or craftspersons' workshops or homes where they create their works. If these are open to the public, you could go and observe and perhaps arrange a later time to discuss their art and process in more depth.

- Arranged setting or context

Arranging a setting or context means you elicit a performance in front of an audience that isn't the usual audience or you arrange an interview to talk with someone about particular topics or experiences. For example, you might arrange a performance by asking someone to prepare a traditional food outside of the usual time or place it would usually be prepared, so you can watch and listen. Or you could observe a process or performance and arrange a follow-up interview with the group or individual at a convenient time.

Getting Started on Fieldwork

When you decide to explore a community and the way its members communicate with each other, you should think carefully about what you hope to learn and what is significant in learning such information. What is your motivation for learning more about this item or performance? Thinking about this will help you make some decisions about who you are in relation to the group you are working with and how you would like to approach your research.

Background Research

Before going into the field, it is usually a good idea to conduct some preliminary research on your topic. You might talk with your instructor or someone you know who has information on your topic to get some background information. You will also need to do some library research. The kind of research you will do depends on your topic, the assignment, the type of folklore you are considering, and how much you already know. For example, one of our contributors, Gary E. A. Saum, began his project, "Roadside Memorials: Material Focus of Love, Devotion, and Remembrance," by looking for research on roadside memorials. When he discovered that little work had been done on the particular topic of vernacular memorial structures, he conducted secondary research in the library and on the Internet about other kinds of vernacular memorials and used this data to provide a foundation for his discussion. Another contributor, Kevin Eyster, begins his essay with some research on the historical background of the event he studies. There are many places to look, beginning with searches of the major folklore journals and database searches for subjects and keywords in your topic. This important step will help prepare you to consider various details of the collection process and of analytical perspectives as you go into the field.

Tools

Once you've decided what you're interested in and have given some thought to your goals for the project, it's time to make contacts and set up opportunities to observe performances and/or talk with people. Of course, the most useful tools in the field are your five senses and your memory, but there are a few things you'll need to gather before you go, to support your natural tools. Depending on the setting, you should have on hand some or all of the following:

- Audio recorder, batteries, power cords, and adapters
- Camera or video recorder, batteries, power cords, and adapters
- Extra film, tapes, memory cards, digital storage devices
- Extension cords
- Pen, pencil, and paper
- Releases and explanations
- Laptop or PDA

Be sure you know how to use all the devices and have practiced using your tools before going on a research jaunt. Also be sure you know how to change batteries, film, and storage cards quickly. The more comfortable you are with these procedures, the more comfortable you will be while you are collecting and the more comfortable your consultants will be. Using audio and video recorders with the longest recording times also reduces interruptions and prevents unnecessary upheaval during performances or conversations with your consultants.

Safety

Most of the time, your own safety while doing fieldwork will not be a major concern, but you should always use common sense any time you are going into a new environment. If you do have any reason for concern, consider taking a partner or arranging to meet in a more comfortable setting.

Release

This recording or recordings (video and/or audio) and any accompanying photographs, notes, and transcripts are the results of one or more voluntary recorded interviews with me. I agree to allow them to be used for the purposes of scholarship and research. I also understand that I have the right to review any recorded materials, as well as written documents, that result from the interviews, and that I may ask to have the materials remain anonymous, or to have them returned to me.

Understood and agreed to:
Name: _____
Address: _____

_____
Phone: _____
Date: _____
Interviewer: _____
Date: _____
Recording number: _____

Releases

When you meet contacts and consultants, always identify yourself and explain the project you're doing and why you're doing it. It is also crucial to get permission to talk with consultants and to observe and record conversations and performances. You need to prepare a written release form that will serve as a record of your consultants' permission and will spell out any special conditions or uses for the material. You need to sign the form along with them to show you agree to the terms.

Above is a sample of a generic release form to illustrate the essential components. You may need to include other details depending on your situation or the kind of work you're doing. For instance, some academic institutions require students to store copies of their audio and visual recordings and written work in the institution's libraries or archives. If this is so in your case, you need to let the consultants know that on the release form. You might also be asked to include notations that key the release to the recorded materials and/or written documents. Consult your instructor to be sure you understand the protocol and have covered all the necessary components of the agreement.

Developing and Asking Good Questions

There are different types of questions you will ask your consultants, depending on the context in which you are collecting your material and the reason for which you're talking with them. The right type of question and the manner in which you ask it are both important. Some questions will be intended simply to gather information—for example, to gain background information on the person with whom you're speaking. Other types include opening questions and follow-up questions—which you might ask during a single interview or in subsequent interviews. Let the consultant lead the conversation, but if there are certain topics you want to address, ask questions that point in that direction. The main thing is to *listen*. Know what you are interested in learning about. You may even need to do some research to know what kind of things you want to ask about or what terminology to use. Establishing rapport with a consultant can be helpful in developing questions and going with the flow of an interview (see the "Rapport" section below).

If you ask a question that your consultant doesn't want to talk about—or a question that is just wrong—how do you recover? What can you do? One thing you can do is stop talking and listen to the consultant. Sometimes we think we need to keep asking questions in order to get good responses, but really we need to listen. Just have a conversation with the consultant and give everybody a break from feeling like it's a formal interview. If a question falls flat or isn't received well, try changing the subject or moving into a more general topic. For example, you might go back to your notes and follow up on an interesting topic that the consultant raised earlier.

In general, when you interview, begin with a clear idea of what interests you and ask questions about those topics. As you continue your interview, keep good notes so you can refer back to something your consultant has commented on for more developed information. These notes will also help you keep track of themes or topics that come up in conversation so you can ask your consultant more about them. Even seasoned folklorists can't always control the shape of their interview process, but the more experienced they become, the more they know how to let consultants lead the conversation in the desired direction.

Some Types of Questions

Opening questions are frequently more broad and open ended than directive or follow-up questions. There might be several points in an interview at which you use opening questions, perhaps as a way to start a conversation or move into a new topic. Here are some examples of such questions:

212

- What do you remember most about the time you lived in [insert town, country, continent, era/decade here]?
- Can you describe what happens when the family gets together for its annual reunion?
- How did you learn this process? Who did you learn from?

Once you have been talking about a topic for a while, there are some other types of more specific *follow-up questions* you might ask:

- Directive questions or comments that pick up on themes or topics:
  You mentioned earlier . . .
  Other people have told me about their memories of the flood. What do you remember about it?
- Questions that elicit interpretations from a consultant, based on something he or she has mentioned:
  Did you believe that would happen?
  Why did you approach the process that way?
  What's the most important part of this process (or preparation for this process)?
  Why do you think those things happen this way?
  What does it mean to you to participate in this?
- Questions that ask for more *specific detail* (could be for follow-ups or gathering background):
  How did your family go about preparation for the meal?
  How old were you when you learned about this?
  When did you change the way you do that?
  What ingredient are you adding here?

Example: Using Open-Ended Questions

The following excerpt from a longer transcript illustrates how asking broader, more open-ended questions can lead to interesting material that might not have emerged if the interviewer had tried to control the discussion with more pointed, directive questions.[54] In this case, the folklorist was doing a fieldwork project about women's work in an industrial town dominated by traditionally male workplaces (coal mines and steel mills, primarily). After an introductory conversation about the town and the kinds of work that men did there, the folklorist asked the consultant, Louise Quigley, a broad, two-part question about her own work: "Did you work?" and "What did you do?" This approach allowed the consultant to choose the order in which she recounted her experiences, as well as the details she wished to emphasize. The interviewer stayed fairly quiet

213

and listened attentively, contributing only a few prompts, and let Louise continue her narrative in her own way.[55]

Martine:	Did you work?
Louise:	Yes, I worked.
M:	What did you do?
L:	I sold *everything*. (laughter) I even sold fire alarms to help out. I'd knock at the door, and the dogs would chase me. I think the fire alarms were six dollars. I *sold* them. And that would help out. Then after the children grew up, I went—I worked for Grant's [Department Store]. From Grant's I went to Barbara Joyce [a women's clothing store] as a cashier, then I went to Fashion Bug, from Fashion Bug I went to Teek's [Shoe Store], and I stayed there a good while. Mmm-hmm.
M:	So you worked . . . all your life, too. . . .
L:	Well . . . after the kids grew up. Not while they were growing up. I didn't want to leave them alone. And, uh, that's about it . . . (pauses) Before I married my husband, I was a singer.
M:	A singer?
L:	Yes. I was going to be a vocalist. I was a whistler, too, like Elmo Tanner used to whistle—*yeearrs* ago! . . . Well, I went to Pittsburgh, to the Club Riviera. I was there, and then there was a twenty-piece band—or twenty-two piece—and they were going to Atlantic City. And, uh, well . . . I just . . . well, when I told my mom, she said "Oh, no way! *No way!*" I was eighteen, and she said, "You are *not* going!" Well, I probably would have made it. But she wouldn't allow me to go, so I met my husband, and married him, and that was that. He told me after we were married that I would still be allowed to go to Atlantic City, and he would come with me, but it never did happen—so. No.
M:	Did you continue to sing—in the choir in church or anything?
L:	Yes, I still do.
M:	Do you still whistle?
L:	Yes.
M:	Do you want to whistle a little bit for me? (Louise laughs) Maybe another time?
L:	Some other time, yes! (she laughs, then pauses) And . . . and after you're married for so long . . . Oh, I still, about six years

214

after we were married, I *still* thought I would go, you know, but ... *Noooo*, you get into the routine where ... (she trails off)

And then thirteen years later I had my *other* son. So. I was well settled and didn't want the singing anymore. So that was it. I did want to go to school. And probably could have gone for music, but my mother absolutely said if I was a boy she would have [let me], but since I'm a girl, it would be a waste. So I never did get to go. And I would have loved to. Oh my. I think education is just, just really something. Mmm-hmm. I wasn't real good in math ... but I went to California [California University of Pennsylvania] and I asked them, "Is there—could I go to college without taking math, no math at all?" And they said "No you can't. We'll get you a tutor." Well, we didn't have that kind of money to get me a tutor, so I didn't go. But I sure did want to go. Mmm-*hmm*.

By waiting until Louise said everything she wanted to say about her desire to pursue a career and an education, the folklorist was able to discover information that direct questions might not have revealed.[56] The personal experience narratives and details that emerged provided fruitful topics for later discussion: the traditional position of women's work in support of male work, the effects of marriage and parenthood on women's occupational opportunities, and educational barriers for working-class women. The folklorist could then follow up on these ideas later with more specific questions.

Field Notes

The primary purpose of field notes is to provide the folklorist with an in-the-moment record of what happened during fieldwork. In the field, a folklorist records her observations in many ways, with audio, video, or photographic equipment, paying careful attention and making precise notes about the details of text, texture, and context. Even when recording, videoing, or photographing, it's important to write down thoughts and ideas to support these other records and to assist with putting together more extensive comments later. Field notes are a kind of running commentary on activities, and they also supplement our memories and responses to the events we take part in during fieldwork. The notes help to explain what was going on and provide the folklorist's perspective on the situation. These comments are useful for the folklorist when planning follow-up interviews and mapping out potential topics for discussion and are also helpful for preparing for future fieldwork.

The folklorist could also refer to the reflexive comments in the notes when analyzing the dynamics of the situation, perhaps to aid in the interpretation of the texts and performances.

There are two kinds of field notes. One is the scribbled thoughts, phrases, questions, observations (including relevant physical or technical details) and impressions the folklorist dashes off *in the field*; the other is a more organized *write-up* based on those quick comments. The write-up is a little more formal and can pull together the perhaps disjointed observations made in the field.

The format for taking field notes and the process of writing them up vary from folklorist to folklorist. Not all notes are exactly the same, nor do they always need to be. With experience and practice, you will find a method and format for your own field projects that work best for your fieldwork and writing style. In some cases, though, the format of field notes—particularly the formal write-ups—is provided for you. Your instructor may have a preferred format that he or she asks you to use in order to ensure uniformity and ease of reading, and some institutions dictate how they want field notes and writes-ups to look, again to ensure uniformity and to simplify the reading and research process. No matter the situation, though, field notes need to be detailed enough to be useful for the folklorist when writing reports, articles, and essays related to field experiences.

Example: Write-up of Field Notes

The following excerpts from a formal write-up of field notes are an example of the kinds of detailed narrative description folklorists may complete as an accompaniment to taped interviews and other field experiences. The project these notes are excerpted and adapted from was a cultural survey supported by the National Park Service, as part of America's Industrial Heritage Project (AIHP). The goal of AIHP was to survey several counties in central and southwestern Pennsylvania, focusing on the industrial, agricultural, and cultural histories of the region. This fieldworker's concentration was on occupational life, primarily coal mining and its impact on the history, community, and expressive culture of the residents of Somerset County, Pennsylvania. As part of this project, fieldworkers were required to supply written daily field notes along with copies of taped interviews, photographs, or videos so future researchers could see the process that the fieldwork followed and perhaps discover new ideas for future projects.[57] The notes also serve the practical function of describing or explaining any confusing spots or technical glitches or features that might affect the recorded materials. These notes are meant for public use, so they are quite detailed and read like a narrative report on the day's fieldwork. This is an excerpt with commentary we've added to illustrate the folklorist's interview process and post-interview ideas.

First of all, the folklorist establishes the factual, dated information and describes the physical context. This information includes who is present at the recording session and where and when it takes place. The folklorist also notes the initial recorded data from which this write-up was developed, with references to the tape log at a few key points. She also notes a few technical details of the taping session that could affect tape quality.

> I met on the evening of June 17, 1990 with Terry and Dorothy Steinkirchner, the owners of the Listie Economy Store in Listie, PA. [Terry's] great-grandfather and grandfather established the store, then his father, Ebby Steinkirchner, took over, and now Terry operates the business. Terry's father still works at the store doing most of the meat cutting. . . . Dorothy's father, Steven Svonavec, is a 95-year old former coal miner and farmer, a Slovakian immigrant. Her brothers, Joe and Butch, own Svonavec Mining Company (strip mining); their sons have taken over the business. . . . We talked in the kitchen of the Steinkirchners' house . . . A kitchen fan kept the room cool on the very warm humid evening I visited, and the whirring and clicking of the blades do show up on the tape. . . .
>
> The Steinkirchners talked mostly about the store and how the business had changed. They said they were much busier before the mines closed, and much of their business then was with the mines. Terry said they used to sell up to five tons of dynamite a week to the small mines surrounding Listie (#A105), and he remembers delivering carbide to the mines with his father. They would take whole truckloads of 100-lb. kegs down to Friedens, Waterloo, Big Seven, Bando, and the mines near Rockwood . . . (#A151). Farmers, too, used more dynamite than they do now, for blasting out stumps, clearing land, and making ditches. . . . (#A168).

Field notes can also help capture details and ideas that it is not possible to explore at the time. Below, the fieldworker records the outline of a story she heard about a local cemetery while she was riding in a truck with her consultants. Since they were on their way to another location, she couldn't ask the driver to stop so she could set up her tape recorder and camera to record this interesting text on the spot. If she decided to learn more or document the narrative, she could arrange to meet the consultants at the cemetery later at a convenient time and ask their permission to record their meeting and perhaps take video or photographs. She could use the earlier nonrecorded experience as background and refer to the more concrete documented information as part of her analysis. The notes help to remind her of the story so she can follow up with her consultants later.

> After the interview, Terry and Dorothy took me on a tour of Listie in their truck. . . . Near the top of one hill, Dorothy pointed out the local cemetery, where members of the Listie Brethren Church and the Listie Catholic (Slovak) Church are buried. She showed me her mother's grave. She said that the Brethren bought the middle section of the property from the Catholics and "now they're all neighbors." Her father, a member of the Catholic Church, likes to joke "We're guarding them," because the Catholics are buried on either side of the Brethren (Protestants), who are "confined" to the middle section.

In the following excerpt, the folklorist notes the shift in scene to a surprise situation—her consultants take her on an unplanned visit to meet another group of family members. She mentions some of the practical problems this lack of planning created but also notes interesting things that came up; even in the tense setting, the folklorist observes material that has potential for more detailed study.

> After the tour, we went to Dorothy's father's house (Steven Svonavec), where he was playing cards with his sons and Joe and Butch (Steve, Jr.) and their wives Grace and Libby. The card game is a twice-weekly—at least—family ritual, with all family members taking part. They were unprepared for the visit, as was I, but Dorothy insisted and assured me it would be fine. I fussed with the tape recorder, and didn't have enough release forms (I arranged to take them over another day), but went ahead and taped a short conversation. . . . We spoke in the basement of Mr. Svonavec's home around a card table. There is a clock ticking loudly in the background of the tape, and Joe occasionally tapped the deck of cards on the table and spit tobacco juice into a tin can on the floor. Toward the end of our talk, he tapped more and more loudly and shuffled the cards.
>
> (The card game, by the way, was invented by Mr. Svonavec and is played only by the Svonavec family. They enjoy it very much and look forward to playing it together every few days. This would be a great angle

to follow up for family tradition. . . . Another interesting note: On the wall, behind framed glass, was a large rosary made of tiny preserved pink roses. I asked about it and Dorothy told me it was used at her mother's funeral—"the last rosary." She said a friend had it framed as a gift for her father. . . . I've never heard of this practice before. Is it widespread? A local custom? Could follow up on this.)

How to recover from a bad question? As the folklorist mentioned in the excerpt above, the situation was not ideal for an interview. Later in the interview, she decided to ask a question she thought would introduce a friendly and entertaining topic to reduce some of the tension—but as you'll see, it seemed to make the consultants more uncomfortable. She records these reactions so she may reflect later on how her presence may have affected what the consultants said—or didn't say—during their initial interview. In this situation, the fieldworker let the discussion unfold in the direction that the consultants wanted to take it and then concluded as quickly as she could. She needed to establish a more professional frame in which to collect information so that the family would be more comfortable, perhaps by asking her original (perhaps more sympathetic) contacts to assist her with arranging a meeting with the family at a more convenient time.

The family was polite, but clearly uncomfortable and a bit unhappy at being interrupted in the middle of their card game. I'm afraid I made the tension worse by asking early in our conversation "What did you used to do for fun in Listie?" In response, and throughout our talk, they stressed the importance of good, hard, serious work, and repeatedly told me they never had time or opportunities for "fun." At the end of the interview, Joe and Steve expressed strong feelings about "fun" as causing the downfall of social and economic structure in the U.S. Mr. Svonavec was less forthcoming than his sons, probably because he kept indicating through grumbles and gestures that he really wanted to get back to his card game. . . . Joe complained about the "rigamaroo" that makes it difficult for his coal company to meet government specs (#A327).

At the end of the write-up, the folklorist listed a few ideas for follow-up, ranging from broad categories to very specific objects or customs. These assisted with planning and acted as reminders of interesting topics to pursue in the future, perhaps even after this particular project was completed.

Notes and Ideas for Future and Follow-up Projects

- Family and occupational PE [personal experience] narratives—connections between work and family lives; mining and farming connections; families connected through community, work.
- Sense of place in terms of family-owned business.
- Ethnic/religious/occupational traditions. . . . Dorothy emphasized that the Catholic Church was a Slovak Catholic church, and the cemetery story confirms the importance of ethnic/religious identity in the town. Many of the miners in Listie were Slovak, and many of the farmers and merchants were German; ethnicity appears to be related to occupation, particularly where the two intersect in Terry and Dorothy's family.
- The Svonavec family's invented card game tradition—both the material and practice of the game itself and the way it figures into family tradition.
- Rosary tradition—this would be fun to learn more about as a traditional craft and vernacular religious practice.
- Politics and social views and their connection with occupation, tradition, sense of place, and family identity.

Transcribing and Transcripts

Transcribing recorded material is a time-consuming but necessary part of fieldwork projects. In planning your project, you need to save a big chunk of time for this activity: transcribing can take four times as long as the recorded session itself. That means for every hour of recorded material, you can expect to take about four hours to fully transcribe the material. This time may vary—yes, it can even take longer—depending on the recording quality and your typing or writing speed.[58] The task may seem daunting, but once finished, you will have a written record of interviews that you can refer to and incorporate into your analysis. The following is an excerpt from a transcript of a longer storytelling session involving five women in their twenties and thirties sharing coming-of-age narratives. (Only four women speak in this particular excerpt.) This segment leads up to a longer narrative told by one of the participants. In this excerpt, you will notice some of the following things the transcriber had to deal with in presenting the information.

- Multiple speakers (identified here by initials to speed the transcribing process)
- Overlapping speakers

220

- Short interjections that sometimes interrupt other speakers
- Participants with the same name or initials
- Points at which specific speakers can't be identified

Transcript

B:	I remember we saw a movie in eighth grade ...
M:	Eighth grade? Wow!
B:	Yeah. I already was ... I mean, I was 11 when I started.
P:	Well, I was nineteen.
M:	You were nineteen?
B:	I was 11. . . . Nineteen? My *gosh!*
MS:	That's older than *me*, man!
P:	I was a late bloomer.
M:	No kidding! (overlapping with B.)
B:	Oh yeah! (overlapping with M.)
P:	So I *really* didn't believe it ...
	[other members of the group comment—Oh, no! Of course! Wow!—but I couldn't sort out who was speaking on the tape]
P:	(continues) I thought Kotex[59] was the biggest rip off in the world. Because all these people would go into the store and buy it ...
B:	Uh-huh.
P:	...you know, when they're 15 or 16 ... [At this point, P. begins a longer narrative about her experience.]

Even in this seemingly insignificant transition section, we get a lot of information. It introduces the topic: the age at which each of the women had her first menstrual period. It establishes the norm within the group as well as the variation: one member of the group started much later than the others, so her experience differed from theirs. The group focused on the difference, and it may be that this unique characteristic of P's experience established a situation that made it okay for her to tell her story. (Here we also see the balance of static and dynamic elements—the general topic is shared by all the women, but the teller's story focuses on the details that make her experience noteworthy.) Another important feature of this segment of the transcript is that it reveals the tone of the conversation: informal, friendly interaction of people who know each other and aren't embarrassed talking about intimate topics around each other.

There has been some debate about how, or whether, to represent accents and regional dialects in transcription. Some people use nonstandard spellings or phonetic representations of pronunciations, while others standardize or clean up speech. In many cases, these decisions are up to the folklorist; in others, there are guidelines provided by an organization or institution with which the transcriber is affiliated. Depending on the purpose of the transcripts, it may be important to capture the individual voice and flavor of the speech, while taking care to avoid implying stereotypes or hierarchical value judgments.

Returning from the Field: Follow-up Research

Once you have returned and organized your materials and your notes, you need to get ready to write about your observations and data. Part of this process includes going back to the library and conducting further research, considering specific aspects of your discoveries in the field. During the fieldwork process you probably will have begun to think about and notice things about the folklore you are collecting and/or the group you are working with that you hadn't thought of before you began. Now you have the opportunity to find out, through your research, what others have had to say about texts similar to those you have examined. What they have said may lead you to discover unexpected avenues to investigate and explore. You might find that others have seen things from a perspective similar to yours, or you might discover in reading other interpretations that you have seen something from a new point of view. In either case, you should be reassured that you will have other critical voices that support yours or that contrast and compare with your ideas. The examples that you'll study in the next chapter should give you some ideas about how to weave together your own research and secondary research. They also illustrate several patterns of organization for the written presentation of your findings.

The People Factor: Interpersonal and Ethical Concerns

The fieldwork process, on the surface, can seem straightforward. You decide on a topic you want to research and figure out how you will make contact with the text and/or people you need to research. You go into the field and collect your data, make and record your observations, then prepare your analysis. But because you're dealing with people (and you're a person), you will encounter issues that are all part of the complex nature of interpersonal interaction, and these are important aspects of the fieldwork experience and interpretation process. As we have illustrated throughout the earlier chapters, folklorists are mindful of the role their own actions and attitudes play in the fieldwork process. Respect for the people and texts with whom they work should be a constant consideration of the folklorist's research process. Above all else when undertaking a fieldwork project, small or large, it is crucial to remember that the folklorist's role never supersedes the roles of those he or she works with in the field. Folklorists recognize that folklore and its meanings are established and shared by groups of people, and always reside within those groups.

Insider and Outsider Roles

As you begin planning your fieldwork, one primary issue to consider is who you are in relation to the groups and texts you will be studying. This isn't a "get in touch with your feelings" exercise but valuable knowledge to have for a number of reasons as you begin your research and even as you work on interpreting your data. This is useful in helping you make choices about how to approach your research. How much will you need to prepare yourself with background research? What biases do you have about the text or people with whom you'll be working? What impact will all of this have on the research you are doing? In other words, you will want to think about your role or *position* in relation to the data you are collecting.

Are you an *insider*, someone who is already a member of the group and may even participate in the particular folklore you are interested in collecting? Are you an *outsider*, someone who does not associate at all with the people you hope to study? Or perhaps you are someone who is a member of a similar group but does not know the specific people and practices of the local group you currently have access to? Such distinctions may not initially be clear cut, but thinking about your position is important in the work you will do.

Consider, for example, the following comments of Jay Mechling, whose work with the Boy Scouts we refer to in chapter 3:

> I come to the study of the Boy Scout experience with the mixed strengths and weaknesses of the insider. This is not a scientifically 'objective' study, if ever such a thing is possible, especially outside the laboratory and in the natural settings of everyday life. My fieldwork with this troop always had as its comparative background my own experiences as a Scout, and it always has as its sense-making framework my ongoing interdisciplinary training and practices, as I drew upon history, folklore, anthropology, sociology, psychology, rhetorical criticism, and other scholarly fields to understand what I was seeing and hearing. (2001, xxi)

223

Mechling is aware of the effect that his position will have on his work, and acknowledging it to himself and the readers of his written interpretation allows potential biases and conflicts to be aired.

Whether you are an insider or outsider will affect the way you position yourself in your interactions with consultants. There are potential complications with either role, though it might seem that researching as an insider would be less difficult. Yet, if you are an insider, you need to consider how to help yourself stand outside to observe and interpret what is happening. This interpretive process can be difficult because behaviors and language seem, to you, to be ordinary. On the other hand, an outsider's stance may be difficult because there is so much unknown to you: the people, the context (physical and psychological), the behavior, the language, and material objects. You may not be sure where to look, what to listen to, or how to behave.

Observation and Participant-Observer Roles

Insider and outsider status are determined by circumstance, things you cannot change when you begin your research. You can, however, choose how you approach your fieldwork, whether as an *observer* only or as a *participant-observer*. An observer watches what people do, examines material objects, and may listen to conversations or stories. He could photograph and seek information about gargoyles and grotesques on property in local neighborhoods. Collecting narratives about people's UFO experiences, through interviews, surveys, or even email also qualifies as observation research. In projects such as this, students are involved in the research ("observation" sounds less active than this type of work really is), but they aren't making regular, experiential contact with the texts and performances.

Participatory observation involves more interaction with members of a group and requires the freedom to adapt to their schedule. A participant-observer spends time with and in the community she is studying. Being a participant-observer could mean that you become an observer within a group in which you already participate; for instance, you record family stories or videotape a Civil War reenactment or study the traditions of the people with whom you play pickup basketball. In other cases, you may choose to involve yourself temporarily in the activities of a group you are interested in. That could mean attending meetings of the Pagan Student Association or riding with a taxi driver for a couple of shifts. This doesn't mean (though it could) completely immersing yourself in a group; it simply acknowledges your active involvement during a folklore performance with the group you're researching. Both observation and participant-observation require the folklorist to consider interpersonal issues such as rapport and ethics, but the position you as the researcher take will affect the way in which you need to think about and prepare for these elements of the research and resultant related interpretation.

Rapport: Creating and Understanding Researcher-Consultant Relationships

Once a researcher has determined what she wants to research, whether a particular type of folklore text or a folk group, she must gain access to the performers or creators of the text or members of the group. In some cases, this may seem quite simple: she may know that the woman who lives two doors down from her meets monthly with a group that quilts. Or she may guess that there is something worth investigating at the lawn mower repair shop with huge wooden animals standing in its parking lot. There may be a playground in her neighborhood where children regularly jump rope after school. These possibilities suggest that physical location won't be an impediment, but what about making contact with the person or people she'd like to observe or talk with, and more importantly, how does she build constructive research relationships with them?

Building rapport requires social awareness and some ability to understand people's communication styles. It requires putting yourself out there to make contact with people and get them to open up to you. If you are not already familiar with people who create or perform the type of texts you are interested in, then you will have to look for contacts through friends, colleagues, classmates, and public directories. Once you have found people to talk with, you will need to develop your relationship. Bruce Jackson, whose book *Fieldwork* provides a good introduction to this type of research, explains that "fieldwork is a dynamic enterprise: each encounter is different from the one before and the one that follows. Collectors, therefore, can never afford to go into collecting sessions without giving careful thought to the structure of the relationships between themselves and the informants" (1987, 70). He finds it difficult to explain how to create rapport, but he does say how it can be damaged or spoiled: basically, by committing typical social faux pas—being dishonest, making (culturally) insensitive comments, and acting inappropriately as related to others' beliefs and values (70–71).

Jackson makes the point that there should be (or is, regardless of whether the fieldworker recognizes it or not) some sort of exchange or mutual understanding between the fieldworker and consultant, and that exchange may not necessarily be based on whether the consultant likes the fieldworker or not (1987, 72).

Circumstance and coincidence may be the strongest influences on rapport building. It might seem that working with a friend or longtime acquaintance would be an ideal fieldwork relationship, but that, too, may not always be the case. As we point out in discussing positioning, a researcher's relationship with consultants alters the context and dynamic of the performance, even if the role of participant-observer is comfortable and the folklorist is accepted by the group members. And that change in position (or relationship) can affect the dynamic enough that the experience doesn't work out as the researcher (or even her consultants) had hoped.

Most interestingly, those people you already know and whose support you have in your work may not turn out to be the best consultants because of that change in the dynamic (see Jackson 1987, 69). It may be that you can work through this potential problem given time and enough audio or video space, and it may be that you simply have to move on and find another consultant or project. The flip side of this is that researchers may make new relationships through fieldwork that would not have existed but for the work they have done. In one of our classes, for example, a student was able to build rapport with her consultant in part because they both sang gospel hymns. At the end of the term, they actually sang together for the class—even though the collection project the student had worked on was not related to music.

Example: Complex Relationships and Responsibilities

A fascinating example of rapport, trust, and the changing dynamics of the relationships among those who are providing texts to fieldworkers and those who are seeking information from the texts can be found in the experiences of Claire Farrer. Farrer's longtime work of researching children's play with the Mescalero Apache changed when she was put in the position of knowing information she didn't want responsibility for and holding that information until the time came for it to be communicated. Bernard Second, a religious leader on the reservation where she worked, informed her that he had dreamed about her and that she was "The One Who is Coming," a person to whom he must pass along knowledge that he could share with no other. Second knew that he would die before Farrer and shared with her certain information that she would need to communicate to a certain person after his death. She was not to record the information but must memorize it, and he could not tell her with whom she should share it—only that she would know (and mustn't give it to the wrong people). Years passed and Farrer doubted that the information was even retrievable from her memory. But then a young man called her and, using a ritual frame, asked her if she knew things he needed to know. That triggered her memory. She realizes now that she only remembers when "the context is appropriate and the questioner asks in a specific way" (2000). Farrer became, in a sense, a keeper of memories which she knows are not hers—and doesn't want. Her responsibility to the Mescalero Apache and perhaps, in some sense, her reciprocal exchange for the work she was able to do with them changed her position in ways one might never imagine.

Ethics

Ethics are an important consideration when performing fieldwork, and because of the intimate nature of the fieldwork folklorists do, they may encounter situations that challenge standard ethical considerations. In some cases, folklorists may develop long-term relationships with their consultants that complicate the ethical issues inherent in such work. Though it's unlikely that you will come across serious ethical issues in your own initial research projects, it's necessary to consider and understand the importance of ethics in fieldwork and to think about the kind of in-depth engagement with culture that folklore can provide.

The act of analyzing context in and of itself may put folklorists on the outside, implying an us/them hierarchy, in which the educated scholar could be assumed to be a more valid interpreter of expressive culture than the group members themselves. In this version of the interpretive process, the folklorist would record the folklore, ask questions of performers and consultants, and perhaps return as often as needed (or possible) to be sure to get a thorough understanding of the material. At this point, most folklorists would have then gone home and prepared the analysis and interpretation, written a scholarly article or a book, and published the work, without discussing their ideas with the performers or consultants. The misconception here is that because folklorists are trained in understanding folklore in ways the consultants (that is, the folk) are not, folklorists' interpretations are always better and more accurate than those of the folk performers and artists. The hierarchical implications of work in which the folklorist's interpretation is the only interpretation, or the only *right* interpretation, conflict with the basic premise of folklore as a process of learning and communicating attitudes, beliefs, and values that are significant to the group sharing them.

Many folklorists advocate an approach to contextual analysis that incorporates the views of folk group members in the interpretation of folklore. That's why most prefer to use terms such as "consultants," "artists," "performers," or "participants" and avoid potentially judgmental terms such as "informant" or "subject." Rather than interpret folklore performances themselves in scholarly isolation, folklorists ask group members about meanings and connections. After they have written about their interpretations, they may share their work and analyses with their consultants and offer the opportunity for them to comment on the folklorist's interpretations or present their own. Approaching fieldwork in this way doesn't mean folklorists do no interpretation at all, though. Jeff Titon (1988) envisions the process as a series of dialogues that are ultimately part of an ongoing discussion among performers, consultants, folklorists, scholars, and the public in general. This approach is referred to as reflexive or *reciprocal ethnography*.[60]

Reciprocal Ethnography

As both an interpretive approach and a method for analyzing and presenting observations about folklore, reciprocal ethnography addresses some of the ethical issues that can arise in fieldwork. As you may recall from reading about interpretive approaches to folklore in the preceding chapter, folklorists recognize that placing their own interpretive spin on the analysis of a text can be ethnocentric, because it often places the text (or at least the interpretation of it) in the cultural context of the folklorist-researcher, not in the context of the group who communicated through it.

To provide a more thorough, balanced interpretation, most folklorists incorporate their consultants' observations and commentary into the analysis of the texts and performances they study. For many, this process of reciprocal ethnography involves providing consultants with drafts of written accounts (essays, articles, books) and requesting their feedback. Consultants then have the opportunity to correct obvious errors (misspellings, inaccurate dates, and so forth), as well as provide their own interpretations of the performances and materials. They can also comment on and critique the folklorists' interpretations. Published accounts of fieldwork and folklore studies incorporate the consultants' and folklorists' reflexive analyses in a variety of ways. Some might present both, side by side, or present the consultants' views when they differ from the folklorists'.

Elaine Lawless has illustrated dramatically why such reciprocal, collaborative approaches are necessary and has demonstrated how folklorists can use reflexive methods to develop their ethnographic works. Lawless (1991, 1992, 1993, 1994, 2000) has reflected upon some of her earlier work, considered ways to more accurately represent her consultants' interpretations, and published accounts of her own reflexive self-analysis and her own position or role in the interpretive process. Lawless's idea is to extend the concept of reciprocal ethnography to include a more collaborative or collective interpretation of the narratives and data collected by the fieldworker. This approach encourages

228

fieldworkers to take into account and give voice to the participants' responses to and understanding of the fieldworkers' interpretations. As Lawless explains, "A reflexive stance should illuminate the biases and preconceptions that inform our interpretations (where *we* are) and move us forward, then, in the direction of collectivity in interpretation and a new authentication of a multivocal kind of ethnography, which includes, as well, where *others* are, but which does not privilege one interpretation over another" (1992, 302). Lawless's work illustrates the dynamic relationships between members of folk groups and the scholars who work with them and demonstrates the fairness and democracy that the reciprocal approach creates and encompasses.

Elaine Lawless is not the only folklorist to support this methodology. One who has applied this approach in the study of oral texts is Kirin Narayan (1995), who worked with a group of Indian women to record and interpret performances of traditional songs. She discusses a few of the problems her fieldwork revealed with "the collection and the presentation of people's own interpretation of their own folklore" (256). Her work illustrates the need for fieldworkers to think reflexively about the influences of their own presence and to consider how best to elicit in-depth responses from consultants. Some of these topics are addressed in a special double issue of the *Journal of Folklore Research*, titled "Issues in Collaboration and Representation" (Brown 2000), in which several scholars consider practical and theoretical concerns that arise during the process. Their comments and questions about how to develop and present shared interpretation in ethnographic accounts demonstrate the potential of the reciprocal approach and suggest ways to apply the methodology in future projects.

Perhaps the most important lesson we are learning from these evolving discussions of this theoretical approach and the work of those who have adopted this methodology is that honest, thorough interpretations of folklore do not occur in a vacuum. They are negotiated articulations of meaning that performers, creators, group members, and scholars form together, as part of an ongoing dialogue or discussion. Certainly, the folklorist's voice is important and holds as much weight as—but not necessarily more than—anyone else's voice in this conversation. It is the folklorist's primary job to shape and provide a framework for the presentation of this shared interpretation. Most scholars working in this area advocate a presentation format that openly acknowledges whose interpretation belongs to whom (performers, scholars, and other commentators) and that reflects—perhaps by recording the dialogue in some way—the nature of the shared process through which interpretations of meaning evolve.

It is important to keep the principles of reciprocal ethnography in mind both in the field and while writing up your analysis. This method acknowledges the collaborative process of folklore, both in the ways it is created and shared among group members and in how it is interpreted and presented by scholars. As Olivia Cadavel reminds us, our ethnographic documents "are not the result of a single voice, and like all representations, they are negotiated" (2000, 190). Cadavel also calls for us to "explore new forms for discursive representation and interpretation. . . . We need to experiment not only with forms of documentation but also with the process of working with 'Others'" (191).

And, as Elaine Lawless says, "Equally important is the reminder to us as scholars that our interpretations are *not* the 'last word,' that our interpretations are not necessarily the right or insightful ones" (1992, 310). Because this methodology acknowledges the consultants' authority to determine in part what happens to the folklore they share, it can help mediate ethical dilemmas that can be part of the fieldwork process. As scholars continue to explore the potential of the collaborative, reciprocal process, greater opportunities for interpreting folklore and thinking about the very nature of the field will certainly emerge.

Example: Giving up the Last Word

In over forty years of work with Hugh Yellowman, a Navajo, and his family, Barre Toelken made numerous audio recordings. Based on these, and from the process that created them, Toelken learned and wrote much about the Navajo culture and its verbal lore. Throughout the years, Toelken grew close to the family (they had adopted him in the 1950s; 1998, 384). It's possible that Toelken's long-term relationship with them made it more likely that he would feel a great responsibility for what would happen to the tapes after his death. However, this ethical question takes on greater implications than the personal and is therefore an important and interesting case for us to consider.

One of the concerns the Navajo had in allowing Toelken to make and keep recordings was that some of the stories were seasonal and were only to be told at certain times "defined by the larger movements of nature, not by the immediate agendas of humans" (1998, 381). Because of the rapport Toelken had built with the Navajo, Yellowman trusted Toelken's promise that he would play the tapes only when cultural rules deemed appropriate, so Toelken was able to record a great deal of Navajo verbal lore. Toelken's perspective and the manner in which he eventually dealt with his concern about the recordings of Yellowman's narratives foreground one of the principles of contemporary folklore study: the importance of people and their *real and active* cultural expressions.

Toelken worked to satisfy both his own scholarly interests and the cultural interests of his Navajo family and friends. His concern about the recordings and the cultural guidelines for sharing them, he imagined, would put him at odds with some of his colleagues who previously had told him he owed it to the profession to investigate the relationship of Coyote stories to witchcraft (1998, 385–86). Nevertheless, his decision about how to handle the tapes after Yellowman's death was founded on his belief that traditional stories "exist in the minds of narrators and audiences and are brought to dramatic reality when they are told in a living cultural context" (386).

After Yellowman's death, Toelken visited with Helen Yellowman, Hugh's widow, and discussed what should be done with the tapes. Concern that the tapes could someday be played at the wrong time, among other issues, convinced Toelken to return the tapes to her to be destroyed (1998, 385). In retrospect, Toelken admits he could have discussed with Yellowman himself how the tapes should be handled, though the issues would still have been difficult: they were "not about ownership, sovereignty, or hegemonic control over the texts, but prudent husbandry of potentially dangerous spoken words." He voices the ethical issue behind such dilemmas simply—as a need to collaborate with fieldwork consultants, "who are, after all, our colleagues and teachers—in the shaping and limiting of the fieldwork project. . . . We play by their rules, not ours" (388).

Conclusion

Toelken sums up many of the important issues and challenges folklorists face when taking part in fieldwork. He hopes his own experience can help folklorists understand that they can "learn more and do better work when scholarly decisions are guided by the culture we study, even when taking this course causes disruption in our academic assumptions" (1998, 381). He believes that "the best reason for studying culturally situated expressions is precisely that we can perceive and understand the culture's worldview better" (384). Respect for the cultural beliefs and values of our consultants is the ethical bottom line for folklorists.

231

CHAPTER 8

Examples of Folklore Projects

To give you an idea of how folklorists—both experienced and novice—handle writing about their fieldwork, we've gathered together six projects for you to read and consider. The researcher-authors have put a great deal of time and energy into their work and its presentation. We are excited by the variety we have to show you: these are researchers and writers with varying levels of experience, and they have approached their work with different research methodologies. We think each of these projects presents interesting discoveries about group interaction and expressive culture, and each does so within its own unique structure, reflecting the type of information gathered and the way in which the researcher-author thinks it comes across most clearly and effectively. Through each of these examples, you can see some of the underlying research strategies and how the researcher's involvement with consultants and their beliefs, values, behaviors, and texts shapes each ethnographic project individually (and sometimes how that research process affects the researchers themselves).

We've discovered these authors and their essays through our work and that of our colleagues as writing and folklore instructors.

Each of these essays incorporates description and interpretation important to writing up research. The description may be of a place, a process, a text, or the people involved, depending on what is important to the presentation of the folklore and to the interpretation of the researcher-author and the consultants. Information drawn from interviews may be summarized, but it is often included in the voices of the consultants themselves. Please note that in some cases, the researcher-authors used pseudonyms for their consultants, because of the personal nature of the experiences and insights reported.

One of the Guys

Joe Ringler

> *Joe researched and wrote this ethnography of a fire station for a first-year writing class. One feature we really like about his project is the level of connection Joe made with his consultants at the fire station. As a first-term, first-year student, Joe was welcomed by the crew at the station, and that made his work with them personally as well as academically fulfilling. He spent a full term on the project, observing, interviewing, and generally just spending time at the station.*
>
> *"One of the Guys" illustrates the type of project that a novice folklorist might take on without extensive research other than fieldwork, with a particular focus on the culture of a group. In this case, there is not as much analysis as in the other studies, which required more background research in addition to work with the people and texts themselves. Joe's research as a participant-observer provides him the kind of detail needed for the narrative style of this essay. We think this description of the station and activities of the unit shows, as Joe points out, the importance of camaraderie among the firefighters.*

A Fire Station?

I arrived at Station 121 at about 3:30 Monday afternoon, Oct. 2nd. I had to hitch a ride from a police officer because I was confused about the location of the engine house. As the policeman escorted me to Station 121 he mentioned to me that the area was not a safe neighborhood for individuals to walk through. The officer exclaimed that the area has a high crime rate. This point that the police officer presented caused the butterflies in my stomach to flutter. I was already nervous about talking to the firefighters about my project, and he had to throw that information to me. The police officer pulled into the sloping driveway as my mind began to think of negative situations that I could be getting myself into. I thought about how the firefighters would reject my plans to observe them and send me off to walk home by myself through a neighborhood that wants to eat my raw flesh. I told the policeman thanks as he drove away to leave me stranded in the driveway.

I stood on the site of the fire station on the corner of High Street and Maple Ave. I examined the apartments and houses that surround the engine house. The buildings were not as shabby and run down as I had imagined. The area was not out of the ordinary. Just a simple looking neighborhood. Let's just say I have seen worse. I turned and directed myself towards the tan colored brick building.

This single story building with a brick exterior had three sections with the north and south ends of the building serving as garages. Both the garages appeared to have enough space in them to hold several emergency vehicles. Seeing what was in the building was difficult due to the fact that the garage doors were closed. The south garage was a bit longer than the north garage and the south side was only about 50 feet from the road. This fire station reminded me of an auto shop, based on the size and construction of the garage. Normally, I would think an engine house would be a two-story building with a dark brick complexion, from what I have seen on TV programs. I would have missed Station 121 if the policeman had not dropped me off. The fire station was camouflaged, so it fit in with the community that surrounded it. I began to assume that there was nothing special about the space I was to encounter. I became disappointed as I continued to walk around the place.

The center section of the building appeared to be the offices and living quarters, which the firefighters occupied between fires. In the front, this section extended past the two garages. In between the driveways, and in front of the center portion of the station, laid a small yard with a couple of small trees, and a flagpole with the American Flag and another flag underneath that read Division of Fire. I looked behind the building to see how far out it extended. The building was pretty much even in the back. There were two separate parking sections at the back of Station 121, also.

As I walked around the south side of the station, I entered what appeared to be a playground for little toddlers. It was interesting because there were no swings or slides. Just sand boxes and animal figures. Was this part of the fire station? This was one more aspect of the surroundings that made the station blend in with the area. I began to think that the surroundings of the place indicated something about who the men were. Frustration rose inside of me as I continued back towards the front of Station 121.

I walked into the south garage because one of the doors happened to be open. I walked inside smelling a hint of diesel fumes and gazed at the fire truck. Engine 121 was written in white letters on the truck's side; the vehicle reminded me of a semi. This piece of equipment struck me funny because of its shape. I was used to seeing long, red, Twinkie shaped vehicles. It had all the necessary pieces of equipment that define a fire truck, such as the lights, sirens, tools, and the large back end where the water was stored. The color, of course, was red. What made it different was the large compartment in between the cab and the tank. The compartment stood above the rest of the truck like a rectangular box and looked like a large phone booth. I assumed that the firefighters rode in this section when on a run due to the fact that it had seats, and in front of the seats was the fire gear that the men wore. Just as I had with the station, I began to feel disappointed with the way the truck looked. The truck was unique but strange. I began to feel like I had chosen a bad station at which to do my research.

Beside the fire truck was a chief's car that two men were climbing out of.

Chief and Captain

"How can I help you?" asked a man who was thin, about my height, had a mustache and was wearing navy blue pants and a navy blue, collared shirt. The right side of his shirt had stitching that read BN. Chief R Cassidy. "He is the chief," I thought, as I read the name. The left side of his shirt had a circular patch. The patch had a flame in the middle and the name of the city and phrase "Division of Fire," circling around the flame. The tension that I acquired after the trip with the police was easing some. I explained to Chief Cassidy that I was doing a fieldwork project for a class and wanted to do it on a fire station.

"Well I got a lot of paper work to do, but Bobby can take you to the Captain's office and he will answer any question you have." Bobby was a short husky fire fighter and wore the same type of clothing as the Chief only his shirt was not a collared, button up shirt. The right side of his shirt was embroidered with the words R. Cornell. He didn't say anything but just motioned his hand for me to follow him through a set of double doors just inside the garage. I entered into the center part of the building and found myself in a hallway that reminded me of a hospital hallway. The Chief, who was walking behind us, went into the first room that was on the left. A sign beside the door read "Chief's Office." I followed the firefighter, Bobby, in through the second door on the left.

"This is Joe, and he wants to do an English project on our station," Bobby said. "Hi, my name is Wes Freeman, the captain of Station 121, B Shift." Captain Freeman was a tall man with a mustache and glasses. He shook my hand firmly and asked me to have a seat in a chair facing perpendicular to his desk. The position of his chair made me turn a little so that I could face him. He was wearing a navy blue uniform just like Chief Cassidy and Bobby. His name was stitched in yellow letters on his shirt on the right side of his chest.

I told him my name and explained to him that I was doing ethnographic research for English. I told him that the assignment required me to pick a group, observe them, and describe the culture within this particular group. I explained that I wanted to examine a fire station because I was interested in what firefighters do.

"I'm just going to visit a couple times a week and observe the atmosphere here," I explained. In a deep voice, Captain Freeman described to me that Station 121 was divided into three groups.

"B Shift, which is the unit I am part of, A Shift, and C Shift all occupy this location. All of these units have a different personality. B Shift is a bunch of good guys," he exclaimed. "There are many decorated men in this outfit." I thought about the truck, the building, and the community, thinking that if they are a bunch of good guys, then why don't they deserve better. I decided that since B Shift is the group that I had first made contact with, I would probably just observe them. He gave me a calendar of days each group worked. "B Shift works on the days that are green."

"Would you like to ride on the engine?" he asked. I was trying to sound calm but was actually excited that he offered.

"Sure!" The word jumped right out of my mouth.

"Well let me ask the Chief if it would be ok," said Wes. He asked the Chief, as he had just strutted into the room.

"Sure, then he can help put out the dumpster fires that the college kids light." I laughed at the statement but Chief Cassidy just looked at me as if I was one of the students at the local college that lights the dumpster fires.

"Let me introduce you to the guys," said Captain Freeman. I followed him out to the dining room where the majority of the men were. They all wore the same uniform as the Chief and Captain. There were ten firefighters that occupied the room. Trevor, Mitch, Brett, Captain, Chief, Ryan, Andre, Bobby, PJ, and John were the names of the men. Captain Freeman spoke and his deep voice rang out telling the men about the assignment that I was working on.

"Can we treat him like the rest of us?" said the firefighter named Trevor.

"I don't think that would be a good idea," said Captain with a small laugh in his voice. I agreed with the Captain for I didn't think that I wanted to be one of these guys.

Dining Room: The First Encounter

The dining room was the focal point for social gathering as the men were all in different locations throughout the room. Firefighters Mitch and Bobby were assisting the cook, Ryan, in the kitchen area. I could smell the aroma of deep fried foods. They were peeling potatoes and slicing them into thin slices, and throwing them into the humongous skillet full of oil. The cook, who was also a firefighter, was breading the fish.

Mitch looked at me and asked if I was going to eat. Mitch was medium height, had a mustache and he reminded me of a fellow from back home by the way he talked and looked. "It is some good food. The cook here can make some good grub." I mentioned that I would stay to eat depending on the time.

"Hey Joe," the noise came from Trevor. I turned around with the kitchen area to my back. Trevor was a tall man that had a bushy dark mustache. He was sitting on one of the long tables that occupied the dining area. His smile was goofy as he looked at me. "Do you like deep fried hotdogs?" His eyes made a clown-like stare as he was waiting for an answer. I was puzzled at the question.

"What do you mean?"

"Don't listen to him." Sitting at the second table was a man named Brett. "Owens has got some problems," he said. Brett had a somewhat thin body but his head did not seem to be proportionate to the rest of his body. He looked like a guy that would get teased by someone like Trevor. He explained the story behind the deep fried hot dogs to me. "A guy that used to be in the B Shift hated hotdogs. So one day we breaded a hotdog and fried it in some oil. He was thinking that it was fish and took a bite of it. The guy about lost the rest of his meal." Trevor was telling the story to PJ at the same time Brett told it to me, so there were two versions of the story coming out.

When Brett had finished telling me about the fried hot dog, I took the opportunity to gather some basic information from him. "So what do you do?" I asked.

"Well I am a paramedic. I ride in the medic and tend to all medical situations." Brett was not getting into the excitement as much as Trevor. He was not as loud as the rest of the bunch but he laughed along with all the jokes and dished out some remarks back to Trevor.

Some of the firefighters were sitting down near the television set and talking amongst each other. Captain Freeman sat down in one of the comfortable chairs that was in front of the television. This old style TV was elevated on an old desk. The television looked like it had been bought from Goodwill or was donated to the station. The Captain was watching some program while the Chief kept making comments about the show.

"Oh man," said the Chief, "that has got to hurt." A man on the show was injured by a piece of wood lodged in his nose. The live program was about the city's hospitals. Apparently some firefighters from the division were on the program, as the Captain would yell out who the medics and firefighters were that were bringing in the injured man.

"So how was your day," I asked as I interrupted Captain Freeman's interest in the TV.

"Well I have not been here all day; I've been in court. I lost 800 dollars in the court today. Are you married, Joe? If not keep it that way." I figured out that he was going through a divorce and that his marriage was not working too well. The Captain showed no signs of discouragement but he made jokes about his situation. I began to realize that the joking language was part of this group. A majority of what the firefighters said was some kind of joke. The phone rang. Chief Cassidy strutted to the phone, which hung just above a desk with a stack of papers on it. The Chief picked up the receiver in a cool manner and eased into a comfortable chair next to the desk full of papers. The man was so calm and relaxed as he talked on the phone. He had to deal with a complaint from the city but did not get excited about the complaint. The Chief hung up the phone and it was time to eat.

I decided to stay because the fish looked wonderful. I got in line with the rest of the men as we served up our own food, one at a time. The homemade potato chips and baked vegetables, as well as the tender fish, were delicious. Mitch was right about Ryan making some good supper. The men continued to talk and watch TV as they ate their greasy yet wonderful meal.

Engine 121: Firefighter of Steel

After supper I decided to check out the truck. Engine 121 was a primary artifact in the station. I followed PJ out to the south garage where Engine 121 was parked. I smelled the scent of diesel as I entered the garage.

"This truck doesn't really look like a fire truck," I said.

"Yeah, I know, the city bought us this piece of junk but it gets the job done. I wish we had a better truck though," PJ said. "It has all the necessary things that an engine is suppose to have." He opened up the many doors and all sorts of mechanisms were inside. Axes and sledgehammers were in one compartment while another compartment had chainsaws, coats, and wrenches. There were medical supplies such as a large tackle box full of all the necessary items that a paramedic would use in a medical run. Ladders were tied along the side of the engine and hoses were rolled up neatly for easy access on the top of the tank. This truck had tools that I have never even heard of. "This is a Halligan tool," said PJ as he pulled out a rod that looked like someone had welded all kinds of prying tools to it. "You can get into anything with this tool," said PJ. "This and the striking tool can get you into any building at anytime." The striking tool looked similar to an ax but had a lip on the back of the ax. Engine 121 had everything, and I would like to say it even had a kitchen sink. (The water tank, hoses, and valves of course.) I was amazed at all that Engine 121 was capable of supplying.

The engine was beat up and rough looking. The poor thing had scratches along the sides of the truck from tree branches. Paint from hitting cars and gates to restricted areas was part of the truck. These marks gave the truck character and a personality. It began to appear like another one of the men. It was another brother that has a job to do when a call comes in. Engine 121 had numerous tools and resources that helped this team of firefighters function well together.

From High Street to Hell

The fire station got to experience some action when a call came over the loud speaker. The woman on the intercom spoke in an operator's voice. All the men froze for a brief moment as they listened to her voice. "Battalion fire grounds, 4407 Cranston Street, Engine 121 of Station 121."

"Let's go, Joe," said PJ, "this is a good one." The men put down what they were doing immediately. Trevor, Bobby, and John stopped their horse-playing almost instantly. All of the firefighters' facial expressions were serious as they ran toward the garages. I ran behind PJ as he sprinted to the truck. I jumped into the large phone booth cab and waited only a brief moment as PJ and Trevor jumped in on both sides of me. Captain jumped in the front passenger side and John jumped in as the driver of the engine. Bobby and the Chief got in the chief's car or what the firefighters called the Chief's Buggy. In the south garage Brett and Mitch got into Medic 121, while Lieutenant Andre jumped into EMS 13.

I was surprised how they were almost fully geared up when they got into the vehicles. These men were quick getting their gear on. Inside the cab of Engine 121 PJ and Trevor were putting on their heavy coats and strapping on the oxygen tanks. Bobby drove out of the garage in a hurry with the lights flashing and the sirens on. The truck came to life as the engine started and its sirens began to scream. The truck reacted in the same way as the firefighters. It got serious and the truck's engine was pumping like the men's hearts. The lights began to flash with alertness, just as the firefighters' eyes scanned in swift motions. The engine screamed as it flew down the road. I found my adrenaline stirred up as we flew down the road dodging cars and trucks on the street. I looked at Trevor as he sat down after putting on his oxygen tank. His expression looked like he was already thinking about what lay ahead. I could tell his mind was concentrating on the job.

"Get out of the way," yelled John. The truck honked at a small compact car that was slow to get over. The medics were behind the truck following at the same speed. The house was just down the street from the station, and we got there in little time.

"I see smoke," yelled Captain. I, too, saw the house had smoke rising from the roof. The fully geared men ran out of the truck in the blink of an eye as the door slammed shut. John stretched out the hose as the others were starting to cut and pry off the plywood that covered what used to be a door of this old run down apartment. I jumped out and stood on the sidewalk watching along with other civilians in the area. John turned on the water and the truck filled up the hoses with water while Captain, PJ, and Trevor went in the smoking building. Andre, Brett, Mitch, and Bobby were outside knocking out the windows for ventilation so that the heat would not engulf the men inside. They also had the medic gear ready in case somebody was hurt. Other emergency vehicles came to the scene to back up the men of Station 121. The ladders were set up and another group of firefighters from another station pulled a man out of the apartment next to the burning one. The Chief was quickly walking around busily talking into the portable radio. He was making sure everything was going well.

The quick actions of the firefighters put out the fire. However, their movement was not as swift once the fire was out. Through the windows I saw the men were walking throughout the whole building making sure that the fire was totally extinguished. I could see the flashlights flashing against the wall and the men pacing back and forth by the windows looking for any indication of fire.

"What happened?" I asked.

"There was a living room fire. Would you want to see it?" said Captain Freeman. I put on a fire helmet (for safety reasons) and walked in the apartment. He went through with me the route that they took to get the fire. The route looked difficult because of the large amount of household appliances that were in the way. The fact that the smoke was blocking their vision at the time of the fire, so they had no idea the appliances were there, must have made it all the more difficult. "We want to attack all fire from behind, that way you don't push the fire back and cause more damage to the house," he explained. The firefighters had charged into a building that they had never seen the inside of before, being blinded by smoke, and risking their lives to put out a fire. We entered the room that had been on fire; the living room was black and charred. It almost had an artistic look to it, like somebody painted the room black and made the smoke designs. I was impressed with the whole situation as we walked back out of the building.

Outside, the men were rolling up the hoses and putting the medic gear away. After they cleaned up they sat on the back of Engine 121 and relaxed along with the truck as it hummed steadily. Captain Freeman sat on the back with a smile as all the men joked about the girls they had seen the other day. Trevor looked at another firefighter while taking off his coat.

"I am getting too old, man." They both laughed at the comment. PJ got teased a little about the job he did, even though they all know he did a good job. They were back to the way they had been before the fire, but their bodies were tired from the work. They seemed proud of what they had done. They kept asking me what I had thought about the fire. My adrenaline was down and I found myself somewhat exhausted from the experience.

Just then, I saw my friend ride up to the scene in his car. I remembered that I had not driven to the station, so I had to get going. "I got to go guys. I will catch you later."

"Make sure you bring back some ladies next time Joe," yelled Trevor. All the men smiled as I walked away.

Down Times

Station 121 experiences a large amount of down time during certain parts of the day. They must somehow find ways of making the down times entertaining. I opened the door to Station 121 as Bobby greeted me. "Hey Joe what's going on? Have you had any wrecks lately?" I smiled and continued to walk to the dining room.

"There he is," yelled Mitch. "It's Crash."

Trevor added, "No it's Crash's buddy." I was now a little embarrassed but found the comments to be humorous.

"What happened?" John asked.

Mitch explained the situation to John. "So Joe was wanting to leave the scene last week, and his friend was there to pick him up. Joe needed to get his bag, and Lieutenant (Andre) was taking him up to the station in EMS 13 to retrieve his things. Joe's buddy was following Andre too close. Andre was going to pull up some and then back up; however, his buddy didn't realize what his plans were and Andre backed into Joe's buddy, hitting his bumper."

John was laughing a little, "Man that sounds pretty funny."

Lieutenant walked into the room. "Hey, how's it going?" He slapped me on the back. "That whole wreck thing last week was all just one big mistake. Like I said earlier if it was my vehicle I would have just let it go. If I had known it was your friend I would have just let the whole situation go."

I mentioned, "It's OK. My friend didn't really think the whole situation was all that big of a deal."

Playing board games and making jokes at each other's expense can be a good source of entertainment for the men at the station. PJ, Mitch, Trevor, and John were all sitting at the table playing the game Aggravation. They were laughing and joked around as they continued to throw the dice on the table making a

241

clackety noise, as the dice would strike the table. Trevor looked at PJ in a goofy way that I had seen before.

"Hey PJ did you get laid last week after your girlfriend saw you in action?" He was waiting for an answer from the young firefighter. Mitch and John both laughed at the statement.

"No, because she wasn't too happy."

"Why was that?" asked John. John was a hair older than PJ.

"Well her car got broken into and her speakers were stolen earlier that evening."

"Man that is not good. It stinks especially that you didn't get laid." Trevor threw down his dice and moved his marble kicking one of Mitch's marbles back to the start.

Mitch yelled out, "Oh man, why did you have to do that!"

"So Joe, do you have a psychoanalysis of us all yet?" said Mitch.

"Yea he has Trevor written down as an idiot," joked John. Mitch was laughing along with PJ.

"Well, John, I might be an idiot but we all know that you are a Momma's boy." John made another statement that just dug him a hole. Mitch, Trevor, and PJ were laughing so hard that their faces were turning red.

The men were all relaxing after a hard day's work. The laughing and joking around got their minds off of the stressful day. They also got their minds off the long night that awaited them.

"The boys joke around to loosen up all the tension. It is all fun and games," said Chief Cassidy. "With a group of guys like these fine men you can't lose your optimistic view," added Chief. I looked around as I thought about how the men were keeping the down time up. Not a single man in the outfit had a sad face. Their language to each other kept the smiles up. They reminded me of how brothers or close friends would treat each other. These men were almost like a family. The Chief and Captain were no exceptions in the fun. They put in their jokes as well.

"Did you go to Circleville [the market/festival] and get yourself some pump-kins, Chief?" asked Captain.

"Why do I need to buy me a pumpkin if I got one that drives me around?" The Chief was pointing to Bobby as he was getting some milk out of the refrigerator.

The men of Station 121 harass each other for the simple fact that the jokes keep them together. It unites the team together in a weird sort of way. They build friendship and bond through all the craziness. When they teased me, I felt like they liked me, like I was a part of the group. I found myself very comfortable with the men. I was no longer an outsider who was uncomfortable there.

This change had happened ever since the accident with my friend "Crash." They included me in the jokes and even made fun of me along with the rest of the group as I hung out during the slow times of Station 121.

A Few Good Men

I was talking to Andre in EMS 13 while waiting for the police to secure the scene of a robbery. Andre was the Lieutenant and was also a medic at Station 121.

"We are waiting for the police to make sure everything is safe so we can do our job," he said.

I asked, "Is it me or do all cops seem to be unfriendly?"

"Well you are right about that, about the cops seeming to give off bad vibes. Cops want to help but they look at the situation differently. They look at the people to see if there is any suspicion, and that is part of their job. But firefighters look at people just like you would. When cops are around somebody is usually going to get in trouble. When firefighters come around we are usually there to help people. That is generally what the public thinks. I would not want to be a cop that is for sure. I like what I do, it's a good job." The run was canceled and we headed back to the station.

Back at Station 121 I began to talk to Brett and asked him why this group of guys was different than other groups of firefighters.

"Well I guess because we all have different interests, and it also depends on how busy a station is, too."

"Is Station 121 busy?" I asked.

"Yeah I would consider it one of the busier stations. The other stations have good guys but each station does things together differently. I mean we do stuff as different as what type of cleaner to mop the floor with or even how we attack a fire. Of course we all have the same basic way of fighting fires, but there might be something different in how we go about it. Some stations have crazy guys in the station that livens up the place a bit, and others have older firefighters that are near retirement that want to take things slow. It is also how we interact with each other. The whole difference is like me saying that my family is different from your family."

"So you consider these guys a second family?" I said.

"Well of course," Brett responded. "There are things I tell these guys that I don't even tell my wife."

Mitch jumped in and said, "And then we tell his wife." Brett just sort of smirked at Mitch as he made the comment.

"So why are these men a bunch of good guys?"

Brett answered right away. "I know we screw off and mess around a lot, but when it comes down to business I know that these guys will back me up. We have trust in each other due to the personality of each man. When I go into a fire they are behind me fighting as hard as I am. That is why I like working here so much. I mean, some stations have firefighters that won't even go into fires. They will leave you with all the work, and when it is all over they will tell me that I did a good job. Also these guys at Station 121 don't feel like they're better than the others. Sure some have high honors but it doesn't matter. We help each other out because we want to. The Chief and Captain are no exceptions either. They will help with the dishes and cleaning and we make it easier on the Chief and Captain by doing stuff without being told. We act like a family and I really enjoy working here."

Trevor came into the conversation and said, "Hey Joe, if you want to interview somebody, you talk to the Cook, Ryan. He has the highest honor that a firefighter can get. And not only does he have the highest honor, he is considered a true American Hero." Trevor was not joking around this time. He was serious about what he was saying because he lacked the goofy look.

The chief told me about Ryan's honor. He had gone into the flames and helped carry out victims trapped in a fire, burning himself in the process. I looked at Ryan sitting in the recliner watching television, quietly by himself. I never realized that true heroes do what needs done without any complaints and ask for very little in return. He seemed like a really nice guy, even offered me some White Castle hamburgers, and for some reason I did not talk to him. I missed an opportunity to interview him, and I wish I hadn't.

Conclusion

After my experience with Station 121, B Shift of Battalion 5, I discovered once again a few things about life. I found the old saying of not judging a book by its cover to be true. I also found that sometimes the best have an appearance of looking like the worst. Being a hero is not on the outside.

I first looked at Station 121 as a place with little potential and nothing of great character. The location was odd, the surrounding of the place hid the station, the fire truck was weird looking, and the neighborhood had a reputation for crime. The place had little in its appearance that suggested it had good qualities. In fact I first thought it had bad qualities. It appeared that the culture of this station received little attention from other cultures. But I realized that the outside had little to do with the personality of the group, as well as its receiving attention.

I got inside and saw how the firefighters interacted together, and began to get a different perspective on the way the place operated. They played games, ate together, joked around, and had fun. They treated each other like brothers and did many activities together. I could tell that B Shift of Station 121 was a true family. When the time came to do their job, they did what they had to, and helped each other out without any questions. This trust was practiced in and outside of the engine house. The men of B Shift, Station 121 were there to do their job, the best that they could without really caring about what others think or what kind of recognition they received. I read a quote from Tom Brokaw just recently in a *Reader's Digest Magazine*. "Heroes are people who rise to the situation and then slip away quietly." I thought the quote fit well with these men. They put out the fires and help sick and injured people, putting their lives at risk a lot of times, and then slip back to Station 121 to have some fun.

My time at this place was greatly enjoyable, and has impacted my life. I had a lot of fun riding in Engine 121, watching the men put out the fires, and help injured victims, watching TV, hearing jokes, and even eating some good food. My time at Station 121 has caused me to look for the odd-looking Engine 121 every time I hear sirens. Anymore I can't help stopping and looking at a picture of a firefighter in a newspaper or on television. This time with Station 121, B Shift has caused me to feel like an insider to the bigger culture of firefighting. I wanted to be a part of this group, and I am considering making firefighting my profession when I get out of college. My stay at Station 121 made me a firefighter at heart.

Gay Rituals: Outing, Biking, and Sewing

Mickey Weems

Mickey has done extensive work looking at gay rituals and culture and is always interested in new ways to understand ritual and new perspectives on gay culture and its parameters.

"Gay Rituals: Outing, Biking, and Sewing" provides an example of the way a folklorist develops and builds on a theory through secondary and primary research, and how a folklorist is always open to new information and perspectives (and impromptu editorial feedback). In original drafts of this essay, Mickey looked at a wider variety of subject matter, and we said, "Hey, we really like the part about Kevin and the photo. What if

> *you looked at a few specific types of 'coming out' experiences and
> narratives? An approach like that would be really useful for stu-
> dents with less experience at gathering and analyzing folklore."
> Not only did he jump on that approach, but somehow along the
> way, one of us became one of his consultants.*
>
> *Mickey's experience with research and writing about folklore
> at the graduate level adds depth to his presentation, but we feel
> that his essay still presents a very readable and doable approach
> to fieldwork for undergraduate students as well.*

The gay community* is composed of people from every ethnic group and
religious background. We think of ourselves as an intercultural collective whose
members celebrate rather than hide their sexual orientation. Our most recognizable symbol is the rainbow, which represents all races and ethnic groups.

Yet, gays are a people set apart. We have distinctive folkways, reflected in the
manner in which we conduct our personal lives, festivals, and memorials. Some
of our folk performance genres are rituals in themselves. Our performance rituals often involve the following characteristics: revelation and celebration of identity, tolerance of difference, spirituality (without religious denomination), and
the inclusion of non-LGBT (Lesbian, Gay, Bisexual, and Transgender) people.

The most important characteristic is the expression of identity, both as individuals and as communities. Gay ritual performance often resembles theater,
but lacks the "make-believe" framework that sets theatrical performance apart
from ritual performance. Many LGBT expressions of identity are better understood as rituals of encounter that reveal personal truths of the performer than
theatrical display.

The line between theater and ritual is not always clear. Drag performance,
for example, may take place on stage and be highly scripted. Nevertheless,
most drag kings and queens consider their art to be much more than illusion.
Personal truths are summoned forth that may be difficult to express outside of
the dress codes and gendered mannerisms that frame drag performance, both
on stage and off. The same can be said about festive events that are more than
just parties, such as feminist community-building in women's music festivals,
the performance of nonviolent masculinity in the gay male dance circuit, and
erotic sado-masochistic bonding in the leather community.

---

*   For the sake of style, I treat the terms "gay" and "LGBT" as synonyms.

Three gay ritual frames will be examined in this essay: 1) coming out, 2) pride parades, and 3) the AIDS Quilt. Each of these represents a different aspect of identity expression by the individual, the community, and by loved ones in memory of the deceased.

Because of a tremendous respect for individual expression, many rituals in the gay community do not look like rituals at first glance because there may be no set pattern or script that must be followed. These rituals are based upon a common framework for performance rather than a strictly coded set of behaviors. As such, we can expect a broad range of behaviors within these ritual frames. The case studies following each example will help illustrate the rich variety of possibilities that can be enacted within the ritual frame.

Coming Out: The Revelation of Self

The "Ur-ritual" of gay rituals is *coming out*, an encounter set up by gay people in order to reveal their sexuality. The term "coming out" is taken from a popular aphorism referring to personal, potentially devastating, secrets: they have *skeletons in the closet*. A homosexual who is afraid for others to know is said to be "closeted" or a "closet case." To "come out of the closet" is to be open about one's sexuality.

People may come out in any number of fashions. They may prepare and rehearse a script to use during a dinner date or family gathering. They may "explode out of the closet" with a dramatic public scene, or they may subtly drop clues that lead their chosen audience to the revelation. They may even choose to have others "out" them (reveal their sexuality). It may be done spontaneously in a fit of anger or when feeling comfortable enough to speak from the heart. Usually, the same person will not come out the same way to everyone—performance varies according to audience.

Coming out involves a degree of risk. Usually, the hapless audience has no idea what is going on before it happens. The person coming out may not be sure how the recipient of the news will take it. This is one reason why there are few rules that define the coming-out ritual: it involves presenting intimate, potentially volatile news that could change or even hurt a relationship. Care is usually taken so that the potential for disaster can be lessened. Coming-out rituals are frames for self-revelation and are constructed based on the individual's own assessment of how best to go about it.

The process of coming out is not limited to gays because coming out involves much more than just the self-outed individuals. It often puts their straight friends and family in an awkward situation: should *they* come out as the parents, brothers, sisters, and friends of gay folk? Organizations such as PFLAG (Parents,

Families, and Friends of Lesbians and Gays) are designed to offer help and community to loved ones who support their gay friends and family members.

Case Study: Kevin Mason

Kevin Mason is a young man in his twenties who works in a bill-processing office with mostly middle-aged women. His way of coming out to them was to place a picture on his desk. When people passed by and made small talk about the picture, he would tell them, "Oh, that's my boyfriend," as if it were nothing exceptional. When asked if he feared being fired or ostracized for being so blatant, Kevin said, "I will not work in an environment where I have to hide who I am."

Reactions to Kevin's coming-out performance ranged from startled surprise to amused acceptance. Brandon, a member of staff support, asked Kevin about the picture and was caught completely off guard by the answer. Brandon had assumed that Karen, Kevin's best friend whose picture was also on his desk, was Kevin's girlfriend. Not knowing what to say, Brandon could not bring himself to talk to Kevin directly and talked instead through the other women in the office to get the full story. Kevin's co-worker Tamika, on the other hand, "scolded" Kevin when she found out. He should have told her earlier!

Kevin has learned from past experience that lack of communication can lead to disaster. When he was in high school, he had a crush on one of his closest friends. During a game of "truth or dare," Kevin wondered aloud to his friends if he were bisexual. Word got to his parents, who consulted with a family physician. The well-meaning doctor feared that homosexual feelings would make Kevin suicidal, so he insisted that Kevin be institutionalized. All of this went on without once consulting Kevin.

Although it broke their hearts, Kevin's folks reluctantly agreed to follow the doctor's advice. Kevin was ordered by his father to pack a bag. "We're going somewhere" was the only answer he received. His parents took him to a psychiatric ward.

Kevin's mother and father visited him as often as they could and wrote to him every day. During one of their visits, a nurse took his father aside. She asked him if his love for his son changed when he found out that Kevin was gay. His father said no, and she suggested that Kevin didn't change either. There was nothing wrong with his son, she said. This advice led to Kevin's release after 33 days in the ward. For the duration of his stay, Kevin was never told why he was there.

The problem for Kevin and his family was that they had no means by which they could talk about this issue with each other. Their silence led to tremendous pain for all involved.

248

"I do not hold anything against my parents for what they did," Kevin said. "They were just ignorant of the situation. Since then, they have taken the initiative to learn who I am and the community that I belong to."

Kevin believes in what he calls "passive education," that the best way to prevent homophobia is for gays to be open about who they are in everyday life. He feels that gays should not be visible only on TV sitcoms or the news. He recognizes, however, that each gay person must decide when, where, and how the coming-out ritual should take place.

Pride Parades: Coming Out as a Community

Every year, most major cities in the US, Canada, Western Europe, and South Africa have "pride parades" commemorating an incident that happened in New York City in 1969. On June 28th, police raided the Stonewall Inn (51-53 Christopher St.), a Greenwich Village gay bar. At the time, it was against the law for people to cross-dress or dance with somebody of the same sex. A crowd gathered outside of the Inn, taunting the police and cheering the people who were being arrested. Things got out of hand when an officer pushed a woman in men's clothing and she pushed back. The crowd threw coins at the police (symbolizing the bribes that they regularly garnished from Stonewall). Coins then escalated to rocks and bottles. This in turn led to three days of civil unrest known as the Stonewall Rebellion. One of the highlights of the rebellion was a chorus line of drag queens that would form in front of the riot squad and sing:

We are the Stonewall girls
We wear our hair in curls
We wear no underwear
We show our pubic hair

Mercifully, no one was killed during the unrest.

A year after the rebellion, the first pride parade was organized in Greenwich Village, which was followed by a dance party. Since that time, parades have sprung up in many more cities and countries.

Pride parades are a form of public *coming out* for both individuals and groups within the larger gay and straight communities. The usual trappings of American parades can be seen, such as floats and marching bands. In addition, there will usually be drag kings and queens, straight PFLAG allies, go-go dancers in skimpy outfits, and "dykes on bikes," lesbians on motorcycles who work as security. All of these performances express the affirmation of gay identity in its myriad manifestations.

Case Study: Gloria McCauley

When it comes to pride parades, Gloria McCauley has lots of experience. She was in charge of security for the Columbus, Ohio pride parade for ten years.

Her very first pride parade, however, put her in an awkward position. Her debut within this very public ritual frame had to be incognito. Unlike Kevin, Gloria could not openly reveal her sexual orientation due to a custody battle over her oldest child—if she had come out as a lesbian, she would have lost her daughter. "I drove a fire truck down the city's main street," she said. "When a news camera was in the vicinity, the people on my truck would warn me and I would place a balloon attached to the side view mirror in front of my face" (Gloria had drawn a face on the balloon).

As security director for the pride parade, Gloria worked with an unofficial group called "Dykes on Bikes," a lesbian motorcycle security patrol. The *lack* of rehearsal and regulation was a vital part of their performance. These women rarely came to planning sessions. Thirty or forty of them would show up on the day of the parade, brief the "newbies" (those who had never done it before), and begin their patrol of the parade area.

The Dykes on Bikes (DOB) would ride on either side of the parade in a corridor between the bystanders and the paraders. Although there was no dress code, many of the women would dress in no-nonsense "biker" outfits with leather jackets, t-shirts, and jeans. They would ride ahead of the parade and make sure that there were no problems with traffic or protesters. They acted as a living, mobile, and protective frame in which the LGBT community could safely be as extravagant as it wanted to be.

Gloria trusted the patrol to do the right thing without her constant supervision. A lead biker would be picked, somebody who had been doing this for a few years and respected by the rest of the group. After that, Gloria let them do their job. This is an interesting reflection of Gloria's own relationship with the pride parade planning committee. Like the DOB, Gloria would rarely attend planning sessions. "I had my job to do and I expected the committee to trust me enough to do it without their supervision."

In order to counter some of the negative verbal impact of anti-gay Christian groups, Gloria and the DOB came up with a performative strategy. Some of the protesters would bring megaphones to ridicule the marchers or preach to them as they passed. Gloria would have the bikers position themselves in a row between the marchers and the protesters. With their backs turned to the protesters, the DOB would then rev their engines, drowning out the megaphones (and creating lots of exhaust fumes).

Gloria recalled one particular biker who would make it a point to always break the rules. This woman was the group's trickster. Sometimes she would ride around without a shirt on. She would have her girlfriend ride on the bike with her, but have her up front and facing her instead of on the back. Sometimes they would simulate having sex on the bike. Initially, Gloria was scandalized by this rebel's behavior. But after a year or so, she grew to expect it and even appreciate it. "She broke the rules because she was so full of life," Gloria said. "It was her way of enjoying the parade and entertaining the crowd."

One thing that Gloria noticed was that DOB members, who normally wore street clothes and motorcycle helmets when they rode their bikes, dressed up for their patrol duties and rode without their helmets. "Some women would break out their leather chaps, vests, or biker jackets only for this occasion," she observed. Gloria attributed this to the ritual *persona* (performance identity) of the Dykes on Bikes—they were not simply a security patrol. She felt that this is the reason why they wore no helmets. "This was a pride parade," she said. "They would show their faces because they wanted to be a part of it."

The AIDS Quilt: Performance of Remembrance

Reputed to be the largest folk project in America, the AIDS Quilt began in November of 1985. Cleve Jones, the founder of the Quilt, was attending a public memorial at the San Francisco Federal Building, which had its walls covered with cardboard posters, each bearing the name of somebody who had died of AIDS. Jones looked at the building and noted how the cardboard pieces resembled a patchwork quilt, each poster a piece in the overall blanket. He was inspired.

From the start, production of the Quilt has brought friends and family together. Jones and his friend Joseph Durant made the first two Quilt panels in February of 1986 in Jones's backyard for their friends Marvin Feldman and Ed Mock. These 3-ft by 6-ft cloth rectangles (the dimensions of a grave) were the prototypes for thousands more to come.

When the AIDS Quilt organization began showing the panels, they ran into trouble with some of the families of the deceased, who were upset that their loved ones were being "outed" as victims of AIDS. These families considered death by AIDS complications as scandalous. Many panels have been sent in with only the vaguest of indicators as to whom they memorialize. Nevertheless, those who made them felt it important to do something in honor of someone who made a difference in their lives, someone who might have been forgotten simply because the cause of death was considered shameful. The Quilt itself does not discriminate on the basis of sexual orientation; all who have died of AIDS are eligible. There are children, housewives, priests, athletes, fathers, and mothers among the myriad drag queens, leather daddies, hairdressers, and show-tune aficionados.

The first official display of the Quilt occurred in August of 1987 in the high front window of the San Francisco Neiman Marcus store. Approximately forty panels were shown. On October 11, 1987, nearly 2000 panels were shown on the National Mall in Washington, DC. On October of 1992, 20,064 panels were displayed in the Mall. The last showing of the entire Quilt was in 1996 with more than 40,000 panels.

Panels are usually the size of the first two made by Jones and Durant. They are sewn together into *blocks*, 12-ft by 12-ft squares made up of eight panels. These blocks (over 5,000) are currently stored in a warehouse in Atlanta, where they are occasionally summoned forth for displays across the nation. An average of one panel a day arrives at the warehouse, which has a sewing room for repair and block-making, a temperature-controlled storage space for the Quilt "at rest," offices for staff, and a room full of file cabinets that hold the memorabilia (letters, pictures, wedding rings, teddy bears, etc.) that people send in with the panels.

The AIDS Quilt generates performances of its own in its production and its display. The production of a panel is a private affair, while the display of the Quilt creates a frame for both public and private encounters, both among the living and between the living and the deceased. Quilt displays usually include a reading of the names of those who have died from AIDS in the tradition of Holocaust memorials. The Quilt blocks are shown either hanging on walls or laid out on the floor or ground.

In my interviews with people who have made panels (and with my own experience encountering the Quilt), the deceased are often a palpable presence during production and display. I never felt alone in its presence, even when I was the only living person in the room.

Case Study: Martha Sims, Tom Wulff, et al.

"We waited long enough, didn't we?"

This rhetorical question was asked by those who worked on a Quilt panel for Tom Wulff of Cleveland, Ohio. In 1986, Tom died from complications associated with AIDS. It was not until two years later that some of his friends memorialized him with a green 3-ft by 6-ft cloth rectangle that featured a large white cat and "Tom Wulff" written in big letters, surrounded by the sun, moon, and stars.

It is not unusual for people to wait a few years to make a Quilt panel. When asked why, the most common answer is, "We waited until it felt right." Those who worked on Tom's panel knew about the AIDS Quilt Project (officially known as the Names Project) before he died. Nevertheless, it took two years for them to put together Tom's memorial.

Martha Sims is a folklorist at The Ohio State University. She became a close friend of Tom's in the early 1980s. She is unique among those who worked on Tom's panel in that she is not gay.

Martha showed me a small teddy bear that Tom had given her. He made it himself; the bear was sewn together with neat stitches out of burgundy calico cloth with tiny flowers. It wears a sparkling link taken from a vintage rhinestone bracelet. The face has a comical yet serious expression. It is the only teddy bear I have seen with movable arms and legs.

"Tom was fond of making teddy bears," Martha told me. Some of the leftover bear cloth was used to make his Quilt panel. The big white cat in the panel (Tom was a cat lover) has a collar made from the same rhinestone bracelet as the link worn by Martha's bear.

Two of the most popular symbols found in the AIDS Quilt are, in fact, cats and teddy bears.

In order to include the stories of others who had worked on Tom's panel in this case study, Martha asked four of them who lived in Cleveland (Laura Sims, Susan Ballard, Judy Maruszan, and Nancy Stemmer) to come together in early 2004 and audiotape their reminiscing. I have listened to this impromptu performance several times. "The girls," as Martha calls them, had created a framed collage with the pictures of the quilters placed around the central image of the green panel itself. Both the audiotape and the collage can be seen as layers in the Quilt's performance of remembrance.

"The girls" reconstruct the timeline of the panel's creation in terms of other events in their lives, such as Pro-Choice rallies, AIDS activism, and hair not yet turned grey. The inspiration for Tom's panel was the first DC Quilt display in 1987.

After much discussion, chair scraping, and the sound of dishes, they conclude that the first concrete meeting to create the panel occurred at a dinner at Sue and Laura's with Judy and Tom's artist friend Jeff Roche on April 10, 1988. Within two months, Tom's panel was finished and on display.

While the group is chatting and sifting through memorabilia, a sought-after bit of evidence pops up unexpectedly from the pictures and news clippings, as if by magic. The speakers announce, "Tom's here." The ease by which Martha and the others speak of Tom in their presence indicates a remarkably comfortable relationship between the living and the dead. The usual feelings of alienation, despair, and sorrow that accompany memories of the deceased are tempered with a casual acceptance, the assurance that Tom is not lost to them.

They happily entertain the idea that he is present among them, the same feeling many people have when they experience the Quilt in person.

This is perhaps the most profound effect of the Quilt: it brings together this world and the next, even when it is not present.

Conclusion: Performing Ourselves

In the course of our lives, all of us have several roles that we play, some of which are carefully scripted. But we tend to view unscripted and individualistic expressions of ourselves as more realistic and genuine. The people in the case studies of this essay purposefully avoided a clearly defined ritual script in favor of a ritual frame that promoted spontaneous interaction. This affinity for the unscripted allowed them to 1) construct an intimate setting for the possibility of genuine encounter, and 2) within that frame, encourage people to lower the barriers between them.

Tolerance and inclusion are the desired results of these rituals. Kevin's coming out was a request for tolerance that included non-LGBT people as a matter of course. Although they are primarily lesbians, Dykes On Bikes have allowed men among their number. Martha did not need to be gay to work on Tom's Quilt panel (the Quilt was born inclusive: its first two panels were for Marvin Feldman, a Jewish man, and Ed Mock, an African American). We can see these same dynamics in the Gay Games (sexual orientation is not an issue for participation), the gay men's dance circuit (anyone can come and dance), and women's music festivals (although men may not be allowed to attend some festivals, all women, regardless of sexual orientation, are invited). Tolerance and inclusion are the reasons why coming out, pride parades, and the AIDS Quilt can be spiritual but not necessarily religious, at least in terms of creed or denomination. Although situated in a secular frame, these rituals are imbued at times with a pervasive sense of compassion, solidarity, and spirituality without any of the social markers of religion.

Let us not suppose, however, that religion and religious symbolism are forbidden within the ritual frame. Gay folk have come out using the language of religion to explain who they are in terms of their relationship with God. Pride parades have religious groups who march in support of the LGBT community (as well as groups who curse it from the sidelines). The AIDS panel for Marvin Feldman has pink and blue stars of David on it.

For gay rituals, the outward trappings of religion are important only as accessories for the expression of identity, as means for sharing who we are. The rituals of outing, biking, and sewing are designed to transcend difference. At their heart, they are intrinsically transcendent.

Roadside Memorials: Material Focus of Love, Devotion, and Remembrance

Gary E. A. Saum

> *Gary researched and wrote this essay for an intermediate composition class that used folklore as its critical content perspective. His initial work on the project included secondary research through library and Internet sources, and this research provided the groundwork for his examination of roadside memorials, a subject which hadn't at that time been written about much.*
>
> *When he was working on this project, Gary was majoring in anthropology, so he had some academic background in the study of cultural texts, and the folklore "lens" inspired him to make contact with and discover the insights of the people to whom the memorial was most significant. We're really impressed by his sensitivity in working with the family and keeping their feelings and intentions in mind throughout the research process; he allowed their voices to come through in evaluating the meaning and significance of the memorial.*
>
> *"Roadside Memorials" illustrates a project that incorporates secondary and primary research and focuses on a single, multi-dimensional text.*

First Impressions

The small feminine figure kneeled on the cold ground in the dark February night. A small firebrand burned bright as the figure used it to light a candle. The woman placed the candle in a luminary; it was one of eight that were arranged in a circle around the small memorial. Because of the distance and the darkness I could not make out the finer details of the inner circle, but I could tell that there was a cross at the center of the arrangement of luminaries. I was touched by this scene and could only think one thing; someone was missing a loved one. I have passed this shrine several times over the last few months, and each time I do I wonder whom the shrine memorializes, and who built it.

Death is a difficult issue to cope with, and sudden tragic death, like those caused by automobile accidents, is probably one of the hardest forms of death to deal with. I once heard it said that death is easy for the dead, but death is hard on the living. One way to work through the pain of death is to remember the person that has passed on. Some remember the dead through construction of memorials, such as, *ofrenda, assemblages,* or roadside memorials. Roadside memorials are a unique, complex, purposeful and public way of remembering a loved one that has passed on. Their design, content, and meaning varies greatly from builder to builder.

Origins

Over the last few decades a new grieving phenomena has become more apparent throughout the United States, Mexico, and several other countries. The focus of this phenomenon, the roadside memorial, is so ubiquitous that no doubt you have probably seen what I am talking about, the little white cross, engraved with a name. Roadside memorials are known by many different names such as roadside shrines, death markers, roadside crosses, and are usually adorned with flowers, pictures, candles, or other mementos. Located at the site of traffic fatalities, these memorials offer a way for friends, family members, and loved ones to remember someone lost to them in a traffic fatality. These memorials also allow the public and the community to participate in the loss and remembrance experiences as well. How did this ritual of building memorials at accident sites get started?

There is an indication that this tradition started out as pile of stones called a *descanso* during the Taos rebellion in New Mexico in 1847 (Gonzales and Rodriguez 1998). *Descanso* means "resting place" in Spanish, and originally these may have simply been resting places for pallbearers as they moved the coffin from the church to the cemetery (Gonzales and Rodriguez 1998). According to another source, "*Descansos* are from an ancient Spanish tradition." Furthermore, "When the Spanish came to the new world and comrades died on the trail, markers where [sic] left at the site" (*Descansos, Roadside Memorials and Crosses 2004,* 1). In yet another source, Mike Cochran indicates that prior to the 1900's *descansos* also served as early markers of a place where a robbery and a murder had occurred. Additionally, per Cochran, this tradition goes back to a pre-Columbian era Mexican tradition of using piles of stones or crosses to mark the death of loved ones (*Descansos, Roadside Memorials and Crosses 2004,* 2). Based on these conflicting accounts, this tradition seems to have an unclear origin but it appears to have eventually evolved into an elaborate public display of loss, grief, and remembrance of a person.

Moreover, there is evidence that material remembrances, like the mementos left at roadside memorials, have been a part of Latin American culture for centuries. In the book, *Milagros: Votive Offerings From the Americas,* Martha Egan indicates that currently in Latin America there is a tradition of leaving offerings of thanks at the altars or statues of a saint for a miracle performed by that saint (1991, 1). Often times these offerings directly reflect the nature of the miracle, and come in the form of a metal charm called a *milagro.* For example, a miniature metal pair of eyes might be left in thanks for an eye related miracle, or a miniature metal torso of a pregnant woman might be offered for a fertility related miracle. However, some of the offerings come in a form less related to the miracle, and are similar to items adorning roadside memorials (Egan 1991, 1). Egan goes on to say that *milagros* (the miniatures offered to saints as "thanks") are part of an ancient folk custom that most likely spread to the new world by Catholics that followed similar traditions on the Iberian Peninsula (1991, 2–7).

In a manner similar to the *milagros,* over the last few decades, the simple pile of stones that marked a resting place for pallbearers has evolved into a marker that represents the spot where someone died. Additionally, it seems likely that, given the importance of memory to the human condition, various offerings such as ball caps, photos, notes, stuffed animals, etc., became an integral part of the construction of the *descansos* and reflect the human need to remember the life that was. When and how this happened is hard to say.

Egan's history of *milagros* may explain the way that various elements of roadside shrines have come to be associated with the simple pile of stones and/ or crosses that make up the core of the roadside shrine tradition. Catholicism was imported to the new world by the Spanish and became the predominant religion of Latin America. Additionally, roadside shrines appear to have started in the new world either as an imported Spanish tradition or as a tradition borrowed from the Spanish by the Indians. Therefore, it stands to reason that the various "offerings" left at roadside shrines grew out of the Spanish tradition of leaving offerings of thanks to the various Catholic saints. However, the offerings at roadside shrines are not left as thanks for miracles, but are instead left to memorialize the victim.

To memorialize a life cut short by tragedy is an apparent goal of the roadside shrine. Memory is very important to the human condition and especially to the Latino community. Virgilio Elizondo summarizes the importance of memory in the Latino community:

> Memory is the soul of a people. Without it we are just individuals living and working in a common space . . . Throughout the Bible, God always

257

calls upon the people to remember their ancestors, to remember what God has done for them. The living memory of how God has walked with us through deserts and mountains, through triumph and defeat, through enslavement and freedom, through life and death is the source of our strength. (Olmos, Ybarra, and Monterrey 1999, 20)

Remembering A Life Cut Short

Roadside memorials serve a number of different functions for the people that construct them: shrines to honor the spirits of the dead, public altars to an "interrupted journey," and to some they represent holy ground (Gonzales and Rodriguez 1998). Furthermore, they may also serve as a focus to remember the lost loved one, a location at which to hold prayer vigils, a way to assuage guilt, or a place to drop off mementos (News-Sentinel Staff 2004, 6). Alternatively, they may serve as warnings that people die on the road or that one should not drink and drive (News-Sentinel Staff 2004, 6). Some of the messages may be less obvious, "drive safely, never leave the house without kissing loved ones goodbye, and don't leave angry" (Gonzales and Rodriguez 1998). The meaning or purpose of each shrine is as varied and individual as the person it commemorates.

Likewise, their construction and design is unique from one shrine to the next. Some of the typical elements that a shrine might consist of include crosses (usually wooden), pictures, flowers, clothing, statues, a pile of rocks, baseball caps, flags, stuffed animals, letters, figurines, metal plaques, wreathes, candles (News-Sentinel Staff 2004). Roadside memorials may not always take the same form. One memorial in New Mexico is in the form of a bed of flowers (Gonzales and Rodriguez 1998). Another memorial is "marked with two crosses complete with hand written notes to Duncan [the victim]. Messages scrolled across the emergency lane read, 'Julie loves you,' 'Rest in peace' and 'I will miss you Mr. Duncan'"(News-Sentinel Staff 2004, 4). Still another memorial is in the form of "a large wooden sign urging motorists not to drink and drive" (News-Sentinel Staff 2004, 6). Designing and building these memorials can be a way to work through the grieving process according to Becky Gould, a social worker in California (News-Sentinel Staff 2004, 2).

Eric, A Life Interrupted

The powerful emotions I felt emanating from the woman lighting the candles that February night stayed with me and resurfaced when I needed to pick a topic for this paper. I have seen several roadside memorials prior to seeing this one. However, this was the first time that I had ever seen anyone interacting with a memorial. Seeing the human interaction drove home the reality of the situation. Here was someone that had known the victim and that had been affected by his or her death.

As I learned more about the complexities of these roadside phenomena, I knew it would help me understand if I could talk to the woman that had been lighting the candles. At first I was apprehensive about approaching the lady as she was lighting the candles, because I didn't want to intrude on her "personal time" so I put off contact for a while. However, one Saturday afternoon in May I was passing by the roadside memorial and I noticed a man attending to the memorial. He was just exchanging old luminaries for new ones, and I figured approaching him at this time would be less "intrusive" on someone's "personal time" than dusk would be. I pulled over, parked, got out of my car, and walked over to the man.

A man of average height and weight was replacing old plastic milk jug lumi-naries with new ones as I approached and did not see me until I said, "Excuse me." The man turned around, straightened up, and said, "Hi."

I introduced myself and explained that I was researching and writing a paper on roadside memorials for a class that I was taking at OSU.

He introduced himself as Phil Bohn, the father of the victim, and he indi cated that he would be happy to set up a time to talk and he also said that he was fairly sure that Eric's mother, Marlene, and Eric's bother, Ryan, would be will-ing to talk to me too. Phil told me the roadside memorial was made to honor his son Eric who died due to injuries sustained in an automobile accident at this spot last October. Eric was 17, and he had been a junior at Worthington Kilbourne High School.

The following week Phil and I set up a time to meet. I arrived at the Bohn house at seven on a Wednesday night. Hanging up over the garage is a banner indicating that a Worthington Kilbourne high school baseball player lives here, and it has "Eric" written on it in black marker. Mr. Bohn, a pleasant man of average height and stature, greets me at the door. Mr. Bohn introduced me to Marlene, Eric's mother. She is also of average size and she has short dark hair. We decided to conduct the interview at Marlene's kitchen table, and the three of us took our seats and I began. "What I'd like to do is have you tell me about Eric, and the memorial and anything that you feel comfortable with telling me" I said, as I turned my tape recorder on. The story of Eric's untimely death started at 5:30 pm, Saturday, October 25th, 2003.

"This one Saturday afternoon we were here and all of a sudden the door rang," Phil Bohn began to tell the story. "And a girl came to the door and it was the first time we'd seen her. It was a friend of Eric's, but not his girlfriend, and she came over to pick him up. Eric was anxious to get out the door, and trying to get out the door, but we were talking to her. She was very pleasant with us too. As

259

they walked out the door, Eric had a shit-eating grin on his face. You know, here he was getting picked up by a good looking girl and we looked out and she was driving a Corvette." Eric and his friend got into the Corvette and drove away.

Both of Eric's parents had gone to bed prior to Eric's return. "We got a call [around 12:45 am] and it was from Eric's best friend and he said, 'Eric's been in a bad accident,' and he thought he was taken to Riverside Hospital. And then of course Marlene and I are both about losing it, and you know, trying to rush to get out of here."

By the time Eric's parents got to the hospital, the doctors were working on Eric in the trauma unit. Shortly afterwards, a couple of Eric's friends arrived at the hospital. The friends had been following the car Eric had been riding in, and were able to fill in the details of the accident for Eric's parents.

Eric had been a passenger in the Corvette, when the driver lost control and went left of center. Then an oncoming car struck the Corvette in the passenger side door, causing extensive injury to Eric. Corvettes are made of fiberglass so there was not much to protect Eric from the force of the impact. Ironically the driver of the Corvette walked away from the crash with only minimal physical damage. Eventually, Eric's parents were able to talk with the doctors that were treating Eric. "They [the doctors] were going to take him up to surgery," Phil continued, "and they said, 'There is a slight chance that Eric might live.' He was very, very critical."

"This is the way the doctor put it to me, 'Your son has not one life threatening thing, but six life threatening things wrong with him,'" Marlene related, choking back a tear.

By Sunday afternoon there were over a hundred students, friends, family, and neighbors at the hospital to show their support for Eric and his family.

"[By late Sunday afternoon] He wasn't getting any better and we met with the doctor. The doctor came in and laid it on the line to us as far as, you know, what was going to happen. Whether it was today or tomorrow, he [Eric] was going to be brain dead. He would just be living on a machine," Mr. Bohn related. Furthermore, the hospital staff had given Eric 32 pints of blood. So Eric's parents made the decision to remove Eric from life support.

Emotion and pain invaded Mr. Bohn's voice as he related, "We went out and told our family that was mostly gathered in the [ICU waiting] room that Eric was going to pass away." Mr. Bohn's voice became thick with pain, "and then right outside the door were all of our friends and neighbors that were there and I went out and told them too."

After Eric's girlfriend [not the driver] and Eric's family had a chance to say goodbye to Eric, Mr. Bohn and Ryan, Eric's brother, went down to where all of

Eric's friends and fellow students were gathered and Mr. Bohn informed them, "God's going to get another angel. Eric's going to pass on."

It was around 6:20 pm on Sunday the 26th that Eric's life support was turned off. ". . . And it was about a minute later or so that Eric was gone," Mr. Bohn related. "Sunday night, the boys [Eric's male friends] got together at Eric's friend's house and made the cross for the site. They got together because his dad had power tools and he had some wood. So all the boys got together, made the cross, painted it, and put in 'R.I.P. E.R.B.' and 'October 26th, 2003.' And they took it over to the site, and put it there because it was still a fresh site to a certain extent because of the fact that there were still rubber gloves on the ground, there were pieces of fiberglass, and somebody found the back of Eric's cell phone battery, things like that. And they decorated the cross because they wanted a memorial site close by," Phil related. Over the next few days some of Eric's friends started leaving mementos at the site.

Marlene related how this cross with a few mementos became transformed and now includes luminaries. "December 17th, it was a Friday night, and Compassionate Friends [a support group for parents that have lost a child] around the world lit a candle for parents who have lost a child. So, we were going to go downtown to a church and light a candle with Compassionate Friends. And we were tired and it was cold. So we decided to light them [candles] at the site. So my sister-in-law made luminaries out of milk cartons. Eight of us went down there, and we had our own little ceremony at 7 o' clock. And I said to Eric, 'You know what, for my love and dedication to you, I [am] going to light these every night. Because I want to let you know that you're loved.' And I've lit them every night, and when I can't his dad lights them for me. It doesn't matter if it is raining, and in the snow I make snow angels and write on the side, 'I love you Eric.'"

"A lady wrote me a beautiful letter [and left it at the site] and said, 'I don't know you but every time I see you I cry because of your love and devotion to your child.' . . . That's why I do it. It's all about Eric; it's not about anybody else. And people wave, honk and holler and say, 'We love you Eric.'"

Elements: Expressions of Love, Respect, and Mementos

Eric's memorial consists of many of the classical roadside memorial elements: a stuffed animal, candles, a picture, notes, for example. I asked Mr. Bohn to tell me something about the significance of the various elements.

Mr. Bohn explained, "A lot of the pieces and parts were put there by the kids [Eric's friends]. Especially on the cross. Somebody put an Ohio State knit cap on there, it was winter, had to keep his head warm."

261

"Eric would make hemp [macramé] bracelets once in a while, and ah, the day of the funeral home [the viewing] the kids had made a bunch of hemp bracelets, and ah, they put one of those on there. And somebody else had another little thing they put on there that they'd had. I don't know necessarily all the significance some of those gifts [have] because they're personal between he [Eric] and his friends too. Ah, Eric was a camper to a certain extent. Marlene had got him that little statue of a bear camping with his backpack. Marlene had done the little angel and a couple of other little things."

"Oh you know, kids will be kids, and there is a bottle of, I think, Pabst Blue Ribbon beer or Labatts laying near there and it's never been opened and it's never been touched."

" . . . [Eric's] girlfriend put the candles, the little votive candles [candle holders] that hang down from each side of the cross. That was a little thing there that she gave. People had given other little gifts for the cross there, the little touches that people wanted to make."

"The circle of friends was given by one of Eric's good friends, and his mom. People put little things there, just like that rock with that hand written message on it. It's just the significance there that people want to have a little memorial. It makes it a little easier for them because they don't have to go all the way out to the cemetery, which isn't close by. So this is a close avenue for them to pay their respects and ah, do whatever they want for Eric."

"The baseball, one of his friends [left it at the shrine]. Somebody brought over their old Worthington travel baseball and youth boosters baseball cap. They put that on there."

"There're a lot of little touches around there from a lot of people. It's just a way to carry on his memory and allow him to know that we're always thinking of him too."

"It means a lot. It means a lot," Mr. Bohn repeated the last phrase as if lost in reflection and trailed off.

The Effects of Death: Devotion, Grief, and Change

Marlene started to explain how her life has been affected by Eric's tragic death. "I am very angry over all of this. Ok? I have never returned to work. I am a registered respiratory therapist. I have been off work seven months now, and I am not returning to respiratory therapy. I can't. I cannot do it right now. Emotionally and physically I can't do it. So that's what it's done to my life. You see? And my other son [Ryan] says, 'I see you quiet and introverted.'"

"You can't make sense out of something which doesn't make sense," Marlene continued.

"Every day I get up and I say, 'My God. My God. What has happened here?' I think the most traumatic part of all of this is going to the cemetery, and you see your son's name on that marker." Pain entered Marlene's voice. "I wrap my arms around his grave and kiss him, on the tombstone at least. That's what none of you sees. . . . Every morning when I get up I kiss his picture a million times." The doorbell rang and Marlene left us to answer the door.

"I commend Marlene for the determination and everything else, for going over there [to the memorial site] day in and day out, for always lighting the candles and everything else. Because, when I've done it for her in her absence, I've become very emotional that whole week or whatever the period of time I'm doing it," Phil related.

Returning, Marlene continued, "My whole life is still about Eric. I know I have Ryan, and Ryan's a part of my life. But Ryan sees me include Eric in everything we do. There's never a day that Eric Bohn is not in my life. I feel bad for his brother. Ryan doesn't deserve this; he's a great kid. But he lost a brother and part of a Mommy."

"If I talk to someone on the phone, they know that my child has been killed in a terrible car accident. You see? I get cards from Verizon people and people I don't even know that say, 'I'm very sorry about your tragic loss.' I think that's what I like the most, that people are kind. You do have people that are not kind, because, they say 'God had a purpose for this.' Then I go ballistic and say. 'No god would do this to me, so don't talk like that. Fate did it and irresponsible parents did it. Don't tell me God had a purpose for this," Marlene continued.

"Sometimes things change and good comes out of these things. . . . My life has changed forever. His life," Marlene pointed to Ryan, who, by now, had joined us at their kitchen table, "has changed forever. His father's life has changed forever. And maybe I'll go to a different profession from this. I'll tell my story if anything happens."

"If I feel anything from Eric's death, that you will all see that will change me, is I will tell my story of Eric Bohn. And I will help others cope with death the way I had. I'm gonna tell them it's ok to stand on the back step and say 'Fuck you! Fuck the world! Fuck everybody because I hate life!' And it's ok to do that, but you think you're losing your mind when you're doing it. But you're not hurting anyone. I'm on my own property and this is what's going to happen to you. I hope someday I can help people and say this is what I went through and I'm a survivor," Marlene continued.

"I'm a different Marlene than I was six months ago, and I'll never be that Marlene again. I'm this Marlene. I'm a changed Marlene, and I'm trying to cope with that. I'm changing. I don't know how to cope with that. And he's changing,"

Photos by Gary E. A. Saum.

Roadside memorial for Eric with objects at the base of the memorial.

Marlene motioned towards Ryan. "And he's changing," Marlene pointed to Phil. "I think the hard thing is people don't know how to accept us any more because we've all changed. . . . They think you've changed and you have because your son's dead. And I'm living a different life now."

"So your life has changed, and we're taking a courageous walk. This is a courageous journey and I don't know where we're going or what we're doing," Marlene indicated.

Meaning and Need

Marlene's idea about helping others cope with death and loss demonstrates that roadside shrines have different meanings and functions for the people that built them. Additionally, those meanings differ from builder to builder, and reflect the needs of the survivors. Eric's shrine is interesting because it reflects two different groups of builders. First, we see the spontaneous cross construction, by Eric's peers and friends, the night of his death. Then, a few months later, Marlene added the luminaries and started tending to it every night. So we have two different groups with two different sets of meanings. Yet Phil and Ryan also attend the memorial from time to time and I wanted to get their thoughts on the significance of Eric's roadside memorial.

"Ryan, what does the memorial mean to you?" I asked.

"I just think like the major significance is that it's kinda like a remembrance, remembrance of him, for everyone, all his friends. It's kind of like a little site where everyone can go and just think their piece. It's almost like a little gravesite. It's just something where people can go instead of going all the way out to the cemetery," Ryan responded.

"Also, I just think it's some place . . . [that] shows you'll never forget about him. We all think about him a lot, he goes through my mind probably twenty-some times a day. It just shows how much we do care about him," Ryan continued.

Ryan went on to explain his view of the significance of the candles. "It's kind of like the little candle symbolizes that his [Eric's] flame won't go out and his memory won't go out either."

Ryan then described the feelings he gets when he lights the candles at Eric's roadside memorial. "I've done it [lit the candles] and I've enjoyed it a lot too."

"It's an emotional time though," Phil interjected.

"It is emotional. But, I mean it's just something like a little part of your day that you can devote to Eric and just let him know that you're still remembering him and lighting a candle. It's almost like going to church for God," Ryan said.

"Have you left any mementos at the memorial?" I questioned Ryan.

"No. I have not personally. No I haven't. I view it [the memorial] as somewhere else. Like I have my own memory. Like I live in the house still and I can go in his room and stuff like that. So that's [the roadside memorial] more of like an outlet for other people, the community, not the immediate family, [but] like his friends, definitely. His friends always leave stuff there," Ryan replied.

"Sometimes, the creators of roadside memorials think of the site as sacred ground. Do you think of Eric's site in that way, or do you think Eric's friends perceive it that way?" I asked Ryan.

"I just think it's something that's really nice to be able to go there and say their piece and ... if they have any problems, it's kind of like an outlet," Ryan answered.

Although Marlene did not create the memorial, she has taken on the role of caretaker of the memorial and explained what this role and what the memorial means to her. "I try to leave everything that the children have given him. However, when something like a [stuffed animal] bear begins to get really yucky, then I dispose of them because I like to keep it [the memorial site] clean and picked up."

"I tell the children [Eric's friends] all the time that they're welcome to come to the site, and they're welcome to light one candle, but Mommy has to light the rest of them. So I give them free reign, that they can do whatever they want if I light the candles," Marlene indicated.

In the course of our discussion, Marlene told me about a news story that WBNS had done recently about Eric's roadside memorial. "I think Channel 10 said it the right way, 'A son has died but his memory is going on. His mom, his brother, and his father are keeping his memory alive.' These candles are doing it because that's how people look at it every day. They see Eric Bohn was killed here and that's a memory and they won't forget our son. You see? And I think that's what I like about it," Marlene related.

"Do you think of the memorial as sacred ground?" I asked Marlene.

"I really don't know what I feel. I guess because the kids put the cross there I just went there because the kids went there. I don't think it's sacred to me now, but it's very special to me now. And I talk to him. While I light the candles I'm always saying, 'Mommy's here, Mommy's here. Mommy misses you. Mommy loves you,'" Marlene answers.

"So for you it's more of a point of connection with Eric then," I conjectured.

With pain in her voice, Marlene answered, "There you go. Yeah that's what it is. Uh huh."

Marlene continued, "And I tell him what I did today; 'today I worked in the yard', and, 'Ryan's coming home'. And I tell him everything I'm doing. And I miss him and I love him. . . ."

Marlene started to cry, "This pain is so hard every day. I cry every day. I was really close to Eric. I like being a Mommy. My heart's broken and you can't mend a broken heart. It won't even scar, it's got a hole in it."

Phil rejoined the conversation, "It is a place for us [Eric's family] to do something on a regular basis. But I think we extend it ... where his friends can go to express their emotions, and they do. On the six month anniversary you," Phil turned toward Marlene, "had several of the kids. . . ."

"I had 14 kids there" Marlene interjected.

266

"14 kids sitting on the hillside," Phil continued.

"Yea, and they did it [got together on their own]. I just had to go light the candles. They were playing music and crying, and they sat there for a while," Marlene stated.

"Phil, what does the memorial site mean to you?" I query.

"A couple of things. It brings back a very emotional aspect of my life, a very tragic aspect of my life, because that's where it happened. And it's the times where I have lit the candles—I am emotionally more distraught that whole period of time I am lighting the candles, and it affects me even more so. But because I have my time with Eric . . . at home, it's a calming process. At times it's not very calming when you go there. It's a process just through the healing process, not only for us but also [it] allows the kids a place to mourn. And it allows us a place to mourn outside of [the home]. It's something that everybody can relate to."

"I haven't personally taken anything over there and placed it at the site. I have those mementos by his picture at home. I can do it that way. It's a very tragic memory," Phil related.

"I don't get sad. I do. I cry but . . ." Marlene started.

Phil interjected with a question to Marlene. "But it's your moment with Eric. Right? Specifically between you and him. Isn't it?"

"Yeah," Marlene agreed.

"'Cause I talk to him too and I play his music," Phil added.

"There's always someone here [at home] with me. [However,] when I go to that site by myself at night, I'm by myself with Eric. And I talk to him and I don't have to share him," Marlene explained.

It was now 9:30 pm and two and a half hours had passed quickly and it was almost dark as Marlene continued. "If right now I'm being anxious it's because I need to get my candles lit. That is so important to me. Even if I'm out for dinner or something and while we're waiting for a table or something I'll go and tell them to sit and wait while I go light the candles, come back, and meet them. That's how important it is. I look so forward to doing that."

"Every time I drive past the site, it brings back that tragic memory. It [also] brings back a lot of good memories that I can relate to," Phil stated.

"So we're keeping his memory alive," Marlene added.

Conclusion

Roadside memorials represent a multitude of purposes to different people. They allow people a tangible way to remember the victim of a traffic fatality. These memorials also offer a public forum to express grief over the loss of a friend or loved one as we see in the case of Eric's friends' spontaneous creation of the cross the night of his death. They can be reflective of the victim, and the victim's connection(s) to the people creating and/or maintaining them, as exemplified by the different "personal" mementos left at these memorials. Additionally, they may serve as a material focus for love, remembrance, devotion, and communication, as Marlene's nightly candle lighting solemnity demonstrates.

Works Cited

Bohn, Marlene, Phil and Ryan. Personal Interview. 19 May 2004.

Egan, Martha. 1991. *Milagros: Votive Offerings From the Americas.* Santa Fe: Museum of New Mexico Press.

Gonzales, Patricia, and Roberto Rodriguez. 1998. "Public Shrines Are Reminders of Interrupted Journey." *Column of the Americas.* 30 October. <www.voznuestra. com/ Americas/_1998/_october/30>. Accessed April 21, 2004.

Descansos, Roadside Memorials and Crosses. 2004. <www.jetcityorange.com/ photos/galleries/descansos/>. Accessed April 21.

News-Sentinel Staff. "Roadside Memorials Left By Loved Ones For All To See." *Lodi News-Sentinel.* 2004. <www.lodinews.com/articles/2004/4/24/news>. Accessed April 24.

Olmos, Edward James, Lea Ybarra, and Manuel Monterrey. 1999. *Americanos: Latino Life in the United States.* New York: Little, Brown and Company.

Appendix: An Inventory Of The Elements That Make Up Eric's Roadside Memorial

- Eight milk bottle luminaries surround the shrine.
- A white cross with "R. I. P. E. R. B." and "10 26 03" written in black marker is the core of the shrine.
- Blue Baseball cap with red embroidered "W" on it hangs on the central upright of the cross.
- Underneath the baseball cap is a red and white OSU knit cap.
- A laminated photograph of Eric is attached at the intersection of the crosspieces.
- Green strips of cloth wrapped around the arms of the cross hold on a metal bracelet and a red beaded rosary. On the rosary is a blue cloth bracelet with "wrapped in his love" printed on the bracelet.
- Under the green cloth and wrapped around the neck of the cross is a white macramé necklace.
- Two votives are fastened to and hanging off of either end of the cross arm.
- A red heart is tied to the bottom of the cross.

- A blue stuffed animal bear is sitting behind the cross.
- A full bottle of Labatt beer is behind the cross, between it and the blue bear.
- Two green glass candleholders sit beside and behind the cross.
- A white porcelain angel sits on the left side of the cross.
- A clear glass candleholder is left of the angel.
- Small stuffed animal "baseball" bear sits in front of the angel.
- A small enamel "Worthington, Ohio" pin is attached to the jersey of the baseball bear.
- A used white baseball lies to the right of the baseball bear.
- A "circle of friends" candleholder sits in front of the cross.
- A small metal cross with "hope" imprinted on its base is located behind and to the right of the circle of friends.
- A white and pink heart shaped candleholder is to the right of the circle of friends.
- Inside of the candleholder is a black and white hacky sack.
- A painted resin "camping bear" candleholder is to the right and behind the heart shaped candleholder.
- A copper candleholder with stars punched out of it with "wish" in the middle of a large star sits to the right of the camping bear.
- In front of the baseball bear, three hand-sized rocks hold up a fourth. The fourth rock has "R. I. P. E. R. B. with love, always & forever. SS, CO, SP" written on it in permanent black marker. One of the three "pedestal" rocks holds down a faded hand-written note.
- A small green and white plastic frog lies on its side to the left of the cross.
- A small white crystal square with "love" etched on it sits in front of the cross between the cross and the circle of friends.
- One loose jingle bell is situated between the frog and the cross.

"Down on Main Street": The 152nd Bellville Street Fair and Homecoming

Kevin Eyster

> *Kevin is a professor in the English and Communication Arts Department at Madonna University in Livonia, Michigan (a suburb of Detroit), and was also an NEH Distinguished Teaching Professor in the Humanities from 2001 to 2003. He has written and published on folklore and literature, with a focus on southern authors, such as William Faulkner, Zora Neale Hurston, and Eudora Welty.*
>
> *He originally wrote this essay for a presentation at an American Folklore Society Conference. In "Down on Main Street," Kevin illustrates how a small community can provide rich material and information for a folklore project—in this case, one that focuses on an annual local festival that celebrates community values and identity. The essay incorporates interviews, personal observations, and information from publications about local history to provide a clear look at an evolving community tradition.*

In a small town in north central Ohio, the Bellville Fair convenes in September. Street fairs have long been a part of Bellville community life, beginning in 1850 with the first Richland County Fair. The following year that fair was relocated to Mansfield, but in 1860 a Bellville agricultural society held the first annual Bellville Agricultural Fair. Referred to locally as the Bellville "World's Fair," the Fair occurs over a four-day period, Wednesday through Saturday, between September 10th and 19th, because it always has been an agricultural event tied to harvest. Over the past century and a half, the Fair has sustained traditional events while new activities have been added along the way.

Covering approximately a quarter of a mile on Main Street between the town's three traffic lights, the Fair comprises a multitude of Midwestern Americana. There are livestock and agricultural displays by local farmers and members of the 4-H Club. Needlework is located in the historical society building, an art show in the library, and the fire station houses flowers, baked and canned goods, and honey and candies.

270

Photos by Gordon Eyster.

The merry-go-round in its proper place.

Bellville's bandstand, originally built in 1879.

The all-important agricultural display.

There are two lengthy rows of restored antique tractors, exhibits by local merchants and businesses. Carnival rides and "games of skill" (Craig Roberts, personal interview) provided by the J and J Carnival Company of Canton, Ohio, food stands by concessionaires from throughout northern Ohio, and home-cooked meals served by local churches and by such organizations as the Eastern Star and the local high school's Athletic Boosters' club. The Lions' Club serves refreshments and Bob Evans' sausage sandwiches.

271

The midway on Main Street.

Musical performances range from the high school band to gospel to bluegrass to contemporary pop and rock. There is square dancing, clogging, and a teen dance on Saturday night. There is a 4-H style show, and a Fair queen is crowned each year on the first night. For children there are pet and doll shows as well as the Kiddie Pedal Pull, a miniature tractor pull, if you will. The popularity of the actual tractor pull resulted in its being scheduled in the 1980s on the Sunday before the four-day period of all other events. The tractor pull and the horse show, which takes place on Saturday afternoon during the Fair, occur at other sites in close proximity to Main Street.

The sights, sounds, and smells of this yearly gathering remain with fairgoers long after the events have concluded, as made evident from anecdotes and personal narratives to stories and photographs in the local paper, the *Bellville Star*. The Fair has both an aesthetic and emotional appeal for many that attend. Residents and former residents plan their schedules to accommodate the Fair and view the homecoming element as an opportunity to visit with family and friends.

As a former resident and regular fairgoer throughout my own life, I see this brief essay as part of what may well develop into what ethnographer Beverly Moss would call a more extensive "topic-oriented ethnography" (1993, 155) but for now is more interpretive than empirical, a narrative more telling about the methodologist perhaps than the methodology. In essence, I'm telling, as Moss aptly suggests, "a story about a community—a story told jointly by the [fieldworker] and members of the community" (1993, 154). This paper and any further work I do on the topic are relevant to the study and preservation of Ohio folklore and to fairs, festivals, and celebrations throughout the United States.

The folkloric concepts most relevant to my work thus far are "survival" and "continuity." As folklorists Robert Georges and Michael Owen Jones suggest in general terms, "whether or not they are judged to be survivals, all examples of folklore provide evidence of continuity in human behavior through time" (1995, 67). As one of only two surviving or remaining independent agricultural street fairs in the state of Ohio, the Bellville Fair sustains continuity because of the continued involvement of local residents in planning and participating in the four days of events.

The Bellville Agricultural Society Fair Board, the governing body that runs the Fair, which consists of four officers and twelve directors, is a chartered member of the Ohio Fair Manager's Association. A pamphlet entitled *Redbook* includes rules that govern the Fair Societies in Ohio (Ohio Department of Agriculture 2011). While almost all of the eighty-eight counties in Ohio hold some kind of annual celebration, only nine independent fairs in the state not associated with a county fair remain. Of the nine remaining independent fairs, only two take place on public property, and only two receive state funding and are state sanctioned—the Bellville and Loudonville Street Fairs. It is the continued emphasis on agriculture and the use of public property as well as the overall success of these fairs that sustains their state funding and sanctioning.

Bellville Fair Board officers and member directors are paid $3.00 for each meeting they attend, and they celebrate their hard work and dedication with a Christmas banquet every year. Four member directors are elected every four years, and there are no term limits. This summer I interviewed two present members and one former member. Craig Roberts, superintendent of Bellville's Division of Water and Wastewater, is a third-generation member of the town's Fair Board. Craig's maternal grandfather, his father, and his brother also have been Board members. One of twelve Board member directors, Craig has been formally involved with the Fair's planning for twenty-four years. Born in September of 1954 during the Fair, Craig indicated that he has been indirectly involved "forever" (personal interview). His responsibilities include overall scheduling, coordinating and emceeing the Kiddie Pedal Pull, and planning all of the nightly entertainment. In 2002, for example, he was the point person in planning an event acknowledging the first anniversary of September 11th, a ceremony that included honoring police officers and firefighters. Along with his position as Superintendent of Water and Wastewater, Craig is one of fifteen residents who are volunteer firefighters.

When I asked Craig how things get done, he indicated that 20% of the set-up and tear-down is done by Board members and a handful of volunteers. The remaining 80% is completed by those directly involved in the production of various parts of the Fair—concessionaires, the carnival company, local merchants and farmers, and so on. He also suggested that the Ohio Fair Manager's Association place greater emphasis on the agricultural dimension than the Board and the residents, who believe what is more significant is community involvement. When I asked Craig about the folkloric concepts of survival and continuity, he replied in the following way:

> The . . . most important [way to maintain] this fair's success is [to make sure] that . . . future generations of the [Clear Fork] valley . . . keep the spirit of homecoming alive. This [success] has been accomplished through the multi-generations of families that have put so much time and energy into the continued existence of this event. One of the secrets to maintaining a tradition is to grow but not to change [unnecessarily]. You must keep a balance between [growth and change]. The [idea] is to keep enough traditional activities to renew the spirit of days gone by and at the same time spark new interest for the younger generations to become excited at the prospect of participating as adults to keep the fair going on [indefinitely]. Very little at the fair has actually changed over the years. We now have exciting steel rides instead of pony rides, high tech entertainment mixed with . . . bluegrass and gospel, different types of foods but still some of the same concessionaires that have been here over fifty years.

Basically, continuity is achieved in four significant ways: through the continued emphasis on homecoming and agriculture, through the ongoing involvement of generations of families in the Fair's production, through the continual return of particular highly popular concessionaires, and by the Board's willingness to respond positively to fairgoers' interests and concerns.

One of the most interesting anecdotes Craig shared with me was the criticism the Board received in 1985 when they decided to move the merry-go-round off of Main Street and onto the village green. While the Board's rationale was to make the flow of fairgoers a smoother process walking up and down Main Street, the townspeople responded with letters to the editor in the *Bellville Star* and a signed petition condemning the move and asking that the ride be returned to its original place (Cherp 1946). The Board not only moved the ride back they also hammered a railroad spike into Main Street to mark the ride's permanence. Instead of being seen by residents as an impediment, the merry-go-round was a necessary icon, a symbol of continuation that interestingly stops the flow of people so that they anticipate and expect to stand and talk with family and friends.

Two other residents involved in ensuring the Fair's success are the present and former Board Presidents, Bob McConkie and Freeman Swank. When Freeman stepped down in 1972 to begin a series of terms as Richland County's County Commissioner, Bob accepted the position he has held ever since. As former dairy farmers—each passed on his business to a younger family member—both Freeman and Bob, as one would expect, emphasized the agricultural dimension of the Fair.

Born in 1924, Freeman attended his first fair as an infant. At the age of 24, he accepted the position of Board President in 1948. He recalls being the one who "saved the Fair" in 1949 when $600 needed to be borrowed from the local Farmer's Bank in order to pay the Premiums to ribbon winners for the various agricultural and artistic exhibits. He attributes the Fair's success to its agricultural connection and to the Board and community's relationship with county and state government.

Born in 1934, Bob also attended his first Fair as an infant. He is most proud of how well the finances have been handled since he was elected Board President, noting in particular the fine work of recently retired Fair Board Treasurer Herb Woodward. He recalled a time when the meager sum Board members were to be paid couldn't be met. Along with the agricultural continuity, Bob is pleased that his son Rob has become a Board member director as well.

One significant change occurring over the past twenty years noted by Craig, Freeman, and Bob has been the volume of people attending the Fair. Twenty-five years ago it was only Friday and Saturday nights that were packed, but since the early 1980s all four nights bring in large crowds. Whereas this change is pleasing to local vendors, concessionaires, and the Carnival Company, it has created headaches regarding parking and for those locals who question the influx of residents from other communities who have no annual street fair celebrations themselves.

While there clearly is willingness to accept and entertain all that attend the Fair, the spirit of homecoming is deep-rooted and most important. I would like to conclude with the following quotation. It is a statement published in the *Bellville Star* on September 12, 1946, by the editor, Gregor Cherp. He wrote:

> If past years provide any criterion many thousands of people [including] former local residents and folks from many miles about . . . will [travel

to] Bellville this weekend to meet and visit with friends and relatives they haven't seen in many . . . years. (1946)

The survival and continuity of the Bellville Fair, then, depends on a variety of factors. As both a participant and an observer, I look forward to attending many more Bellville Street Fairs and expanding this narrative to include more of the voices and visions of the people involved in such a special cultural event.

Works Cited

Cherp, Gregor. 1946. *The Bellville Star*. Editorial. 12 Sept. N.p.

Georges, Robert A. and Michael Owen Jones. 1995. *Folkloristics: An Introduction*. Bloomington, IN: Indiana University Press. Print.

McConkle, Bob. Personal interview. N.d.

Moss, Beverly J. 1993. "Ethnography and Composition: Studying Language at Home." *Methods and Methodology in Composition Research*. Edited by Gesa Kirsch and Patricia A. Sullivan. Carbondale, IL: Southern Illinois University Press. 153-171. Print.

Ohio Department of Agriculture. 2011. County and Independent Agricultural Societies. "*Redbook*": *Laws and Rules*. Print.

Roberts, Craig. Personal interview. N.d.

Swank, Freeman. Personal interview. N.d.

Food for Thought: Power and Food in Hurston's *Their Eyes Were Watching God*

Emily Yu

Emily wrote this essay for a Twentieth Century American Literature course during her master's degree program at the University of Northern Colorado. Her interest in foodways developed because of her own experiences and the influence of her Chinese background on food and food events. She has been intrigued by the contrast between the practices of her own family and those of more traditional Chinese families and American families.

Prior to her taking the class for which she wrote the essay, Emily had taken several courses in cultural studies. When reading Zora Neale Hurston for the course, she discovered many interesting parallels in how power and hierarchy were conveyed through these food events. To develop the essay, she

> used secondary research and close readings of both the text
> and Hurston's autobiography. This is her first scholarly essay
> about folklore.
>
> "Food for Thought" is an accessible essay that shows some-
> thing about the general ideas of power and hierarchy conveyed
> through foodways that Emily was initially struck by, and it
> also serves as a solid example of an interpretation of folklore
> and literature.

Food plays an important role in its representation of cultural identity. The practices surrounding food in relationship to its culture, also known as food-ways, "bind individuals together, define the limits of the group's outreach and identity, distinguish in-group from out-group, serve as a medium of inter-group communication, celebrate cultural cohesion, and provide a context for perfor-mance of group rituals" (Keller and Mussell 1984, 5). Foodways are a represen-tation of the cultures and the cultural groups that practice them. They dem-onstrate the power relations found within their given social group, and their practices illustrate the forms of cohesion for a group's identity. Both foods and foodways contain cultural significance as symbols of these power relations. Zora Neale Hurston demonstrates the relationships of power between the characters through these foodways and food symbols in *Their Eyes Were Watching God*.

Many of Hurston's recent critics have either focused on the folkways or the rhetorical strategies found within the novel. Both topics regard Janie's ability, or inability, to discover herself as a result of both of these subjects. For Margaret Marquis, food is a direct indication of the ability to communicate through body language and hunger rather than in words. This form of food communication also foreshadows events and reveals the growth, both spiritually and physically, of Janie Crawford. Marquis states:

In the numerous scenes involving love, flirtation and food, Hurston cre-ates a society that acknowledges food relationships as both necessary and positive, or, in the case of Tea Cake's death, predictors of doom. It is appropriate that Janie's life and strength are continually represented by her physical presence and awareness and also by food, the source of human vitality. (2003, 87)

Marquis provides an explanation for the use of food imagery, specifically the character names taken from food items, as a means of communicating desire.

However, she does not address the other events that use food as a means of communicating power. The characters communicate with a language that is infused with food references, and they manipulate Janie, and other characters, through food and hunger. Characters like Tea Cake and Janie eventually learn about the power they possess over others and within the community through cooking and feeding foods to others. Food actively participates as a means of expression in *Their Eyes Were Watching God* because words, and other communicative forms normally associated with power, cannot.

Hurston was very aware of the demonstrative value of food within a cultural community. During her experiences in Jamaica, she learned that food even communicated gender practices and sexuality during various food events. Specific meals would hold a cultural significance that was understood to be extremely masculine or feminine. She participated in the curry goat food event and discovered "[t]his feast [was] so masculine that chicken soup would not be allowed. It must be soup from roosters. After the cock soup comes ram goat and rice. No nanny goat in this meal either. It is ram goat or nothing" (Hurston 1983, *24)*. Food in this instance represented much more than nourishment for the community. The cock soup and ram goat were specifically chosen to dominate the participants with masculinity. They also represented a culture that Hurston later found to be particularly critical towards educated and independent women. The meal, which was the earlier part of a marriage custom, demonstrated the power relations between the man and the woman, as well as the gender roles within their entire Jamaican community.

A similar power relation occurs with the demarcation of gender roles for Janie. However, the feminization of Janie is not pronounced by a masculine authority within her culture. Instead, she was informed of her role as a woman by her grandmother Nanny. Nanny frequently referred to Janie as "Honey" and "Sugar," constraining Janie within the role of a sweet, fluid girl. Nanny's goal was to provide Janie a comfortable and safe life as the wife of Logan Killicks. She forced Janie into a specific role based on values symbolized by the foods served at Janie's wedding. Nanny and Mrs. Washburn had prepared "three cakes and big platters of fried rabbit and chicken. Everything to eat in abundance" (Hurston 1998, 21). The three cakes mentioned in Janie's wedding were also present in the wedding ceremony Hurston attended while in Jamaica. Within the same masculine meal of curried goat and cock soup, "[t]hree women with elaborate cakes upon their heads were dancing under the arch at the gate. The cakes were of many layers and one of the cakes was decorated with a veil" (Hurston 1983, 23). The cakes in this ceremony were personified to represent the bride and her bridesmaids. The division between the feminine cakes and the

278

masculine, and more substantial, main courses illustrate the gendered power relations between men and women within the marital institution.

The disappointment in Janie's first marriage leads her back to Nanny's house in order to receive further instructions on her domestic role. She indicates to Nanny that her new house "was absent of flavor" while Nanny was preparing "beaten biscuits" in Mrs. Washburn's kitchen (Hurston 1998, 22). The demonstrative qualities of food discuss the issues that Janie cannot vocally emote to her grandmother. Janie's issues with Logan concern sexual gratification. The absence of flavor indicates Janie's lack of sexual interest in Logan's blandness—something that women cannot openly suggest or discuss about their husbands. Meanwhile, Nanny's task within Mrs. Washburn's home indicates that her role in society is of a "beaten" woman, someone who is not independent or able to give Janie advice about improving her marital situation. As Nanny prepares "beaten biscuits," she is also trying to "beat" Janie into the submissive role of Logan's wife. Nanny assumes that she can coerce Janie into settling for Logan because of his secure position within the local farming community. Her impressions of Janie reflect the assumption that Janie is malleable dough that can be kneaded and pounded on to fit within a specific social role.

Although the impression left by Nanny "was still powerful and strong," Janie was able to escape from her marriage through the intervention of Jody Starks.[†] The interaction between Jody and Janie was addressed through a double entendre of food references:

> "You married? You ain't hardly old enough to be weaned. Ah betcha you still craves sugar-tits, doncher?"
> "Yeah, and Ah makes and sucks 'em when de notion strikes me. Drinks sweeten' water too."
> "Ah loves dat mahself. Never specks to get too old to enjoy syrup sweeten' water when it's cool and nice."
> "Us got plenty syrup in de barn. Ribbon-cane syrup. If you so desires." (Hurston 1998, 28)

[†] According to Sigrid King, "Hurston's naming of Starks is ironic for several reasons. The word stark is often used as a synonym for barren, and Joe Starks and Janie never have any children [...] Stark's name is also ironic because of his focus on capitalistic pursuits. Starks's wealth gives him a false sense of power because the townspeople resent him and the things he does to gain his wealth." The name of Starks also foreshadows Jody's death because his refusal to eat Janie's food leaves him stark as well.

279

Through making idle conversation after receiving a glass of water, Jody attempts to establish a hierarchy with Janie as a young baby "hardly old enough to be weaned." This also has an implication of a new life for Janie, starting out again as if she were reborn. His "sweet" talk uses literal sweets such as sugar-tits and sweeten' water to entice Janie to run away with him as part of this new beginning. In addition, his attitude towards sweetening syrup implies that he "[n]ever specks to get too old to enjoy" both the syrup and Janie. Janie is able to respond to his desires for both by answering that she has "got plenty syrup in de barn." The negotiation of Janie and Jody's marriage takes place within this context. Jody's initial attempt in establishing a hierarchical system of power is thwarted by Janie's ability to reciprocate and form an equal relationship. Jody is offering Janie a new life, while Janie offers to fulfill whatever Jody's desires will be. Marquis argues that, "[u]nlike many women who are uneasy with their relationships with food, Janie recognizes not only the physical need to eat but also the urge to eat, and as the urge for sexual intimacy" (2003, 86). However, Janie is negotiating for more than just a satiation of sexual hunger. She is also attempting to negotiate a kind of freedom that allows her to do what she pleases "when de notion strikes." Jody's temporary concession to Janie's reciprocity is the main reason Janie chooses to follow him. She realizes that she has no form of reciprocity in her relationship with Logan, and Jody's sweet words, also coinciding with his offerings of candy, convince Janie to leave her first marriage.

In general, feeding and cooking provide both power and authority to many of the characters in *Their Eyes*. The primary example of this demonstration of power relations occurs when Janie refuses to cook for her husbands. In the first instance, Logan interrupts the cooking of his last breakfast from Janie in order to complain about her role in his household. His demands for her to assist him with manure shoveling, and the shift in her role as his wife, provide Janie a reason for leaving with Jody. She finally decides to leave Logan in the same moment she finishes cooking Logan's hoe-cake. It was only after she "[t]urned the hoe-cake with a plate and then made a laugh" that we are aware of Janie's "turn" of fate (Hurston 1998, 32). The focus of this turning act within Janie's cooking exemplifies the new direction she is about to take with Jody. Her flippant decision of leaving Logan for Jody shows that her power over Logan is strong enough to break their marriage vows.

In contrast, Jody inadvertently chooses to end his relationship with Janie through his refusal to eat her food. "She was worried about his not eating his meals," not because he was simply avoiding Janie's cooking, but his refusal of her cooking represented his way of repressing her voice. Jody refused to listen to Janie, and he insisted that she was trying to poison him. Ironically, his mind is poisoned by a hack root-doctor due to his refusal to communicate with Janie. However, she doesn't state that she has a problem with his direct refusal to communicate with her. Instead, she describes her problem with Jody's behavior as his accusations of her poisoning him. She states, "Tuh think Ah been wid Jody twenty yeahs and Ah just now got tuh bear de name uh poisonin' him! It's 'bout to kill me, Pheoby. Sorrow dogged by sorrow is in mah heart" (Hurston 1998, 82-3). It is evident to the reader that the issues surrounding Jody's death are really concerned with the hindrance of communication, yet Janie herself cannot state this to Pheoby. The reason for this is that Janie has no authority through verbal communication. As a woman in the Eatonville community,‡ she has never had much power through her voice. However, her power and authority are vested in her communication skills through cooking. She feeds Jody, and Jody can listen through eating what she serves. Once Jody ceased eating, Janie lost her only means of communication and authority. His refusal to eat with her also stigmatized her within the Eatonville community. She could no longer claim the same privileges of authority as Jody. She was ignored by the community while "[t]his one and that one came into her house with covered plates of broth and other sick-room dishes without taking the least notice of her as Joe's wife" (Hurston 1998, 83). The community took over her responsibilities of feeding Jody, thus removing all her power.

With her third husband, Janie discovers a different form of power that can be shared within a relationship. Vergible "Tea Cake" Woods is the only husband that does not confine Janie to a specific role within their marriage. Tea Cake is willing to share the responsibilities of their relationship, and he demonstrates this through sharing the responsibilities in cooking. During their courtship, Tea Cake constantly provided Janie with food, and he took pleasure in feeding her. He would "pick some lemons and squeezed them for her"; "had a string of fresh-caught trout" that he cleaned; he made breakfast for her and insisted that she "get her rest"; and he took her to buy groceries for the "big Sunday School picnic" (Hurston 1998, 102-08). In previous marriages, the thought of sharing the task of finding and preparing food was never mentioned. Janie was in control of the kitchen, and none of her former husbands were interested in sharing this responsibility. Tea Cake, however, is completely engrossed with the process of gathering and cooking food. He insists upon sharing these tasks with Janie. Tea Cake doesn't interrupt and try to redefine Janie's role, like Logan, nor does

‡   In the "[Eatonville] Anthology" Hurston depicts an economy of hunger and need in which women are dependent—toothless, pleading, jealous, and helplessly pregnant [. . .] In those stories Hurston presented to her audience a stereotypical image of women in the black township of Eatonville as mute and suffering (Dalgarno 525).

he completely avoid any communication through cooking, like Jody. Instead, Tea Cake, as his name suggests, is incorporated into the power and authority Janie holds within the kitchen.

While Tea Cake moves into the realm of Janie's kitchen, he simultaneously moves her out of the kitchen and into the community. With Jody, Janie was always placed on the outside of the community identity. She was not a member of Eatonville, and this was obvious from her inability to participate in their porch talk. With Tea Cake, however, she is encouraged to pick beans in the muck just like everyone else. In addition to her work in the fields, she becomes even more inculcated as a group member because of Tea Cake's popularity and their evening meals. "The house was full of people every night," and each social group activity encouraged Janie's association with the muck community identity (Hurston 1998, 132). Janie learns to cook for the entire community, thus solidifying her identification as a community member. She would boil "big pots of blackeyed peas and rice. Sometimes baked big pans of navy beans with plenty of sugar and hunks of bacon lying on top," and she would share these foods with the other muck workers nearly every night (Hurston 1998, 132). This became a ritualized social event at Janie and Tea Cake's home. Janie's act of serving food to the community "is a sign of hospitality and sociability [. . .] [These foodways provide] the kind of impression one hopes to make, the image one wants to project, and the relationship binding those who gather to eat" (Kaplan 1998, 130). The relationship between Janie and Tea Cake became an emblem for the relations between the other members of the community. They noticed the displays of affection, and they were at ease once Janie and Tea Cake unabashedly played in the bean fields. The social gatherings at their home solidify this image of equality within their relationship. The community in the muck, with Janie as one of its members, shares their power and author-ity equally among all the members in the same manner they share their meals each evening. The community truly exemplifies Foucault's notion of power. He states:

> The omnipresence of power: not because it has the privilege of consoli-dating everything under its invincible unity, but because it is produced from one moment to the next, at every point or rather in every relation from one point to another. Power is everywhere; not because it embraces everything, but because it comes from everywhere. (1990, 93)

As an active member of the muck community, Janie is now incorporated into the power relations that constantly move from point to point. No one member of the community has more power than the other for any length of time. The muck becomes a collective of members who are willing to share everything.

Unfortunately for Janie, her time with Tea Cake would not last. The bite from a rabid dog took away Tea Cake's appetite for both Janie and for food. No matter what Janie would cook, Tea Cake could not eat it. He could no longer share in the production of food, and he was unable to communicate to Janie in the same way he had before. His inability to ingest food and water became indicative of the end of their marriage:

> Tea Cake took [the water] and filled his mouth then gagged horribly, dis-gorged that which was in his mouth and threw the glass upon the floor. Janie was frantic with alarm.
>
> "What make you ack lak dat wid yo' drinkin' water, Tea Cake? You ast me tuh give it tuh yuh."
>
> "Dat wather is somethin' wrong wid it. It nelly choke me tuh death. Ah tole yuh somethin' jumped on me heah last night and choked me. You come makin' out ah wuz dreamin'." (Hurston 1998, 174-5)

Tea Cake's accusations of the water's contamination emulate the accusations Jody threw at Janie about being poisoned. The repeated scene is a haunt-ing reminder of what happens when the various forms of communication eventually break down between Janie and her husbands. Once she is unable to either feed them or cook for them, the relationship can no longer exist. In both Jody and Tea Cake's cases, the only resolution to this lack of communi-cation is death.

The result of Tea Cake's death eventually causes Janie to leave the muck and return to Eatonville. The opening of the novel establishes Janie's power after her return from the shared authority of the muck community. The men and women of Eatonville, gaze at her from afar, "Seeing the woman as she was made them remember the envy they had stored up from other times. So they chewed up the bad parts of their minds and swallowed with relish" (Hurston 1998, 2). Without Janie physically cooking anything, she meta-phorically forces the members of the Eatonville community to swallow the envy that her image force-feeds to them. Janie's previous experience with power and authority in the muck provide her with the ability to maintain her power in Eatonville.

Upon Janie's return, she finds companionship in her friend, Pheoby, who is already waiting with a plate of mulatto rice to feed Janie. Both Pheoby and Janie are in a reciprocal relationship of feeding—Pheoby provides the physical food, while Janie satiates "Pheoby's hungry listening" with her life story (Hurston 1998, 10). The result of this framed narrative is Janie's realization that the Eatonville community is "parched up from not knowing things" (Hurston 1998, 192). Their knowledge of Janie's story cannot be filled unless Pheoby becomes the messenger to feed them. Even then, Janie explains to Pheoby that the talk amongst the community members "don't amount tuh uh hill uh beans when yuh can't do nothin' else. And listenin' tuh dat kind uh talk is jus lak openin' yo' mouth and lettin' de moon shine down yo' throat. It's uh known fact, Pheoby, you got tuh *go* there tuh know there" (Hurston 1998, 192). An image of force feeding appears with her comments on the moon shining down into their throats. After Janie's experiences with her three husbands, she realizes that force-feeding is simply another means of governing others without equal reciprocity. Janie provides Pheoby with the tools to inform the community of her return, but she understands that she cannot force Pheoby to feed them this information. The result, however, is that the Eatonville community can never "ingest" Janie's gained knowledge regarding power or the discovery of her identity. Janie remains on the outside of this group because of both their refusal to eat and their inability to understand.

In *Their Eyes Were Watching God*, food imagery, foodways, and feedings all demonstrate the power relations and dynamics that constantly flow through the characters' lives and communities. They provide a form of communication to the attentive observer, and they communicate the cultures that produce and participate in them. For Janie, they illustrate the constant fluctuation of her power and authority within her relationships and her memberships within Eatonville and the muck. Food is no longer just a form of sustenance; it becomes the very essence of a cultural text.

Works Cited

Dalgarno, Emily. 1992. "'Words Walking without Masters': Ethnography and the Creative Process in *Their Eyes Were Watching God.*" *American Literature* 64.3: 519-541. Print.

Foucault, Michel. 1990. *The History of Sexuality: An Introduction: Volume 1.* New York: Vintage Books. Print.

Hurston, Zora Neale. 1983. *Tell My Horse.* Berkeley: Turtle Island Foundation. Print.

———. 1998. *Their Eyes Were Watching God.* New York: Harper Perennial. Print.

Kaplan, Anne R. et al. 1998. "Introduction: On Ethnic Foodways." *The Taste of American Place: A Reader on Regional and Ethnic Foods.* Edited by Barbara G. Shortridge and James R. Shortridge. Lanham: Rowman and Littlefield. 121-133. Print.

Keller, Linda Brown and Kay Mussell, eds. 1984. *Ethnic and Regional Foodways in the United States: The Performance of Group Identity.* Introduction. Knoxville: The University of Tennessee Press. Print.

King, Sigrid. 1990. "Naming and Power in Zora Neale Hurston's *Their Eyes Were Watching God*." *Black American Literature Forum* 24.4. 2004. <http://0-web24.epnet.com.source.unco.edu/citation.asp?>. Accessed Nov 14. Web.

Marquis, Margaret. 2003. "'When de Notion Strikes Me': Body Image, Food and Desire in *Their Eyes Were Watching God*." *Southern Literary Journal* 35.2: 79-88. Print.

McGowan, Todd. 1999. "Liberation and Domination: *Their Eyes Were Watching God* and the Evolution of Capitalism." *MELUS* 24.1: 109-128. Print.

The Hookah Folk: Understanding Hookah Smokers as a Folk Group

Joshua Smith

Josh researched and wrote this essay after some initial work he and a small group of introductory folklore classmates did looking at hookah lounges. As he notes in the essay, he was already personally involved in the local hookah community as a customer. The early research he did with his group indicated there was little on this practice as a growing American cultural phenomenon, so he was interested in pursuing it further.

As an insider first to the social community and then to the behind-the-scenes elements of the business, he is able to present interesting and complex views of the culture and the performance aesthetics of a hookah barista's work. Since he grew to be a skilled performer of the art (attested to by the clients at Shisha) and brought to it his aesthetic standards as a member of the social culture, he examines this material practice as a cultural participant as well as a researcher.

Josh's opportunity to devote an entire summer to his research provides this essay with a broad look at the Midwest American hookah culture in addition to a close-up of the process of crafting a high-quality product influenced by both standards of ethnic traditions and local customs.

For many of us our initial introduction to hookah smoking came in Disney's classic *Alice in Wonderland* (Geronimi, Jackson, and Luske 2010). In her adventures a shrunken Alice meets Absalom, a caterpillar who, between puffs of his

285

hookah, questions Alice's identity. The caterpillar calmly inhales from the hookah pipe and forms smoke rings that shape into letters and ask Alice a fateful question: "WHO R U?"

Like a caterpillar trying to understand Alice's identity, I sought, through this ethnography, to better understand a cultural practice and its links to folk group identity. It seemed to me that many hookah smokers placed a great deal of value upon the performance and aesthetics of this tradition and not only strongly identified with the practice but found their own particular texture in the practice. Smokers create an identity based upon their choice of hookah establishment and their particular preferred flavors.

Most of the literature dealing with this topic focuses on health concerns and policy making, seemingly ignoring ethnic and cultural facets. The practice of hookah smoking, though, seems strongly tied to ethnic and family values, and practitioners often place a strong emphasis on the aesthetics of the hookah assembly, including the quality of the water pipe itself and the mixing of flavored tobacco to create new, exciting flavors for consumption.

The ethnographic methods utilized in this research include observation, interviews, and participation. Long before engaging in this study, I was a participant in this tradition; however, by obtaining summer seasonal employment as a barista in a hookah lounge, I was able to become heavily immersed in the practice and culture and find ample opportunity for interviewing and observation. I was also heavily exposed to the aesthetics of preparation through my job training. Since my methods included participation both in the practice and in serving others, it seems appropriate to deliver my findings in first person, so to communicate my own thoughts and feelings about the experience along with my analysis of the subject. I will begin by describing my immersion into the culture and employment as a barista, followed by a description and analysis of a few factors contributing to the traditional practice.

A New Craft

My adventures with hookah began with what I dub "habit stereotyping." I'm uncertain if this concept is already labeled under another name, but I'm referring to the tendency to group a behavior with other behaviors based upon a few, small similarities. When I was initially invited to smoke hookah, I immediately grouped hookah with other forms of tobacco use, especially cigarettes. Being that I had spent a fair amount of my youth convincing my parents to cease their habit of cigarette smoking, I had a strong adversity toward any form of tobacco use. I politely declined my initial invitation to visit a hookah lounge, which, strangely enough, came from my freshman year resident advisor in the dormitories.

After this invitation hookah was somehow hidden from my social radar for two years. I accepted the second invitation extended to me not from an urge to explore a new culture or curiosity toward a new activity but merely because of attraction toward the person who offered the invitation. This person who introduced me to this tradition would later become my fiancée and is soon to be my wife. I am a perfect cliché of the age-old adage that a flattering female can convince a man to do anything.

My initial voyage brought me with a group of friends, including my soon-to-be fiancée, to Gypsy Café, a local hookah lounge in the Short North area of Columbus, a mere five minute drive from The Ohio State University campus. I had, by this point, already sampled recreational tobacco use through the occasional cigar—but hookah smoking was radically different. Compared to that from a cigar, hookah smoke was smooth, sweet, and moist, and it was tangible, most likely due to the moisture contained in it. Upon exhalation I could literally feel the soft caressing of the smoke as it drifted across my skin. Hookah smoke also gave me a strong feeling of relaxation of both the body and mind. It was very different from other induced forms of relaxation, such as that of alcohol. Whereas alcohol operates through the medium of myopia, hookah seemed to slow down my thoughts and speech, allowing me to focus effortlessly on individual thoughts. Indeed, this observation was supported in an interview with Khalid, the owner of another local hookah lounge, Cleopatra's, or Cleo's for short. Khalid noted in the interview that hookah allows one to take each thought, normally intermingled with other thoughts and difficult to separate, and set them apart, side by side, before the smoker, allowing the individual to deal with each thought one by one. This report agrees with my experience: I've found that while smoking hookah my conversations reach a new depth and focus.

This alteration in my ability to focus is probably what brought me back to hookah as since this initial exploration I have come to enjoy the practice and moved from smoking socially to using the hookah while studying, researching, or writing. After classes I would venture toward one of the various hookah lounges, typically Gypsy Café, Cleo's, or Shi-sha. Gypsy Café and Cleo's were both within walking distance of the south campus area, and Shi-sha was a short distance from the north campus area. As I became a regular at each of these places, I came to understand that each hookah lounge offered a unique culture: it seemed to me that Gypsy was more of a relaxed social environment and Cleo's had more of a partyesque atmosphere. Any of these locations were exceptional places for studying during the afternoon, just after they opened for business. Hookah smoking tends to be a night-time activity, so during the earlier hours after opening, I would find the locations empty of large social groups and, as a result, quieter. During the day these places also tended toward softer music, often indie rock, which also contributed toward a less social and more focused mood.

When the sun set, however, each of these places radically changed, and this is where the distinct personality of each hookah lounge began to show. Cleo's, partially due to its location, became a hotspot for teenagers just barely old enough to smoke: the lights were dimmed, and strobe lights and disco-balls accompanied an atmosphere heavily influenced by hip-hop and rap. Periodically the patrons of Cleo's would engage in rap battles or dance offs.

Gypsy and Shi-sha offered a different atmosphere from Cleo's, but the two were fairly similar to each other as they were owned by the same family. The distinctions were not so much in the business itself as in the different feel of the patrons of each. Shi-sha was closer to campus and attracted a larger student-based population than Gypsy, which attracted many shoppers from the trendy Short North neighborhood and young, urban dwellers seeking excitement. Both played similar music and offered nearly identical menu items, utilizing the same style of hookah pipes and tobacco as well as supplementing the hookah menu with food items such as baklava and falafels and beverages such as exotic teas, chai lattes, and coffee-based drinks. Both Shi-sha and Gypsy Café became social hot spots after the sun set, but Shi-sha always seemed more geared toward social gathering itself whereas Gypsy Café appeared to be more of a place to wind-down after a night of partying at the various local bars and clubs.

All three of these venues I honestly loved and frequented. Which venue I visited depended upon my mood: If I was looking for an atmosphere that offered high excitement, I would head toward Cleo's and observe (usually not participate in) the hip-hop and rap scene. If I wanted relaxing conversation I would head north toward Shi-sha. If I simply wanted to wind down for the evening and collect my thoughts I would smoke at Gypsy Café.

It was far too convenient that at my time of graduation Shi-sha began hiring baristas. Since I needed summer employment this seemed a perfect opportunity to kill two birds with a single stone: I would earn my living through employment as a barista and utilize the opportunity to exercise my ethnographic methods in personal research. By this point I recognized that hookah smoking was something new that deserved study and focus. I had found little literature concerning hookah. That was the beginning of a summer full of ethnography surrounding the tradition that I had come to love. I applied, and during the interview I explicitly stated my intentions to research the practice and even asked about the possibility of interviewing the owners. Thus began my true studies.

Learning the Craft

Ethical practices required I be very upfront in my job interview, so when I spoke with the manager of Shi-sha café, I discussed the reason I sought employment and the nature of my project. We seemed to share a mutual excitement toward the project. Mona, the interviewer and manager, was the daughter of the owners. Again, the same family owned and operated both Gypsy Café and Shi-sha and so controlled the atmosphere and aesthetics of each: they sold the same brand of tobacco, often played similar music, and typically attracted a similar crowd.

Despite having been a fanatical hookah smoker, I walked into this job almost completely naïve as to the actual workings of the hookah pipe. This was quickly addressed by Mona's training. Her training was simple, quick, and efficient, and enabled me to serve hookah pipes to customers within an hour.

The hookah water pipe is assembled from a variety of pieces: The base holds the water and is similar in shape and appearance to a vase. The stem is usually metal, is approximately the same height as the vase, and has a thin tube that protrudes below the level of the water; a disk-shaped metal tray is placed atop the stem to catch embers that may drop from the heated coal. A clay bowl contains the tobacco leaves. The hose, usually several feet long, has a wooden handle at the end from which one smokes. The hose attaches to one side of the stem just above the connection to the base.

The base is filled approximately two-thirds full with water, so that the metal tubing from the stem rests just below water level. The stem is sealed to the base with a rubber seal, preventing air leakage. An additional rubber seal connects the hose to the stem, again preventing unwanted air leakage. With the base, stem, and hose assembled, one is ready to begin concocting the tobacco mix (more on this specific art later). Once the appropriate tobacco leaves for the desired flavor have been mixed, they are placed into the clay bowl. A square piece of foil, usually four inches by four inches, is then laid over the top of the bowl, and the edges of the foil are wrapped around the sides of the bowl, forming a sealed cover. Using a thumb tack small holes are poked through the foil covering to create as many tiny holes as possible to allow for sufficient airflow. Finally a heated coal is placed atop the foil and the bowl is sealed to the top of the stem, just above the tray, with a final rubber seal. The hookah is now ready to smoke.

Creating a Third Place: Shi-Sha Café Case Study

Ray Oldenburg, in *The Great Good Place*, describes what he calls 'third places'. A third place is a place other than home (the first place) and work (the second place) that cultivates its own community and social environment, a place visited for the pleasure of familiar faces and lively conversation (Oldenburg 1999). Some prominent examples include coffee shops, salons, and bookstores. Oldenburg notes, however, that America seems to be lacking in third places. Due to suburbanization and the subsequent commuting required between home and work, Americans tend to directly leave the stress of work, drive home, and close the garage door behind their car, skipping a potentially critical part of their social lives.

Hookah lounges may be filling this gap in the social lives of Midwestern Americans, especially those of college age. Hookah lounges have exploded in popularity in urban centers across the Midwest, and Shi-sha is a prominent example. Ray Oldenburg lists eight criteria that are critical markers of an ideal third place, all of which Shi-sha exemplifies; Shi-sha may be an indication that hookah lounges, while certainly unhealthy in frequent practice, fill an important social need in Midwestern communities.

The atmosphere is a critical facet of a true third place: it must be on neutral ground, be accessible and accommodating, and maintain a low profile (Oldenburg 1999). Shi-sha is just north of campus in the "Old North," allowing students to escape from campus. The hours are long—three in the afternoon until four in the morning—welcoming afternoon studiers as well as night owls and partiers. It is a frequent stop after an exciting, energetic night at the nearby bars. It is often also deemed a "hipster location." It draws very little attention, apart from the thickly sweet smell one may notice walking by, and it utilizes very little advertising. Instead, word of mouth allows patrons to invite others of their choosing. Of my twenty plus interviews of over fifty people, all but one reported having been introduced to hookah smoking and Shi-sha by a friend, and the one patron who discovered it on his own did so simply by peering in the windows curiously as he walked down High Street.

It is not merely the physical or anti-commercial atmosphere that cultivates the distinctive culture, but more importantly, the people and their activities. Other criteria listed by Ray Oldenburg and exemplified by Shi-sha are that a third place attracts regulars whose main activity is conversation and that these people would describe their third place of choice as a home away from home (1999). Indeed, all of the patrons who self-identified as regulars during interviews described Shi-sha as a second home, one regular even declaring that she had nicknamed Shi-sha "the living room of campus." These regulars, for the most part, know one another solely from contact made when frequenting Shi-sha. Many of them have established relationships that transcend the boundaries of the third place but still revolve around interaction within it. Randy, for example, noted that most of the other regulars have his phone number, and should he decide to skip a night of smoking and perhaps stay in his apartment, he can expect several text messages requesting he make an appearance. Misha, who was described by Mona as the most prominent regular, has been attending Shi-sha since before its current owners acquired the establishment. Misha reports regularly visiting the hookah lounge for several hours a day, three or four days a week, often more, for nearly a decade.

The regulars and their conversations are as much a part of the atmosphere of Shi-sha as the building and the owners are, if not more. They become the face of the establishment: Randy reported that he feels a duty to welcome any newcomers and introduce himself even though he is only a patron and not employed by Shi-sha. I often observed him offering to share seating and hookahs with newcomers. Misha also seems to feel a responsibility toward the place, though her engagement is perhaps less social and more pragmatic. I often observed her troubleshooting malfunctioning hookahs for less experienced patrons or helping them move their hookah pipe across the room (improperly carrying a hookah can easily result in damage and, sometimes, injury from the burning coal). I have observed Misha both warmly welcome and assist new customers and rebuke and chastise intoxicated or inconsiderate customers, even to the point of driving them out. Other patrons describe Misha as a mother figure of Shi-sha, a matriarch who nourishes the establishment and its patrons while wholeheartedly defending them from those who might intentionally or unintentionally cause harm.

Performing the Craft

As I learned to prepare the hookahs and made natural mistakes I was corrected both by my employers and the regulars; thus my employment as a hookah barista quite literally became a performance, which allowed for study and analysis of the aesthetics of the practice.

My critics as a hookah barista were the customers. Newcomers, with their undeveloped palates and naïve aesthetic expectations, were the easiest to please. The regulars, however, could be severely demanding, though I should note that their demands were never rude or harsh, just quite particular. Misha's palate was quite developed, and she would request specific orders, noting the exact proportions she desired, such as one-quarter guava, one-half mango, and one-quarter vanilla. Other patrons, such as Randy, would not demand particular portions but still, with a developed palate, presented a taste difficult to please.

One of his favorite mixtures, which he called orange cream, was a combination of orange and vanilla, and too much or too little of each flavor would result in due criticism. The hookah flavors require considering a variety of factors, and the regulars' palates proved a trustworthy source of criticism.

As my relationship with the regulars and my comfort as a barista evolved my concern with the aesthetics of the performance of the craft became more apparent. The order would be placed, and when I received it from my co-workers, I would often step into the main lounge and draw the customer out on their particular wants and desires. This was more often necessary with newcomers since I came to understand the tastes and desires of the regulars and didn't need such explicit instruction. Newcomers often did not know how to choose a flavor in accordance with their tastes and desires. In this conversation I would break down the elements of hookah smoking (discussed more thoroughly below), ask them to prioritize their preferences, and then offer a set of flavors that would maximize their priorities. With this information I would assemble their hookah, deliver it, and wait for feedback. After a few hits I would inquire as to their pleasure or displeasure and, if necessary, adjust the mixture accordingly.

It was through this system that I learned the most. The initial conversation allowed me to establish a set of criteria, offering me a connection to my audience that I would utilize in the assembly. Indeed, as a performance, hookah preparation became a method of communication between myself as the performer and the smokers as the audience. The conversations before and after came to serve as a frame, especially for the newcomers. Customers who reported never having smoked before often received a very particular performance as I would take their order, explain to them the practice and the traditions surrounding hookah, and after preparation and delivery, sit with them and teach them how the pipe functioned, conversing with them as to their opinions of hookah.

The ultimate artistic and expressive freedom came when either newcomers or regulars asked for my special. Whenever this order was placed, I used the aforementioned conversation concerning their preferences. Working with the aesthetics I had learned, I would deliver a new concoction and eagerly await judgment. As I learned the most desired flavors and mixtures, the feedback guided my analysis of the hookah art and eventually led to my invention of popular, appreciated flavors. I was learning the craft as a observant scholar as well as a performing member of the group.

Aesthetics of the Craft

The discussion of aesthetics is best divided into three critical components: tradition (Toelken 1996), the degree to which the text preserves more traditional ideas about the practice versus entails experimentation; practicality, or the utility and function of the text; and skill (Pocius 2003), or the consensually valued expressive details within a folk group. I will analyze the aesthetics of hookah preparation with these lenses in relation to the idea of emergence (Bauman 1984), the new practices that emerge from more traditional practices.

Tradition

Hookah originated as a practice in the Near and Middle East (Griffiths, Harmon, and Gilly 2011), and appears, from my observation and interviews, to be strongly tied to ethnic identity. Indeed, of the seven hookah lounges in the central Columbus area, all are owned by first-generation immigrant families except for one: Smoking Buckeye. Shi-sha and Gypsy Café are owned by Ethiopians, Cleopatra's is owned by a family of Arabs from Qatar, and Leno's is owned by Libyans. Such Columbus ethnic groups as Libyans, Somalians, and Egyptians frequent, as well, hookah lounges. The lounges often serve a variety of ethnic dishes and beverages with the hookah: gyros, falafels, chai lattes, Arabic teas, and more.

It seemed, from my interviews with the owners of these lounges, that all are eager to share their cultural practice with any who are interested. Khalid, the owner of Cleo's, always seemed eager both to serve the hookahs and to explain the traditional practice and the importance of hookah smoking in his home, Qatar. He noted that among the plethora of flavors available to smoke, only a few are traditional and utilized by Arabic smokers, flavors such as double apple and white grape. He also explained that hookahs were traditionally flavored with molasses and honey, but as the shi-sha tobacco has become more industrialized, more efficient methods of sweetening have been utilized, such as glycerin. This has also led to new flavors marketed toward American smokers, such as chocolate and café latte.

The single domestically owned and operated hookah lounge, Smoking Buckeye, pushes the boundaries of the practice by combining traditional ethnic elements with American foods and flavors, offering shi-sha tobacco flavors such as strawberry margarita and pink lemonade. Their food and beverage menu lacks ethnic foods but instead offers pizza, smoothies, and root beer floats. Emerging from this experimentation a different practice altogether has arisen, utilizing alternative liquids in the base of the hookah, such as soda flavors, juice, and, outside the lounge, wine. By using sodas and juices the smoke takes on a new flavor and a different moisture consistency. As several smokers reported from home practice, adding alcohol such as wine gives the smoke an intoxicating effect. Utilizing alternatives to water in the base of the hookah is not a new practice but is uncommon in hookah lounges; rather, it seems from interviews that only smokers in their own homes once performed this practice.

The atmosphere of Smoking Buckeye is also Americanized, as suggested by the name of the establishment. The owners have sought to intermingle the ethnic practice of hookah with the Buckeye football fanaticism prevalent among the college and local fan populations. The patrons of Smoking Buckeye are, consequently, different than those that frequent the other six lounges. The owners explained to me that they see a large number of football fans, who visit after noticing the shop on their way to Ohio State's football stadium. This past autumn Smoking Buckeye began hosting football parties, displaying the football games on a large wall-mounted flat-screen television.

This emerging practice, a creolization of the ethnic tradition with American culture, is not well received by all. The owners of Smoking Buckeye reported several cases of threats and even vandalism, and they believe that it is largely tied to racial identity and their experimentation. As they began pushing the boundaries of tradition associated with hookah smoking and intermingling cultures, they became a target, they believe, of some of the families who own the more traditional hookah lounges. They noted that it doesn't seem to be merely a matter of business competition, as new hookah lounges are opening throughout Columbus without similar targeting. They believe that the threats and violence are due to a combination of racial identity issues and the emergence of new practices surrounding the tradition.[§]

The traditional aspects of hookah aesthetics are also displayed in the patrons' choices of flavors. As previously noted, Khalid listed double apple and white grape as prominent traditional flavors, and, indeed, the ethnic-identifying patrons interviewed often described double apple as their favorite flavor. Two Arabs that frequented Shi-sha often explicitly requested from me, as their barista, fresh, clean hookahs void of any lingering flavors. Double apple, in particular, is an exceptionally strong flavor with, peculiarly enough, a taste similar to that of black licorice. Another group of Ethiopian regulars also regularly requested double apple. Most American smokers, however, avoided double apple due to the strong black licorice flavor. This had an effect on the performance feedback, requiring me to consider the personal preference of the smokers as affected by the role of tradition in their practice. The smokers whose initial involvement

---

§   The attribution of the cause of the violence to the combination of racial identity issues and the emergence of new practices is the opinion of the owners of the establishment. Further investigation would be required to confirm or deny it.

with hookah began through strong ethnic ties, such as those introduced to hookah by their families, were more likely to prefer the traditional flavors and would judge the aesthetics of my performance differently than the American smokers. That required me to consider an additional criterion in my barista work.

Most smokers seemed to prefer a mixture of traditional flavors such as guava, mango, and white grape with Americanized flavors such as mint or cherry. Unlike the displeasure they expressed toward the emerging practices at Smoking Buckeye, ethnic smokers did not frown upon most 'Americanized' flavors, though they rarely used them, and some even allowed some experimentation with their mixtures.

Practicality

There are certain parts of the hookah that, if prepared improperly, result in malfunctions, such as smoke that was too thin or flavor that was lacking. Fixing these problems was not always simple but did not pertain, necessarily, to artistic skill. It is important, for example, to poke a large quantity of small holes into the foil covering the bowl. Too few holes results in a lack of airflow, and holes that are too large may result in pieces of coal drifting into the pipe itself so that the smoker inhales small, crumbling pieces of coal. Obviously these small pieces of coal are undesirable, though one of my co-workers would often downplay the issue by calling the coal-pieces "Scooby snacks" and dismiss them as rare occurrences that are simply a risk of smoking.

The seals are also important practical elements of the functioning *nargileh* (another name for the hookah pipe), though they may require more improvisation to fix. As described above there are three rubber seals. The seal between the base and the stem is largest and thickest and rarely tears or leaks. The smaller seals, however, connecting the hose to the stem and the bowl to the stem often tear. These problems, I was taught by my coworkers, could easily be solved with makeshift seals assembled from napkins. Tearing a small piece off a napkin and wrapping it around the seal would stop the excess leakage. Because the paper would eventually become moist, these makeshift seals were usually only good for a single use and, when the hookah was cleaned and prepared for a subsequent use, required replacing. Of course the issue of seals relates to product design, but seals naturally wear with use and improvisational fixes were considered critical knowledge for a barista.

Skill

As my performance evolved, I came to appreciate the various aspects of hookah smoking. Certain details of the craft greatly affect the experience.

Through conversation and feedback I came to recognize several important factors that influenced the desirability of the smoke: the thickness of the smoke, the strength of the "buzz," the flavor, and the burn. As I gained experience as a barista, I learned how to best control these qualities, through my own practice of hookah smoking as well as from the feedback of customers. It is impossible to separate my interpretation as a scholar from my work as a barista; both identities influenced and guided my understanding of these elements.

It should be stated that not all flavors are created equal; that is, not all flavors mix and burn alike. Vanilla, being heavily sweetened, includes a greater amount of molasses, and the leaves contain more moisture than flavors such as guava. This must be taken into consideration when mixing hookah flavors. Rose and jasmine burn with a thicker smoke, while vanilla or orange will often result in a very thin smoke. Thus, in order to increase the thickness of the smoke in the aforementioned "orange cream" flavor, I could use a slight pinch of jasmine. Jasmine is a flowery flavor, and not all customers enjoy this taste, especially in combination with orange and vanilla, but if the Jasmine leaves are placed at the bottom of the bowl, they will receive less heat and less of their flavor will appear in the smoke, giving a bolder, thicker smoke to the orange cream flavor without compromising the taste.

Certain flavors also offer a strong kick, or buzz, the physiological relaxation effect. These flavors include mint, double apple, white grape, and watermelon, to name a few. If a customer requests a strong buzz, I may suggest one of these flavors; if none of these are desired, a small amount, again placed at the bottom of the bowl, can bolster the buzz without altering the preferred flavor combination.

The flavor is the most apparent of all of the factors, and often the only factor considered by new smokers. Taste can be controlled primarily through two methods: the proportions used of different tobacco flavors and the depth the leaves are placed in the bowl. Certain flavors are stronger, such as mint, and require a smaller proportion. Guava, however, is a stronger flavor that requires a higher proportion. One can also manipulate the taste, as described above, by placing the stronger flavor at the bottom. Because it receives less heat, the bottom layer produces less flavor than the top layers.

The final factor is the burn. Certain flavors will burn hotter and quicker than others. This is most important to consider with citrus flavors such as orange and lemon. The citrus-based flavors tend to burn much more quickly and can result in a harsher smoke that burns the throat. The taste may also change as the citrus flavors burn out leaving the remaining flavors that burn slower. Again, this is an important consideration with orange cream. As the orange flavor burns out, all that remains is the strong, sometimes too-sweet vanilla. This can be solved by creating three layers: a layer of orange on top, vanilla in the middle, and a second layer of orange beneath the vanilla. Vanilla is too sweet to place immediately beneath the coal, but by splitting the layer of orange a backup layer of orange is available after the top layer loses flavor. If the top layer of orange is light it also reduces the burn of the harsh smoke produced, and the vanilla, producing a smoother flavor, complements the orange and aids in preventing the harsh smoke feeling.

Conclusion: Communicating Identity through Craft

The current literature concerning hookah and the practice mostly deals with health risks, and while these risks must not be ignored, the social aspects surrounding the practice of smoking shi-sha are clearly worthy of study. There exists a sense of expressive communication between several potential classifications of folk groups. Some ethnic minorities share hookah smoking as an aspect of their culture and become tradition bearers across continents, and their mobility in new societies creates new folk groups, such as the hookah-smoking community within Columbus, Ohio. Though these two folk groups intermesh, their communication and identification is very different.

Hookah seems to serve as a cultural placeholder for such ethnic minorities in Columbus. Very few Americans can boast the experience and knowledge of the practice that those born into the tradition have acquired, perhaps before immigration to the United States. In establishing a hookah lounge, they may safely integrate their culture into, and offer new experiences to, American society in a controlled manner that reduces the risk of losing their distinctive experience within an overwhelming and absorbing American culture. The establishments owned and operated by these tradition bearers preserve culture also through ethnic foods and beverages and even their atmospheres, thereby striving for the "salad bowl" mixture that keeps cultures integrated yet whole, as opposed to the "melting pot" in which distinctive identities are absorbed into the identity of American culture as a whole. This may begin to explain the issues facing Smoking Buckeye—perhaps the creolization of the culture of Ohio State Buckeye fanaticism with tradtional ethnic practices is viewed as threatening the unique cultural identities.

But an additional folk group created by emergent American tradition bearers who now identify with the practice also exists, though perhaps not with the status of an ethnic group. In Columbus these smokers consist mostly of college students or young adults living in the area. This folk group can be further subdivided based upon location, as each lounge offers a unique atmosphere and personality and consequently draws a distinctive crowd. These distinctions may seem minor to non-smokers, but smokers, based upon interviews, seem to strongly identify with their personal lounge of choice. They sometimes carry stereotypes of the smokers of other lounges: "Only underage smokers go to Cleo's" or "I felt like the people at Shi-sha were too immature." Clearly the identification is more specific than suspected from an external view, though these stereotypes do not completely prevent smokers from visiting multiple lounges. Layers of group identification are expressed.

This analysis of hookah smoking in a Midwestern community would be incomplete without addressing the issues of exoteric and esoteric communication, which is where the subdivision of groups becomes most apparent. As mentioned above, ethnic minorities and immigrants operating and patronizing the establishments may experience a sense of solidarity and unity surrounding the practice but also exoterically welcome new smokers into the practice and into the overarching folk group of hookah smokers. Yet they still preserve their individual identities by maintaining many of the primary elements of the tradition. Other smokers become members of a separate folk group who identify their status with the practice. Many of the smokers interviewed noted that nonsmokers may have assumptions and stereotypes about the practice, which in their exoteric perspective link hookah smoking with illicit drug use: "A lot of people think hookah pipes are bongs." Thereby the communication of smokers' identity takes on a sort of rebellious nature. Subdividing further, within the group there exists simultaneous unity and differentiation—two smokers that identify with different lounges may still share a hookah in the home or even in a lounge.

Certainly hookah smoking carries different meanings and communicates different things to different people based upon folk group identification, so analysis becomes increasingly complex due to the differing strata of smoker folk groups. Study of the culture proves just as important as the study of the health risks posed by smoking. By studying hookah we may gain more insight into the creolization and integration of cultural traditions. This study is, by no means, comprehensive. A single summer of employment, observation, and interviews will not suffice for that, but perhaps it will serve as a diving board for the study and preservation of a tradition that may, despite the risks involved, offer the American Midwest new cultural ties and a much-needed environment for social interaction.

Works Cited

Bauman, Richard. 1984. *Verbal Art as Performance.* Prospect Heights, IL: Waveland.

Geronimi, Clyde, Wilfred Jackson, and Hamilton Luske, directors. 2010. *Alice in Wonderland:*

Special Un-anniversary Edition. United States: Walt Disney Video.

Griffiths, Merlyn A., Tracy R. Harmon, and Mary C. Gilly. 2011. "Hubble Bubble Trouble: The Need for Education about and Regulation of Hookah Smoking." *Journal of Public Policy and Marketing* 30 (1). 119–32. doi:10.1509/jppm.30.1.119.

Oldenburg, Ray. 1999. *The Great Good Place*. Cambridge, MA: De Capo Press.

Pocius, Gerald. 2003. "Art." In *Eight Words for the Study of Expressive Culture*. Edited by Burt Feintuch. 42–68. Urbana, IL: University of Illinois Press.

Toelken, Barre. 1996. *The Dynamics of Folklore*. Logan, UT: Utah State University Press.

CHAPTER 9

Suggestions for Activities and Projects

The best part of learning about folklore is getting involved in a project and discovering firsthand what folklore is and how it works. The following suggested activities cover introductions to topics, methods, library research, and fieldwork and can easily be built into longer, in-depth writing and research projects. There are five categories of activities here:

> Group and Classroom Activities
> Personal Reflection
> Library Research
> Fieldwork Projects
> Integrated Projects (these combine reflection, library research, and
>> fieldwork)

Some of the activities within the different categories are similar to each other, but they are presented with different approaches or goals in mind. For instance, in the "Group and Classroom Activities" category, we suggest you write about a familiar object in order to practice detailed observation and description skills. In the "Personal Reflection" category, we again ask you to write about an object, but this time in a more reflective essay, in order to interpret how the object conveys group identity.

You might do some of the activities as separate, discrete assignments, use them as launching pads for longer projects, or do some brainstorming at the beginning of the course and determine a direction for an extended, integrated project that you work on throughout the term. In any case, we hope these suggestions get you thinking about the countless possibilities for folklore study.

Group and Classroom Activities

The following suggested activities are designed to help you start experiencing and thinking about folklore with your peers and fellow students. These activities will work within the classroom with groups of fellow students or can be done on your own outside the class with friends or family members. They easily lend themselves to in-class discussion and presentation of your observations.

1. Get together with friends, family members, or classmates and share some contemporary legends you have heard. While the group talks, jot down a few notes about the topics and types of stories those present tell. For example, you might think about whether tellers and/or listeners express belief in the events of the stories or note how people begin and end the narratives. Share your observations with others in your class. You might also write a short report on what you heard and learned. If others in the group have been doing the same activity, share how your observations and notes differ from and are similar to theirs. Note: You might also share belief behaviors (superstitions), family holiday traditions, and so forth, rather than contemporary legends.

2. With at least one other classmate or friend, go to a public place like a coffee shop, mall, or park. Sit or stand a few yards from each other. For about fifteen minutes, note everything going on around you. When you have finished, get together with your friends or classmates and share your observations. How are they similar and different? What might account for the similarities and differences?

3. Tape a conversation between yourself and one or two other people; you may also tape a performance such as a series of songs or stories, including audience reactions. The tape should be about a half hour long. Later, transcribe the entire tape, taking care to identify speakers and to note any sounds or other interferences that could affect a reader's understanding of the transcribed event. Share your transcript with fellow students and talk about your taping and transcribing experiences. What did you learn that will be helpful when doing fieldwork in the future?

4. Write a detailed description of a familiar object or artifact. Provide a physical description and tell as much as you know about the creation, use, and/or significance of the object—but do not reveal what

301

the object is. Share your description with others. Can they discover what the object is? Can they sketch it? Can you identify the objects others describe? Another activity might be to have one person in your group, or perhaps your instructor, bring an unusual or unfamiliar object to class. Each person would then write a description and talk about possible contexts in which this object might have been created and/or used.

5. Locate an article that surprises you in a folklore journal—that is, it is about a topic you might not have imagined being in a folklore journal, or being folklore at all. Read the article, then take a copy to class with you and talk about what surprised you, what you learned as you read the article, and any questions you have about the topic.

    (Some prominent print folklore journals are: *Journal of American Folklore, Western Folklore, Folklore Forum, Contemporary Legend, Fabula, Folklore Fellows Communications,* and *Journal of Folklore Research.* Some electronic journals: *De Proverbio* and *New Directions in Folklore.*)

Personal Reflection

The following suggestions are mainly reflective writing assignments that focus on how you experience and respond to folklore. You might share these as part of peer discussion and writing or editing projects and/or develop them into longer writing projects.

1. Write about a folk group of which you are or have been a member. Focus on who's in the group, how one becomes a member, group hierarchy, why members are members, and so forth. What characteristics do the members of each group share? How did the group form? Is it a group based on a shared interest? Proximity? Occupation? What special traditions, customs, or verbal expressions do the group members share that let them and others know they are members of the group?

2. Have you taken part in a ritual that marks an important event in one of the groups you belong to? Describe the ritual and talk about what it meant to you—did your status change? Did you feel a greater sense of belonging? Did you gain any special privileges or responsibilities as a result of taking part in the ritual?

3. Describe and discuss a unique expression used only by members of your family. Do you know who originated it or why or how it came about? In what circumstances might the expression be used? Who would use it and why? What significance does this expression have for you?

4. Select an object that expresses some aspect of a group you belong to. What makes it important? In what ways have you (or others) used or displayed this object that illustrates its importance? What does this object say about you and/or the group's culture, beliefs, values, ethnicity, worldview?

5. Identify a belief behavior you have taken part in or still continue to practice. What is the behavior and in what contexts does it occur? To what degree does belief in the behavior influence its performance? What values or attitudes are expressed through the behavior?

Library Research

A great way to extend our understanding of folklore and deepen our theoretical background is to find out what others have said and written about it. These activities are meant to give you experiencing finding, analyzing, and responding to the work of other folklorists as you explore your own ideas about texts and performances.

1. Locate an article in a folklore journal that interests you. Write a summary of the article and then jot down at least five questions you have for further research. Now explore those related topics using your library's search tools. List other articles that have to do with those topics.

2. Look more closely at the history of a particular genre or type of text. For example, you might research what folklorists have written about folk art and what types of creative texts they have studied, or consider how people have studied fairy tales or trickster tales. What has changed? How have definitions of the genre or type of text evolved? What types of conclusions can be seen in interpretations of these texts? Has there been any controversy or debate about *how* such work should be categorized or studied?

303

3. Examine the work of a particular folklorist. What kind of connections can you make between the different types of research the folklorist has done? Who does she or he seem to be influenced by? How does his or her career illuminate the history of the discipline?

4. Find out about a proverb that is well known in a culture that is different from your own. What are some ways it might be used? What has been said about the text's meanings and origins?

Fieldwork Projects

At the heart of most folklore projects is fieldwork, which includes observation and recording and analysis of performances, as well as interviews and conversations with group members. The following suggested projects provide experience with the tools and methods of fieldwork.

1. Get together with the members of a group and observe them interacting with each other in a space or event which is typical of their group. Describe the interactions and setting (context) of the event. Try to determine different roles or hierarchies within the group and describe them. In your field notes, speculate about the importance of these roles and formulate questions *for yourself* about interactions to look for. (You may also begin drafting questions to ask participants if you choose to interview them for a longer ethnographic project.)

2. Record a song or musical performance by an individual or group. Be sure to record details of text, texture, and context. In what ways is this a folk performance? What makes it "folk?" Ask the performers to explain the significance the performance has to them.

3. Interview a local folk artist or crafter about his or her work. Tape your interviews and take photographs or video. Present a slide show, PowerPoint presentation, or short film about the artist at work and his or her discussion of the creative process. Include the artist's commentary about his or her work.

Integrated Projects—Bringing It All Together

You may already be thinking of ways to combine the activities and writing and research projects described above. Here we offer a few ideas for creating integrated reflection, research, and fieldwork-based projects that could develop into extensive ethnographic projects. The three parts of the proposed projects are not necessarily progressive steps toward a completed presentation; they may be accomplished in order, but there is a great deal of overlap. For example, it is likely that you will continue research and personal reflection as you conduct fieldwork and will perhaps revisit all three types of experiences as you write your analysis. Keep in mind these are only examples of the kinds of things that could be done—the possibilities for extended research are limitless.

In each of the following suggested projects, incorporate your personal and fieldwork observations, library research, and discussions with consultants into your conclusions.

1. Traditional Behavior

    a.   In what ways do the traditional behaviors of a group you belong to help to express its identity to others? Discuss an example of a particular text (verbal, customary, or material) that illustrates how your selected group uses folklore to maintain and express identity.

    b.   Conduct research about how folklore helps to maintain and express identity, both within a group and outside it. What have others said about tradition and identity?

    c.   Talk with members of a particular group about their ideas and experiences related to folklore, tradition, and so forth. How do they perceive folklore? Tradition? How important are the group's traditions and customs in the views of the group members? Record their stories and comments and discuss their interpretations.

2. Changes in Groups and Traditions

    a.   Many of us belong to groups that change over time. Describe a group you have belonged to that has changed. What led to the change? What was the outcome? How have the group's traditions developed to accommodate the changes? Or, how has the group adapted to the changes in its traditions?

b. Conduct research about group dynamics and how groups change. What have folklorists said about the effects of change on groups? On tradition? What kinds of changes have people examined? What are your ideas about group evolution, based on your research?

c. Talk to members of a group that has changed or disbanded—perhaps a group that existed because of age or situation and then changed when members grew out of the group or moved away—a high school band, a scout troop, a group of cabin mates at summer camp, or former neighbors, for instance. What are their thoughts about the group's evolution? What experiences do they perceive as being an essential part of their "groupness?" What was or is important to them about their experiences as part of that group? In what ways do group members still identify themselves as part of that group?

3. Verbal Expressions

a. Describe and discuss how a group you belong to uses special verbal expressions. Do you know who originated particular expressions or why or how they came about? In what circumstances might the expressions be used? Who would use them and why? What significance do these expressions have for you?

b. Find out what folklorists have said about how and why group language originates and how groups employ these verbal texts. Talk about some of the expressions others have studied and draw some conclusions of your own about how and in what contexts verbal "folk" sayings have significance.

c. Record some instances of the performance of a group's verbal expressions. Talk to members of the group about the unique verbal expressions the group uses. What are their thoughts about where they came from and how they are used? Do they use the expressions regularly? How do they interpret their importance, personally and to the group? Consider the relationships among group members, the contexts in which the expressions occur, and the larger social, cultural, or group meanings the expressions convey.

4. Legend Trips

a. Talk about a legend trip you have participated in. Provide details about the location, any actions or expressions that must be performed, and the narrative that accompanies the trip. Who did you go with on the trip and why? What did you do?

b. Do some research about a legend trip you have participated in. Are there similar legends in other places? Has anyone studied the same legend you took part in? What do folklorists say about the significance of legend trips? Do you agree or disagree with their interpretations as related to the trip you are discussing?

c. Conduct some fieldwork about a legend trip. Take part in a trip, record any discussions or comments by the participants, take photos or a video. Talk with the participants and conduct follow-up interviews about the experience. How do they describe and interpret the trip? What significance do they see in the experience? What does it mean to them?

5. Foodways

a. Talk about a food tradition associated with a holiday or special event in a group you are part of. How is the food prepared? Who prepares it? What ingredients are essential for this food and why? How is it served? Describe a particular time when this food is served and talk about what the food, its preparation, its serving, and/or consumption mean to you.

b. Find out about foodways and how folklorists have studied the significance of food customs and traditions related to a particular holiday. Choose a particular food or food custom and examine what has been said about its origins, changes, and/or importance. Discuss how the custom has been interpreted and/or offer your own theories and observations in light of your research.

c. Interview members of a group about a traditional holiday food or food custom. Find out how it is prepared, when and why it is served, who prepares and consumes it, and so on. Take photographs and record people's comments and perhaps take part in the customary preparation and consumption of the food. Ask group members what the food or food custom means to them and how they perceive its significance within the holiday context.

Stuck for ideas? To get ideas for projects—

Talk with others. Brainstorm with family members, friends, fellow students.

Think about groups. Make a list of groups you belong to and note any customs, material objects, or verbal expressions that are traditional for those groups.

Read the newspaper. Many times ideas can be found in current events. There might be a story about a local craftsperson, for instance, or an announcement of a community yard sale or local church dinner. These kinds of events are often filled with traditional activities that you might find interesting.

Think about genres. We know we've said genre isn't the most important way to think about folklore, but genre classifications can help you think about the kinds of texts you encounter every day. Check the first chapter of this book for some examples of types of verbal, material, and customary texts to help get the wheels turning.

Notes

1. One growing area is the application of the folklore approach in industrial settings. Formally trained folklorists sometimes go into a business or other organization and use ethnographic fieldwork techniques to make observations and conduct interviews about the traditions and culture of the workplace. The managers and workers can learn about each others' esoteric and exoteric perceptions from the folklorists' observations and use that understanding to solve workplace challenges.
2. "Aesthetic qualities" refers to artistic or creative dimensions. We discuss aesthetics in much more detail in chapter 5, "Performance."
3. We'll talk more extensively about these dynamic and conservative characteristics in chapter 3, "Tradition."
4. See Brunvand, *The Study of American Folklore* (1998) and Toelken, *The Dynamics of Folklore* (1996). Brunvand labels this mode of expression *oral* rather than *verbal*, but Toelken uses *verbal*. We prefer Toelken's term to clearly indicate that folklore does exist in written form as well as oral.
5. A more elaborate, purposeful type of custom is *ritual*, a category of folklore that we discuss in depth in chapter 4.
6. Goffman (1974). Also see chapter 4, "Ritual," for a discussion of framing and rituals, and chapter 5, "Performance," for more about frames as markers of performance.
7. See for example, Rosemary V. Hathaway, "The Unbearable Weight of Authenticity: Zora Neale Hurston's *Their Eyes Were Watching God* and a Theory of 'Touristic Reading,'" *Journal of American Folklore*, 117. 464 (Spring, 2004), pp. 168-190.
8. A *variant* is a particular local or vernacular version of a text. Individual performers or creators of texts may produce their own individual variants as well.
9. Signs and symbols.
10. Folklorists who study material folk texts and objects.
11. Ethnocentric attitudes or actions focus on a specific cultural or ethnic group's perspective.
12. Among them Dan Ben-Amos.
13. Law and Taylor published a book about their craft: *Appalachian White Oak Basketmaking* (1991).
14. Alan Dundes talks in more detail about part-time folk groups in "Who Are the Folk?" (1980).
15. Some of these ideas have been challenged: see "Functionalism" in chapter 6, "Approaches to Interpreting Folklore."
16. If you have seen the film *High Fidelity* (directed by Stephen Frears 2000) or read the novel upon which it was based (Nick Hornby 1995), you may be familiar with the

behavior of a group of fictional record store employees. These fictional employees have their own folklore, similar to the types of folklore shared by other retail occupational groups.

17. Bonnie Blair O'Connor (1995) provides a model for less ethnocentric belief study, incorporating and valuing a community's own ideas about its health-related beliefs and practices. Her work illustrates the necessity of being aware of how various belief systems within and outside a group support, oppose, and otherwise interact with each other.

18. The term *cultural evolution* has often been used to describe the assumption that human societies develop along a timeline, from less sophisticated to sophisticated, or primitive to civilized. Romantic era notions of cultural evolution assumed the opposite, that humans had de-evolved from a pure, natural state to a corrupt, artificial state. We discuss these theories in more depth elsewhere in this chapter.

19. Dundes presents this definition in several essays. See, for example, "Brown County Superstitions" (1961); and "Structural Typology" (1963).

20. This category of narrative was originally referred to by the term *urban legend*; however, most folklorists prefer the term *contemporary legend*, since the stories are about contemporary events that take place in contemporary settings, but not always in urban areas.

21. Turner refers to the work of Brunvand (1981), Gary Alan Fine (1980), and Koenig (1985) to show how widely known and studied the Kentucky Fried Rat legend is.

22. Elizabeth Chiseri-Strater and Bonnie Stone Sunstein also draw on the work of Geertz, as well as Ruth Benedict, Barbara Myerhoff, and Ward Goodenough, to visualize culture as "an invisible web of behaviors, patterns, rules and rituals of a group of people who have contact with each other and share common languages" (2001, 3).

23. To avoid the connotations of "making things up" or "fakeness" that the term *invention* can imply, some folklorists prefer the term *emergent tradition* to describe and discuss the ways traditions change and arise within groups. See chapter 5, "Performance," for more discussion of emergence.

24. See, for example, Thomas, "Ride 'Em Barbie Girl" (2000).

25. Folklorists, fine artists, anthropologists, and others who study the work of self-taught artists debate the term used to identify such artists. Labels such as "outsider," "visionary," "art brute," and "primitive," to name a few, join "folk" as terms for debate. (See, for example, the work of Henry Glassie, Michael Owen Jones, and Simon Bronner.)

26. Jack Santino (1992) applies this term to folk art in "The Folk *Assemblage* of Autumn: Tradition and Creativity in Halloween Folk Art."

27. Blow Oskar is a figure based on Miller's cousin, who used to honk, or "blow," his car horn when he would pass by Miller's house.

28. Victor Turner ([1908] 1969) writes about liminality as a state of being "betwixt and between" the role or position that someone regularly takes and another role. In Turner's definition, the person is essentially stripped of even his or her typical status.

29. In the traditions of some churches, full immersion baptism ritual occurs, perhaps not coincidentally, at about the time of puberty but is not overtly connected with the physical changes that begin at this time. This is considered the time when children are old enough to use reason and make conscious choices. There is acknowledgment of the

310

child's stepping into a new age of spiritual, social, and intellectual matu.
the overt recognition and celebration of physical and sexual maturity.

30. If more than one person is baptized, the final prayers take place after the last c.
has been immersed.

31. Shuman does point out a few exceptions that apply to the reciprocity expectation. For
instance, if the exchangers are equal in status, the foods exchanged are similar. People
give more elaborate gifts to rabbis, single men, the ill, and the elderly; but single men,
the ill, or elderly give only small gifts, or no gifts, in return (497).

32. Ellis tells us that a number of folklorists (Linda Dégh, Kenneth Thigpen, Gary Hall, and
William Clements, among others) have done studies of trips to single locations or single
legend motifs (1982–83, 61).

33. *Bar Mitzvah* means "son of the commandment" and *Bat Mitzvah* "daughter of the
commandment."

34. The nine African American Greek-letter societies.

35. *Communitas* refers to the sense of unity that forms within a group when its members bond together outside (sometimes in opposition to or separated from) the larger
society.

36. For in-depth discussions and extensive collections of proverbs, see the work of Wolfgang
Mieder (1999).

37. Bauman's article was originally published in 1977; page references are to the 1984
printing.

38. See Dundes, "Texture, Text, and Context" (1964).

39. Henry Glassie has examined vernacular architecture, including Pennsylvania barns. See,
for example, *Pattern in Material Folk Culture* (1968).

40. Jones goes on to say that this "aesthetic impulse" makes all folklore art. That doesn't
mean that all folklore is "folk art." Some folklorists do study folk art as a kind of "art for
art's sake" *genre* created by individual artists within folk groups.

41. The names of the characters in the story have been changed at the performer's request.

42. The study of performance is frequently considered an interpretive approach. Because
the study of performance is as much about how texts are collected and defined as it is
about how they are interpreted, it has been covered in depth in the preceding chapter.

43. Mullen, in his own overview of American belief scholarship (2000), acknowledges the
drawbacks of functionalist analysis and provides a more complex discussion of the
ways a functionalist approach might be applied through detailed contextual analysis
and reciprocal ethnography. See Elaine Lawless (1992) for discussion of reciprocal
ethnography.

44. See Antti Aarne and Stith Thompson's *The Types of the Folktale* (1987) and Stith
Thompson's *Motif Index* (1955).

45. See, for example, Lau (1996).

46. Bettelheim's work has been questioned, but many still refer to *The Uses of Enchantment*
in specific discussions of fairy tales.

47. *Projection*, according to Freud, is a defense mechanism in which a person applies his
or her own impulses to someone else because she or he is afraid of or uncomfortable
with them. The *Oedipal and Electra complexes* ("family romance") are understood by

311

Freudians to be developmental stages in which a male or female child is attracted to the parent of the opposite sex. Normal emotional and sexual development requires that children grow out of this phase and separate romantically from their parent.

48. Dundes refers to Mary and Herbert Knapp (1976), Simon Bronner (1988), Janet Langlois (1978), and Jan Harold Brunvand (1986).

49. The "vanishing hitchhiker" legend often includes some reference to a marker proving the truth of the narrative, often, as Brunvand states, a purse or some other accessory or piece of clothing, wet spots, or footprints in the car (cited in Dundes 2002, 80).

50. An exception is Jay Mechling's work in *On My Honor: Boy Scouts and the Making of American Youth* (2001), in which Mechling delves into theories about psychosexual development of young boys as expressed through the verbal, customary, and material lore of Boy Scout troops—though Mechling's work, too, has been critiqued as being essentialist, based on a composite vision of "Troop 49" in which psychoanalytic explanations for adolescent behaviors are put forth. See Bender (2004).

51. Even texts some might consider fixed or static (published creative works or material objects) are considered from this perspective, often layered with aesthetic and literary theory and critique. An example is some of the work of Daniel R. Barnes (2003), which weaves literary and folklore analyses of the uses of riddling in Emily Dickinson's poetry with discussions of the poet's personal correspondence with her family and friends.

52. *Hegemony,* as used here, refers to the influence of a dominant group over the beliefs, practices/customs, and material items—specifically, foodways, in Montano's essay—of a subordinate group.

53. *Counterhegemony* is the opposition by those less in subordinate or less powerful positions to hegemonic power and/or control over folklore and cultural practices.

54. Bruce Jackson (1987) discusses these differences briefly in "Fieldworker Roles" in *Fieldwork.* A good practical guide to fieldwork is available from the American Folklife Center (2010).

55. In this transcript and in all the examples of transcribed text in this chapter, italics indicate the speaker's emphasis of words or sounds. Parentheses enclose actions such as laughter or pauses, and square brackets enclose the folklorist's interpolations or explanations of information that may be unfamiliar to the reader.

56. Jeff Todd Titon discusses the ways nondirective interviewing can work in eliciting life stories, which he argues are different from oral histories, biographies, and personal histories but can provide the folklorist with much "folk-cultural information" (1980, 287).

57. Complete versions of these field notes are housed along with photographs and the formal analytical report written at the end of the project in the Special Collections of Indiana University of Pennsylvania, AIHP Manuscript Group 76.

58. For most short fieldwork projects, it's possible to just listen to the recording and type or scribble down the words, using the rewind, pause, and fast-forward buttons to review or move through previously transcribed portions. For bigger projects or lengthy recordings, though, you might consider borrowing or renting a foot-powered transcription machine that allows you to slow down, pause, or speed up while keeping both hands free for typing. You could check with your university or local library to see if they have these machines available for student use.

59. This is an example of a brand name commonly used as a generic term. Other examples are Xerox, Kleenex, and BAND-AID.
60. Elaine Lawless uses the term *reciprocal ethnography* to describe the process of shared interpretation. See "Women's Life Stories" (1991), and "'I Was Afraid Someone Like You'" (1992).

References

Aarne, Antti, and Stith Thompson. [1961] 1987. *The Types of the Folktale: A Classification and Bibliography*. Translated and enlarged by Stith Thompson. 2nd rev. ed. Folklore Fellows Communications no. 184. Helsinki: Suomalainen Tiedeakatemia, Academia Scientiarum Fennica.

Abrahams, Roger. 1977. "Toward an Enactment Theory of Folklore." In *Frontiers of Folklore*, edited by William Bascom, 79–120.

———. 1983. *African Folktales*. New York: Pantheon.

American Folklife Center. 2010. *Folklife and Fieldwork: An Introduction to Field Techniques*. Washington, DC: Library of Congress.

American Folklore Society. 2010. "Folklore Commons: About Folklore: What Is Folklore?" http://afsnet.org. Accessed November 20.

Babb, Jewel, and Pat Little Dog. 1994. *Border Healing Woman: The Story of Jewel Babb*. Austin: University of Texas Press.

Babcock-Abrahams, Barbara A. 1975. "A Tolerated Margin of Mess: The Trickster and His Tales Reconsidered." *Journal of the Folklore Institute* 11(3): 147–86.

Barnes, Daniel R. 1979. "Toward the Establishment of Principles for the Study of Folklore and Literature." *Southern Folklore Quarterly* 43:5–16.

———. 2003. "Emily Dickinson's Riddling." Paper presented at the Center for Folklore Studies Alumni Lecture. Columbus, OH: The Ohio State University. 19 Nov.

Bascom, William R. 1965. "Four Functions of Folklore." In Dundes, *The Study of Folklore*, 279–98.

Bauman, Richard. 1971a. "Differential Identity and the Social Base of Folklore." In Bauman, "Toward New Perspectives in Folklore," 31–41.

———, ed. 1971b. "Toward New Perspectives in Folklore." Special issue, *Journal of American Folklore* 84 (331).

———. 1984. *Verbal Art As Performance*. Prospect Heights, IL: Waveland.

Ben-Amos, Dan. 1971. "Toward a Definition of Folklore in Context." In Bauman, "Toward New Perspectives in Folklore," 3–15.

———. 1976a. "Analytical Categories and Ethnic Genres." In Ben-Amos, *Folklore Genres*, 215–42.

———, ed. 1976b. *Folklore Genres*. Austin: University of Texas Press.

———. 1984. "The Seven Strands of Tradition: Varieties in Its Meaning in American Folklore Studies." *Journal of Folklore Research* 21 (2–3): 97–131.

———. 1993. "'Context' in Context." *Western Folklore* 52 (2–4): 209–26.

Bender, Nathan E. 2004. Review of *On My Honor: Boy Scouts and the Making of American Youth,* by Jay Mechling. *Journal of American Folklore* 117 (463): 108–9.

Bennett, Gillian, and Paul Smith. 1996. *Contemporary Legend: A Reader.* New York: Garland.

Berger, Harris M., and Giovanna P. Del Negro. 2002a. "Bauman's *Verbal Art* and the Social Organization of Attention: The Role of Reflexivity in the Aesthetics of Performance." In Berger and Del Negro, "Toward New Perspectives on *Verbal Art as Performance*," 62–91.

———, eds. 2002b. "Toward New Perspectives on *Verbal Art as Performance.*" Special issue, *Journal of American Folklore* 115 (455).

Berger, Peter L., and Thomas Luckmann. 1966. *The Social Construction of Reality: A Treatise in the Sociology of Knowledge.* Garden City, NJ: Anchor Books.

Bettelheim, Bruno. 1976. *The Uses of Enchantment: The Meaning and Importance of Fairy Tales.* New York: Random House.

Bird, S. Elizabeth. 1994. "Playing With Fear: Interpreting the Adolescent Legend Trip." *Western Folklore* 53 (3): 191–209.

Blank, Trevor, ed. 2009. *Folklore and the Internet: Vernacular Expression in a Digital World.* Logan: Utah State University Press.

Borland, Katherine. 2003. Personal communication.

Botkin, Benjamin A. 1938. *Supplementary Instructions to the American Guide Manual: Guide for Folklore Studies, Federal Writers Project.* In the *Harvard College Handbook for Students: Folklore and Mythology.* Harvard College, 2010-2011. http://isites.harvard.edu/icb/icb.do?keyword=k69286&pageid=icb.page349142.

Bradshaw, Thelma Finster. 2001. *Howard Finster: The Early Years, a Private Portrait of America's Premier Folk Artist.* Birmingham, AL: Crane Hill Publishers.

Bronner, Simon. 1986. *American Folklore Studies: An Intellectual History.* Lawrence: University Press of Kansas.

———. 1988. *American Children's Folklore.* Little Rock, AR: August House.

———, ed. 2005. *Manly Traditions: The Folk Roots of American Masculinities.* Bloomington: Indiana University Press.

Brown, Mary Ellen, ed. 2000. "Issues in Collaboration and Representation." Special issue, *Journal of Folklore Research* 37 (2–3).

Brunvand, Jan Harold. 1981. *The Vanishing Hitchhiker: American Urban Legends and Their Meanings.* New York: W. W. Norton.

———. 1986. *The Mexican Pet.* New York: W. W. Norton.

———. 1998. *The Study of American Folklore: An Introduction.* 4th ed. New York: W. W. Norton.

Cadavel, Olivia. 2000. "'Show Trial' or 'Truth and Reconciliation?' A Response." In Brown, "Issues in Collaboration and Representation," 185–95.

Castro, Rafaela G. 2001. *Chicano Folklore: A Guide to the Folktales, Traditions, Rituals and Religious Practices of Mexican Americans.* Oxford: Oxford University Press.

Chiseri-Strater, Elizabeth, and Bonnie Stone Sunstein. 2001. *Fieldworking: Reading and Writing Research.* Boston: Bedford/St. Martin's.

Correll, Timothy Corrigan, and Patrick Arthur Polk. 2000. *Muffler Men.* Jackson: University Press of Mississippi.

de Caro, F. A. 1986. "Riddles and Proverbs." In Oring, *Folk Groups and Folklore Genres,* 175–97.

315

Deemer, Polly Stewart. 1975. "A Response to the Symposium." In Farrer, "Women and Folklore," 101–9.

Dorson, Richard M. 1976. *Folklore and Fakelore: Essays toward a Discipline in Folk Studies.* Cambridge, MA: Harvard University Press.

Dundes, Alan. 1961. "Brown County Superstitions." *Midwest Folklore* 11:25–56.

———. 1963. "Structural Typology of North American Indian Folktales." *Southern Journal of Anthropology* 19:121–30.

———. 1964. "Texture, Text, and Context." *Southern Folklore Quarterly* 20:251–65.

———, ed. 1965. *The Study of Folklore.* Upper Saddle River, NJ: Prentice Hall.

———. 1980. "Who Are the Folk?" In *Interpreting Folklore,* 1–19. Bloomington: Indiana University Press.

———. 2002. *Bloody Mary in the Mirror: Essays in Psychoanalytic Folkloristics.* Jackson: University Press of Mississippi.

Ellis, Bill. 1982–83. "Legend-Tripping in Ohio: A Behavioral Study." *Papers in Comparative Studies* 2: 61–73.

———. 2001. "A Model for Collecting and Interpreting World Trade Center Disaster Jokes." *New Directions in Folklore* 5. http://www.temple.edu/isllc/newfolk/wtchumor.html.

———. 2002. "Making a Big Apple Crumble: The Role of Humor in Constructing a Global Response to Disaster." *New Directions in Folklore* 6. http://www.temple.edu/isllc/newfolk/bigapple/bigapple1.html.

Farrer, Claire, ed. 1975a. "Women and Folklore." Special issue, *Journal of American Folklore* 88 (347).

———. 1975b. "Women and Folklore: Images and Genres." In Farrer, "Women and Folklore," v–xv.

———. 2000. "Whose Lore, Whose Culture?: Post NAGPRA Intellectual Property Rights." Paper presented at the Annual Meeting of the American Folklore Society, Columbus, OH, 27 Oct.

Feintuch, Burt, ed. 1995. "Common Ground: Keywords for the Study of Expressive Culture." Special issue, *Journal of American Folklore* 108 (430).

Fine, Elizabeth C. 2003. *Soulstepping: African-American Step Shows.* Urbana: University of Illinois Press.

Fine, Gary Alan. 1980. "The Kentucky Fried Rat: Legends and Modern Society." *Journal of the Folklore Institute* 17 (2–3): 222–43.

———. 1992. *Manufacturing Tales.* Knoxville: University of Tennessee Press.

Foote, Monica. 2007. "Userpicks: Cyber Folk Art in the Early 21st Century." *Folklore Forum* 37 (1): 27–38.

Foster, Michael Dylan. 2010. "The Fall and Rise of the Tourist Guy: Humor and Pathos in Photoshop Folklore." Paper presented at the American Folklore Society Meeting, Nashville, TN, 14 Oct.

Frank, Russell. 2009. "The *Forward* as Folklore: Studying E-mailed Humor." In Blank, *Folklore and the Internet: Vernacular Expression in a Digital World,* 98–122.

Geertz, Clifford. 1973. *The Interpretation of Cultures.* New York: Basic Books.

Georges, Robert, and Alan Dundes. 1963. "Toward a Structural Definition of the Riddle." *Journal of American Folklore* 76 (300): 111–18.

Gilman, Lisa. 2011. Review of *Manly Traditions: The Folk Roots of American Masculinities*, edited by Simon Bronner. *Journal of American Folklore* 124 (491): 110–12.

Glassie, Henry. 1968. *Pattern in the Material Folk Culture of the Eastern United States*. Philadelphia: University of Pennsylvania Press.

———. 1975. *Folk Housing in Middle Virginia*. Knoxville: University of Tennessee Press.

———. 1992. "The Idea of Folk Art." In Vlach and Bronner, *Folk Art and Art Worlds*, 269–74.

———. 1995. "Tradition." In Feintuch, "Common Ground: Keywords for the Study of Expressive Culture," 413–31.

Goffman, Erving. 1974. *Frame Analysis: An Essay on the Organization of Experience*. New York: Harper and Row.

Goldstein, Diane E. 1995. "The Secularization of Religious Ethnography and Narrative Competence in a Discourse of Faith." *Western Folklore* 54 (1): 23–36.

Goldstein, Kenneth S. 1991. "Notes Toward a European-American Folk Aesthetic: Lessons Learned from Singers and Storytellers I Have Known." *Journal of American Folklore* 104 (412): 164–78.

Greenfield, Verni. 1986. *Making Do or Making Art: A Study of American Recycling*. Ann Arbor, MI: UMI Research Press.

Greenhill, Pauline. 2006. Review of *Manly Traditions: The Folk Roots of American Masculinities*, edited by Simon Bronner. *Journal of Folklore Research* 43 (2): 197–99.

Handler, Richard, and Jocelyn Linnekin. 1984. "Tradition: Genuine or Spurious?" *Journal of American Folklore* 97 (385): 273–90.

Hathaway, Rosemary V. 2004. "The Unbearable Weight of Authenticity: Zora Neale Hurston's *Their Eyes Were Watching God* and a Theory of 'Touristic Reading.'" *Journal of American Folklore* 117 (464): 168–90.

Hobsbawm, Eric, and Terence Ranger. 1983. *The Invention of Tradition*. Cambridge: Cambridge University Press.

Howard, Robert Glenn. 2009. "Crusading on the Vernacular Web: The Folk Beliefs and Practices of Online Spiritual Warfare." In Blank, *Folklore and the Internet: Vernacular Expression in a Digital World*, 159–74.

Hufford, David J. 1995. "The Scholarly Voice and the Personal Voice: Reflexivity in Belief Studies." *Western Folklore* 54 (1): 57–76.

Hufford, Mary. 1991. "American Folklife: A Commonwealth of Cultures." American Folklife Center. Library of Congress. http://www.loc.gov/folklife/cwc/cwc.html.

———. 1995. "Context." In Feintuch "Common Ground: Keywords for the Study of Expressive Culture," 528–49.

Hyde, Lewis. 1998. *Trickster Makes This World: Mischief, Myth, and Art*. New York: Farrar, Straus & Giroux.

Hymes, Dell. 1974. *Foundations in Sociolinguistics: An Ethnographic Approach*. Philadelphia: University of Pennsylvania Press.

Jackson, Bruce. 1987. *Fieldwork*. Urbana: University of Illinois Press.

Jansen, William Hugh. 1965. "The Esoteric-Exoteric Factor in Folklore." In Dundes, *The Study of Folklore*, 43–51.

Jones, Michael Owen. 1987. *Exploring Folk Art: Twenty Years of Thought on Craft, Work, and Aesthetics*. Logan: Utah State University Press.

Jordan, Rosan A., and Susan J. Kalcik. 1985. Introduction to *Women's Folklore, Women's Culture*, edited by Rosan A. Jordan and Susan J. Kalcik, ix–xiv. Philadelphia: University of Pennsylvania Press.

Kapchan, Deborah. 1995. "Performance." In Feintuch, "Common Ground: Keywords for the Study of Expressive Culture," 479–508.

Kapchan, Deborah A., and Pauline Turner Strong. 1999. "Theorizing the Hybrid." *Journal of American Folklore* 112 (445): 239–53.

Kirshenblatt-Gimblett, Barbara. 1975. "A Parable in Context: A Social Interactional Analysis of Storytelling Performance." In *Folklore: Performance and Communication*, edited by Dan Ben-Amos and Kenneth S. Goldstein, 105–30. The Hague: Mouton.

Knapp, Mary, and Herbert Knapp. 1976. *One Potato, Two Potato . . .: The Secret Education of American Children.* New York: W. W. Norton.

Koenig, Fredrick. 1985. *Rumor in the Marketplace: The Social Psychology of Commercial Hearsay.* Dover, MA: Auburn House.

Langlois, Janet. 1978. "'Mary Whales, I Believe in You': Myth and Ritual Subdued." *Indiana Folklore* 11:5–33.

Lau, Kimberly J. 1996. "Structure, Society and Symbolism: Toward a Holistic Interpretation of Fairy Tales." *Western Folklore* 55 (3): 233–43.

Law, Rachel, and Cynthia Taylor. 1991. *Appalachian White Oak Basketmaking.* Knoxville: University of Tennessee Press.

Lawless, Elaine. 1991. "Women's Life Stories and Reciprocal Ethnography as Feminist and Emergent." *Journal of Folklore Research* 28 (1): 35–61.

———. 1992. "'I Was Afraid Someone Like You . . . an Outsider . . . Would Misunderstand': Negotiating Interpretive Differences between Ethnographers and Subjects." *Journal of American Folklore* 105 (417): 302–14.

———. 1993. *Holy Women/Wholly Women: Sharing Ministries through Life Stories and Reciprocal Ethnography.* Philadelphia: University of Pennsylvania Press and the Publications of the American Folklore Society, New Series.

———. 1994. "Writing the Body in the Pulpit: Female-Sexed Texts." *Journal of American Folklore* 107 (423): 55–81.

———. 2000. "Reciprocal Ethnography: No One Said It Was Easy." In Brown, "Issues in Collaboration and Representation," 197–205.

Lévi-Strauss, Claude. 1971. *The Naked Man: Introduction to a Science of Mythology.* Vol. 4. New York: Harper and Row.

Library of Congress. 1998. "American Life Histories: Manuscripts from the Federal Writers' Project, 1936–1940." American Memory: Historical Collections from the National Digital Library. http://www.memory.loc.gov/ammem/wpaintro.

Limon, J. E., and M. J. Young. 1986. "Frontiers, Settlements, and Development in Folklore Studies, 1972–1985." *Annual Review of Anthropology* 15: 437–60.

Lloyd, Timothy Charles. 1981. "The Cincinnati Chili Culinary Complex." *Western Folklore* 40 (1): 28–40.

Lord, Albert. 1960. *The Singer of Tales.* Cambridge, MA: President and Fellows of Harvard College.

Magoulick, Mary. 2000. "Native American Cultural Renewal and Emerging Identity in Michigan Ojibwe Narratives and in Erdrich's *The Antelope Wife*." PhD diss., Indiana University.

McNeill, Lynne S. 2009. "The End of the Internet: A Folk Response to the Provision of Infinite Choice." In Blank, *Folklore and the Internet: Vernacular Expression in a Digital World,* 80–97.

Mechling, Jay. 2001. *On My Honor: Boy Scouts and the Making of American Youth.* Chicago: University of Chicago Press.

Mieder, Wolfgang. 1999. "Popular Views of the Proverb." *De Proverbio: An Electronic Journal of International Proverb Studies* 5(2). http:www.deproverbio.com/DPjournal/DP,5,2,99/MIEDER/VIEWS.htm.

Montaño, Mario. 1997. "Appropriation and Counterhegemony in South Texas: Food Slurs, Offal Meats, and Blood." In Tuleja, *Usable Pasts: Traditions and Group Expressions in North America,* 50–67.

Motz, Marilyn. 1998. "The Practice of Belief." *Journal of American Folklore* 111 (441): 339–55.

Mould, Tom. 2005. "'Running the Yard': The Negotiation of Masculinities in African American Stepping." In Bronner, *Manly Traditions: The Folk Roots of American Masculinities,* 77–115.

Mullen, Patrick B. 1988. *I Heard the Old Fishermen Say: Folklore of the Texas Gulf Coast.* Logan: Utah State University Press. First published 1978 by University of Texas.

———. 2000. "Belief and the American Folk." *Journal of American Folklore* 113 (448): 119–43.

———. 2003. Email correspondence.

———. 2008. *The Man Who Adores the Negro: Race and American Folklore.* Urbana: University of Illinois Press.

Myerhoff, Barbara G. 1977. "We Don't Wrap Herring in a Printed Page: Fusion, Fictions and Continuity in Secular Ritual." In *Secular Ritual,* edited by Sally F. Moore and Barbara G. Myerhoff, 199–224. Amsterdam: Van Gorcum/Assen.

Myerhoff, Barbara G., Linda A. Camino, and Edith Turner. 1986. "Rites of Passage: An Overview." In *Encyclopedia of Religion,* edited by Mircea Eliade. New York: Macmillan.

Narayan, Kirin. 1995. "The Practice of Oral Literary Criticism: Women's Songs in Kangra, India." *Journal of American Folklore* 108 (429): 243–64

National Pan Hellenic Council. 2011. "NPHC Policies: Step Show Conduct." National Pan-Hellenic Council Policy Statements. http://www.nphchq.org/policies.htm#step. Accessed May 17.

Neustadt, Kathy. 1992. *Clambake: A History and Celebration of an American Tradition.* Amherst: University of Massachusetts Press.

Noyes, Dorothy. 2003. "Group." In *Eight Words for the Study of Expressive Culture,* edited by Burt Feintuch, 7-41. Urbana: University of Illinois Press.

O'Connor, Bonnie Blair. 1995. *Healing Traditions: Alternative Medicine and the Health Professions.* Philadelphia: University of Pennsylvania Press

Oring, Elliott, ed. 1986a. *Folk Groups and Folklore Genres.* Logan: Utah State University Press.

———. 1986b. "Folk narratives." In Oring, *Folk Groups and Folklore Genres,* 127–30.

———. 1986c. "On the Concepts of Folklore." In Oring, *Folk Groups and Folklore Genres,* 1–22.

Pocius, Gerald. 1995. "Art." In Feintuch, "Common Ground: Keywords for the Study of Expressive Culture," 415–31.

Prahlad, Sw. Anand. 2005. "Africana Folklore: History and Challenges." In "Africana Folklore," edited by Sw. Anand Prahlad. Special issue, *Journal of American Folklore* 118 (469): 253–70.

Primiano, Leonard Norman. 1995. "Vernacular Religion and the Search for Method in Religious Folklife." *Western Folklore* 54 (1): 7–56.

Propp, Vladimir. 1968. *The Morphology of the Folktale.* 2nd ed. Austin: University of Texas Press.

Radner, Joan Newlon. 1993. Preface to *Feminist Messages: Coding in Women's Folk Culture,* edited by Joan Newlon Radner, vii-xiii. Urbana: University of Illinois Press.

Radner, Joan N., and Susan S. Lanser. 1987. "The Feminist Voice: Strategies of Coding in Folklore and Literature." *Journal of American Folklore* 100 (398): 412–25.

Santino, Jack. 1988. "Occupational Ghostlore: Social Context and the Expression of Belief." *Journal of American Folklore* 101 (400): 156–67.

———. 1992. "The Folk *Assemblage* of Autumn: Tradition and Creativity in Halloween Folk Art." In Vlach and Bronner, *Folk Art and Art Worlds,* 151–69.

Sawin, Patricia E. 2002. "Performance at the Nexus of Gender, Power, and Desire." In Berger and Del Negro, "Toward New Perspectives on *Verbal Art as Performance,*" 28–61.

Shuman, Amy. 2000. "Food Gifts: Ritual Exchange and the Production of Excess Meaning." *Journal of American Folklore* 113 (450): 495–508.

Shuman, Amy, and Carol Bohmer. 2004. "Representing Trauma: Political Asylum Narrative." *Journal of American Folklore* 117 (466): 394–414.

Siple, Bruce. 2005, 2010, 2011. Personal communication with the authors.

Stahl, Sandra K. D. 1977. "The Personal Narrative as Folklore." *Journal of the Folklore Institute* 14:9–30.

Tallman, Richard S. 1974. "You Can Almost Picture It: The Aesthetics of a Nova Scotia Storyteller." *Folklore Forum* 7:121–30.

Tedlock, Dennis. 1971. "On the Translation of Style in Oral Narrative." In Bauman, "Toward New Perspectives in Folklore," 114–33.

———. 1992. "Ethnopoetics." In *Folklore, Cultural Performances, and Popular Entertainments: A Communication–Centered Handbook,* edited by Richard Bauman, 81–85. New York: Oxford University Press.

Thomas, Jeannie Banks. 2000. "Ride 'Em, Barbie Girl: Commodifying Folklore, Place, and the Exotic." In *Worldviews and the American West: The Life of the Place Itself,* edited by Polly Stewart, Steve Siporin, C. W. Sullivan III, and Suzi Jones, 65–86. Logan: Utah State University Press.

———. 2003. *Naked Barbies, Warrior Joes, and Other Forms of Visible Gender.* Urbana: University of Illinois Press.

Thompson, Stith. 1955. *Motif Index of Folk Literature.* 6 vols. Bloomington: Indiana University Press.

Titon, Jeff Todd. 1980. "The Life Story." *Journal of American Folklore* 93 (369): 276–92.

———. 1988. *Powerhouse for God: Speech, Chant, and Song in an Appalachian Baptist Church.* Austin: University of Texas Press.

Toelken, Barre. 1976. "The 'Pretty Languages' of Yellowman: Genre, Mode and Texture in Navaho Coyote Narratives." In Ben-Amos, *Folklore Genres,* 145–70.

———. 1996. *The Dynamics of Folklore.* Logan: Utah State University Press.

———. 1998. "The Yellowman Tapes, 1966–1997." *Journal of American Folklore* 111 (442): 381–91.

Tuleja, Tad. 1997. *Usable Pasts: Traditions and Group Expressions in North America.* Logan: Utah State University Press.

Turner, Patricia. 1992. "Ambivalent Patrons: The Role of Rumor and Contemporary Legends in African-American Consumer Decisions." *Journal of American Folklore* 105 (418): 424–41.

Turner, Victor. 1969. *The Ritual Process: Structure and Anti-Structure.* Chicago: Aldine.

van Gennep, Arnold. [1908] 1960. *The Rites of Passage.* Translated by Monika B. Vizedom and Gabrielle L. Caffee. Chicago: University of Chicago Press.

Vlach, John Michael, and Simon J. Bronner, eds. 1992. *Folk Art and Art Worlds.* Logan: Utah State University Press.

Weems, Mickey. 2008. *The Fierce Tribe: Masculine Identity and Performance in the Circuit.* Logan: Utah State University Press.

Wertkin, Gerard C. 1998. "Authentic Voices, Stammered Words." In *Light of the Spirit: Portraits of Southern Outsider Artists,* edited by Karekin Goekjian and Robert Peacock, 10–17. Jackson: University Press of Mississippi.

Westerman, William. 2009. "Epistemology, the Sociology of Knowledge, and the Wikipedia Userbox Controversy." In Blank, *Folklore and the Internet: Vernacular Expression in a Digital World,* 123-158.

Wilson, William A. 1988. "The Deeper Necessity: Folklore and the Humanities. *Journal of American Folklore* 101 (400): 156–67.

Yoder, Don. 1974. "Toward a Definition of Folk Religion." *Western Folklore* 33 (1):2–15.

Index

322